Juanjo Moyano Vázquez

1001 GAMES AND
EXERCISES OF PADEL

WANCEULEN
INTERNATIONAL

Tittle:	1001 GAMES AND EXERCISES OF PADEL
Author:	JUANJO MOYANO VÁZQUEZ
Editorial:	WANCEULEN EDITORIAL DEPORTIVA, S.L. C/ Cristo del Desamparo y Abandono, 56 41006 SEVILLA www.wanceulen.com infoeditorial@wanceulen.com
I.S.B.N.:	978-84-9993-392-4
Dep. Legal:	
©Copyright:	WANCEULEN EDITORIAL DEPORTIVA, S.L.
First edition:	Year 2016

*For Carol, who has been my right hand and part of my head
in the realization of this book. Thanks for your time.*

Nico and Leo, who will be the future.

*To all my pupils, colleagues and teachers with
its indirect assistance created this work.*

*To my father, who always told me I could get everything I set my
mind whenever I work hard so my dreams always be realized.*

CONTENTS

Foreword by Carolina Navarro, Cecilia Reiter and Vanessa Zamora 9

Introduction: 10 Things teaches padel 11

Graphic symbols and references...15

Exercises Forehand and Backhand 17

Exercises Wall (SF, SL, SDP) 45

Exercises Volley...69

Exercises Lob...125

Exercises Serve 130

Exercises Volley Tray (Bd) 131

Exercises Shot...148

Combination Exercises: Forehand Backhand Wall 163

Combination Exercises: Forehand Backhand Lob..........171

Combination Exercises: Forehand Backhand Volley.......174

Combination Exercises: Forehand Backhand Shot /
Volley Tray (Bd)...182

Combination Exercises: Lob Shot Volley Tray (Bd)........184

Combination Exercises: Forehand Backhand Wall Volley...........186

Combination Exercises: Forehand Backhand Wall Shot..........190

Combination Exercises: Forehand Backhand Volley Shot 190

Combination Exercises: Forehand Backhand Volley
Volley Tray (Bd)...200

Combination Exercises: Wall Lob Volley 201

Combination Exercises: Wall Lob...................................202

Combination Exercises: Wall Volley 202

Combination Exercises: Wall Shot 236

Combination Exercises: Wall Volley Tray (Bd)...............240

Combination Exercises: Wall Volley Shot 241

Combination Exercises: Wall Volley Volley Tray (Bd) 254

Combination Exercises: Volley Shot...258

Combination Exercises: Volley Volley Tray (Bd) 274

Combination Exercises: Volley Tray (Bd) Shot 284

Combination Exercises: Forehand Backhand Wall Volley Shot........293

Combination Exercises: Serve Volley...294

Combination Exercises: Serve Shot..296

Combination Exercises: Lob Volley 297

Combination Exercises: Serve Volley Shot 299

Combination Exercises: Serve Volley Volley Tray (Bd) Shot 301

Combination Exercises: Rest or return Volley Volley Tray (Bd) 305

Varied Exercises 306

Competition Exercises..308

Peque-Pádel: Children Exercises 341

Sheet format class 351

Padel reviews 353

Special thanks...355

Thank you note 357

Literature and photography 359

FOREWORD

Padel is a young sport, which is starting a lot of people, which makes it one of the fastest growing sports in Spain today.

By having a few years of life, padel does nos have a high educational level development and today there are only a small number of dedicated coaches who acquaint their knowledge based on experience in working with pupils and professional players.

From this arises the importance of expanding and communicate this knowledge and experience, to continue training instructors and coaches collaborate on a sustained growth of padel sport.

The training itself teach pupils the secrets of the game and the keys that will lead to improve every day. All without distinction can surpass whatever our level of play. Here comes the importance to experience the feeling of taking classes, training, although our goal is not to become professional players.

It is essential to understand that if we learn to play better, surely we manage to fun a little every day and we can get our relationship with the padel takes hold to never stop entertaining and get interested in it.

As professional players, we invite you, from these lines, to let love for this great sport that fascinated currently more than 2 million Spanish players (date 2011, 5 million Spanish players in 2015).

Carolina Navarro, Cecilia Reiter and Vanessa Zamora

INTRODUCTION

10 THINGS TEACHES PADEL

1. Develop good HABITS

In order to succeed, people must develop good habits. Introduction: We are creatures of habit. Sport is not just something to do to look good, gain muscle or lose weight, sport becomes part of our lifestyle.

We set in our daily schedule that gap dedicate ourselves to doing what we like, play padeL, tennis or train, and makes us feel good. Almost without realizing we generate in our lives a discipline that can be applied to any field of the same: work, family, school.

2. Moderation

Everything in life is good in moderation ... as my mother said.

We cannot be on a diet 365 days a year and is not good training 4 months (2 to 3 hours per day) in a row without a break us. When we lose control of things, it is when everything goes wrong. Take a break to recover lost feelings.

3. Discipline is the KEY

Train or play four days in a week and the next do nothing, this does not lead anywhere. The key is to maintain discipline in the middle term training. In life we must perseverance and fight for the goals we have set.

4. Prioritize YOUR life

Look back and assessor what is most important to you. Sport is part of our life, because we understand that an iron and healthy body give us quality of life. Clearly, we are all busy and work stress is very high, but we must always find us a place to train or play a game.

5. Quality, not quantity

Everyone knows that practicing padeL intensity and concentration during training are more important than the number of hours invested in it.

As in the padeL, in life, we sometimes have an abundance of material wealth and that does not necessarily give us happiness, however, the quality of our experiences and the people around us will make our life much more full and happy.

6. Take care of yourself FIRST

Take care of yourself first. To focus on your health and give priority to nutrition, you're taking care of yourself. If we are physically, mentally and spiritually stable, we can offer more to our loved ones.

7. EVERY ACTION has a reaction

A physical change requires dedication, commitment and sacrifice. And the goals we set during training should always be middle to long term. Every choice in life has a consequence, by understanding the results of this long-term decision (training), we can make better decisions applicable to any area of our lives.

8. If you do not have a plan, we will fail.

If we want to achieve some goal in sport, we must understand how nutrition, rest, exercises, motivation, etc. ... each separately influence the final results. Like any situation in life, we must first understand what it takes to get a goal and once that is done, we can only walk the walk.

9. KEEP an open mind.

Continually new studies on nutrition, exercises, health and what was generated dogma, no longer is. We just have to read a nutrition book of the seventies to see how things are constantly changing.

Our knowledge on any subject is always limited, so never make the mistake of believing you know everything, the world is constantly changing and you must be prepared for everything.

10. Enjoy the journey, not just the DESTINATION.

There is always a challenge ahead ... there is always a game we want to win or win a championship. We must be continually motivated to give the best of ourselves, whatever the result. To value life, we have to enjoy the process of it (live) and not focusing so much on the destination, because once we reach our destination, there's always somewhere farther where we want to get ... this desire to resist the comfort , to be evolving is what creates success.

¡¡¡¡¡ Enjoy every day the good that gives us the Padel!!!!!

GRAPHIC SYMBOLS AND REFERENCES

Disciple   ○ *Pupil*   ○ *Instructor*

Reference shooting / shooting area   ●   1

Hitting reference or Pupil Movement

Pupil Displacement

Round-trip journeys Pupil

Shifts in 8

Rotation Pupil

Pupil strike

Instructor strike

Order of strokes   1 2 3 4 5

Fence

Jumping fence

Painted area

Shooting area

Ball trolley

Paddle children

Target hitting Wall or grid

String

Chain rings

Zones marked with ropes or chains

Step Movement Area

D	*Forehand*	**R**	*Backhand*	**SF**	*Output bottom Wall*
SL	*Output sidewall* **SDP**	*Double Wall Outlet*	**CP**	*Against Wall*	
V	*Volley*	**G**	*Lob*	**Rm**	*Shot*
Bd	*Volley Tray (Bd)*	**Sq**	*Serve*	**Rest or return**	*Rest or return*
//	*Parallel*	**X**	*Crossed over*		

15

EXERCISES FOREHAND AND BACKHAND

Exercise 0001   Hits: D

Target: Pregame warm-up or pre class warm-up
Striking sequence: D - D

Description:
The players will hit Forehand in parallel without touching the ball reaches the Wall.

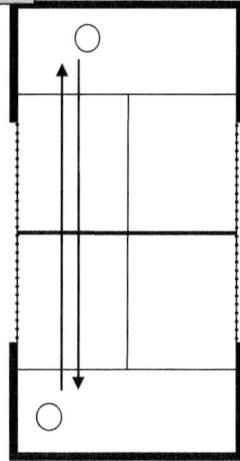

Exercise 0002   Hits: R

Target: Pregame warm-up or pre class warm-up
Striking sequence: R - R

Description:
The players will hit Backhand in parallel without touching the ball reaches the Wall.

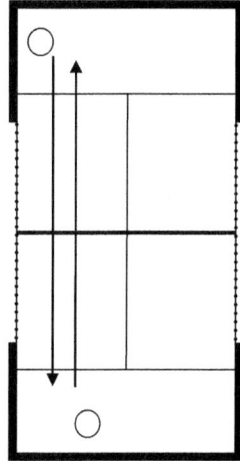

Exercise 0003   Hits: D

Target: Pregame warm-up or warm-up
Striking sequence: D - D

Description:
Players performing hits crossed over forehand. It tries to change the speed and depth without touching the ball reaches or lateral Wall or background.

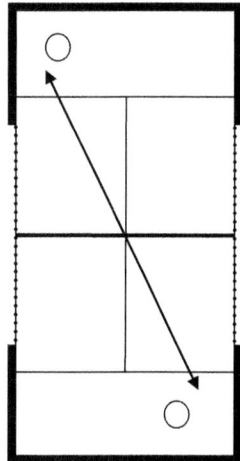

Exercise 0004   Hits: R

Target: Pregame warm-up or warm-up
Striking sequence: R – R

Description:
Players located on the back of the court faced in crossed over, crossed overs made hits crossed over backhand. They will try to change the speed and depth without touching the ball reaches or lateral wall or background.

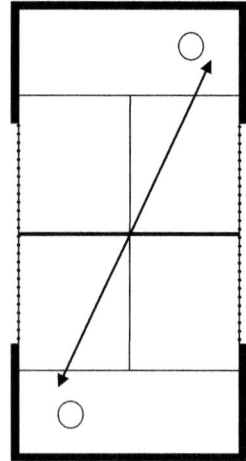

Exercise 0005   Hits: D –R

Target: Pregame warm-up or warm-up
Striking sequence: D – R – D

Description:
Placed a player on one side of the court and two on the other side, a player strike against two players alternating Forehand and Backhand hits. They will try to change the speed and depth without touching the ball reaches or lateral wall or background.
Player 1: // Forehand - Backhand X Player 2: Backhand //
Player 3: Forehand X

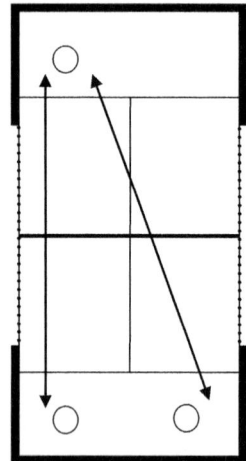

Exercise 0006   Hits: D – R

Target: Pregame warm-up or warm-up and Control of scrimmage
Striking sequence: D – R – D

Description:
Located a player on the bottom of the court up to the T and two on the other end of the court, a player strike against two players alternating Forehand and Backhand hits. They will try to change the speed and depth without touching the ball reaches or lateral wall or background:
Player 1: // Forehand - Backhand X Player 2: Backhand //
Player 3: Forehand X

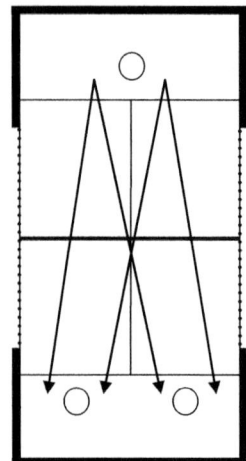

Exercise 0007   Hits: D

Target: Control of scrimmage
Striking sequence: D// – DX – D// – DX

Description:
Control of hitting four players located on the bottom of the court. The one side of Forehand hits performed in parallel and two hits Forehand made in crossed over. They will try to change the speed and depth without touching the ball reaches or lateral wall or background. After striking 2' orientation is changed.

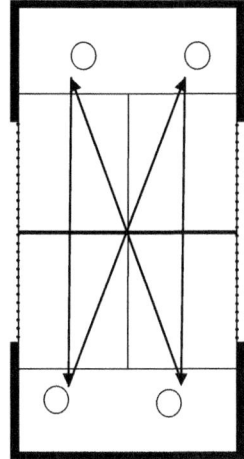

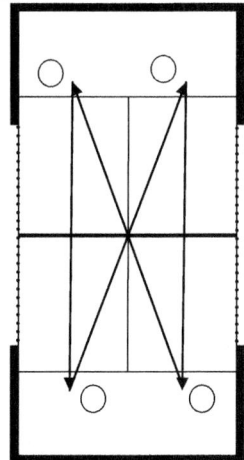

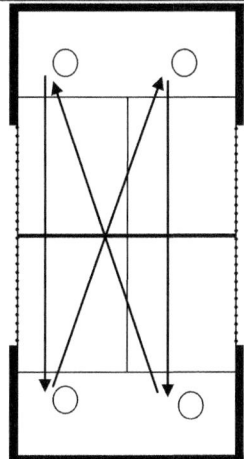

Exercise 0008   Hits: R

Target: Control of scrimmage
Striking sequence: R// – RX –R// – RX

Description:
Control of hitting four players located on the bottom of the court. The one side of Backhand hits performed in parallel and two hits Backhand made in crossed over. They will try to change the speed and depth without touching the ball reaches or lateral wall or background. After striking 2' orientation is changed.

Exercise 0009   Hits: D – R

Target: Control of scrimmage
Striking sequence: D// – RX –D// – RX

Description:
Control of hitting four players located on the bottom of the court. The one side of Forehand hits performed in parallel and two hits Backhand made in crossed over. They will try to change the speed and depth without touching the ball reaches or lateral wall or background. After striking 2'orientation is changed.

Exercise 0010   Hits: D – R

Target: Control of scrimmage
Striking sequence: Free hit without rebound

Description:
Players located on the bottom of the court, two on each side, will perform free hit control without rebound. The above free hits performed in parallel and below in crossed over. They will try to change the speed and depth without touching the ball reaches or lateral wall or background.
After striking 2'orientation is changed.

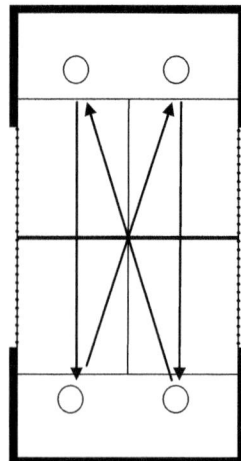

Exercise 0011   Hits: D

Target: Forehand Control of scrimmage moving
Striking sequence: D // – D X

Description:
Located a player in the back of the court, made hits of parallel forehand and crossed over forehand to a target marked on the bottom of the court.
After 10 balls is changed player.

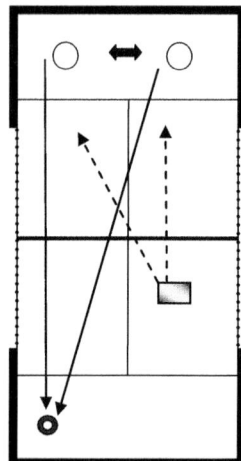

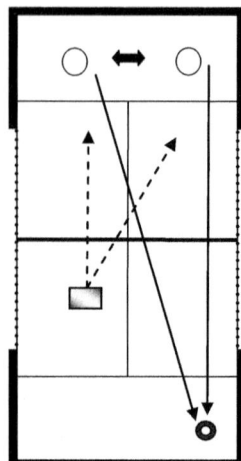

Exercise 0012   Hits: R

Target: Backhand Control of scrimmage moving
Striking sequence: R // – R X

Description:
Located a player in the back of the court, made hits of parallel backhand and crossed over backhand to a target marked on the bottom of the court.
After 10 balls is changed player.

Exercise 0013   Hits: D – R

Target: Control suddenly moving
Striking sequence: D X – R X

Description:
Located a player in the back of the court, made hits of crossed over forehand and crossed over backhand , from different positions, a target marked on the bottom of the court.
After 10 balls is changed player.

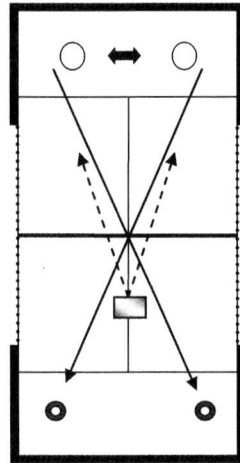

Exercise 0014   Hits: D – R

Target: Control suddenly moving
Striking sequence: D// - R// - DX - RX

Description:
Located a player in the back of the court, made hits parallel forehand, parallel backhand, crossed over forehand and crossed over backhand, from different positions, a target marked on the bottom of the court.
After 10 balls is changed player.

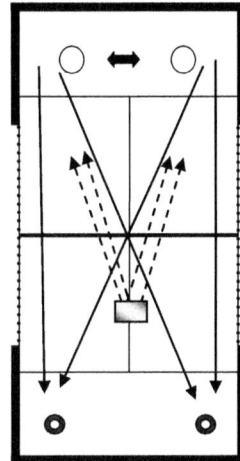

Exercise 0015   Hits: D – R

Target: Control suddenly moving
Striking sequence: D// - R//

Description:
Set the player's position defense in the bottom of the court, made hits of parallel forehand and parallel backhand to the targets marked on the back of the court.
After every shot past the cone.
After 10 balls is changed player.

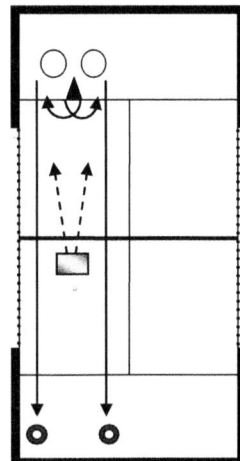

Exercise 0016   Hits: D – R

Target: Control suddenly moving
Striking sequence: DX - R//

Description:
Set the player's position defense in the bottom of the court, made hits of Crossed over forehand and Parallel backhand to the targets marked on the back of the court. After every shot past the cone.
After 10 balls is changed player.

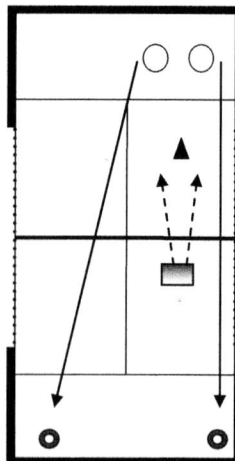

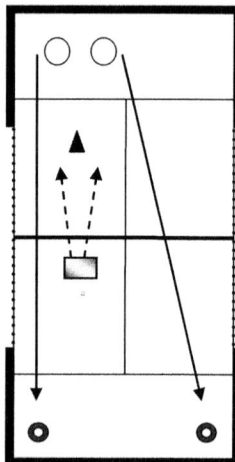

Exercise 0017   Hits: D – R

Target: Control suddenly moving
Striking sequence: D// - RX

Description:
Set the player's position defense in the bottom of the court, made hits of Parallel forehand and Crossed over backhand to the targets marked on the back of the court after every shot past the cone.
After 10 balls is changed player.

Exercise 0018   Hits: D – R

Target: Pregame warm-up or warm-up and Control of scrimmage
Striking sequence: D// – R//

Description:
Control of hitting between two players at the bottom of the court. One of the players strike of parallel forehand and the other parallel backhand, without letting the ball touch the wall reaches bottom.
After striking 2' orientation is changed.

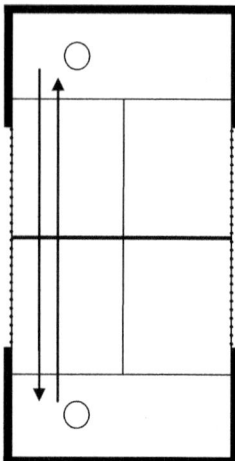

Exercise 0019   Hits: D – R

Target: Pregame warm-up or warm-up and Control of scrimmage
Striking sequence: DX – RX

Description:
Control of hitting between two players at the bottom of the court. One player of forehand hit crossed over and the other crossed over backhand, without letting the ball touch the wall reaches bottom.
After striking 2' orientation is changed.

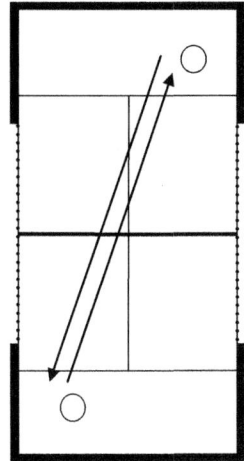

Exercise 0020   Hits: D – R

Target: Forehand and Backhand moving
Striking sequence: DX –R//

Description:
Located player in the position of defense in the bottom of the court, hit a ball of crossed over forehand and touch the cone and then hitting backhand placed in parallel, looking like targets the markings in the corners of the court.
After 10 balls is changed player.

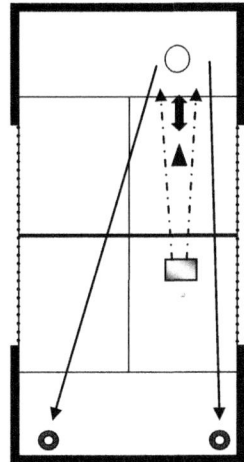

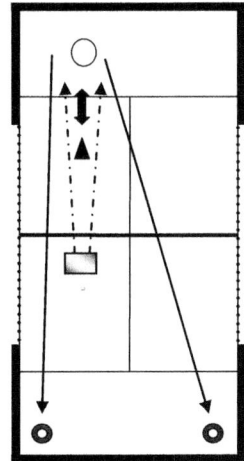

Exercise 0021   Hits: D – R

Target: Forehand and Backhand moving
Striking sequence: D// –RX

Description:
Located player in the position of defense in the bottom of the court hit a ball of parallel forehand and touch the cone and then hitting backhand placed in parallel, looking like targets cones placed in the corners.
After 10 balls is changed player.

Exercise 0022   Hits: D

Target: Control of scrimmage against wall
Striking sequence: D

Description:
Located player on the line of serve, he made short forehand with a boat against the back wall.
Duration of exercise: 1'

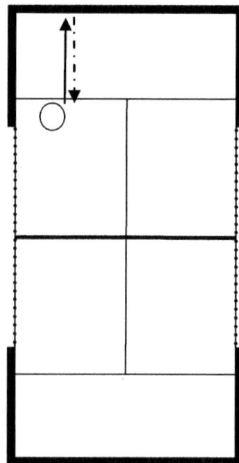

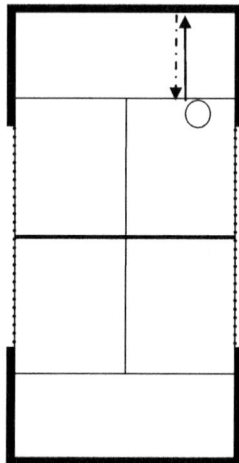

Exercise 0023   Hits: R

Target: Control of scrimmage against wall
Striking sequence: R

Description:
Located player on the line of serve, made short backhand with a boat against the back wall.
Duration of exercise: 1'

Exercise 0024   Hits: D – R

Target: Control of scrimmage against wall
Striking sequence: D – R

Description:
Located player on the service line, made short strokes alternating forehand and backhand with a bounce against the back wall.
Duration of exercise: 2'

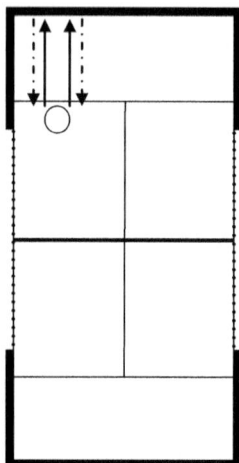

Exercise 0025   Hits: D

Target: Control of scrimmage against wall
Striking sequence: D

Description:
Located half-court player, make long forehand with a bounce against the back wall.
Duration of exercise: 1'

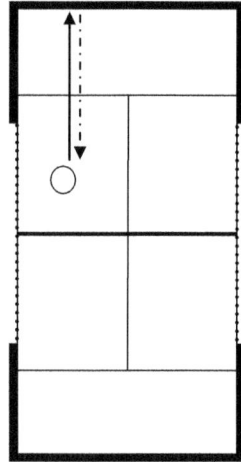

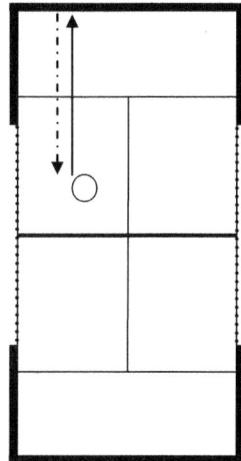

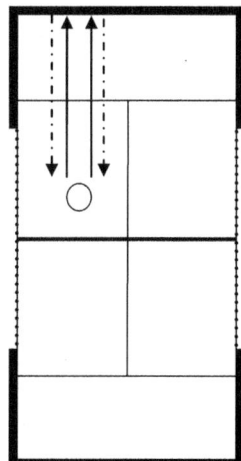

Exercise 0026   Hits: R

Target: Control of scrimmage against wall
Striking sequence: R

Description:
Located half-court player, make long backhand with a bounce against the bottom wall.
Duration of exercise: 1'

Exercise 0027   Hits: D – R

Target: Control of scrimmage against wall
Striking sequence: D – R

Description:
Located half-court player, make long strokes alternating forehand and backhand with a bounce against the back wall.
Duration of exercise: 1'

Exercise 0028   Hits: D

Target: Control of scrimmage against wall and movement

Striking sequence: D

Description:
Located half-court player, alternate long and short forehands with a bounce against the back wall.
Then you can do only with the Backhand.
Duration of exercise: 1'

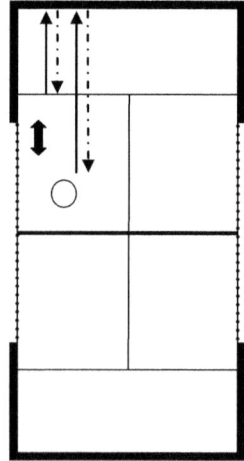

Exercise 0029   Hits: D – R

Target: Control of scrimmage against wall and movement

Striking sequence: DX – RX

Description:
Located half-court player on the midline, alternate forehand and backhand cross over.
After every shot you will pass behind the cone to hit the ball.
Duration of exercise: 1'

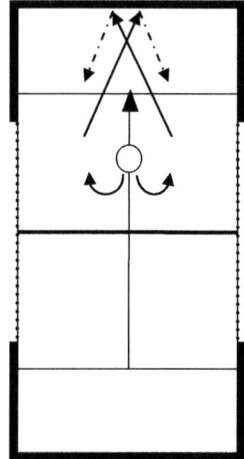

Exercise 0030   Hits: D – R

Target: Control of scrimmage against wall and movement

Striking sequence: D – R

Description:
Located player at the bottom of the court, alternate hits of forehand and backhand into the corner.
Duration of exercise: 1'

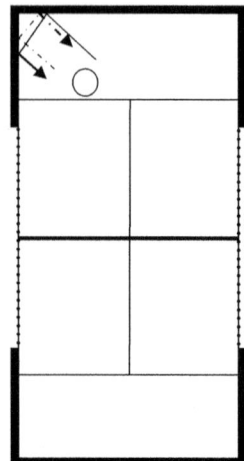

Exercise 0031   Hits: D – R

Target: Control of scrimmage against wall and movement

Striking sequence: D – R

Description:
Located player at the bottom of the court, alternate hits of forehand and backhand into the corner.
Duration of exercise: 1'

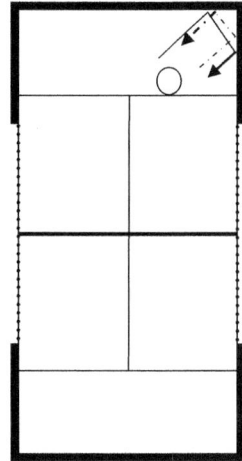

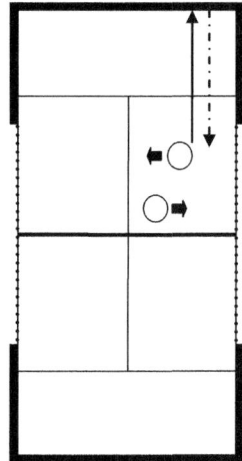

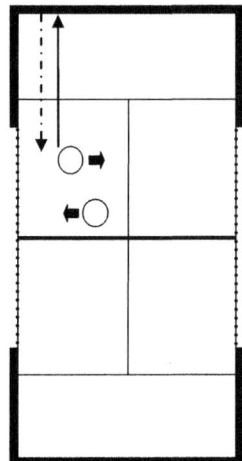

Exercise 0032   Hits: D

Target: Control of scrimmage against wall and movement

Striking sequence: D – D

Description:
Located half-court players, forehand hit in parallel against the wall and leave space for his teammate hit the next ball.
Duration of exercise: 1'

Exercise 0033   Hits: R

Target: Control of scrimmage against wall and movement

Striking sequence: R – R

Description:
Located half-court players, backhand hit in parallel against the wall and leave space for his teammate hit the next ball.
Duration of exercise: 1'

Exercise 0034   Hits: D

Target: Control of scrimmage against wall and movement
Striking sequence: D – D

Description:
Located half-court players, forehand hit twice against the wall and parallel to the back row.
Duration of exercise: 1'

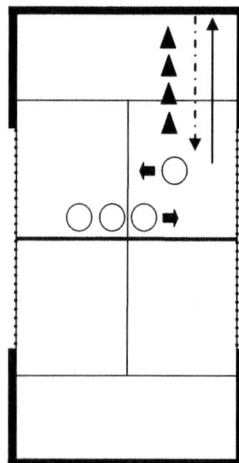

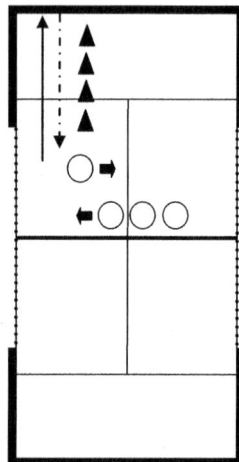

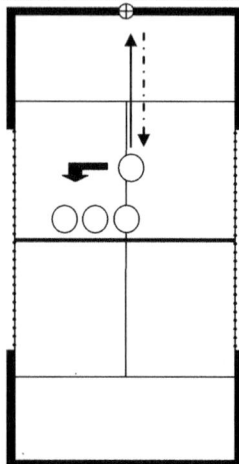

Exercise 0035   Hits: R

Target: Control of scrimmage against wall and movement
Striking sequence: R – R

Description:
Located half-court players, hit twice parallel backhand against the wall and return to the line.
Duration of exercise: 1'

Exercise 0036   Hits: D – R

Target: Control of scrimmage against wall and movement
Striking sequence: Free

Description:
Located half-court players on the midline, they hit on forehand or parallel backhand against the wall and mark the row again.
Duration of exercise: 1'

Exercise 0037   Hits: D – R

Target: Control of scrimmage against wall and movement
Striking sequence: Free

Description:
Located half-court on the halfway line before hitting players will say the name of the next player. The hitting will be free, the ball rebound will have to leave the line of serve and who fail twice will be eliminated.
Duration of exercise: 2' or when there is a winner

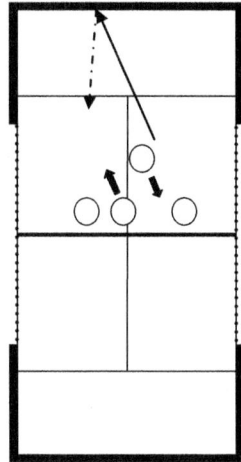

Exercise 0038   Hits: D – R

Target: Alternating forehand and backhand at different depths
Striking sequence: D// - R//

Description:
Located player at the bottom of the court, alternate hits of parallel forehand and parallel backhand looking different depths, with the target of cones placed on the court.
After 12 balls is changed player.

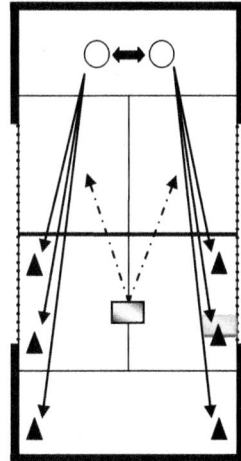

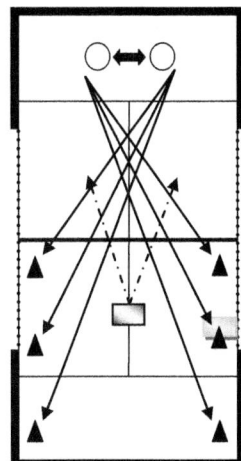

Exercise 0039   Hits: D – R

Target: Alternating forehand and backhand at different depths
Striking sequence: DX – RX

Description:
Located player at the bottom of the court, alternate hits of crossed over forehand and crossed over backhand and looking for different depths, with the target of cones placed on the court.
After 12 balls is changed player.

Exercise 0040   Hits: D – R

Target: Defend background with balls to the middle without rebound
Striking sequence: Free

Description:
With two players at the bottom of the court, they will defend themselves from the balls thrown by the monitor directing his balls to the area marked on the court.
After 10 balls position players alternates.

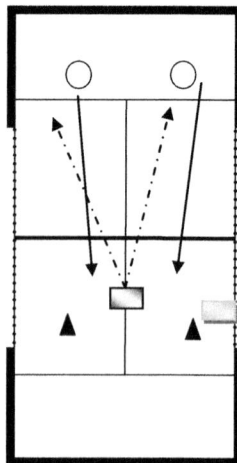

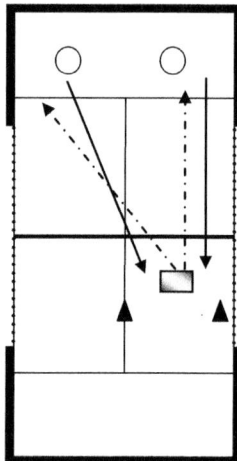

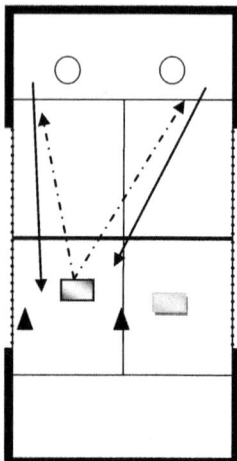

Exercise 0041   Hits: D – R

Target: Defend the background without rebound
Striking sequence: Free

Description:
With two players at the bottom of the court, they will defend themselves from the balls thrown by the monitor directing his balls to the area marked on the court.
After 10 balls position players alternates.

Exercise 0042   Hits: D – R

Target: Defend the background without rebound
Striking sequence: Free

Description:
With two players at the bottom of the court, they will defend themselves from the balls thrown by the monitor directing his balls to the area marked on the court.
After 10 balls position players alternates.

Exercise 0043   Hits: D – R

Target: Forehand and backhand moving
Striking sequence: D// - R//

Description:
Hand balls thrown by the monitor, a player hits performed parallel forehands and parallel backhands with the target of the marks on the corners of the court. After 10 balls is changed player.

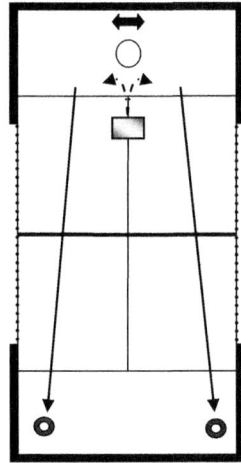

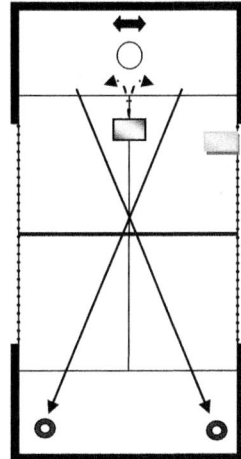

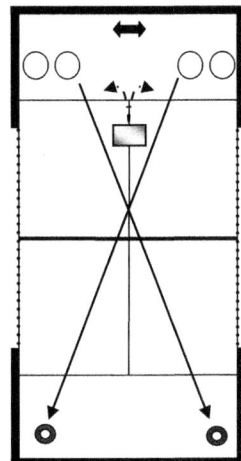

Exercise 0044   Hits: D – R

Target: Forehand and backhand moving
Striking sequence: DX - RX

Description:
Hand balls thrown by the monitor, a player hits performed crossed over forehands and crossed over backhands, with the target of the marks on the corners of the court.
After 10 balls is changed player.

Exercise 0045   Hits: D – R

Target: Forehand and backhand moving
Striking sequence: DX - RX

Description:
Hand balls thrown by the monitor, two players move laterally and the closest to the monitor will hit crossed over forehand and crossed over backhand, with the target of the marks on the corners of the court. The other player made the "mirror".
After 10 balls is changed player.

Exercise 0046   Hits: D – R

Target: Forehand and backhand moving
Striking sequence: D// - R//

Description:
Hand balls thrown by the monitor, two players move laterally and the closest to the monitor will hit parallel forehand or parallel backhand, with the target of the marks on the corners of the court. The other player made the "mirror".
After 10 balls is changed player.

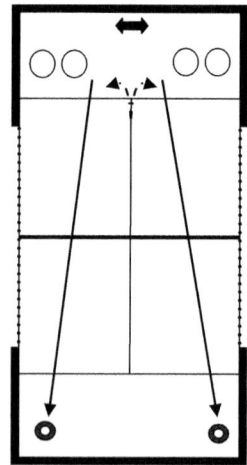

Exercise 0047   Hits: D – R

Target: High ball attack
Striking sequence: DX - RX

Description:
Players located in the bottom line, make an attack on crossed over from forehand or backhand to high balls thrown by the monitor, with the target of the marks on the corners of the court.

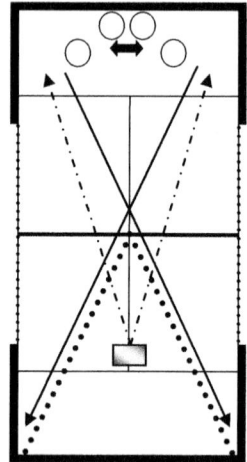

Exercise 0048   Hits: D

Target: Forehand with target
Striking sequence: D – D – D

Description:
Located player in the baseline, make three hits forehand held by each of the rings placed in the string.
After 12 balls is changed player.

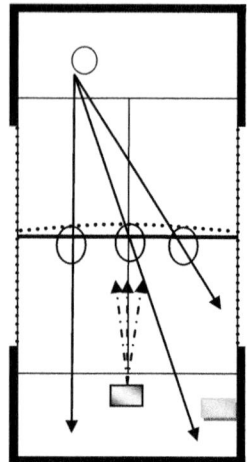

Exercise 0049   Hits: R

Target: Backhand with target
Striking sequence: R – R – R

Description:
Located player in the baseline, make three hits backhand held by each of the rings placed in the string.
After 12 balls is changed player.

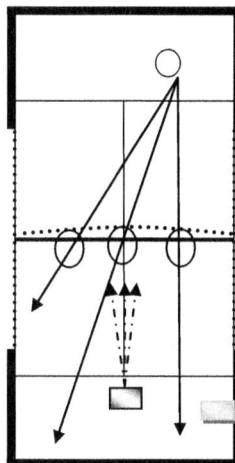

Exercise 0050   Hits: R

Target: Backhand with target
Striking sequence: R – R – R

Description:
Located player in the baseline, make three hits backhand held by each of the rings placed in the string.
After 12 balls is changed player.

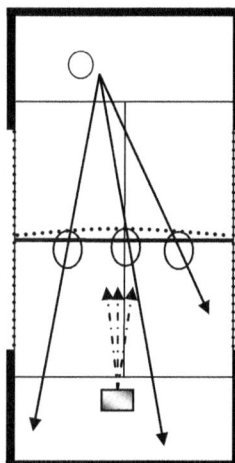

Exercise 0051   Hits: D

Target: Forehand with target
Striking sequence: D – D – D

Description:
Located player in the baseline, make three hits forehand held by each of the rings placed in the string.
After 12 balls is changed player.

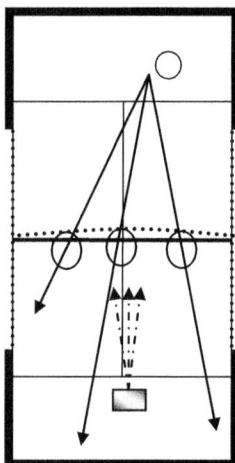

Exercise 0052   Hits: D

Target: Direction and depth
Striking sequence: D

Description:
Located player on the bottom line, make two hits forehand alternating all areas marked on the court.
After 12 balls is changed player.

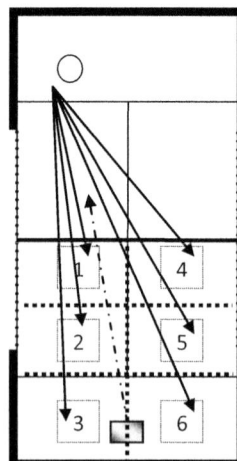

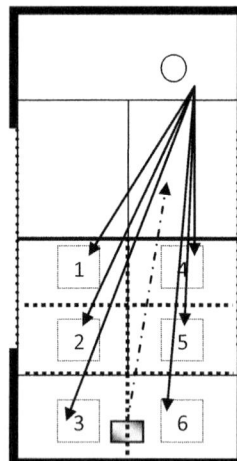

Exercise 0053   Hits: R

Target: Direction and depth
Striking sequence: R

Description:
Located player on the bottom line, make two hits backhand alternating all areas marked on the court.
After 12 balls is changed player

Exercise 0054   Hits: R

Target: Direction and depth
Striking sequence: R

Description:
Located player on the bottom line, make two hits alternating backhand all areas marked on the court.
After 12 balls is changed player.

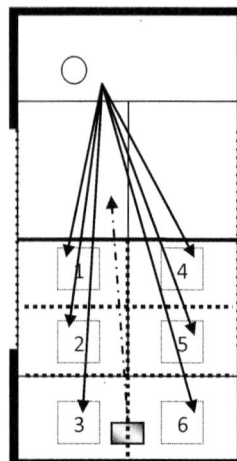

Exercise 0055   Hits: D

Target: Direction and depth
Striking sequence: D

Description:
Located player on the bottom line, make two hits forehand alternating all areas marked on the court.
After 12 balls is changed player.

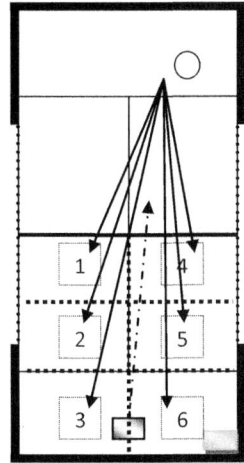

Exercise 0056   Hits: D

Target: Variation forehand hits
Striking sequence: D – D – D – D

Description:
Located player on the bottom line, the player held four hits forehand, below the string, to the various targets located on the court.
After 12 balls you change player

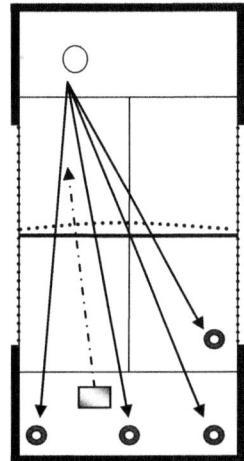

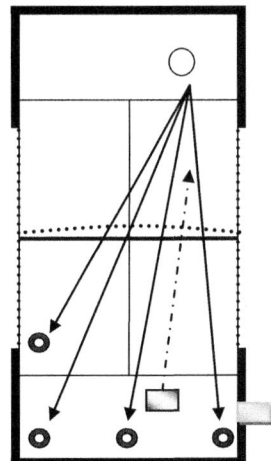

Exercise 0057   Hits: R

Target: Variation bbackhand hits
Striking sequence: R – R – R – R

Description:
Located player on the bottom line, the player held four hits backhand, below the string, to the various targets located on the court.
After 12 balls you change player

Exercise 0058   Hits: R

Target: Variation bbackhand hits
Striking sequence: R – R – R – R

Description:
Located player on the bottom line, the player held four hits backhand, below the string, to the various targets located on the court.
After 12 balls you change player

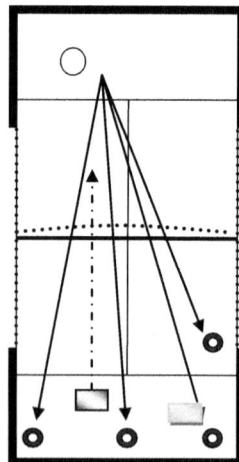

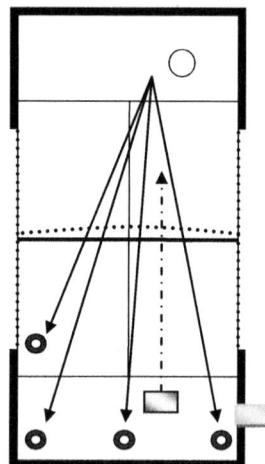

Exercise 0059   Hits: D

Target: Variation forehand hits
Striking sequence: D – D – D – D

Description:
Located player on the bottom line, the player held four hits forehand, below the string, to the various targets located on the court.
After 12 balls you change player

Exercise 0060   Hits: D – R

Target: Reaction to a situation
Striking sequence: D o R

Description:
Sitting on the floor in defense, got up and hit a short ball forward, we return to the cone and sat down to retake the exercise.
After 5 balls you change player.

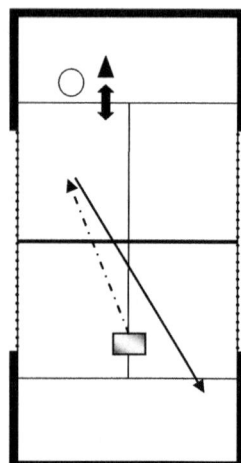

Exercise 0061   Hits: D – R

Target: Reaction to a situation
Striking sequence: D o R

Description:
Sitting at half court, retrieve balls bounce back without background wall exiting the forehand and left. After each recovery, we return to the cone and turn to sit.
After 10 balls change of player.

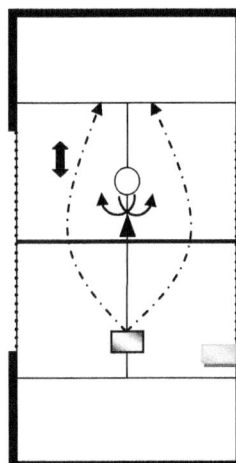

Exercise 0062   Hits: D – R

Target: Reaction to a situation
Striking sequence: D o R

Description:
Sitting at half court, we recover high balls that pass over our head, before bouncing on background wall. After each recovery, we return to the cone and turn to sit.
After 6 balls change of player.

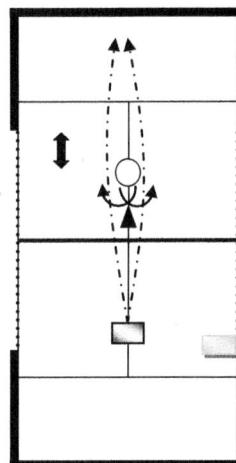

Exercise 0063   Hits: D – R

Target: Reaction to a situation
Striking sequence: D o R

Description:
Half-court sitting with his back to the net, recovered balls on background passing in different directions, before bouncing off the Walls. After each recovery, back to sit next to the cone.
After 8 balls change of player.

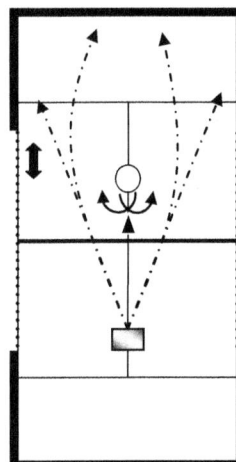

Exercise 0064   Hits: D

Target: Reaction to a situation
Striking sequence: DX

Description:
In defense, one knee on the ground, recovered to lob a ball crossed over to the corner, before it bounces on the walls. After each recovery, we again put ourselves with a knee on defense.
After 5 balls change of player.
Then you can make in the other corner.

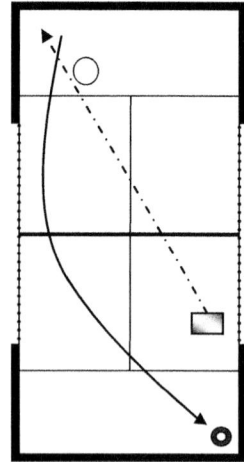

Exercise 0065   Hits: D – R

Target: Control of scrimmage
Striking sequence: DX - RX

Description:
Players placed in two rows at the bottom of the court, the players alternate hits of crossed over forehand and crossed over backhand, with the target of the marks on the corners of the court.
After each blow will change row for the other type of hit.

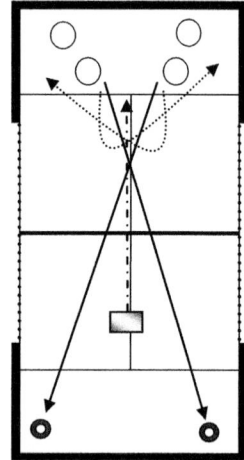

Exercise 0066   Hits: D

Target: Reaction to a situation
Striking sequence: DX – D//

Description:
Set the player at the bottom of the court, hits a crossed over forehand and run forward to hit a short ball Forehand parallel.

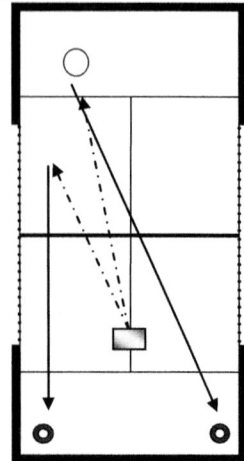

Exercise 0067   Hits: D

Target: Reaction to a situation
Striking sequence: D// - D//

Description:
Set the player at the bottom of the court, hits a parallel forehand and run forward to hitting parallel forehand a short ball that gives first to the grid, with the target of the mark on the bottom of the court.

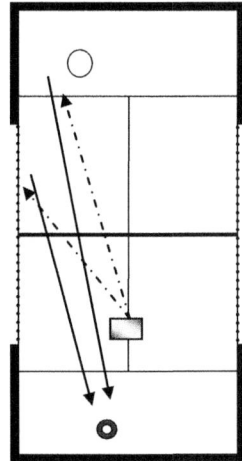

Exercise 0068   Hits: R

Target: Reaction to a situation
Striking sequence: R// - R//

Description:
Set the player at the bottom of the court, hits a backhand stroke parallel and run forward to hitting a short ball parallel backhand giving first grid, with the target of the mark on the bottom of the court.

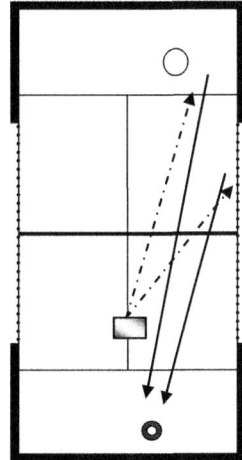

Exercise 0069   Hits: D

Target: Reaction to a situation
Striking sequence: D

Description:
Set the player at the bottom of the court makes a turn and run forward to get a drop shot to hit forehand.

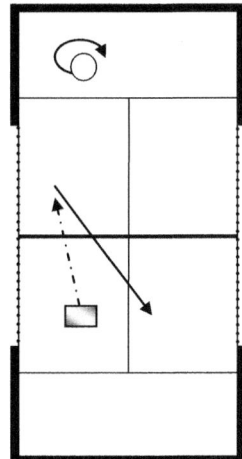

Exercise 0070   Hits: R

Target: Reaction to a situation
Striking sequence: R

Description:
Set the player at the bottom of the court makes a turn and run forward to get a drop shot to hit backhand.

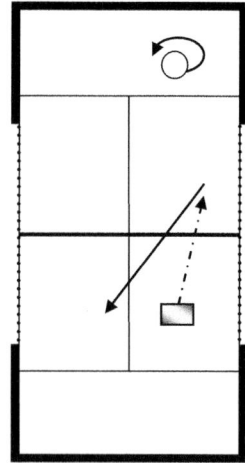

Exercise 0071   Hits: D – R

Target: Control parallel stroke from bottom
Striking sequence: D// o R//

Description:
Located players at the bottom of the court, made hits of forehand or parallel backhand with the target of the marks at the bottom of the court.
After 20 balls position players alternates.

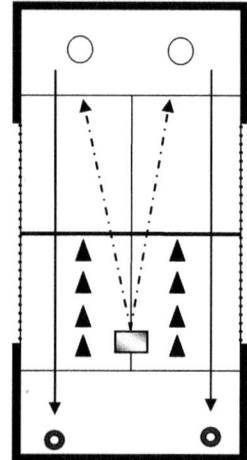

Exercise 0072   Hits: D – R

Target: Control crossed over from background
Striking sequence: DX o RX

Description:
Located players at the bottom of the court, made hits of forehand or crossed over backhand, with the target of the marks at the bottom of the court.
After 20 balls position players alternates.

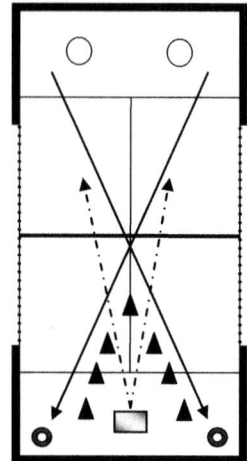

Exercise 0073   Hits: D – R

Target: Control crossed over from bottom
Striking sequence: D// - R//

Description:
Located player at the bottom of the court, parallel alternate stroke backhand and forehand parallel, with the target of the marks at the bottom of the court.
After 10 balls is changed player.

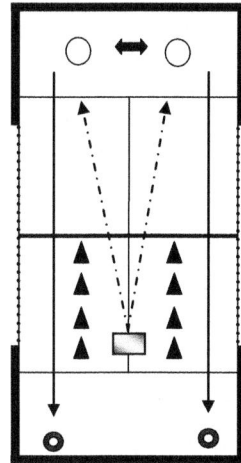

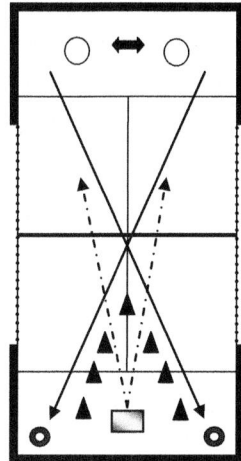

Exercise 0074   Hits: D – R

Target: Control crossed over from bottom
Striking sequence: DX - RX

Description:
Located player at the bottom of the court, alternate stroke crossed over forehand and another crossed over backhand, with the target of the marks at the bottom of the court.
After 10 balls is changed player.

Exercise 0075   Hits: D – R

Target: Control of scrimmage
Striking sequence: D – Free

Description:
Set the player at the bottom of the court, hits a smooth forehand over the bar and again hitting forehand, backhand or cadet after the bounce.
Important control in the first blow to facilitate second.

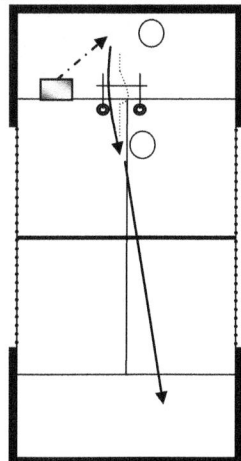

Exercise 0076   Hits: D – R

Target: Control of scrimmage
Striking sequence: R – Free

Description:
Set the player at the bottom of the court, hits a backhand blow soft over the bar and again hitting backhand, forehand or cadet after the bounce.
Important control in the first blow to facilitate second.

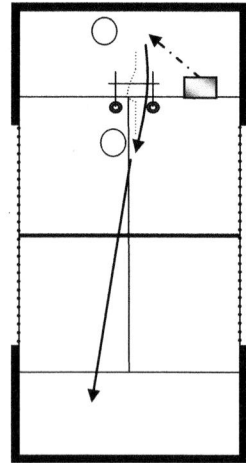

Exercise 0077   Hits: D – R

Target: Striking at different speeds without rebound ball
Striking sequence: D – R – D – R

Description:
Located the player's position backhand side defense, different hits performed both as backhand and forehand, depending on the speed and location of impact of the ball:
.- If it comes easy and slow, will make a lob
.- If it comes hard or difficult, it hit hard for the volley of opposites.
.- If hits high Wall, attack or perform lob, and if you come down, try to lob the knees down well.

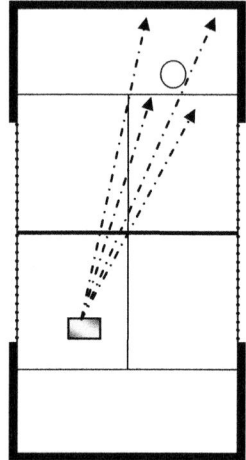

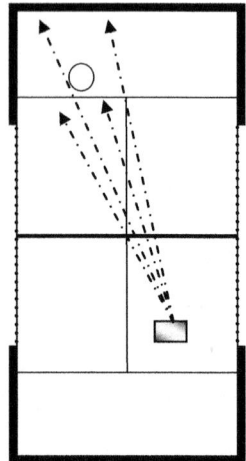

Exercise 0078   Hits: D – R

Target: Striking at different speeds without rebound ball
Striking sequence: D – R – D – R

Description:
Located the player's position forehand side defense, perform different hits, both as backhand and forehand, depending on the speed and location of impact of the ball:
.- If it comes easy and slow, will make a lob
.- If it comes hard or difficult, it hit hard for the volley of opposites.
.- If hits high Wall, attack or perform lob, and if you come down, try to lob the knees down well.

Exercise 0079   Hits: R

Target: Reaction to a situation
Striking sequence: RX – RX

Description:
Set the player at the bottom of the court, hits a crossed over backhand background and run forward to a short ball that gives the grid first making a crossed over backhand.

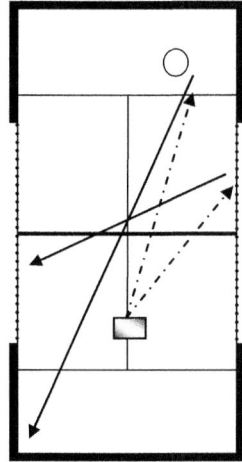

Exercise 0080   Hits: D

Target: Reaction to a situation
Striking sequence: DX – DX

Description:
Set the player at the bottom of the court, hits a crossed over forehand background and run forward to a short ball that gives the grid first making a crossed over forehand.

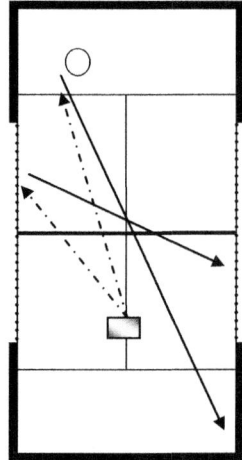

Exercise 0081   Hits: R

Target: Reaction to a situation
Striking sequence: RX

Description:
Set the player at the bottom of the court makes a turn and run forward to get a drop shot to hit crossed over backhand and make a counter left.

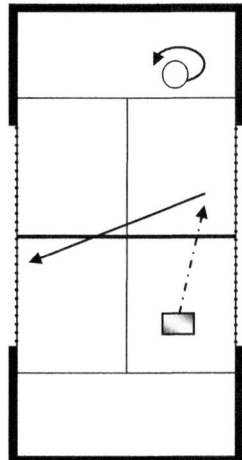

Exercise 0082   Hits: D

Target: Reaction to a situation
Striking sequence: DX

Description:
Set the player at the bottom of the court makes a turn and run forward to get a drop shot to hit crossed over forehand and make a counter left.

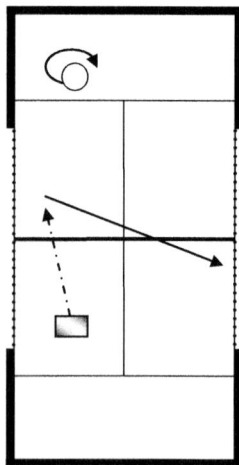

Exercise 0083   Hits: D – R

Target: Control of scrimmage parallel from the bottom
Striking sequence: D// o R//

Description:
Located in the bottom of the court, players will be placed in two rows. The monitor will throw a ball in the middle and leave a player in a row to hit its side and parallel row change.

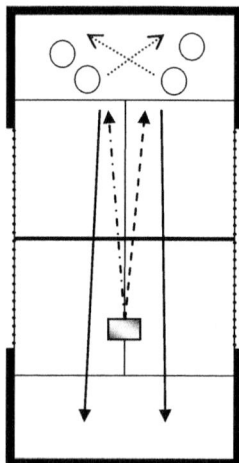

Exercise 0084   Hits: D – R

Target: Control of scrimmage parallel from the bottom
Striking sequence: DX o RX

Description:
Located in the bottom of the court, players will be placed in two rows. The monitor will throw a ball in the middle and leave a player in a row to hit crossed over to his side and change row.

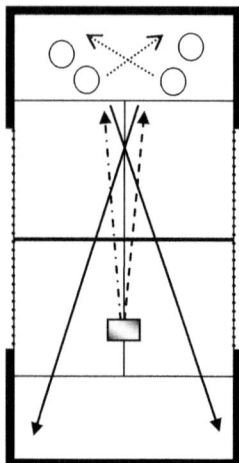

Exercise 0085   Hits: D – R – G

Target: Lob
Striking sequence: D// - RX

Description:
Set the player at the bottom of the court, made parallel forehand lobs and crossed over backhand lobs above the string located between the peaks of the court.
After 10 balls is changed player.

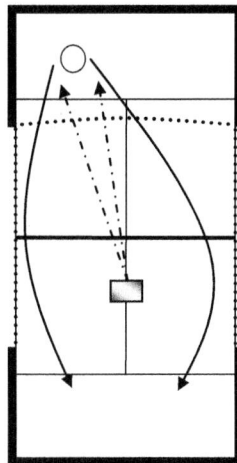

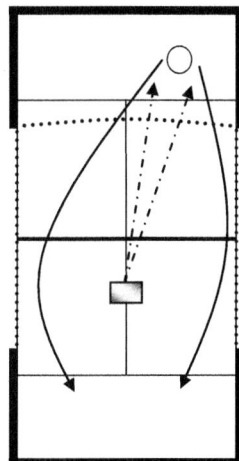

Exercise 0086   Hits: D – R – G

Target: Lob
Striking sequence: DX – R//

Description:
Set the player at the bottom of the court, made crossed over forehand lobs and parallel backhand lobs above the string located between the peaks of the court.
After 10 balls is changed player.

EXERCISES OF WALL: SF, SL SDP.

Exercise 0087   Hits: SF

Target: Control of scrimmage between 4 players with bounce
Striking sequence: SFDX – SFD// – SFRX – SFR//

Description:
Located players at the bottoms of the court, held in control stroke among four players.
The players hit above in parallel after rebound in background wall and hit bottom in crossed over after rebound on background wall.
After 2' position alternates between players.

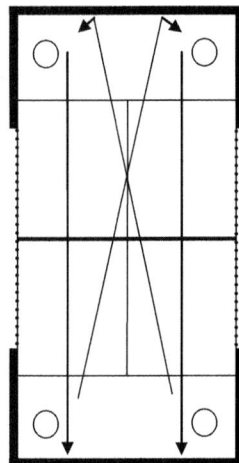

Exercise 0088   Hits: SF

Target: Background wall outlet
Striking sequence: SFD// – SFR//

Description:
Located player in the back of the court, held in control after stroke rebound on background wall alternating hits parallel forehand and parallel backhand to the balls thrown by the monitor in parallel.
After 10 balls is changed player.

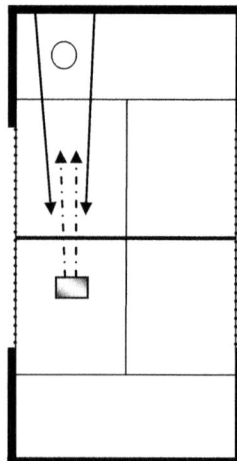

Exercise 0089   Hits: SF

Target: Background wall outlet
Striking sequence: SFDX – SFRX

Description:
Located player in the back of the court, held in control after stroke rebound on background wall alternating hits crossed over forehand and crossed over backhand to the balls thrown in crossed over by the monitor.
After 10 balls is changed player.

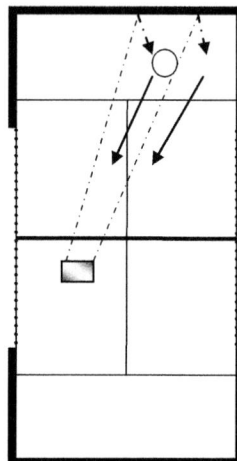

Exercise 0090   Hits: SF

Target: Background wall outlet
Striking sequence: SFDX – SFRX

Description:
Located player in the back of the court, held in control after stroke rebound on background wall alternating hits crossed over forehand and crossed over backhand to the balls thrown in crossed over by the monitor.
After 10 balls is changed player.

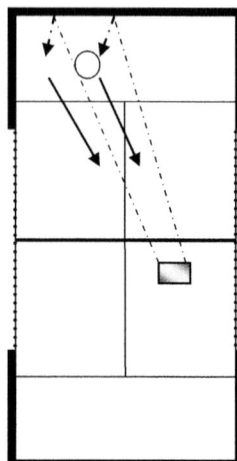

Exercise 0091   Hits: SF

Target: Background wall outlet
Striking sequence: SFD// – SFRX

Description:
Located player in the back of the court takes control after rebound hitting bottom wall parallel alternating strokes forehand and crossed over backhand to the balls thrown in parallel by the monitor, looking as targets the markings on the corners court.
After 10 balls is changed player.

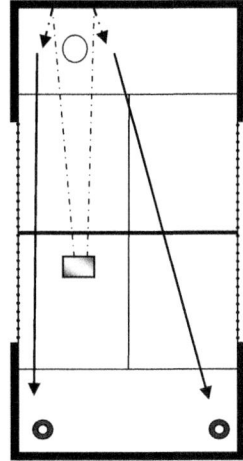

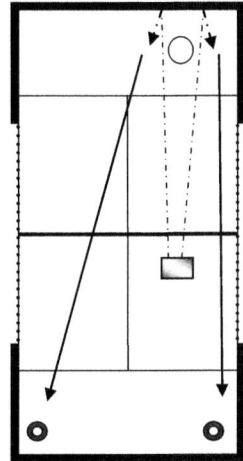

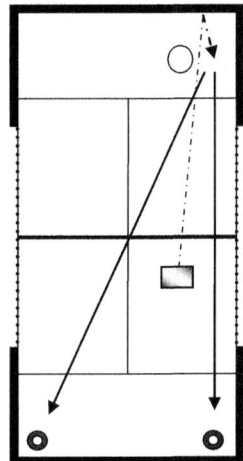

Exercise 0092   Hits: SF

Target: Background wall outlet
Striking sequence: SFDX – SFR//

Description:
Located player in the back of the court takes control after rebound hitting bottom wall parallel alternating strokes backhand and crossed over forehand to the balls thrown in parallel by the monitor, looking as targets the markings on the corners court.
After 10 balls is changed player.

Exercise 0093   Hits: SF

Target: Background wall outlet
Striking sequence: SFRX – SFR//

Description:
Located player in the back of the court takes control after rebound hitting bottom wall parallel alternating strokes backhand and crossed over backhand to the balls thrown in parallel by the monitor, looking as targets the markings on the corners court.
After 10 balls is changed player.

Exercise 0094   Hits: SF

Target: Background wall outlet
Striking sequence: SFDX – SFR//

Description:
Located player in the back of the court takes control after rebound hitting bottom wall parallel alternating strokes forehand and crossed over forehand to the balls thrown in parallel by the monitor, looking as targets the markings on the corners court.
After 10 balls is changed player.

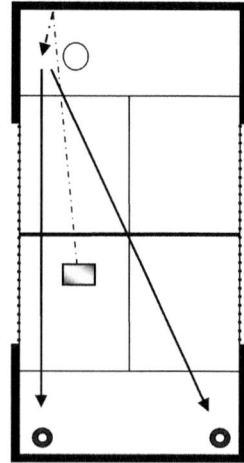

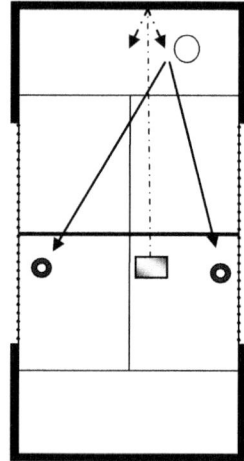

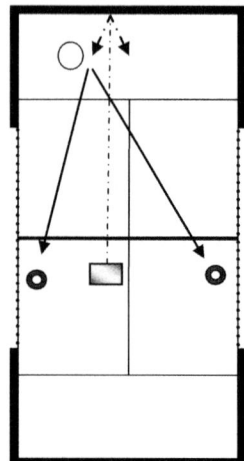

Exercise 0095   Hits: SF

Target: Background wall outlet
Striking sequence: SFDX – SFD//

Description:
Located player in the back of the court takes control after rebound hitting bottom wall parallel alternating short strokes forehand and crossed over forehand to the balls thrown in parallel by the monitor, looking as targets the markings on the corners court.
After 10 balls is changed player.

Exercise 0096   Hits: SF

Target: Background wall outlet
Striking sequence: SFRX – SFR//

Description:
Located player in the back of the court takes control after rebound hitting bottom wall parallel alternating short strokes backhand and crossed over backhand to the balls thrown in parallel by the monitor, looking as targets the markings on the corners court.
After 10 balls is changed player.

Exercise 0097   Hits: SF

Target: Background wall outlet
Striking sequence: SFDX – SFD//

Description:
Located player in the back of the court will stroke monitored after rebound on background wall alternating short hits forehand crossed overs and shorts parallels forehand to the balls thrown in parallel by the monitor, looking as targets the markings close of the net.
After 10 balls is changed player.

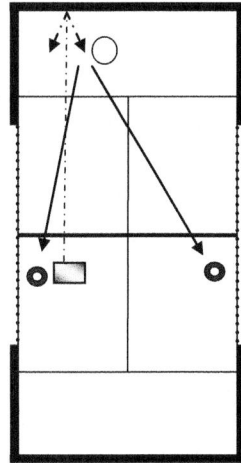

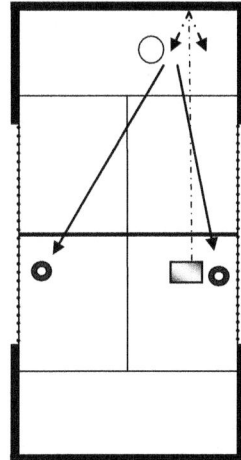

Exercise 0098   Hits: SF

Target: Background wall outlet
Striking sequence: SFRX – SFR//

Description:
Located player in the back of the court will stroke monitored after rebound on background wall alternating short hits backhand crossed overs and short parallel backhands to the balls thrown in parallel by the monitor, looking as targets the markings close of the net.
After 10 balls is changed player.

Exercise 0099   Hits: SF

Target: Background wall outlet
Striking sequence: SFDX – SFR//

Description:
Located player in the back of the court will stroke monitored after rebound on background wall alternating hits forehand crossed over and parallel backhand to the balls thrown in parallel by the monitor, looking as targets the markings near the wall.
After 10 balls is changed player.

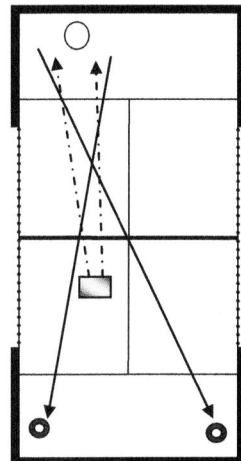

Exercise 0100   Hits: SF

Target: Background wall outlet
Striking sequence: SFD// – SFRX

Description:
Located player in the bottom of the court takes control after rebound on background wall alternating hits parallel forehand and crossed over backhand to the balls thrown in parallel by the monitor, looking as targets tags placed near the wall.
After 10 balls is changed player.

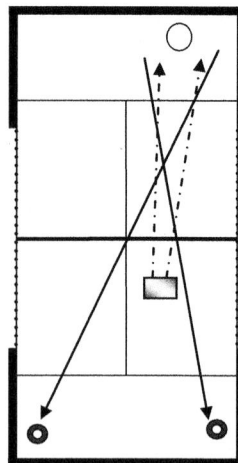

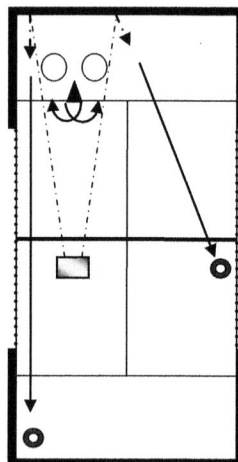

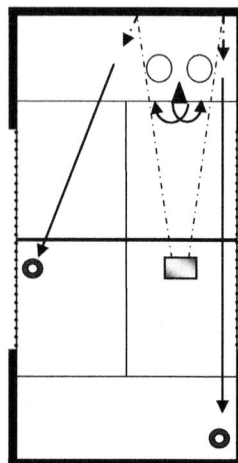

Exercise 0101   Hits: SF

Target: Background wall outlet
Striking sequence: SFD// – SFRX short

Description:
Located in the bottom of the court, after rebound in background wall, the player hit a ball of parallel forehand and pass in front of the cone and then placed backhand hitting short crossed over, looking as targets tags placed one on the corner of the court and the other on the net.
After 10 balls is changed player.

Exercise 0102   Hits: SF

Target: Background wall outlet
Striking sequence: SFR// – SFDX short

Description:
Located in the bottom of the court, after rebound in background wall, the player hit a ball of parallel backhand and pass in front of the cone and then placed hitting short crossed over forehand, looking as targets tags placed one on the corner of the court and the other on the net.
After 10 balls is changed player.

Exercise 0103   Hits: SF

Target: Background wall outlet
Striking sequence: SFD// short – SFR// short

Description:
Located in the bottom of the court, after rebound in background, the player will perform hits from short parallels forehand will scroll across the field and knock of short parallel backhand, looking like targets marks located near the net.
After 10 balls is changed player.

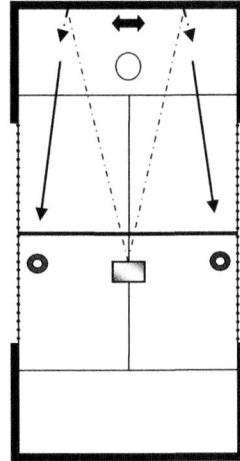

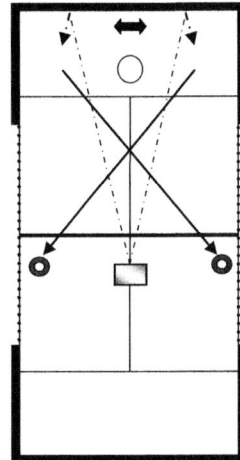

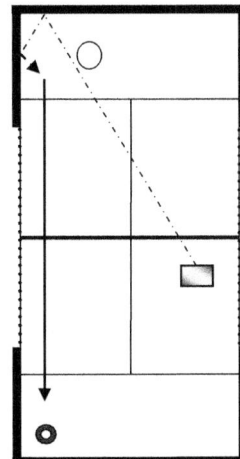

Exercise 0104   Hits: SF

Target: Background wall outlet
Striking sequence: SFDX short – SFRX short

Description:
Located on the bottom of the court, after rebound in Background wall, the player will perform hits short from crossed over forehand, he will move across the field and hits short crossed over backhand, looking as targets marks located near of the net.
After 10 balls is changed player.

Exercise 0105   Hits: SDP

Target: Double bouncing wall
Striking sequence: SDPD//

Description:
Located on the bottom of the court, then rebound in the bottom and side walls, the player will perform hits of parallel forehand looking as the target mark on the bottom of the court.
After 10 balls is changed player.

Exercise 0106   Hits: SDP

Target: Double bouncing wall
Striking sequence: SDPR//

Description:
Located on the bottom of the court, then rebound in the bottom and side walls, the player will perform hits of parallel backhand looking as the target mark on the bottom of the court.
After 10 balls is changed player.

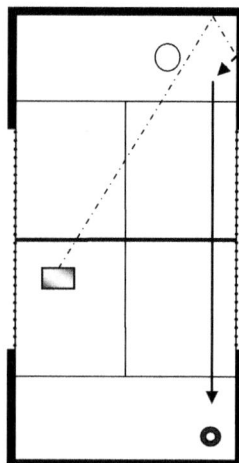

Exercise 0107   Hits: SDP

Target: Double bouncing wall
Striking sequence: SDPD// - SDPDX

Description:
Located on the bottom of the court, then rebound in the bottom and side walls, the player will perform hits and hits parallel forehand and crossed over forehand over targets looking like tags placed in the corners of the court.
After 12 balls is changed player.

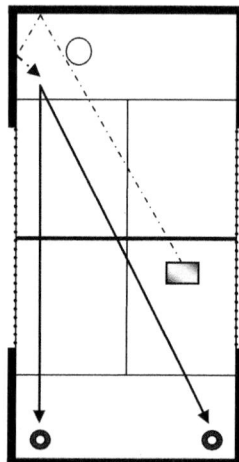

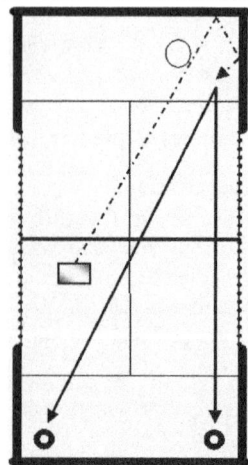

Exercise 0108   Hits: SDP

Target: Double bouncing wall
Striking sequence: SDPR// - SDPRX

Description:
Located on the bottom of the court, then rebound in the bottom and side walls, the player will perform hits and hits parallel backhand and crossed over backhand targets looking like tags placed in the corners of the court.
After 12 balls is changed player.

Exercise 0109   Hits: SDP

Target: Double bouncing wall
Striking sequence: SDPD// - SDPDX

Description:
Located in the bottom of the court, after rebound in the bottom and side wall, alternate player's hits parallel forehand and short crossed over forehand hits looking like targets the markings on the court.
After 10 balls is changed player.

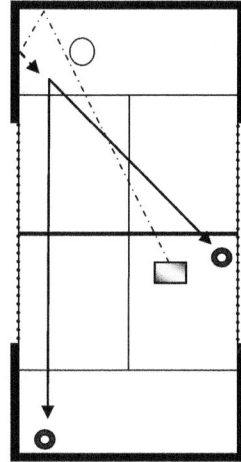

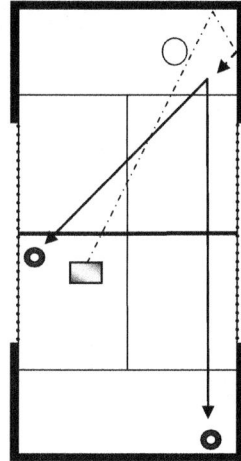

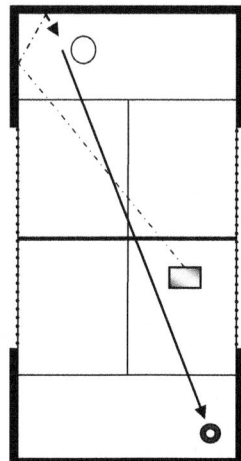

Exercise 0110   Hits: SDP

Target: Double bouncing wall
Striking sequence: SDPR// - SDPRX

Description:
Located in the bottom of the court, after rebound in the bottom and side wall, alternate player's hits and parallel backhand and short crossed over backhand hits looking like targets the markings on the court.
After 10 balls is changed player.

Exercise 0111   Hits: SDP

Target: Double bouncing wall
Striking sequence: SDPDX

Description:
Located in the bottom of the court, after bouncing on the lateral and background wall, player made hits crossed over forehand searching for the target the mark on the back of the court.
After 10 balls is changed player.

Exercise 0112   Hits: SDP

Target: Double bouncing wall
Striking sequence: SDPRX

Description:
Located in the bottom of the court, after rebound in side and bottom walls, the player hits backhand crossed over searching for the target mark on the bottom of the court.
After 10 balls is changed player.

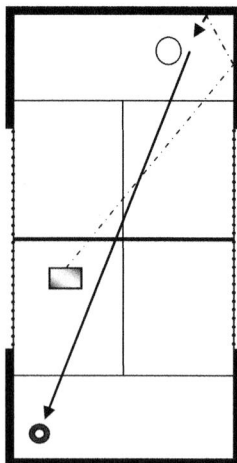

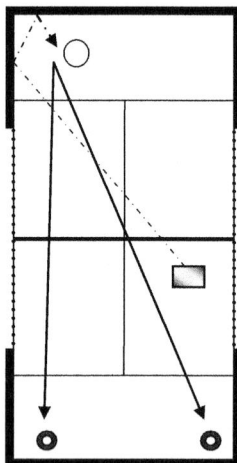

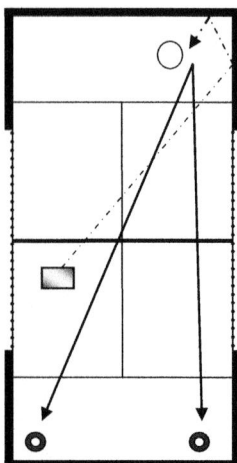

Exercise 0113   Hits: SDP

Target: Double bouncing wall
Striking sequence: SDPD// - SDPDX

Description:
Located in the bottom of the court, after bouncing on the side and bottom wall, alternate player hits of parallel forehand and crossed over forehand searching for the target mark on the bottom of the court.
After 10 balls is changed player.

Exercise 0114   Hits: SDP

Target: Double bouncing wall
Striking sequence: SDPR// - SDPRX

Description:
Located in the bottom of the court, after bouncing on the side and bottom wall, alternate player hits of parallel backhand and crossed over backhand searching for the target mark on the bottom of the court.
After 10 balls is changed player.

Exercise 0115   Hits: SDP

Target: Double bouncing wall
Striking sequence: SDPDX – SDPDX short

Description:
Located on the bottom of the court, then rebound in the side and bottom wall, alternate player hits from crossed over forehand and short crossed over forehand searching for the targets mark on the bottom of the court.
After 10 balls is changed player.

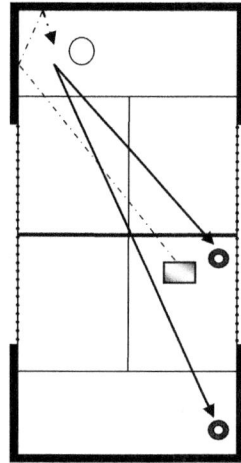

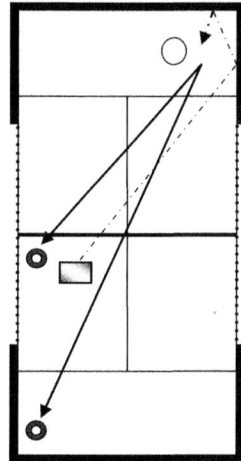

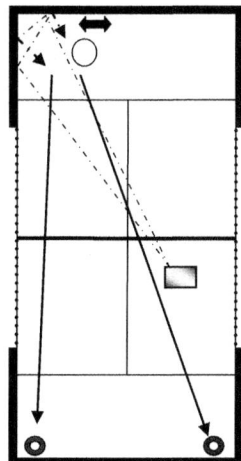

Exercise 0116   Hits: SDP

Target: Double bouncing wall
Striking sequence: SDPRX – SDPRX short

Description:
Located on the bottom of the court, then rebound in the side and bottom wall, alternate player hits from crossed over backhand and short crossed over backhand searching for the targets mark on the bottom of the court.
After 10 balls is changed player.

Exercise 0117   Hits: SDP

Target: Double bouncing wall
Striking sequence: SDPD// - SDPDX

Description:
Located in the bottom of the court, after the double bounce in wall, alternating bottom-side and side-bottom the player will alternate the hits of parallel forehand and crossed over forehand searching for the targets mark on the bottom of the court.
After 10 balls is changed player.

Exercise 0118   Hits: SDP

Target: Double bouncing wall
Striking sequence: SDPR// - SDPRX

Description:
Located in the bottom of the court, after the double bounce in wall, alternating bottom-side and side-bottom, the player will alternate the hits of parallel backhand and crossed over backhand searching for the targets mark on the bottom of the court.
After 10 balls is changed player.

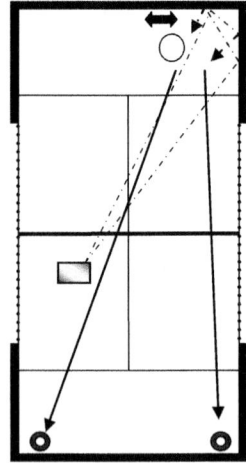

Exercise 0119   Hits: SDP

Target: Double bouncing wall
Striking sequence: SDP// - SDPX

Description:
Located on the bottom of the court, then rebound in the double wall, alternating bottom and side, and side and bottom, alternate player hits the parallels and frees crossed over hits searching for the targets mark on the bottom of the court.
After 10 balls is changed player.

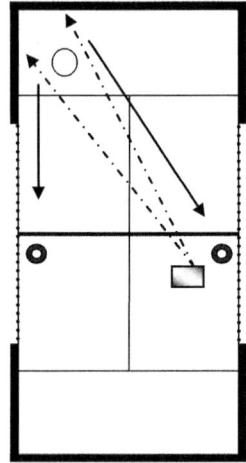

Exercise 0120   Hits: SDP

Target: Double bouncing wall
Striking sequence: SDP// - SDPX

Description:
Located on the bottom of the court, then rebound in the double wall, alternating bottom and side, and side and bottom, alternate player hits the parallels and frees crossed over hits searching for the targets mark on the bottom of the court.
After 10 balls is changed player.

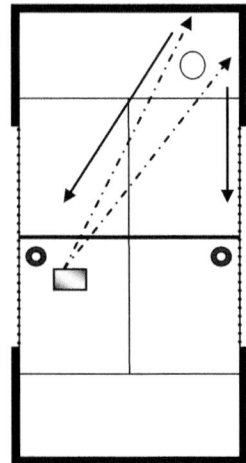

Exercise 0121   Hits: SDP

Target: Double bouncing wall
Striking sequence: SDP - SDP

Description:
Located a player in the back of the court and the other on the net, after the double wall rebound to a ball thrown by the monitor, the baseline player hit to his team mate who made a volley to the player and he returned to the monitor. After this hit, the exercise will continue with the same sequence.
After 2'position players alternates.

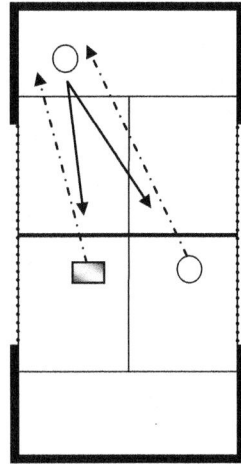

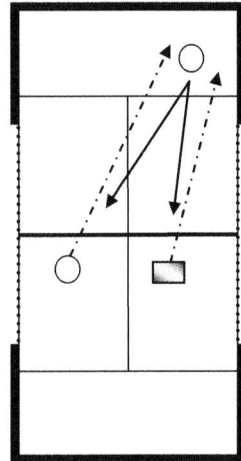

Exercise 0122   Hits: SDP

Target: Double bouncing wall
Striking sequence: SDP - SDP

Description:
Located a player in the back of the court and the other on the net, after the double wall rebound to a ball thrown by the monitor, the baseline player hit to his team mate who made a volley to the player and he returned to the monitor. After this hit, the exercise will continue with the same sequence.
After 2'position players alternates.

Exercise 0123   Hits: SDPG

Target: Turn after double bounce in wall
Striking sequence: Turn – GD

Description:
Located on the bottom of the court, then rebound in the background side wall, the player will make a turn to accompany the ball bounce on its way to lateral wall and background wall and perform a crossed over backhand lob, with the target of the mark on the corner of the court.
After 10 balls is changed player.

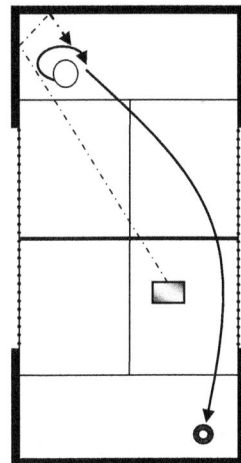

Exercise 0124   Hits: SDPG

Target: Turn after double bounce in wall
Striking sequence: Turn – GR

Description:
Located on the bottom of the court, then rebound in the background side wall, the player will make a turn to accompany the ball bounce on its way to lateral wall and background wall and perform a crossed over forehand lob, with the target of the mark on the corner of the court.
After 10 balls is changed player.

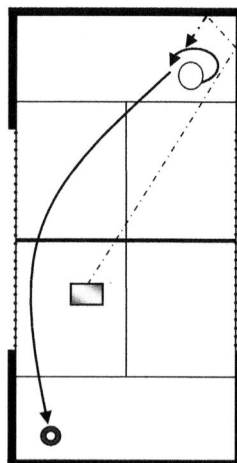

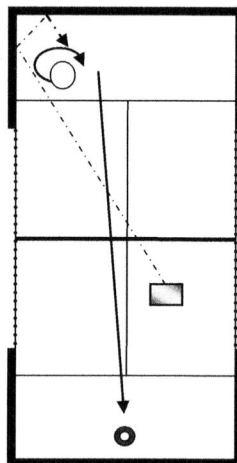

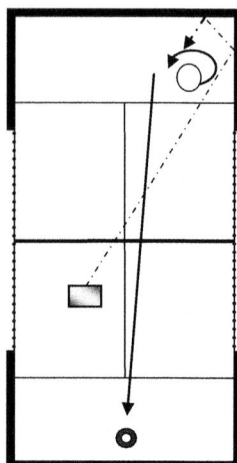

Exercise 0125   Hits: SDP

Target: Turn after double bounce in wall
Striking sequence: Turn – Drop R

Description:
Located on the bottom of the court, then rebound in the background and side wall, the player will make a turn to accompany the ball bounce on its way to lateral wall and background and make a drop backhand to half, with the target of the mark on the bottom of the court.
After 10 balls is changed player.

Exercise 0126   Hits: SDP

Target: Turn after double bounce in wall
Striking sequence: Turn – Drop R

Description:
Located on the bottom of the court, then rebound in the background and side wall, the player will make a turn to accompany the ball bounce on its way to lateral wall and background and make a drop forehand to half, with the target of the mark on the bottom of the court.
After 10 balls is changed player.

Exercise 0127   Hits: SF

Target: Background wall outlet forehand and backhand
Striking sequence: SFD// - SFR//

Description:
Located on the bottom of the court, and then rebound in the background wall players will output the background parallel forehand and parallel backhand from each position, with the target of the marks at the bottom of the court. After each hit, they touch the cone at the grid and return to the starting position.
After 10 balls is changed player.

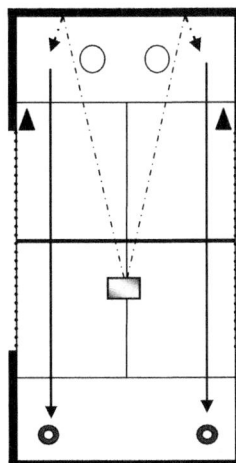

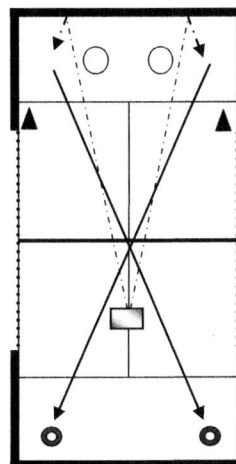

Exercise 0128   Hits: SF

Target: Background wall outlet forehand and backhand
Striking sequence: SFDX - SFRX

Description:
Located on the bottom of the court, and then rebound in the background wall players will output the background crossed over forehand and crossed over backhand from each position, with the target of the marks at the bottom of the court. After each hit, they touch the cone at the grid and return to the starting position.
After 10 balls is changed player.

Exercise 0129   Hits: SF

Target: Variation in output hits background wall
Striking sequence: SFD

Description:
Located in the bottom of the court, after rebound in background wall, player made four starts forehand background to the various targets located on the court.
After 12 balls is changed player.

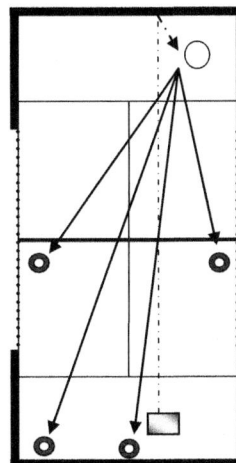

59

Exercise 0130   Hits: SF

Target: Variation in output hits background wall
Striking sequence: SFR

Description:
Located in the bottom of the court, after rebound in background wall, player made four starts backhand background to the various targets located on the court. After 12 balls is changed player.

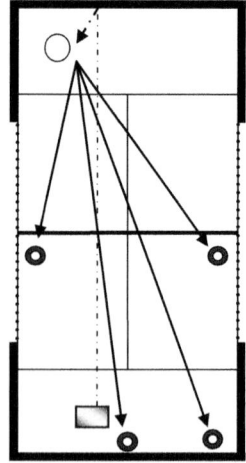

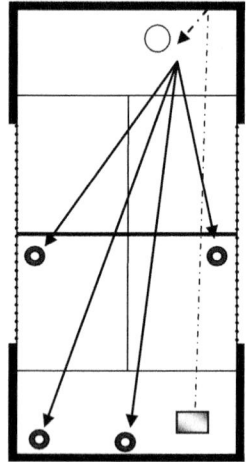

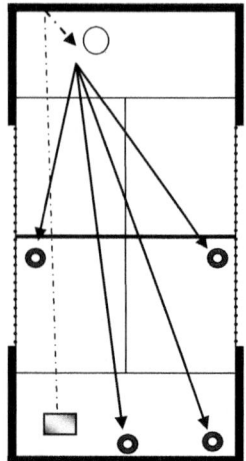

Exercise 0131   Hits: SF

Target: Variation in output hits background wall
Striking sequence: SFR

Description:
Located in the bottom of the court, after rebound in background wall, player made four starts backhand background to the various targets located on the court. After 12 balls is changed player.

Exercise 0132   Hits: SF

Target: Variation in output hits background wall
Striking sequence: SFD

Description:
Located in the bottom of the court, after rebound in background wall player made four starts forehand background to the various targets located on the court. After 12 balls is changed player

Exercise 0133   Hits: CP

Target: Reaction to a situation
Striking sequence: CpD// - CpRX

Description:
Sitting on the floor in the middle of the court, the monitor makes a lob and the player gets up to make a coup of crossed over forehand against wall or parallel backhand against wall, after what will the cone to repeat the exercise.
After 10 balls is changed player.

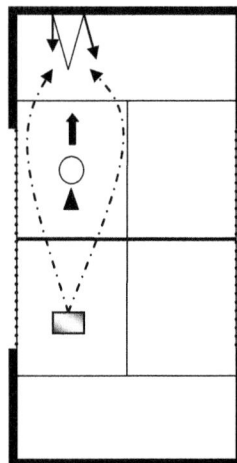

Exercise 0134   Hits: CP

Target: Reaction to a situation
Striking sequence: CpD// - CpRX

Description:
Sitting on the floor in the middle of the court, the monitor makes a lob and the player gets up to make a coup of parallel forehand against wall or crossed over backhand against wall, after what will the cone to repeat the exercise.
After 10 balls is changed player.

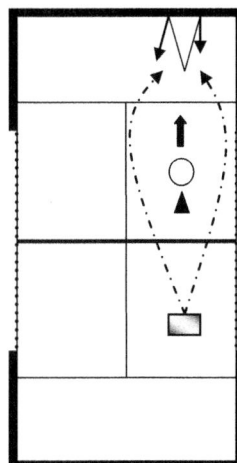

Exercise 0135   Hits: SDP

Target: Reaction to a situation

Striking sequence: SDP

Description:
Sitting on the floor in the back of the court in the position of defense, we got up and respond rebound after two walls. After the coup we turn to sit to repeat the exercise.
After 10 balls is changed player.

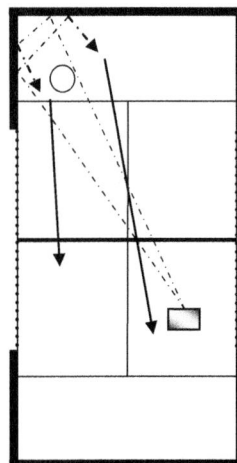

Exercise 0136   Hits: SDP

Target: Reaction to a situation

Striking sequence: SDP

Description:
Sitting on the floor in the back of the court in the position of defense, we got up and respond rebound after two walls. After the coup we turn to sit to repeat the exercise.
After 10 balls is changed player.

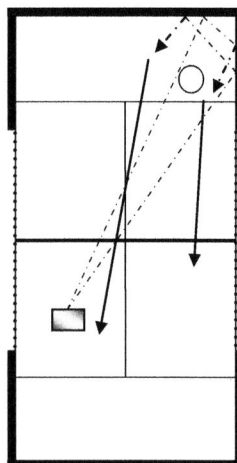

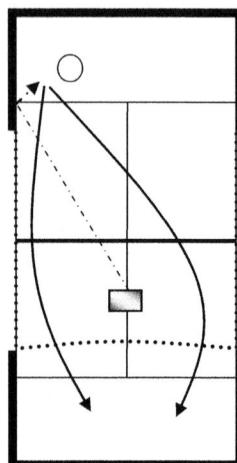

Exercise 0137   Hits: SF

Target: Stroke background output control
Striking sequence: SFDX - SFRX

Description:
Players placed in two rows at the bottom of the court, players will outlet background crossed over forehand and crossed over backhand with the target of the marks on the corners of the court.
After each blow will change row for the other type of hit.

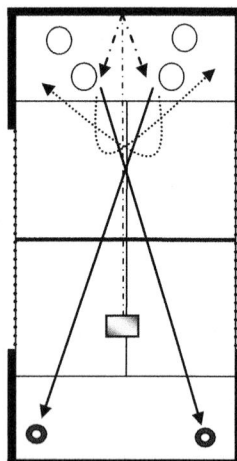

Exercise 0138   Hits: SL

Target: Lob off side
Striking sequence: SLD// - SLDX

Description:
Set the player at the bottom of the court, makes a side exit parallel forehand lob and a side exit crossed over forehand over the string located between the peaks of the bottom of the court.
After 10 balls is changed player.

Exercise 0139   Hits: SL

Target: Lob off side
Striking sequence: SLR// - SLRX

Description:
Set the player at the bottom of the court, makes a side exit parallel backhand lob and a side exit crossed over backhand over the string located between the peaks of the bottom of the court.
After 10 balls is changed player.

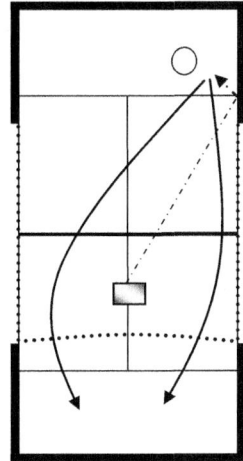

Exercise 0140   Hits: SDP

Target: Lob off double wall
Striking sequence: SDPD// - SDPRX

Description:
Set the player at the bottom of the court, makes a double outlet wall of parallel forehand lob and a double output wall of crossed over backhand lob over the string located between the peaks of the bottom of the court.
After 10 balls is changed player.

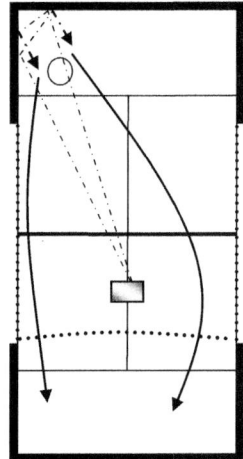

Exercise 0141   Hits: SDP

Target: Lob off double wall
Striking sequence: SDPR// - SDPDX

Description:
Set the player at the bottom of the court, makes a double outlet wall of parallel backhand lob and a double output wall of crossed over forehand lob over the string located between the peaks of the bottom of the court.
After 10 balls is changed player.

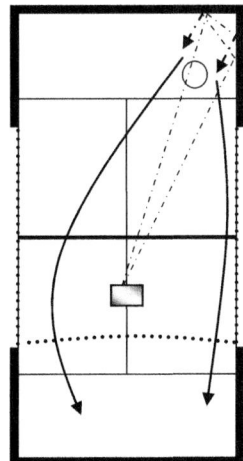

Exercise 0142   Hits: SF

Target: Stroke rebound control
Striking sequence: SFD – SFR

Description:
Control of scrimmage between two players hitting after rebound, background output parallel, parallel forehand output or parallel backhand output.
Once the player has hit it must touch the cone located in front of him and the striking work in motion.

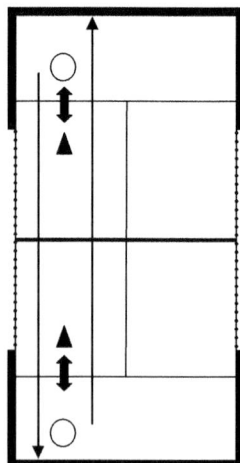

Exercise 0143   Hits: SF

Target: Control of scrimmage between 3 players with rebound
Striking sequence: SFD// – SFRX – SFR// – SFDX

Description:
Control of scrimmageled between three players hit forehand or backhand after rebound background wall.
The top player will perform parallel hitting after rebound.
Players below striking held in crossed over after rebound in the bottom wall.
After 2' position alternates between players

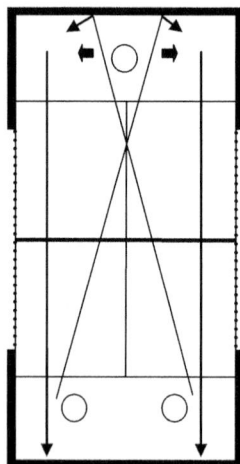

Exercise 0144   Hits: SL – G

Target: Lob side exit
Striking sequence: SLDG// - SLDGX

Description:
Set the player at the bottom of the court, makes an output side parallel forehand lob with and an output side crossed over forehand lob over the string located between the peaks of the court.
After 10 balls is changed player.

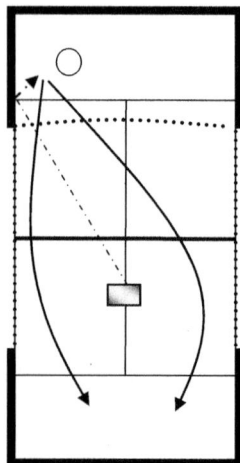

Exercise 0145   Hits: SL – G

Target: Lob side exit
Striking sequence: SLRG// - SLRGX

Description:
Set the player at the bottom of the court, makes an output side parallel backhand lob with and an output side crossed over backhand lob over the string located between the peaks of the court.
After 10 balls is changed player.

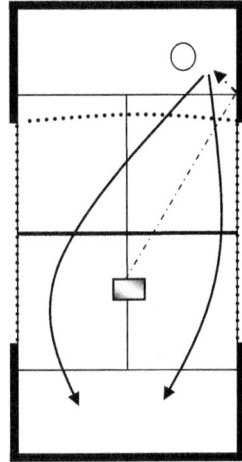

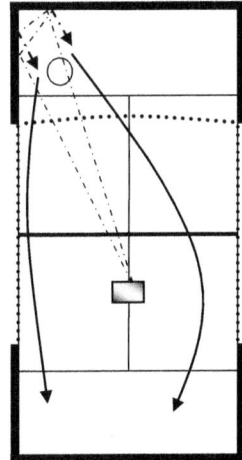

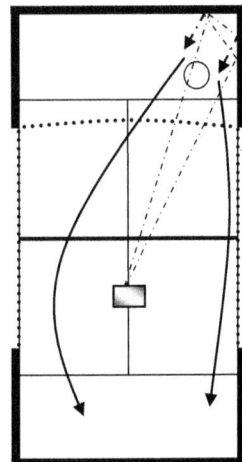

Exercise 0146   Hits: SDP – G

Target: Lob off double wall
Striking sequence: SDPD// - SDPRX

Description:
Set the player at the bottom of the court, makes a double wall outlet with parallel forehand lob and double wall output of crossed over backhand lob over the string located between the peaks of the court.
After 10 balls is changed player.

Exercise 0147   Hits: SDP – G

Target: Lob off double wall
Striking sequence: SDPDX – SDPR//

Description:
Set the player at the bottom of the court, makes a double wall outlet with parallel backhand lob and double wall output of crossed over forehand lob over the string located between the peaks of the court.
After 10 balls is changed player.

Exercise 0148   Hits: SF

Target: Stroke exit checks background
Striking sequence: SFD// o SFR//

Description:
Players located on the back of the court, held parallel output line output line parallel forehand or parallel backhand with the target of the marks on the corners of the court.
After each stroke, the player will touch the cone hits for moving.
After 10 balls position players alternates.

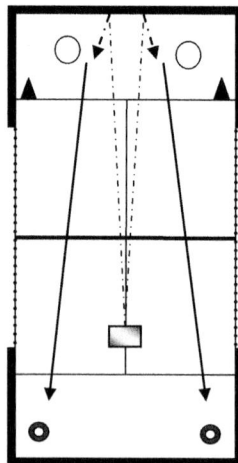

Exercise 0149   Hits: SF

Target: Stroke exit checks background
Striking sequence: SFDX o SFRX

Description:
Players located on the back of the court, held crossed over output line output line crossed over forehand or crossed over backhand with the target of the marks on the corners of the court.
After each stroke, the player will touch the cone hits for moving.
After 10 balls position players alternates.

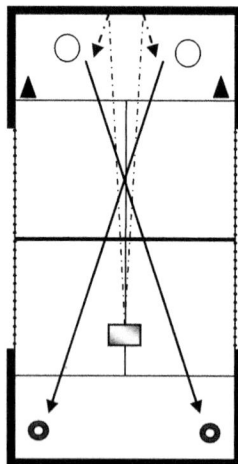

Exercise 0150   Hits: CP

Target: Against wall of forehand
Striking sequence: 8 in cones - CPD

Description:
Set the player at the bottom of the court, hits a cone 8 and run at the ball that you throw to make a smooth forehand against wall against the monitor.
I work only with a ball to adjust the movement and the player has to play it to control and monitor hand.

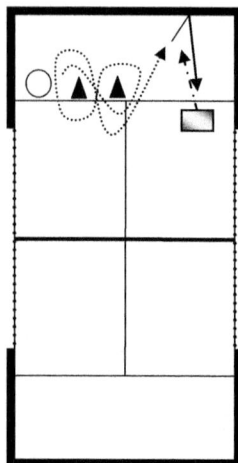

Exercise 0151   Hits: CP

Target: Against wall of bbackhand
Striking sequence: 8 in cones - CPR

Description:
Set the player at the bottom of the court, hits a cone 8 and run at the ball that you throw to make a smooth backhand against wall against the monitor.
I work only with a ball to adjust the movement and the player has to play it to control and monitor hand.

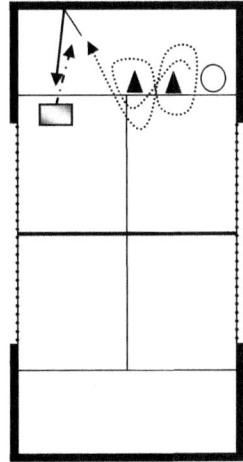

Exercise 0152   Hits: CP

Target: Against wall of forehand
Striking sequence: CPD

Description:
Set the player at the bottom of the court, hits a cone 8 and run at the ball that you throw to make a smooth forehand against wall against the monitor.
We do it with one ball, so that pupils can have the same self well and score well in technical terms which impact both the ball and the bottom wall and commuting to work properly to get well. Important, always turn the body where the ball is going, so we have no injury on knees or lower back.

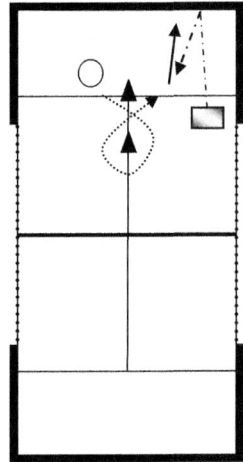

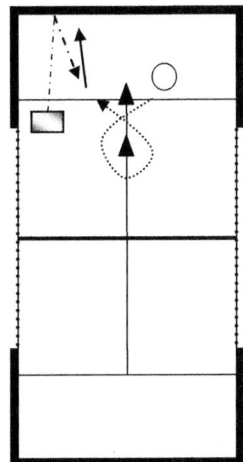

Exercise 0153   Hits: CP

Target: Against wall of backhand
Striking sequence: CPR

Description:
Set the player at the bottom of the court, hits a cone 8 and run at the ball that you throw to make a smooth backhand against wall against the monitor.
We do it with one ball, so that pupils can have the same self well and score well in technical terms which impact both the ball and the bottom wall and commuting to work properly to get well. Important, always turn the body where the ball is going, so we have no injury on knees or lower back.

Exercise 0154   Hits: CP

Target: Against wall of forehand
Striking sequence: 5 Plio - CPD

Description:
Located half-court player, between the cones open and close legs 5 times, and let the ball against background wall and perform of forehand. After each hit, we step on and repeat the punch line (x5).
With one ball more weight in it, we combine physical and technical exercise. We use cones for the pupil to work on them with plyometric exercises. Balls against the wall go hand monitor.

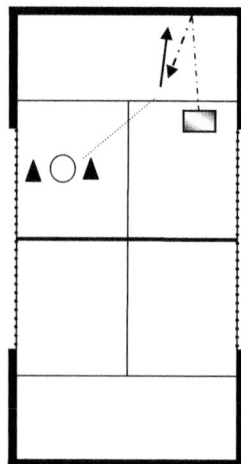

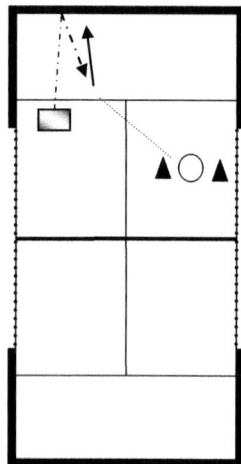

Exercise 0155   Hits: CP

Target: Against wall of backhand
Striking sequence: 5 Plio - CPR

Description:
Located half-court player, between the cones open and close legs 5 times, and let the ball against background wall and perform of backhand. After each hit, we step on and repeat the punch line (x5).
With one ball more weight in it, we combine physical and technical exercise. We use cones for the pupil to work on them with plyometric exercises. Balls against the wall go hand monitor.

Exercise 0156   Hits: SF

Target: Control of scrimmage between 3 players with rebound
Striking sequence: SFD o SFR

Description:
Located players at bottom of the court, one of them alone, hit forehand or backhand after bouncing back wall.
The top player will alternate parallel output background and other output background crossed over.
Players below, one of them held parallel outputs output and the other output background crossed over background, even after rebound.
After 2' position alternates between players.

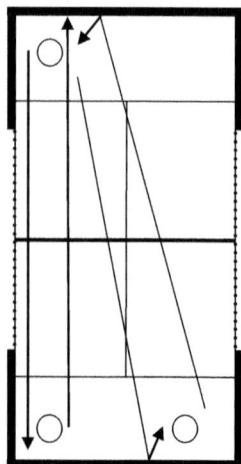

EXERCISES OF VOLLEY

Exercise 0157   Hits: V

Target: Volleys control

Striking sequence: VD// - VRX – VD// - VRX

Description:

Located four players close to the net, above the volleys made in parallel and below volleys in crossed over.

After striking 2' orientation is changed.

After 2' position players alternates.

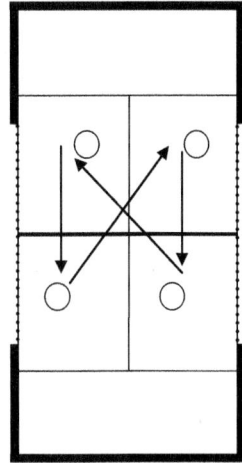

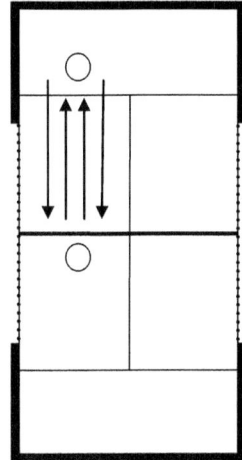

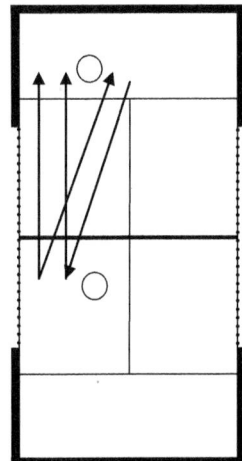

Exercise 0158   Hits: D – R – V

Target: Control volleys between two players

Striking sequence: VD // – VR//

Description:

Placed a player on the net and one in the back of the court, the player in the net will make a parallel forehand volley and a parallel backhand volley against the player who is in the position of defense.

After 2' position players alternates.

Exercise 0159   Hits: D – R – V

Target: Control volleys between two players

Striking sequence: VR // – VR//

Description:

Placed a player on the net and one in the back of the court, the player in the net will make a parallel backhand volley and a parallel backhand volley against the player who is in the position of defense. He will alternate the direction of their volleys.

After 2' position players alternates.

Exercise 0160   Hits: D – R – V

Target: Control volleys with three players
Striking sequence: V// – VX

Description:
Placed a player on the back of the court and the other two in the net, the player of the back of the court defends the volleys of opposites striking once on each side.
After 2' position players alternates.

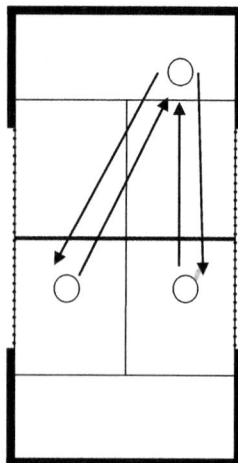

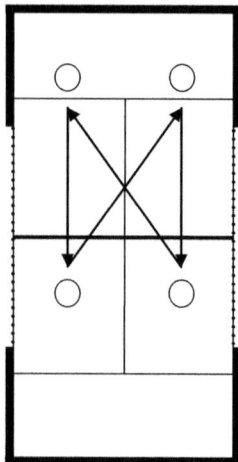

Exercise 0161   Hits: D – R – V

Target: Volley displacement control
Striking sequence: VD – VR

Description:
Set the player at the bottom of the court, he will make backhand volleys and forehand volleys of each shift with cones placed on the court.
After 12 balls is changed player.

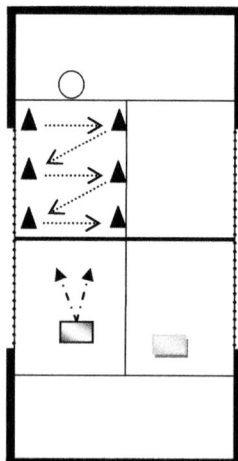

Exercise 0162   Hits: D – R – V

Target: Control volleys with four players
Striking sequence: VX – VX

Description:
Located two players at the bottom of the court and the other two in the net, players perform background parallels hits and the players in the net perform crossed over volleys.
If the exercise is mastered, you can try with two balls at once.
After 2'position players alternates.

Exercise 0163   Hits: V

Target: Control volleys against the wall
Striking sequence: VD

Description:
Located player in the bottom of the court made of forehand volleys against the wall in front of the line serve alternating speed and height.
Duration of exercise 1'

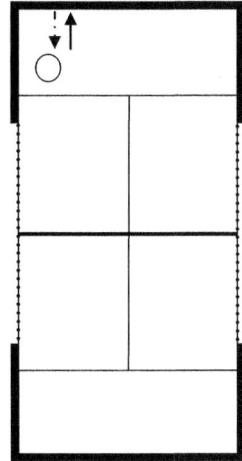

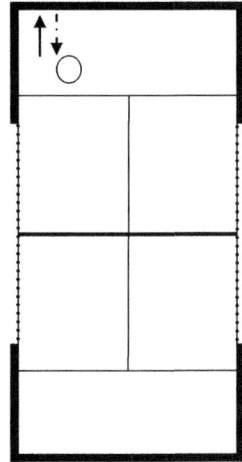

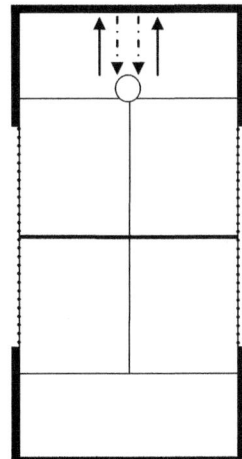

Exercise 0164   Hits: V

Target: Control volleys against the wall
Striking sequence: VR

Description:
Located player in the bottom of the court made of backhand volleys against the wall in front of the line serve alternating speed and height.
Duration of exercise 1'

Exercise 0165   Hits: V

Target: Control volleys against the wall
Striking sequence: VD – VR

Description:
Located player in the bottom of the court made forehand volleys and backhand volleys against the wall in front of the line serve alternating speed and height.
Duration of exercise 1'

Exercise 0166   Hits: V

Target: Control volleys against the wall
Striking sequence: VD

Description:
Located player in the bottom of the court will make a forehand volley against the wall and return to the row.
Duration of exercise 2'

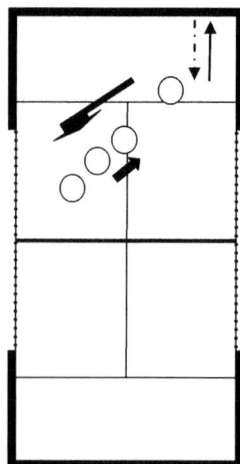

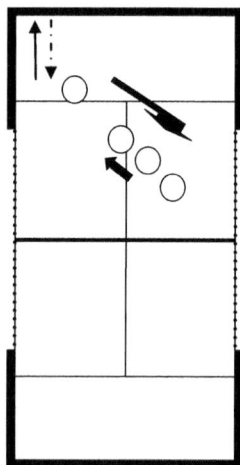

Exercise 0167   Hits: V

Target: Control volleys against the wall
Striking sequence: VR

Description:
Located player in the bottom of the court will make a backhand volley against the wall and return to the row.
Duration of exercise 2'

Exercise 0168   Hits: V

Target: Control volleys against the wall
Striking sequence: V free

Description:
Located half-court players will make a volley and return to the row. Who lost ball stops bouncing.
2' exercise duration or who reaches 5 failures.

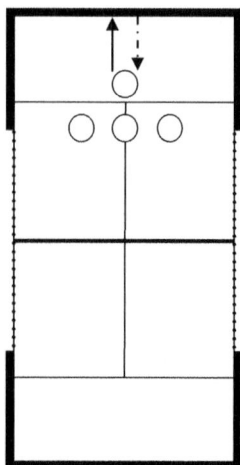

Exercise 0169   Hits: V

Target: Control volleys with 3 players
Striking sequence: V free

Description:
Located players in the net, two on one side and another one, which is one volley after each of his teammates.
After 2' position players alternates.

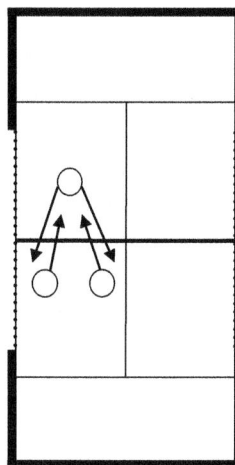

Exercise 0170   Hits: V

Target: Control volleys with 3 players
Striking sequence: VD// - VRX

Description:
Located players in the net, two on either side alone, which it is only will make parallel forehand volley and crossed over backhand volley.
After 2'position players alternates.

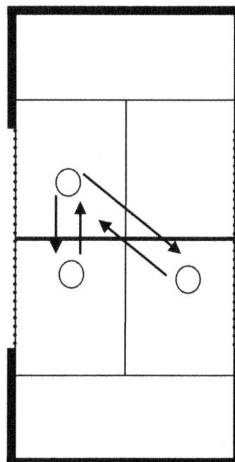

Exercise 0171   Hits: V

Target: Control volleys with 3 players
Striking sequence: VD// - VRX

Description:
Located players in the net, two on either side alone, which it is only will make parallel backhand volley and crossed over forehand volley.
After 2'position players alternates.

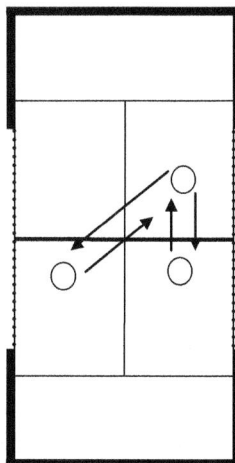

Exercise 0172   Hits: V

Target: Control volleys with 3 players
Striking sequence: V free

Description:
Located players in the net, two on either side alone, which it is alone volley twice each player both forehand backhand.
After 2' position players alternates.

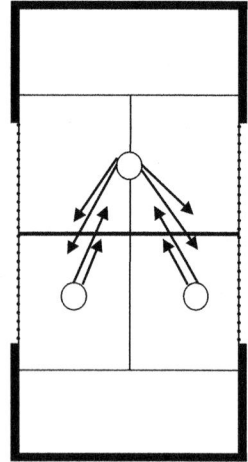

Exercise 0173   Hits: V

Target: Control volleys with 4 players
Striking sequence: V// - VX – V// - VX

Description:
Located players in the net, top players perform crossed over volleys and below players perform parallel volleys.
After 2' position players alternates.

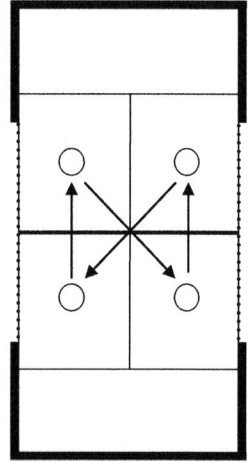

Exercise 0174   Hits: V

Target: Control volleys with 4 players
Striking sequence: VD// - VRX – VD// - VRX

Description:
Located players in the net, top players perform parallel volleys and below players perform crossed over volleys.
After 2' position players alternates.

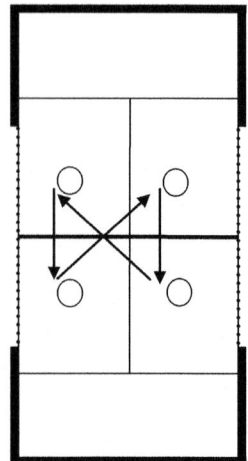

Exercise 0175   Hits: V

Target: Control volleys with 4 players
Striking sequence: V// - VX – V// - VX

Description:
Located players in the net, top players perform parallel volleys and below players perform crossed over volleys, but we work with two balls at once.
After 2' position players alternates.

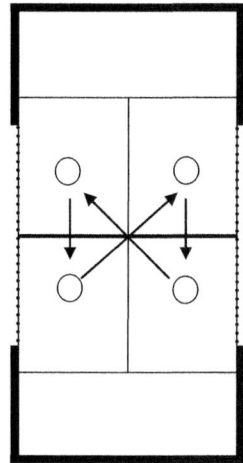

Exercise 0176   Hits: V

Target: Control volley with lateral displacement
Striking sequence: VD

Description:
Players located on the side of the court near the net, players perform three forehand volleys with displacement to the the target marked on the bottom of the court and return to the line.

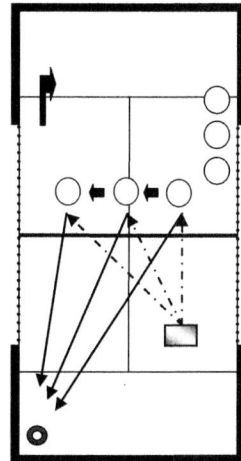

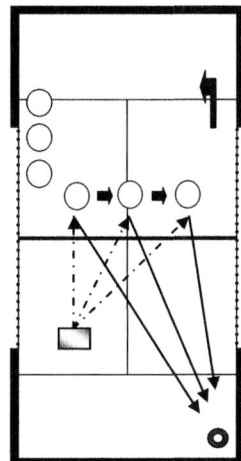

Exercise 0177   Hits: V

Target: Control volley with lateral displacement
Striking sequence: VR

Description:
Players located on the side of the court near the net, players perform three backhand volleys with displacement to the the target marked on the bottom of the court and return to the line.

Exercise 0178   Hits: V

Target: Control volley with displacement
Striking sequence: VD scrolling forward

Description:
Located players on the line of serve, done with forward motion three forehand volleys to cross the target marked on the bottom of the court and return to the line.

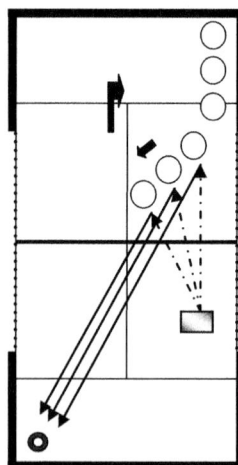

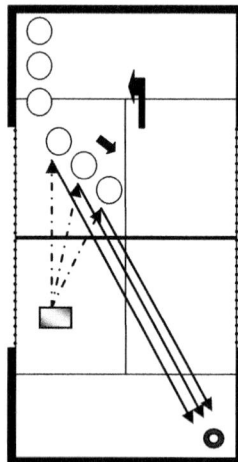

Exercise 0179   Hits: V

Target: Control volley with displacement
Striking sequence: VR scrolling forward

Description:
Located players on the line of serve, done with forward motion three backhand volleys to cross the target marked on the bottom of the court and return to the line.

Exercise 0180   Hits: V

Target: Volleys control
Striking sequence: Alternative volley

Description:
Players located on the midline, made with forward movement, a crossed over volley.
If the number of pupils is odd, will alternate forehand and backhand. If the number of pupils is even, the monitor will alternate the hits for all pupils to work both sides.
Once they realized the coup, again row.

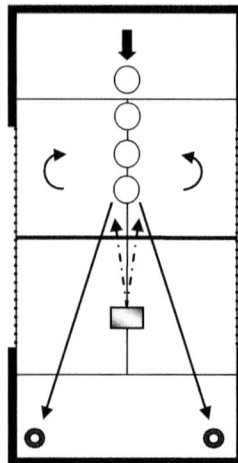

Exercise 0181   Hits: V

Target: Volleys control
Striking sequence: VR// - VDX

Description:
Players located on one side of the court near the net, perform a parallel backhand volley and crossed over forehand volley to the marks on the corners, and return to the line.

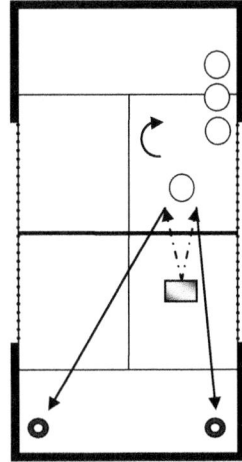

Exercise 0182   Hits: V

Target: Volleys control
Striking sequence: VD// - VRX

Description:
Players located on one side of the court near the net, perform a parallel forehand volley and crossed over backhand volley to the marks on the corners, and return to the line.

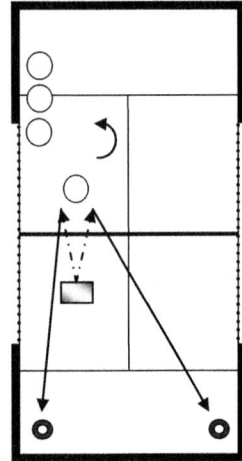

Exercise 0183   Hits: V

Target: Volleys control
Striking sequence: VD// - VRX

Description:
Set the player near the net, perform a parallel forehand volley and a crossed over backhand volley to the marks on the corners.
After 10 balls is changed player.

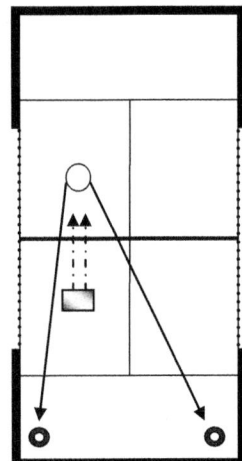

Exercise 0184   Hits: V

Target: Volleys control
Striking sequence: VR// - VDX

Description:
Set the player near the net, perform a parallel backhand volley and a crossed over forehand volley to the marks on the corners.
After 10 balls is changed player.

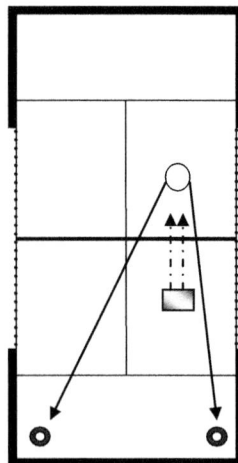

Exercise 0185   Hits: V

Target: Volleys control
Striking sequence: VD// - VDX - VR// - VRX

Description:
Located player near the net, striking perform the following sequence of marks on the corners:
parallel forehand volley, crossed over forehand volley, parallel backhand volley, crossed over backhand volley and continue with the exercise.
After 12 balls is changed player.

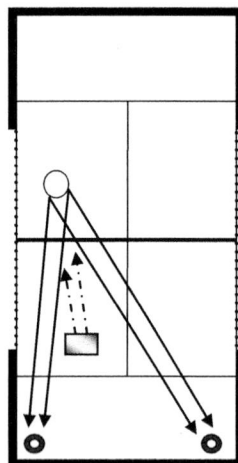

Exercise 0186   Hits: V

Target: Volleys control
Striking sequence: VD// - VDX - VR// - VRX

Description:
Located player near the net, striking perform the following sequence of marks on the corners:
parallel backhand volley, crossed over backhand volley, parallel forehand volley, crossed over forehand volley and continue with the exercise.
After 12 balls is changed player.

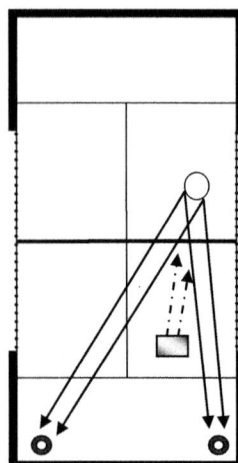

Exercise 0187   Hits: V

Target: Volleys control
Striking sequence: VD// - VDX short with angle

Description:
Set the player near the net, perform a parallel forehand volley and a short crossed over forehand volley with angle to the marks on the court.
After 10 balls is changed player.

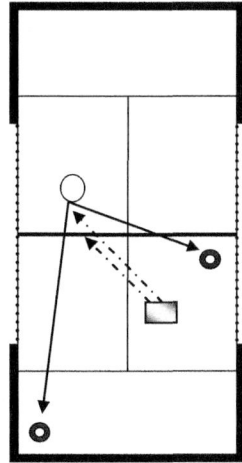

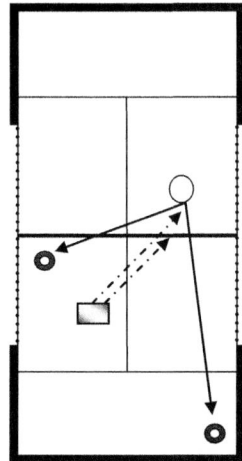

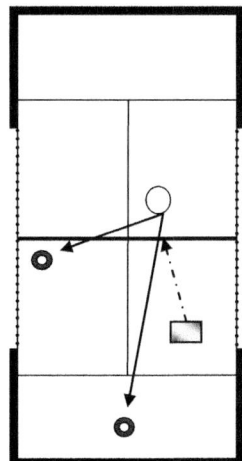

Exercise 0188   Hits: V

Target: Volleys control
Striking sequence: VR// - VRX short with angle

Description:
Set the player near the net, perform a parallel backhand volley and a short crossed over backhand volley with angle to the marks on the court.
After 10 balls is changed player.

Exercise 0189   Hits: V

Target: Volleys control
Striking sequence: VR to the center - VRX short angle

Description:
Set the player near the net, perform a backhand volley to the center and a short crossed over backhand volley with angle to the marks on the court.
After 10 balls is changed player.

Exercise 0190　　Hits: V

Target: Volleys control
Striking sequence: VD to the center - VDX short with angle

Description:
Set the player near the net, perform a forehand volley to the center and a short crossed over forehand volley with angle to the marks on the court.
After 10 balls is changed player.

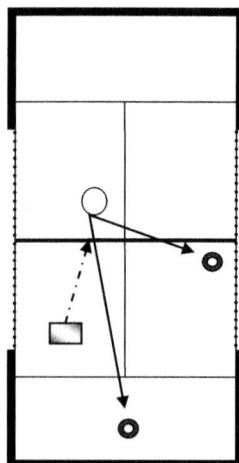

Exercise 0191　　Hits: V

Target: Volleys control
Striking sequence: VR to the center – VD//

Description:
Set the player near the net, perform a backhand volley to the center and a strong parallel forehand volley to the marks on the bottom of the court.
After 10 balls is changed player.

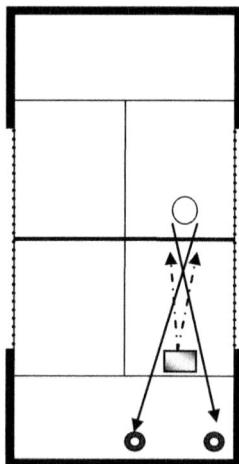

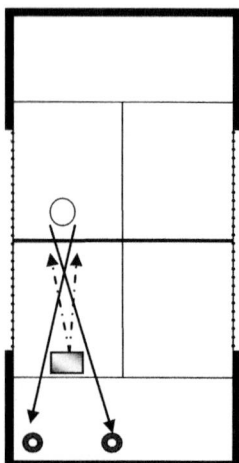

Exercise 0192　　Hits: V

Target: Volleys control
Striking sequence: VD to the center – VR//

Description:
Set the player near the net, perform a forehand volley to the center and a strong parallel backhand volley to the marks on the bottom of the court.
After 10 balls is changed player.

Exercise 0193   Hits: V

Target: Volleys control
Striking sequence: VRX short –VR center – VD// strong

Description:
Set the player near the net, perform a short angled crossed over backhand volley, a backhand volley to the center and a strong parallel forehand volley to the marks on the court.
After 12 balls is changed player.

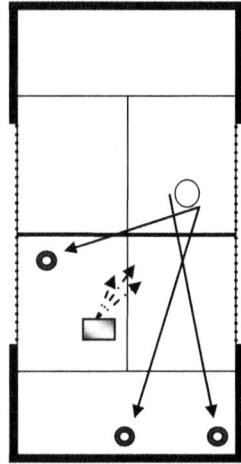

Exercise 0194   Hits: V

Target: Volleys control
Striking sequence: VDX short –VD center – VR// strong

Description:
Set the player near the net, perform a short angled crossed over forehand volley, a forehand volley to the center and a strong parallel backhand volley to the marks on the court.
After 12 balls is changed player.

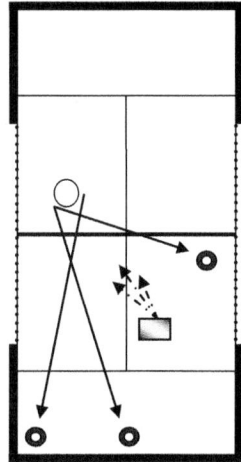

Exercise 0195   Hits: V

Target: Volleys control
Striking sequence: VD// - VR//

Description:
Set the player near the net, perform a parallel forehand volley and a parallel backhand volley to the marks on the bottom of the court, passing behind the cone after each blow.
After 10 balls is changed player.
Then it is done on the other side.

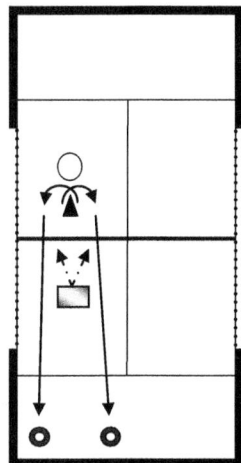

Exercise 0196   Hits: V

Target: Changing volleys
Striking sequence: Volley – Fast Volley - Left

Description:
Set the player near the net, the monitor will throw 10 balls and the player will alternate a left or a quick volley every two normal volleys.
After 10 balls you change player

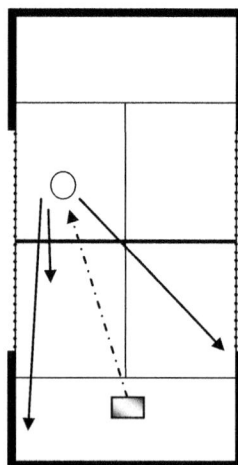

Exercise 0197   Hits: V

Target: Volleys control
Striking sequence: VD// - VRX

Description:
Set the player near the net, perform a parallel forehand volley and a crossed over backhand volley to the marks on the corner, passing behind the cone after each blow.
After 10 balls is changed player.

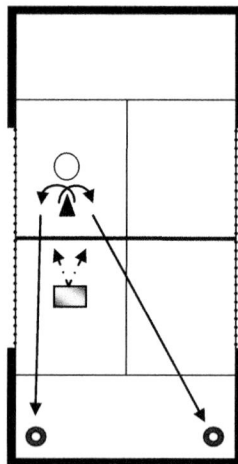

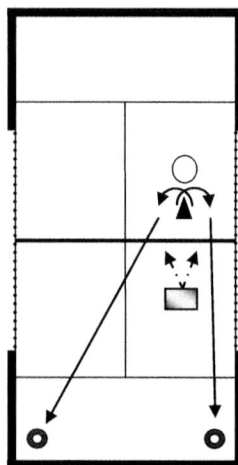

Exercise 0198   Hits: V

Target: Volleys control
Striking sequence: VDX – VR//

Description:
Set the player near the net, perform a parallel backhand volley and a crossed over forehand volley to the marks on the corner, passing behind the cone after each blow.
After 10 balls is changed player.

Exercise 0199   Hits: V

Target: Volleys control
Striking sequence: VDX – VR//

Description:
Set the player near the net, perform a short crossed over forehand volley and an angled parallel backhand volley to the marks on the court, passing behind the cone after each blow.
After 10 balls is changed player.

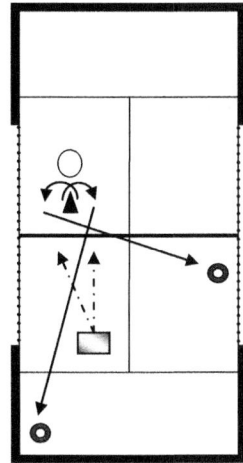

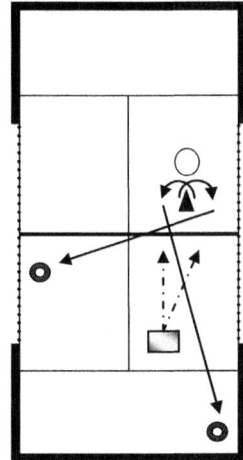

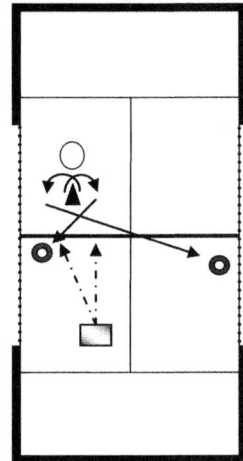

Exercise 0200   Hits: V

Target: Volleys control
Striking sequence: VRX - VD//

Description:
Set the player near the net, perform a short crossed over backhand volley and an angled parallel forehand volley to the marks on the court, passing behind the cone after each blow.
After 10 balls is changed player.

Exercise 0201   Hits: V

Target: Volleys control
Striking sequence: VDX short – VR// short

Description:
Set the player near the net, perform a short crossed over forehand volley and an angled parallel backhand volley to the marks on the court, passing behind the cone after each blow.
After 10 balls is changed player.

Exercise 0202   Hits: V

Target: Volleys control
Striking sequence: VRX short – VD// short

Description:
Set the player near the net, perform a short crossed over backhand volley and an angled parallel forehand volley to the marks on the court, passing behind the cone after each blow.
After 10 balls is changed player.

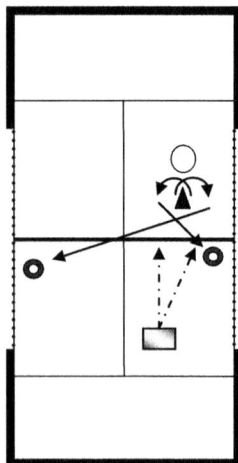

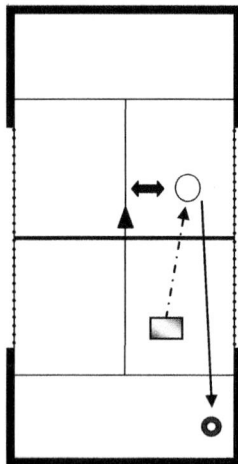

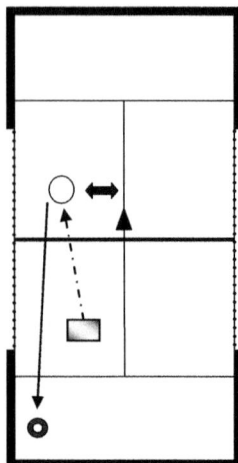

Exercise 0203   Hits: V

Target: Backhand volley on the move
Striking sequence: VR//

Description:
Located player near the net, perform a parallel backhand volley to the mark on the court and then touch the blue cone at the middle of the court.
After 10 balls is changed player.

Exercise 0204   Hits: V

Target: Forehand volley on the move
Striking sequence: VD//

Description:
Located player near the net, perform a parallel forehand volley to the mark on the court and then touch the blue cone at the middle of the court.
After 10 balls is changed player.

Exercise 0205   Hits: V

Target: Moving volleys
Striking sequence: VR// – touch cone – VRX

Description:
Set the player near the net, perform a parallel backhand volley, touch the blue cone and make another short backhand volley with angle to the target of the marks on the court.
After 10 balls is changed player.

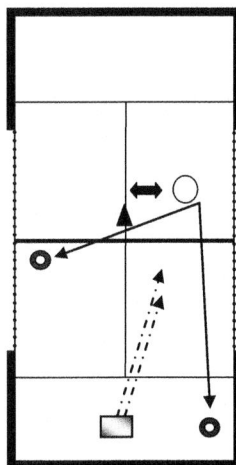

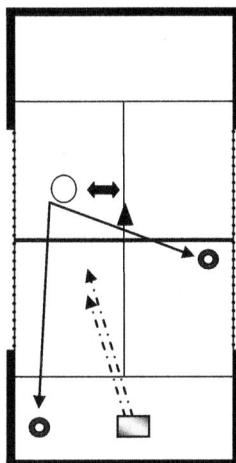

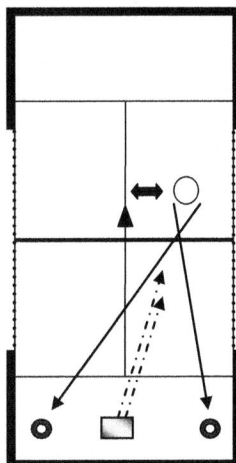

Exercise 0206   Hits: V

Target: Moving volleys
Striking sequence: VD// – touch cone – VDX

Description:
Set the player near the net, perform a parallel forehand volley, touch the blue cone and make another short forehand volley with angle to the target of the marks on the court.
After 10 balls is changed player.

Exercise 0207   Hits: V

Target: Moving volleys
Striking sequence: VD// – touch cone – VRX

Description:
Set the player near the net, perform a parallel forehand volley, touch the blue cone and make another crossed over backhand volley to the target of the marks on the court.
After 10 balls is changed player.

Exercise 0208   Hits: V

Target: Moving volleys
Striking sequence: VDX – touch cone – VR//

Description:
Set the player near the net, perform a parallel backhand volley, touch the blue cone and make another crossed over forehand volley to the target of the marks on the court.
After 10 balls is changed player.

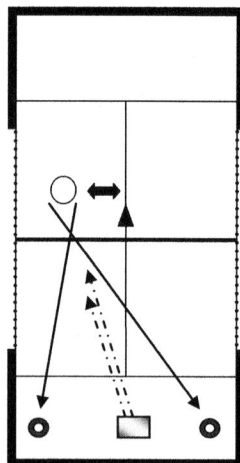

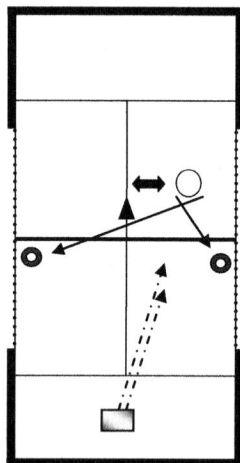

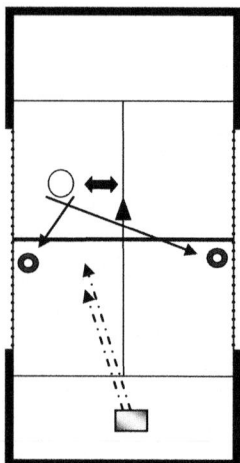

Exercise 0209   Hits: V

Target: Moving volleys
Striking sequence: VD// short – touch cone – VRX short

Description:
Set the player near the net, perform a short parallel forehand volley, touch the blue cone and make another short crossed over backhand volley, with the target of the marks located near the net.
After 10 balls is changed player.

Exercise 0210   Hits: V

Target: Moving volleys
Striking sequence: VR// short – touch cone – VDX short

Description:
Set the player near the net, perform a short parallel backhand volley, touch the blue cone and make another short crossed over forehand volley, with the target of the marks located near the net.
After 10 balls is changed player.

Exercise 0211   Hits: V

Target: Moving volleys
Striking sequence: VD// – touch cone – VR//

Description:
Set the player near the net, perform a parallel forehand volley, touch the blue cone and perform another parallel backhand volley, with the target of the marks at the bottom of the court.
After 10 balls is changed player.

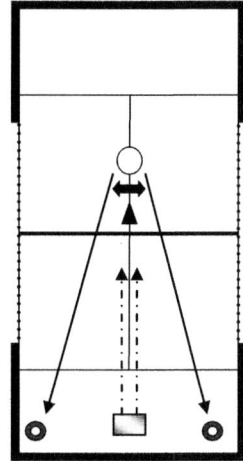

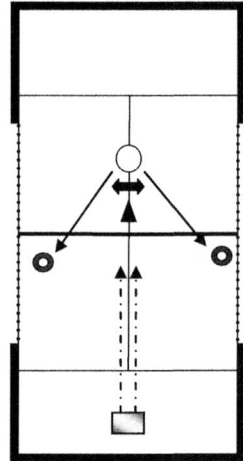

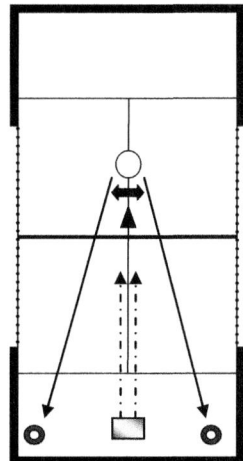

Exercise 0212   Hits: V

Target: Moving volleys
Striking sequence: VD// short – touch cone – VR// short

Description:
Set the player near the net, perform a short parallel forehand volley, touch the blue cone and perform another short parallel backhand volley, with the target of the marks near the net.
After 10 balls is changed player.

Exercise 0213   Hits: V

Target: Moving volleys
Striking sequence: VD//-VD//–touch cone–VR//-VR//

Description:
Set the player near the net, make two parallel forehand volleys, touch the blue cone and performed two parallel backhand volleys, with the target of the marks at the bottom of the court.
After 10 balls is changed player.

Exercise 0214   Hits: V

Target: Moving volleys
Striking sequence: VDX – VRX

Description:
Located player near the net, perform a short crossed over forehand volley, pass behind the cone and perform a short crossed over backhand volley, with the target of marks located near the net.
After 10 balls is changed player.

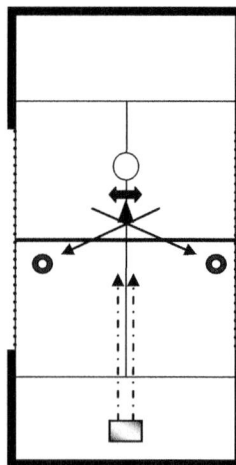

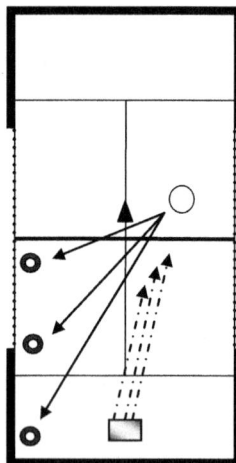

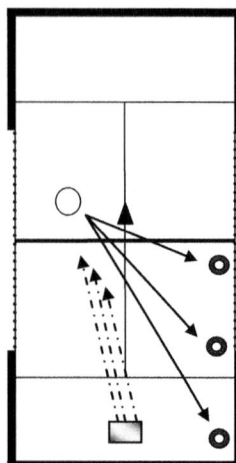

Exercise 0215   Hits: V

Target: Moving volleys
Striking sequence: VDX – VDX – VDX

Description:
Set the player near the net, make three crossed over forehand volleys to the various targets located on the court.
After 10 balls is changed player.

Exercise 0216   Hits: V

Target: Moving volleys
Striking sequence: VRX – VRX – VRX

Description:
Set the player near the net, make three crossed over backhand volleys to the various targets located on the court.
After 10 balls is changed player.

Exercise 0217   Hits: V

Target: Moving volleys
Striking sequence: VRX – VRX – VDX

Description:
Located half-court player, make two crossed over backhand volleys and a crossed over forehand volley from different positions at the same target located on the bottom of the court, and will perform the exercise again.
After 12 balls is changed player.

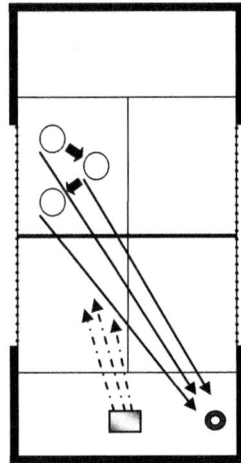

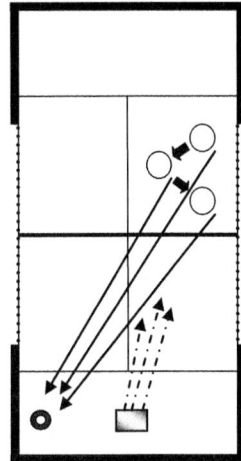

Exercise 0218   Hits: V

Target: Moving volleys
Striking sequence: VDX – VDX – VRX

Description:
Located half-court player, make two crossed over forehand volleys and a crossed over backhand volley from different positions at the same target located on the bottom of the court, and will perform the exercise again.
After 12 balls is changed player.

Exercise 0219   Hits: V

Target: Lock volleys
Striking sequence: VRX

Description:
Set the player near the net, attached to the grid, the player will cover the middle and blocked backhand volley to cross to the mark on the bottom of the court, and will perform the exercise again.
After 10 balls is changed player.

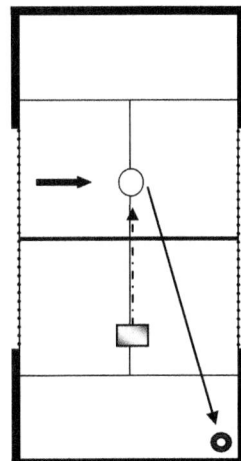

Exercise 0220   Hits: V

Target: Lock volleys
Striking sequence: VDX

Description:
Set the player near the net, attached to the grid, the player will cover the middle and block forehand volley to cross to the mark on the bottom of the court, and will perform the exercise again.
After 10 balls is changed player.

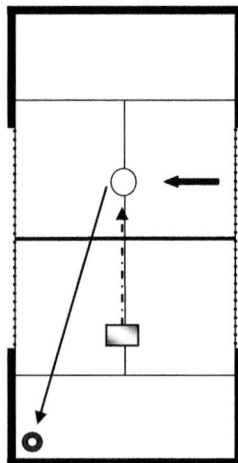

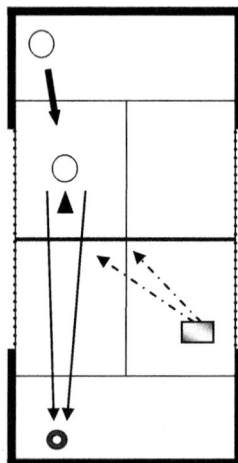

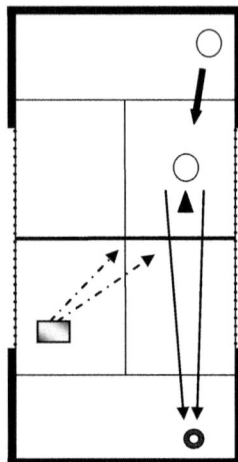

Exercise 0221   Hits: V

Target: Moving volleys
Striking sequence: VD// - VR//

Description:
Set the player at the bottom of the court, will go running to the net and made two parallel forehand volleys and two parallel backhand volleys to the mark on the back of the court and do the exercise again.
After 10 balls is changed player.

Exercise 0222   Hits: V

Target: Moving volleys
Striking sequence: VD// - VR//

Description:
Set the player at the bottom of the court, will go running to the net and made two parallel backhand volleys and two parallel forehand volleys to the mark on the back of the court and do the exercise again.
After 10 balls is changed player.

Exercise 0223   Hits: V

Target: Moving volleys
Striking sequence: VDX short - VR//

Description:
Set the player at the bottom of the court, will go running to the net and volleys take place, and the player will make a parallel forehand to the bottom of the court and another short crossed over backhand to the mark located near the net, and will perform the exercise again.
After 10 balls is changed player.

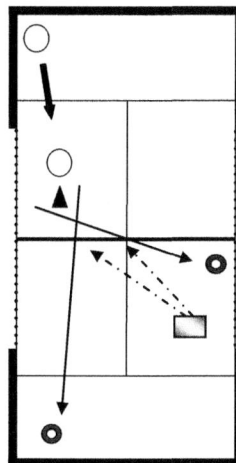

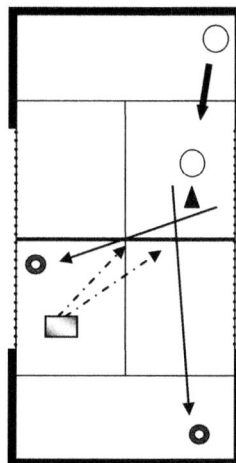

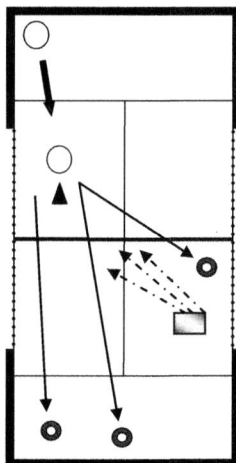

Exercise 0224   Hits: V

Target: Moving volleys
Striking sequence: VD// - VRX short

Description:
Set the player at the bottom of the court, will go running to the net and volleys take place, and the player will make a parallel backhand to the bottom of the court and another short crossed over forehand to the mark located near the net, and will perform the exercise again.
After 10 balls is changed player.

Exercise 0225   Hits: V

Target: Moving volleys
Striking sequence: VD// - VR in the middle - VRX

Description:
Set the player at the bottom of the court, will go running to the net and made a parallel forehand volley to the bottom of the court, another backhand volley in the middle and another short crossed over backhand volley, with the target of the marks on the court, and will perform the exercise again.
 After 10 balls is changed player.

Exercise 0226   Hits: V

Target: Moving volleys
Striking sequence: VR// - VD in the middle - VDX

Description:
Set the player at the bottom of the court, will go running to the net and made a parallel backhand volley to the bottom of the court, another forehand volley in the middle and another short crossed over forehand volley, with the target of the marks on the court, and will perform the exercise again.
After 10 balls is changed player.

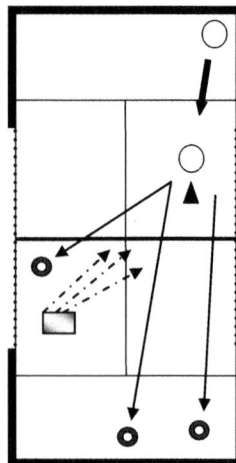

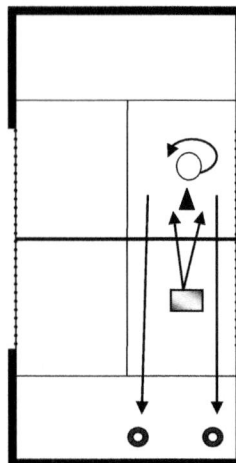

Exercise 0227   Hits: V

Target: Combination of hits with displacement
Striking sequence: VD – VR

Description:
Located players lined up near the net, will hold a forehand volley and a backhand volley against the monitor and return to the line.

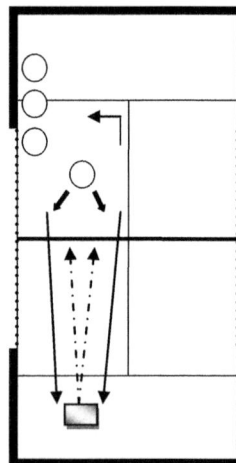

Exercise 0228   Hits: V

Target: Rotating Volleys
Striking sequence: VD// - VR//

Description:
Set the player near the net, takes a turn after each volley parallel forehand volley or parallel backhand volley with the target of the marks at the bottom of the court.
After 10 balls is changed player.

Exercise 0229   Hits: V

Target: Rotating Volleys
Striking sequence: VDX - VRX

Description:
Set the player near the net, takes a turn after each crossed over forehand volley or crossed over backhand volley, with the target of the mark at the bottom of the court.
After 10 balls is changed player.

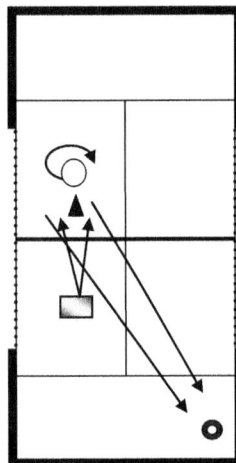

Exercise 0230   Hits: V

Target: Volley displacement control
Striking sequence: VD// – VD// – VD//

Description:
Located player in the back of the court, held parallel forehand volleys, touch the cone your left and advance to the next volley, with the target of the mark at the bottom of the court.
After 12 balls player changes.

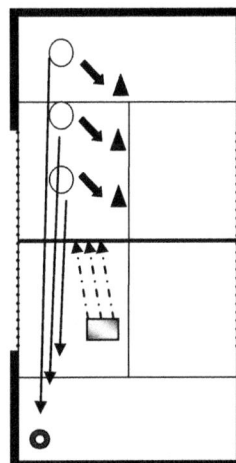

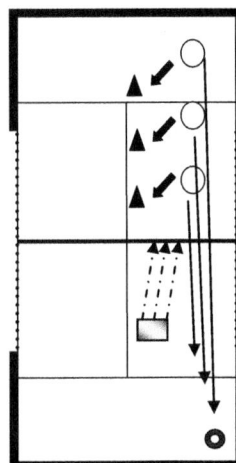

Exercise 0231   Hits: V

Target: Volley displacement control
Striking sequence: VR// – VR// – VR//

Description:
Located player in the back of the court, held parallel backhand volleys, touch the cone of his right and advance to the next volley, with the target of the mark at the bottom of the court.
After 12 balls player changes.

Exercise 0232   Hits: V

Target: Volley displacement control
Striking sequence: VD middle – VD middle – VD middle

Description:
Set the player at the bottom of the court, made forehand volleys to the middle, touch the cone of the left and advance to the next volley, with the target of the mark at the bottom of the court.
After 12 balls player changes.

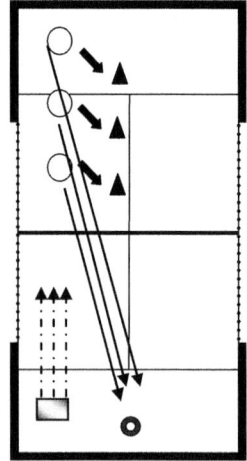

Exercise 0233   Hits: V

Target: Volley displacement control
Striking sequence: VR middle – VR middle – VR middle

Description:
Located player in the back of the court, held backhand volleys to the middle, touch the cone of his right and advance to the next volley, with the target of the mark at the bottom of the court.
After 12 balls player changes.

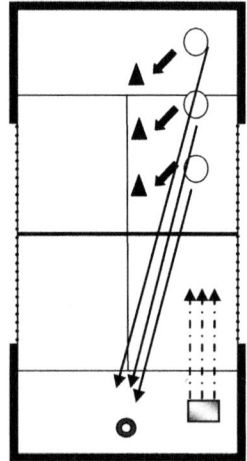

Exercise 0234   Hits: V

Target: Volley displacement control
Striking sequence: VDX – VDX – VDX

Description:
Set the player at the bottom of the court, will crossed over forehand volleys, touch the cone of the left and advance to the next volley, with the target of the mark at the bottom of the court.
After 12 balls player changes.

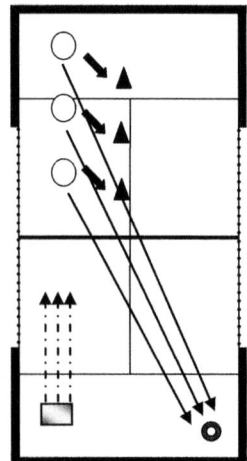

Exercise 0235   Hits: V

Target: Volley displacement control
Striking sequence: VRX – VRX – VRX

Description:
Set the player at the bottom of the court, will crossed backhand volleys, touch the cone of his right and advance to the next volley, with the target of the mark at the bottom of the court.
After 12 balls player changes.

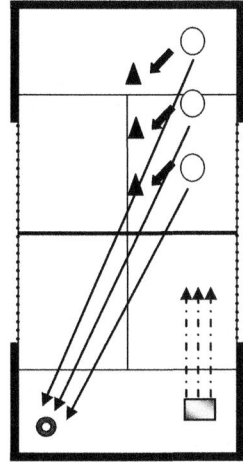

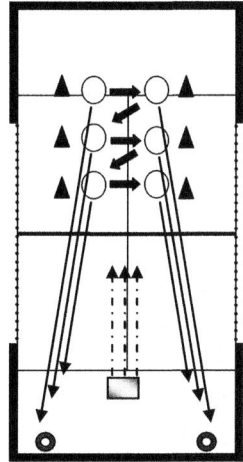

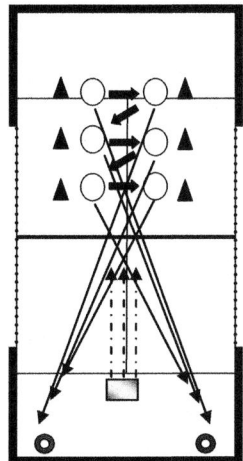

Exercise 0236   Hits: V

Target: Volley displacement control
Striking sequence: VD// - VR//

Description:
Set the player at the bottom of the court and with a zigzag movement forward, the player will perform parallel forehand volleys and parallel backhand volleys to the height of the cones, with the target of the marks at the bottom of the court.
After 12 balls player changes.

Exercise 0237   Hits: V

Target: Volley displacement control
Striking sequence: VDX - VRX

Description:
Set the player at the bottom of the court and with a zigzag movement forward, the player will perform crossed over forehand volleys and crossed over backhand volleys to the height of the cones, with the target of the marks at the bottom of the court.
After 12 balls player changes.

Exercise 0238   Hits: V

Target: Volley displacement control
Striking sequence: VDX - VR//

Description:
Set the player at the bottom of the court and with a zigzag movement forward, the player will perform crossed over forehand volleys and parallel backhand volleys to the height of the cones, with the target of the marks at the bottom of the court.
After 12 balls player changes.

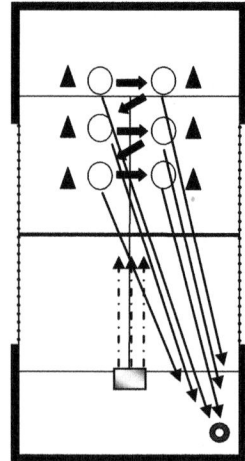

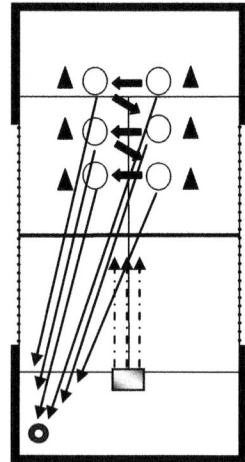

Exercise 0239   Hits: V

Target: Volley displacement control
Striking sequence: VD// - VRX

Description:
Set the player at the bottom of the court and with a zigzag movement forward, the player will perform crossed over backhand volleys and parallel forehand volleys to the height of the cones, with the target of the marks at the bottom of the court.
After 12 balls player changes.

Exercise 0240   Hits: V

Target: Volley displacement control
Striking sequence: VDX - VRX

Description:
Set the player near the net, made crossed over forehand volleys and crossed over backhand volleys through the area marked with the target of the marks at the bottom of the court.
After 10 balls is changed player.

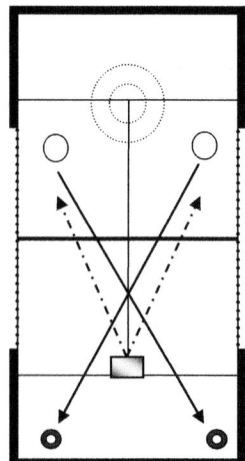

Exercise 0241   Hits: V

Target: Volley displacement control
Striking sequence: VD// - VR//

Description:
Set the player near the net, made parallel forehand volleys and parallel backhand volleys through the area marked with the target of the marks at the bottom of the court.
After 10 balls is changed player.

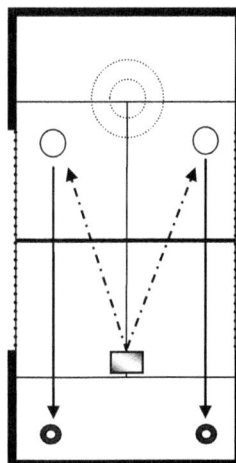

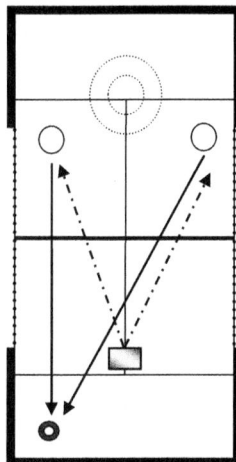

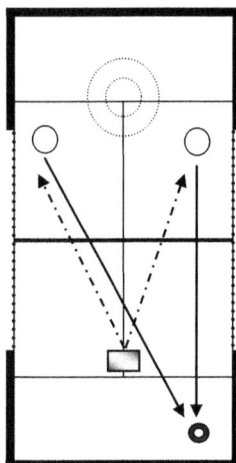

Exercise 0242   Hits: V

Target: Volley displacement control
Striking sequence: VD// - VRX

Description:
Set the player near the net, made parallel forehand volleys and crossed over backhand volleys through the area marked with the target of the marks at the bottom of the court.
After 10 balls is changed player.

Exercise 0243   Hits: V

Target: Volley displacement control
Striking sequence: VDX – VR//

Description:
Set the player near the net, made crossed over forehand volleys and parallel backhand volleys through the area marked with the target of the marks at the bottom of the court.
After 10 balls is changed player.

Exercise 0244   Hits: V

Target: Volley displacement control
Striking sequence: VD// – VR//

Description:
Set the player near the net on the middle line, alternate parallel forehand volleys and parallel backhand volleys at different distances, with the target of the marks on the back of the court.
After 10 balls is changed player.

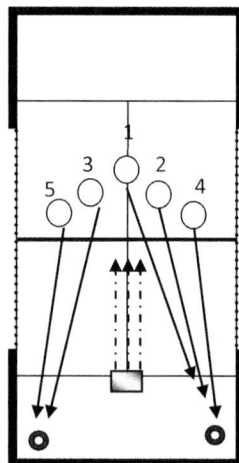

Exercise 0245   Hits: V

Target: Volley displacement control
Striking sequence: VDX – VRX

Description:
Set the player near the net on the middle line, alternate crossed over forehand volleys and crossed over backhand volleys at different distances, with the target of the marks on the back of the court.
After 10 balls is changed player.

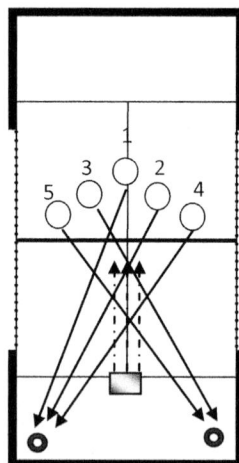

Exercise 0246   Hits: V

Target: Volley displacement control
Striking sequence: VDX – VR//

Description:
Set the player near the net on the middle line, alternate crossed over backhand volleys and parallel backhand volleys at different distances, with the target of the marks on the back of the court.
After 10 balls is changed player.

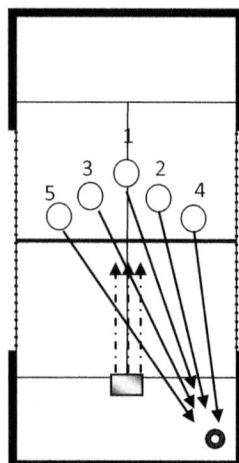

Exercise 0247   Hits: V

Target: Volley displacement control
Striking sequence: VD// – VRX

Description:
Set the player near the net on the middle line, alternate crossed over forehand volleys and parallel forehand volleys at different distances, with the target of the marks on the back of the court.
After 10 balls is changed player.

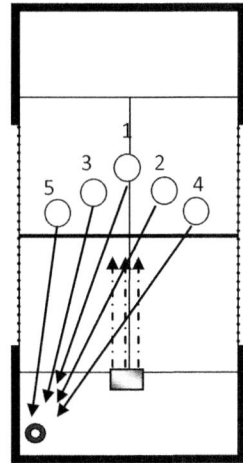

Exercise 0248   Hits: V

Target: Volleys control
Striking sequence: VD// - change – VR// - change

Description:
Players located near the net in two rows, perform a parallel forehand volley and change of line to make a parallel backhand volley and switch back row.

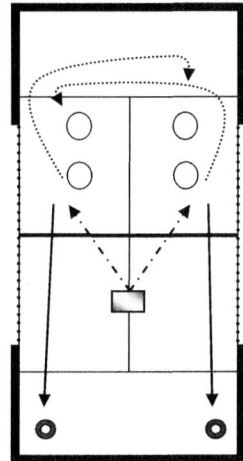

Exercise 0249   Hits: V

Target: Volleys controls
Striking sequence: VDX - change – VRX - change

Description:
Players located near the net in two rows, perform a crossed over forehand volley and change of line to make a crossed over backhand volley and switch back row.

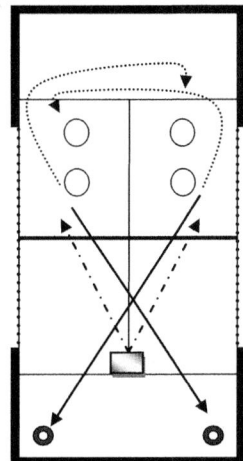

Exercise 0250   Hits: V

Target: Moving volleys
Striking sequence: VD – VD – VD

Description:
Set the player near the net, make three forehand volleys of moving with the target of the mark on the corner of the court.
After 12 balls you change player

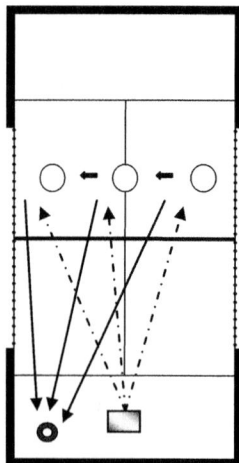

Exercise 0251   Hits: V

Target: Moving volleys
Striking sequence: VR – VR – VR

Description:
Set the player near the net, make three backhand volleys of moving with the target of the mark on the corner of the court.
After 12 balls is changed player.

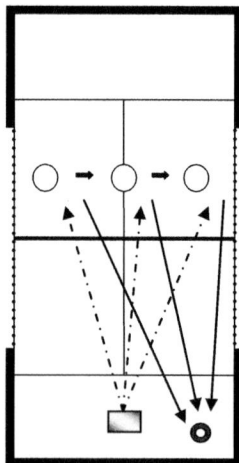

Exercise 0252   Hits: V

Target: Moving volleys
Striking sequence: VD – VD – VD

Description:
Set the player near the net, make three forehand volleys of moving with the target of the mark on the corner of the court.
After 12 balls is changed player.

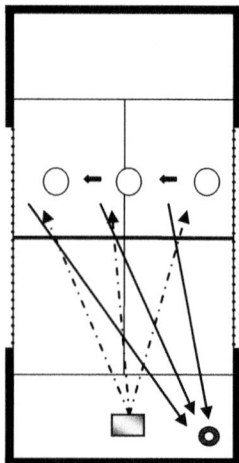

Exercise 0253   Hits: V

Target: Moving volleys
Striking sequence: VR – VR – VR

Description:
Set the player near the net, make three backhand volleys of moving with the target of the mark on the corner of the court.
After 12 balls is changed player.

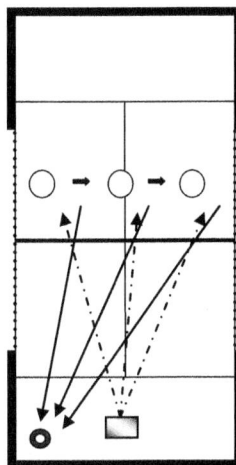

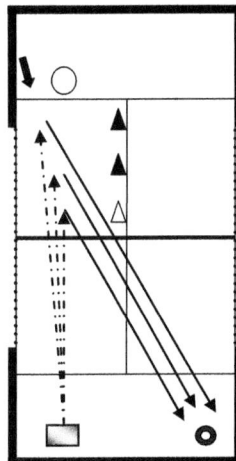

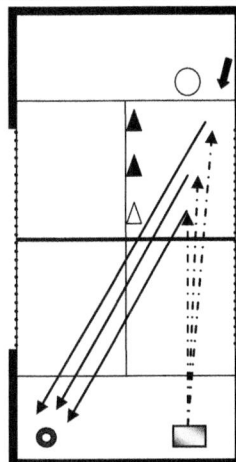

Exercise 0254   Hits: V

Target: Variation volleys
Striking sequence: VDX – VDX – VDX

Description:
Located player on the line of serve, will rise to the net and the height of each cone black made forehand volleys to approach and in the white cone, make a power crossed over forehand volley, with the target of the mark on the corner.
After 12 balls is changed player.

Exercise 0255   Hits: V

Target: Variation volleys
Striking sequence: VRX – VRX – VDX

Description:
Located player on the line of serve will rise to the net and the height of each cone black made backhand volleys to approach and in the white cone, make a power crossed over forehand volley, with the target of the mark on the corner.
After 12 balls is changed player.

Exercise 0256   Hits: V

Target: Volley displacement
Striking sequence: VDX – VDX – VDX

Description:
Set the player to the peak height, moving toward the net making three cross forehand volleys, with the target of the mark on the corner of the court.
After 12 balls is changed player.

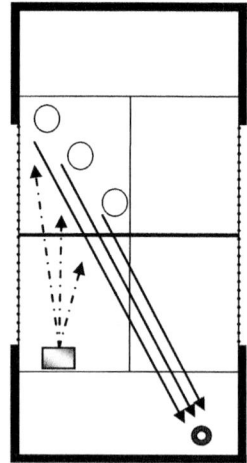

Exercise 0257   Hits: V

Target: Volley displacement
Striking sequence: VRX – VRX – VRX

Description:
Set the player to the peak height, moving toward the net making three backhand volleys cross, with the target of the mark on the corner of the court.
After 12 balls is changed player.

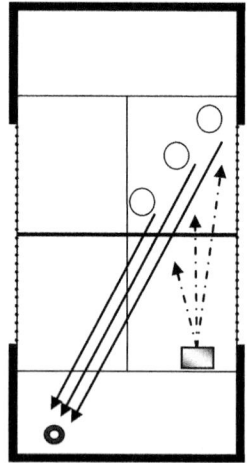

Exercise 0258   Hits: V

Target: Volley displacement
Striking sequence: VDX–VDX–VDX-VD-VD-VD

Description:
Set the player to the peak height, the player will advance to the net to make three crossed over forehand volleys and return to the T for three more forehand volleys, with the target of the mark on the corner of the court.
After 12 balls is changed player.

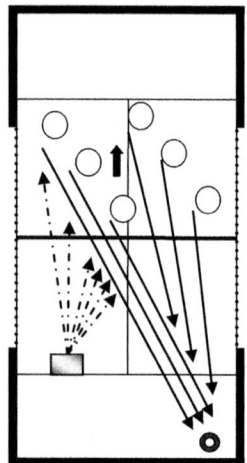

Exercise 0259   Hits: V

Target: Volley displacement
Striking sequence: VRX–VRX–VRX-VR-VR-VR

Description:
Set the player to the peak height, the player will advance to the net to make three crossed over backhand volleys and return to the T for three more backhand volleys, with the target of the mark on the corner of the court.
After 12 balls is changed player.

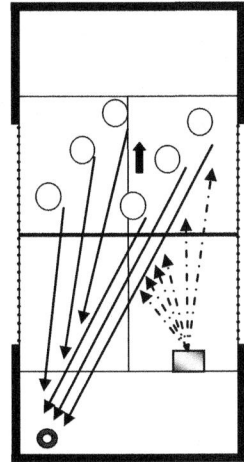

Exercise 0260   Hits: V

Target: Volley displacement
Striking sequence: VDX–VDX–VDX-VD//-VD//

Description:
Located player to the peak height, advance in parallel to the net for making three crossed over forehand volleys and continue with lateral displacement and performing two parallel forehand volleys, with the target of the mark on the corner of the court.
After 10 balls is changed player.

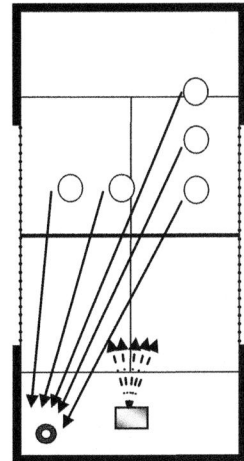

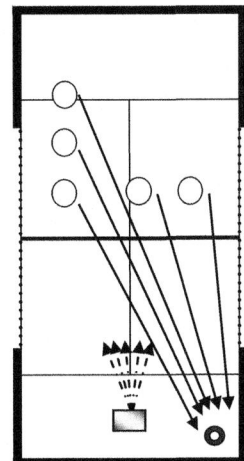

Exercise 0261   Hits: V

Target: Volley displacement
Striking sequence: VRX–VRX–VRX-VR//-VR//

Description:
Located player to the peak height, advance in parallel to the net for making three crossed over backhand volleys and continue with lateral displacement and performing two parallel backhand volleys, with the target of the mark on the corner of the court.
After 10 balls is changed player.

Exercise 0262   Hits: V

Target: Volleys control
Striking sequence: VD// - VD//

Description:
Located two players on the net and two on the bottom line, they held control of parallel forehand volleys.
After 2' position players alternates.

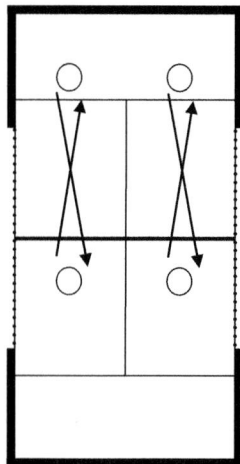

Exercise 0263   Hits: V

Target: Volleys control
Striking sequence: VDX - VDX

Description:
Located two players on the net and two on the bottom line, they held control of cross forehand volleys.
After 2' position players alternates.

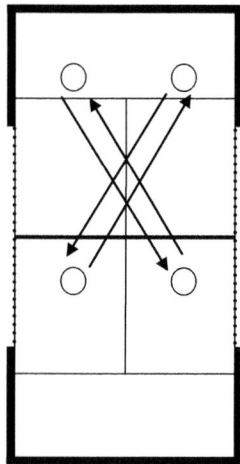

Exercise 0264   Hits: V

Target: Volleys control
Striking sequence: VRX - VRX

Description:
Located two players on the net and two on the bottom line, they held control of cross backhand volleys.
After 2' position players alternates.

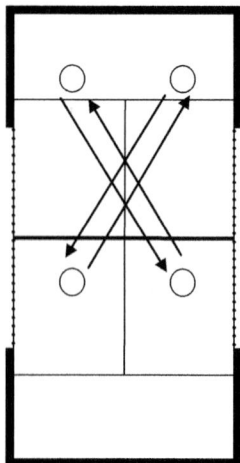

Exercise 0265   Hits: V

Target: Volleys control
Striking sequence: VR// - VR//

Description:
Located two players on the net and two on the bottom line, they held control of parallel backhand volleys.
After 2' position players alternates.

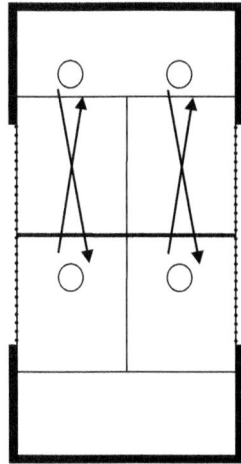

Exercise 0266   Hits: V

Target: Volleys control
Striking sequence: V// - V//

Description:
Located two players on the net and two on the bottom line, perform parallel control volleys with striking free.
After 2' position players alternates.

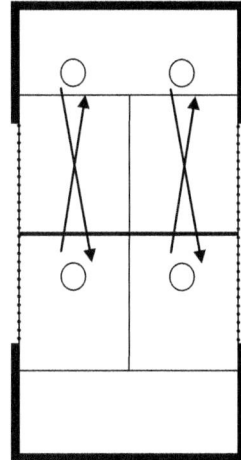

Exercise 0267   Hits: V

Target: Volleys control
Striking sequence: VX - VX

Description:
Located two players on the net and two on the bottom line, perform crossed over control striking volleys free.
After 2' position players alternates.

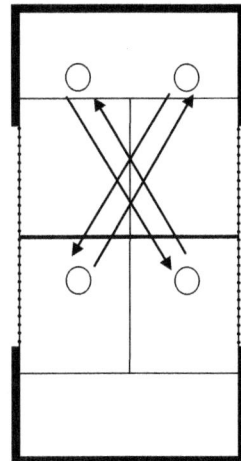

Exercise 0268   Hits: V

Target: Volleys controls
Striking sequence: VD - VR

Description:
Faced two players close to the net, move laterally to touch the opposite grid made of forehand volleys against backhand volleys. If it fails it starts again.

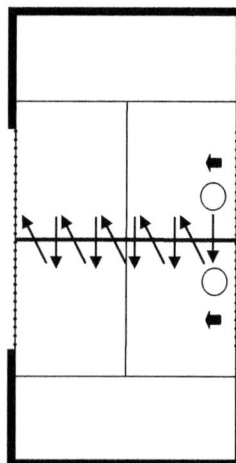

Exercise 0269   Hits: V

Target: Volleys controls
Striking sequence: VD - VR

Description:
Faced two players close to the net, move laterally to touch the opposite grid made of forehand volleys against backhand volleys. If it fails it starts again.

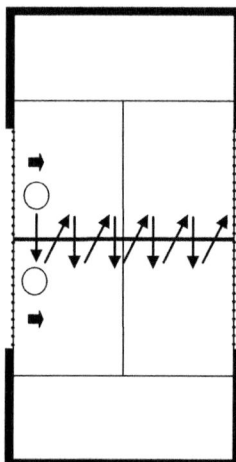

Exercise 0270   Hits: V

Target: Volleys controls
Striking sequence: VD - VR

Description:
Faced two players close to the net, move laterally to touch the opposite grid made of forehand volleys against backhand volleys and return for the same place. If it fails it starts again.

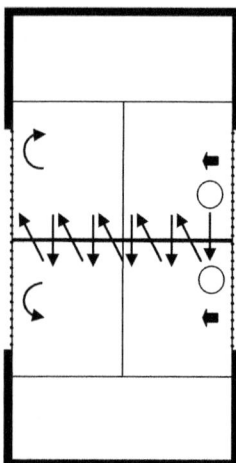

Exercise 0271   Hits: V

Target: Volleys controls
Striking sequence: VD - VR

Description:
Faced two players close to the net, one in the net and the other on the bottom line, move laterally to touch the opposite grid made of forehand volleys against backhand volleys. If it fails it starts again.

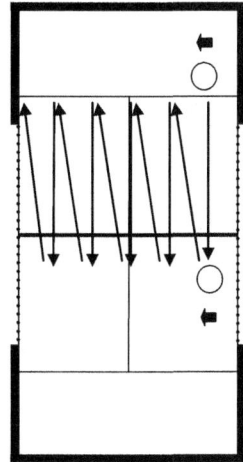

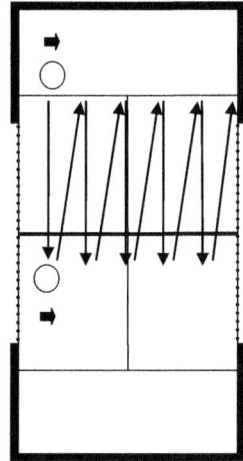

Exercise 0272   Hits: V

Target: Volleys controls
Striking sequence: VD - VR

Description:
Faced two players close to the net, one in the net and the other on the bottom line, move laterally to touch the opposite grid made of forehand volleys against backhand volleys. If it fails it starts again.

Exercise 0273   Hits: V

Target: Volleys controls
Striking sequence: VD - VR

Description:
Faced two players close to the net, one in the net and the other on the bottom line, move laterally to touch the opposite grid made of forehand volleys against backhand volleys and return for the same place.
If it fails it starts again.

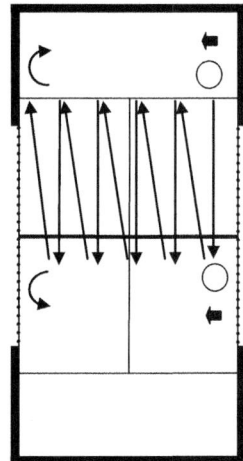

Exercise 0274   Hits: V

Target: Volleys controls
Striking sequence: VD - VR

Description:
Faced two players against each other in the net, players will move laterally to touch the opposite grid made of forehand volleys against backhand volleys. On one side there are two players, alternate hits between them, beating and leaving roommate. If it fails it starts again.

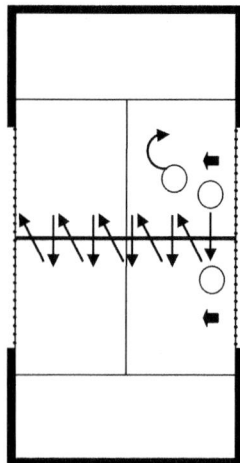

Exercise 0275   Hits: V

Target: Volleys controls
Striking sequence: VD - VR

Description:
Faced two players against each other in the net, players will move laterally to touch the opposite grid made of forehand volleys against backhand volleys and return for the same place. On one side there are two players, alternate hits between them, beating and leaving roommate. If it fails it starts again.

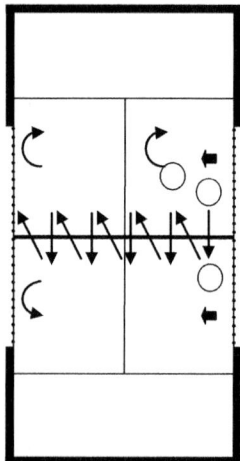

Exercise 0276   Hits: V

Target: Volleys controls
Striking sequence: VD - VR

Description:
Faced two players against each other in the net, players will move laterally to touch the opposite grid made of forehand volleys against backhand volleys. On one side there are two players, alternate hits between them, beating and leaving roommate. If it fails it starts again.

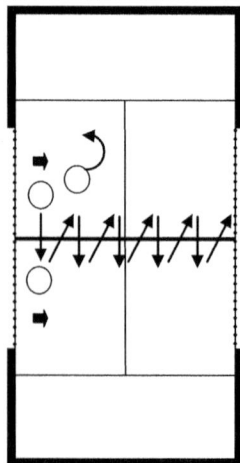

Exercise 0277   Hits: V

Target: Volleys controls
Striking sequence: VD - VR

Description:
Faced two players on the baseline against another in the net, players will move laterally to touch the opposite grid made of forehand volleys against backhand volleys. On one side there are two players, alternate hits between them, beating and leaving roommate. If it fails it starts again.

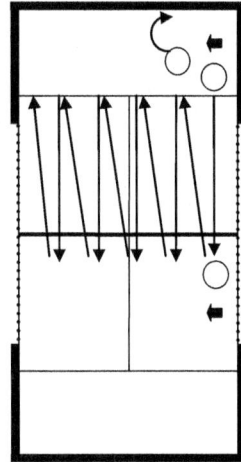

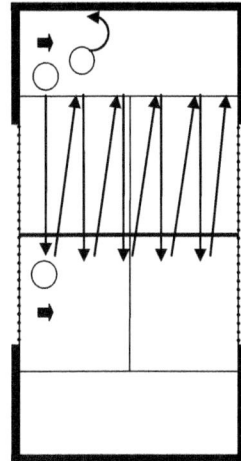

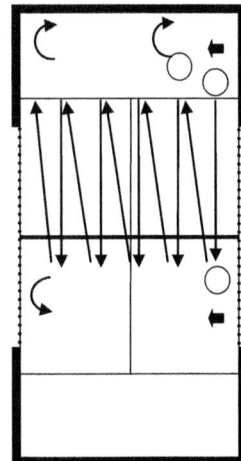

Exercise 0278   Hits: V

Target: Volleys controls
Striking sequence: VD - VR

Description:
Faced two players on the baseline against another in the net, players will move laterally to touch the opposite grid made of forehand volleys against backhand volleys. On one side there are two players, alternate hits between them, beating and leaving roommate. If it fails it starts again.

Exercise 0279   Hits: V

Target: Volleys controls
Striking sequence: VD - VR

Description:
Faced two players on the baseline against another in the net, players will move laterally to touch the opposite grid made of forehand volleys against backhand volleys and return for the same place. On one side there are two players, alternate hits between them, beating and leaving roommate. If it fails it starts again.

Exercise 0280   Hits: V

Target: Volleys controls
Striking sequence: V// - V//

Description:
Faced two players from the bottom of the court, parallel volley advancing to win the net. The volleys continue until the end point.
After 11 points are changed players.

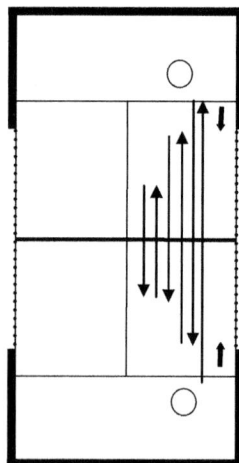

Exercise 0281   Hits: V

Target: Volleys controls
Striking sequence: VX - VX

Description:
Faced two players in crossed over from the bottom of the court, crossed over volley advancing to win the net. The volleys continue until the end point.
After 11 points are changed players.

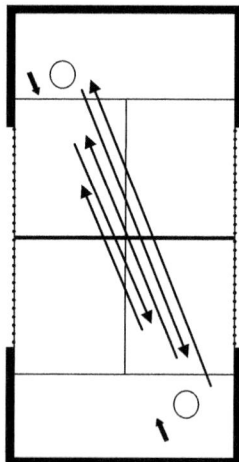

Exercise 0282   Hits: V

Target: Volleys controls
Striking sequence: V// - V//

Description:
Faced two players on one from the bottom of the court, parallel advancing volley to win the net. Players who are together, alternating the striking leaving space for partner after each stroke. The volleys continue until the end point.
After 11 points are changed players.

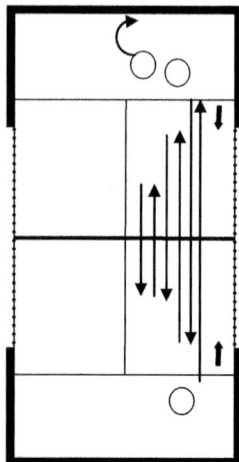

Exercise 0283   Hits: V

Target: Volleys controls
Striking sequence: VX - VX

Description:
Faced two players on one from the bottom of the court, crossed over advancing volley to win the net. Players who are together, alternating the striking leaving space for partner after each stroke. The volleys continue until the end point.
After 11 points are changed players.

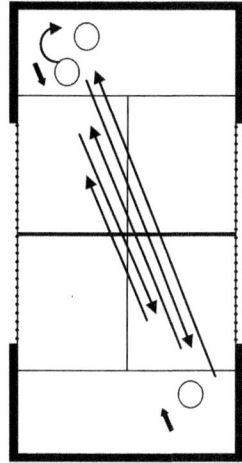

Exercise 0284   Hits: D – V

Target: Volleys controls
Striking sequence: Short ball D – 2VD// - VDX

Description:
Located half-court player, up to a short ball with forehand approach to the environment, it makes two parallel forehand volleys and cross over forehand volley to continue to monitor and finish the point.

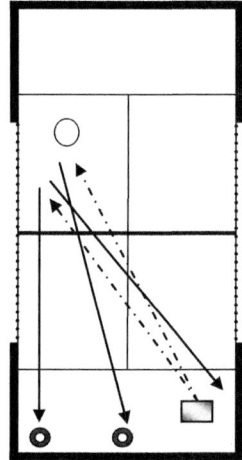

Exercise 0285   Hits: R – V

Target: Volleys controls
Striking sequence: Short ball R – 2VR// - VRX

Description:
Located half-court player, up to a short ball with backhand approach to the environment, it makes two parallel backhand volleys and cross over backhand volley to continue to monitor and finish the point.

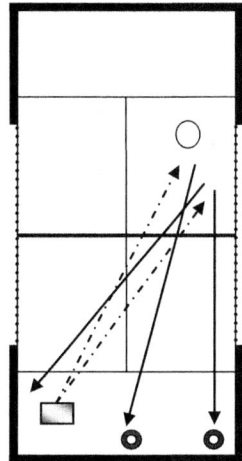

Exercise 0286   Hits: V

Target: Volleys controls
Striking sequence: VD// o VR//

Description:
Located players near the net, perform parallel forehand volleys and parallel backhand volleys with the target of the marks at the bottom of the court and always in the space between the cones and the grid.
After 10 balls position players alternates.

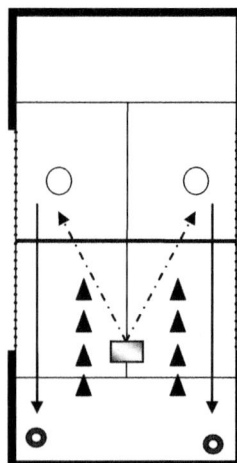

Exercise 0287   Hits: V

Target: Fence jump more volleys control
Striking sequence: Jump – VD – VR

Description:
Set the player at the bottom of the court, hits a jump fence and run at the net to make a forehand volley and backhand volley to hand monitor, and repeat the exercise 10 times.

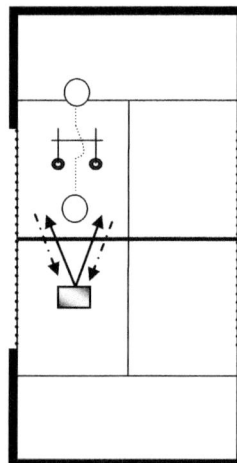

Exercise 0288   Hits: V

Target: Mobility and volleys power
Striking sequence: Jumping cones – VD x5

Description:
Located player on the line of serve, done jumping cone and run at the net to make 5 powers crossed over forehand volleys. We work the hopping tests, the frontal displacement and braking. Remember that we're working speed and strength, not striking technique.

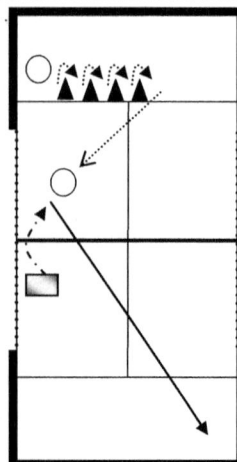

Exercise 0289   Hits: V

Target: Mobility and volleys power
Striking sequence: Jumping cones – VR x5

Description:
Located player on the line of serve, done jumping cone and run at the net to 5 powers crossed over backhand volleys. We work the hopping tests, the frontal displacement and braking. Remember that we're working speed and strength, not striking technique.

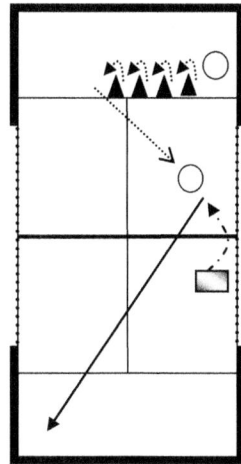

Exercise 0290   Hits: V

Target: Scroll volley
Striking sequence: VRX

Description:
Set the player near the net, held repeats crossed over backhand volley stepping on the white cone on the right foot at the time of striking. After hitting will play the black cone and repeat the exercise. The movement to the coup is crossed over forward.
After 10 balls is changed player.

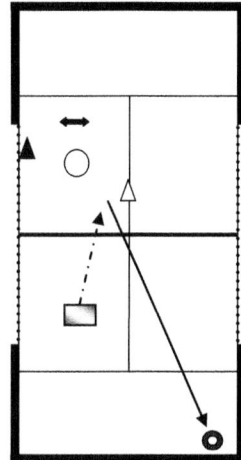

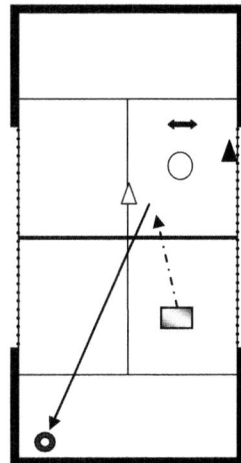

Exercise 0291   Hits: V

Target: Scroll volley
Striking sequence: VD

Description:
Set the player near the net, held repeats crossed over forehand volley stepping on the white cone on the left foot at the time of striking. After hitting will play the black cone and repeat the exercise. The movement to the coup is crossed over forward.
After 10 balls is changed player.

Exercise 0292   Hits: V

Target: Control volleys between 4 players
Striking sequence: V – V – V – V

Description:
They placed four players close to the net, made crossed over volleys to keep the grids without losing concentration with the ball. It is a visual technical exercise.
After 2'position players alternates.

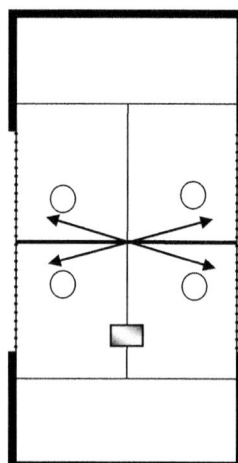

Exercise 0293   Hits: V

Target: Power volleys
Striking sequence: VDX – VR//

Description:
Set the player near the net, alternate crossed over forehand volleys and parallel backhand volleys. It is an exercise of power by which it must attack the ball with the forward leg to give weight to the ball. We do not seek technique but power.
After 10 balls is changed player.

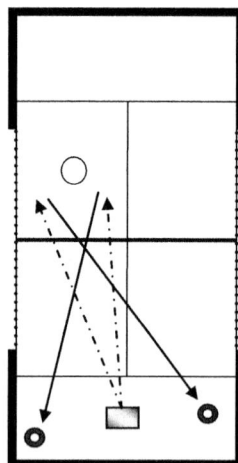

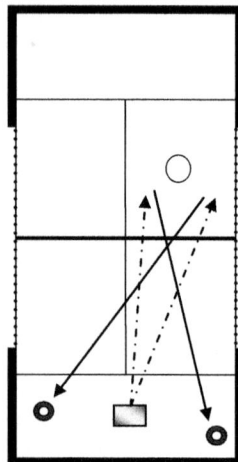

Exercise 0294   Hits: V

Target: Power volleys
Striking sequence: VD// – VRX

Description:
Set the player near the net, alternate crossed over backhand volleys and parallel forehand volleys. It is an exercise of power by which it must attack the ball with the forward leg to give weight to the ball. We do not seek technique but power.
After 10 balls is changed player.

Exercise 0295   Hits: V

Target: Volleys control
Striking sequence: VDX – VR//

Description:
Set the player near the net, alternate forehand volleys to the grid and parallel backhand volleys. The player held six volleys, three of each class, but if you fail you will continue pulling until you get it right. The crossed over forehand volley should be slow to be left in the grid.

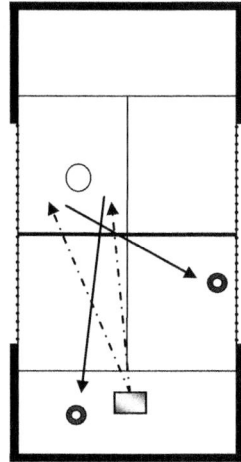

Exercise 0296   Hits: V

Target: Volleys control
Striking sequence: VRX – VD//

Description:
Set the player near the net, alternate backhand volleys to the grid and parallel forehand volleys. The player held six volleys, three of each class, but if you fail you will continue pulling until you get it right. The crossed over backhand volley should be slow to be left in the grid.

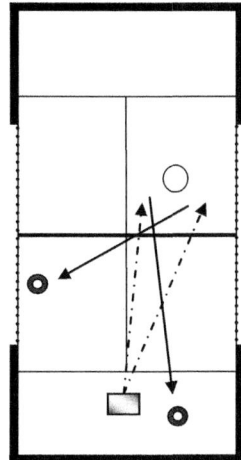

Exercise 0297   Hits: V

Target: Volleys control
Striking sequence: VRX short – VDX

Description:
Set the player near the net, alternate backhand volleys to the grid and crossed over forehand volleys. The player held six volleys, three of each class, but if you fail you will continue pulling until you get it right. The crossed over backhand volley should be slow to be left in the grid.

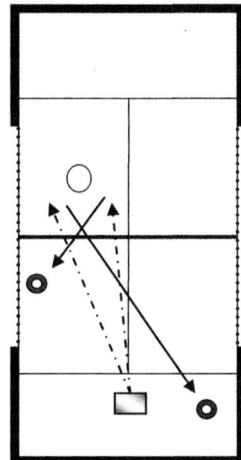

Exercise 0298   Hits: V

Target: Volleys control
Striking sequence: VDX short – VRX

Description:
Set the player near the net, alternate backhand volleys to the grid and crossed over forehand volleys. The player held six volleys, three of each class, but if you fail you will continue pulling until you get it right. The crossed over forehand volley should be slow to be left in the grid.

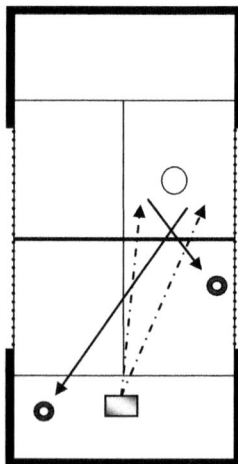

Exercise 0299   Hits: V

Target: Volley displacement control
Striking sequence: VD// - VR//

Description:
Set the player at the bottom of the court up to the T, making advance parallel forehand volleys and parallel backhand volleys in each of the cones, with the target of the marks on the back of the court.

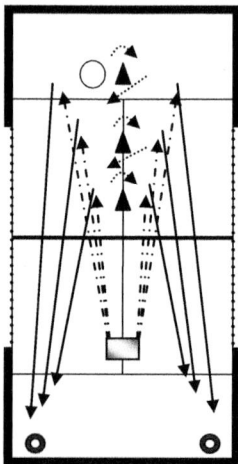

Exercise 0300   Hits: V

Target: Volleys controls
Striking sequence: VD// - VDX

Description:
Players located near the net on the side of the drive, perform a parallel forehand volley and crossed over forehand volley, and rotate in the middle of the circle marked by the monitor.

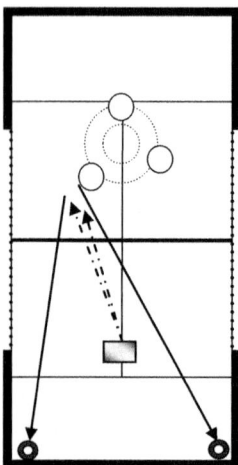

Exercise 0301   Hits: V

Target: Volleys controls
Striking sequence: VR// - VRX

Description:
Located players near the net on the left side, players will perform a parallel backhand volley and a crossed over backhand volley and rotate in the middle of the circle marked on the monitor.

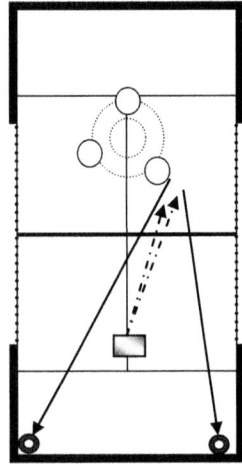

Exercise 0302   Hits: V

Target: Volleys controls
Striking sequence: V

Description:
Located players near the net, perform volleys control between two opposite pairs for the net. As if it were a game of volleyball, players pass the ball across the net and then pass the ball between them a maximum of three times before turning it over to the other side of the net.

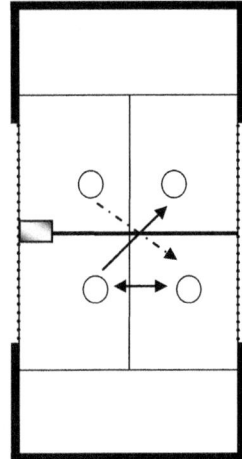

Exercise 0303   Hits: V

Target: Volleys controls
Striking sequence: VD// - VR//

Description:
Located players near the net will hold a parallel forehand volley or a parallel backhand volley and change the row. Exercise dynamic in which the movement must be continuous.

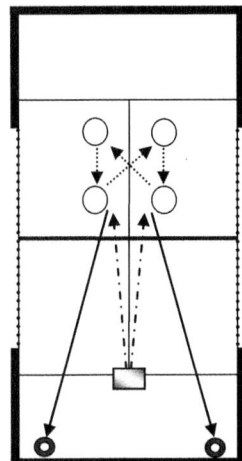

Exercise 0304   Hits: V

Target: Volley displacement control
Striking sequence: VD//

Description:
Set the player near the net, held parallel forehand volleys to the bottom of the court. After each stroke, will be delayed and will touch the cone with the target of making the moving volleys.
After 10 balls is changed player.

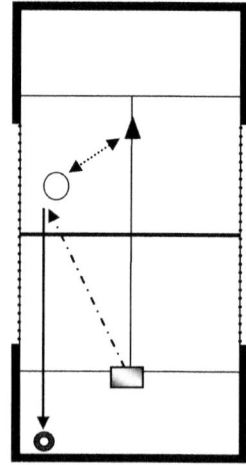

Exercise 0305   Hits: V

Target: Volley displacement control
Striking sequence: VR//

Description:
Set the player near the net, held parallel backhand volleys at the bottom of the court. After each stroke, will be delayed and will touch the cone with the target of making the moving volleys.
After 10 balls is changed player.

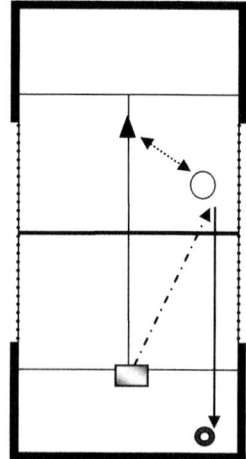

Exercise 0306   Hits: V

Target: Volley displacement control
Striking sequence: VDX

Description:
Set the player near the net, made a crossed over forehand volleys to the corner of the court. After each stroke, will be delayed and will touch the cone with the target of making the moving volleys.
After 10 balls is changed player.

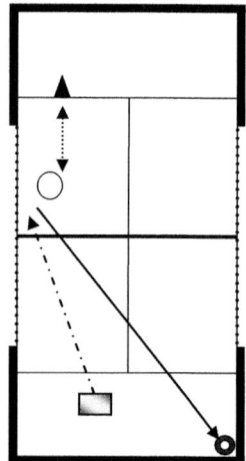

Exercise 0307   Hits: V

Target: Volley displacement control
Striking sequence: VRX

Description:
Set the player near the net, made a crossed over backhand volleys to the corner of the court. After each stroke, will be delayed and will touch the cone with the target of making the moving volleys.
After 10 balls is changed player.

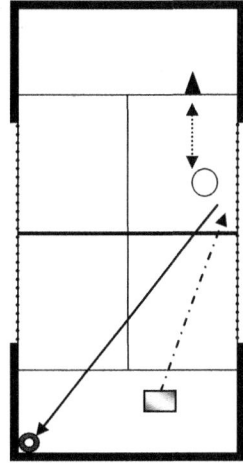

Exercise 0308   Hits: V

Target: Volleys controls
Striking sequence: VD – VD

Description:
Players located close to the net, will perform a forehand volley against the monitor in each of the areas of the court. It is a volley control exercise, in which the players will slow volleys with lateral movement.

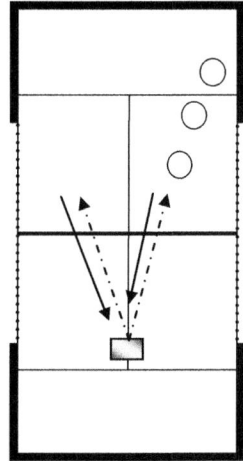

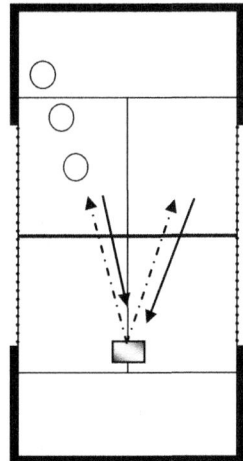

Exercise 0309   Hits: V

Target: Volleys controls
Striking sequence: VR – VR

Description:
Players located close to the net, will perform a backhand volley against the monitor in each of the areas of the court. It is a volley control exercise, in which the players will slow volleys with lateral movement.

Exercise 0310   Hits: V

Target: Volleys controls
Striking sequence: VD// - VR// - VR//

Description:
Set the player near the net, performed in a parallel forehand volley and a parallel backhand volley, and then will move laterally to make a parallel backhand volley at the other side of the court.

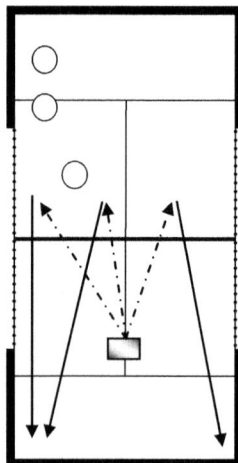

Exercise 0311   Hits: V

Target: Volleys controls
Striking sequence: VR// - VD// - VD//

Description:
Set the player near the net, performed in a parallel backhand volley and a parallel forehand volley, and then will move laterally to make a parallel forehand volley at the other side of the court.

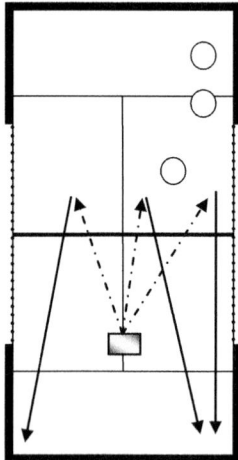

Exercise 0312   Hits: V

Target: Volley displacement control
Striking sequence: V//

Description:
Volleys control exercise, where one player holds the position in the net and the other goes up and down while controlling the parallel volley.
After 2' position players alternates.

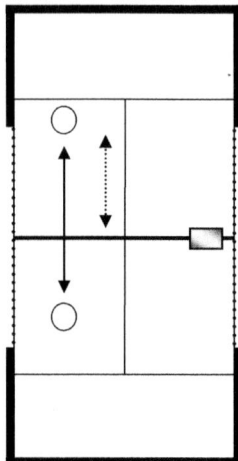

Exercise 0313   Hits: V

Target: Volley displacement control
Striking sequence: VX

Description:
Control volleys exercise, where one player holds the position in the net and the other goes up and down while controlling cross volley.
After 2' position players alternates.

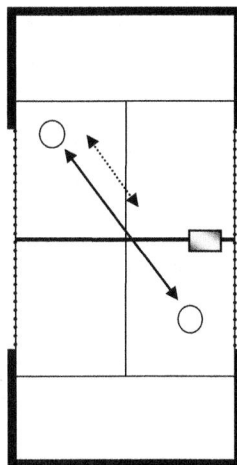

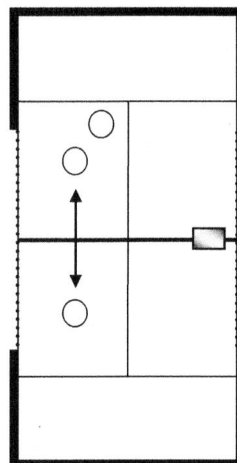

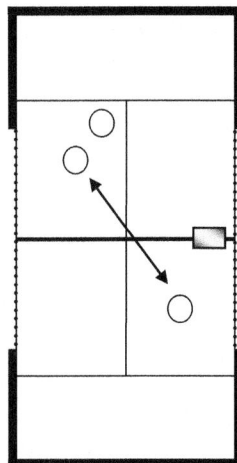

Exercise 0314   Hits: V

Target: Volleys control between 3 players
Striking sequence: V//

Description:
Control parallel volley exercise between three players. Two players who are together held two parallel volleys against his neighbor and will be delayed to make way for his team mate, who will volleying twice parallel and away again.
After 2' position players alternates.

Exercise 0315   Hits: V

Target: Volleys control between 3 players
Striking sequence: VX

Description:
Control parallel volley exercise between three players. Two players who are together held two crossed over volleys against his neighbor and will be delayed to make way for his team mate, who will volleying twice crosses over and away again.
After 2' position players alternates.

Exercise 0316   Hits: V

Target: Volley displacement control
Striking sequence: VD// - VR//

Description:
Players located near the net, held parallel forehand volleys and parallel backhand volleys. After each stroke, the marks will surround ahead to return to make a volley. After 10 balls position players alternates.

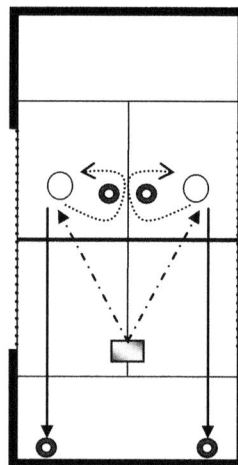

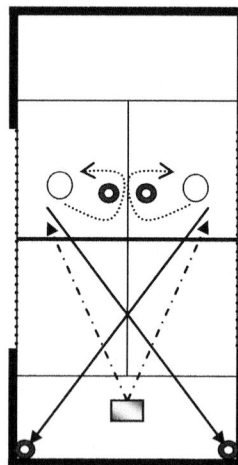

Exercise 0317   Hits: V

Target: Volley displacement control
Striking sequence: VDX - VRX

Description:
Players located near the net, held crossed over forehand volleys and crossed over backhand volleys. After each stroke, the marks will surround ahead to return to make a volley.
After 10 balls position players alternates.

Exercise 0318   Hits: V

Target: Volley displacement control
Striking sequence: VD// - VR//

Description:
Players located near the net, held parallel forehand volleys and parallel backhand volleys. After each stroke, they will surround the brands to return to make a volley. After 10 balls position players alternates.

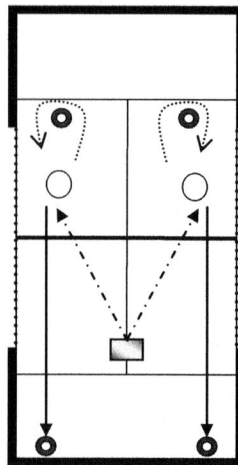

Exercise 0319   Hits: V

Target: Volley displacement control
Striking sequence: VDX - VRX

Description:
Players located near the net, held crossed over forehand volleys and crossed over backhand volleys. After each stroke, they will surround the brands to return to make a volley.
After 10 balls position players alternates.

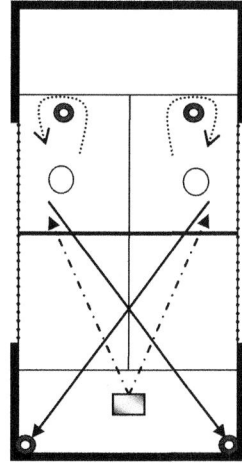

Exercise 0320   Hits: V

Target: Volley displacement control
Striking sequence: VD//

Description:
Located player in the line of serve held parallel forehand volleys to the mark on the back of the court. If the volleys are well made, will progress to the next cone but if it fails, repeat to do it correctly.

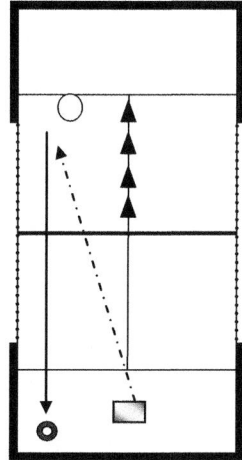

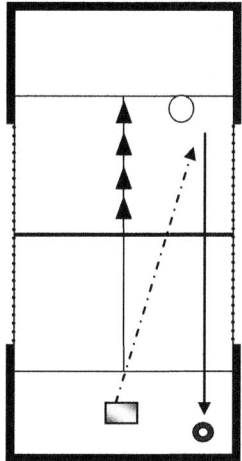

Exercise 0321   Hits: V

Target: Volley displacement control
Striking sequence: VR//

Description:
Located player in the line of serve held parallel backhand volleys to the mark on the back of the court. If the volleys are well made, will progress to the next cone but if it fails, repeat to do it correctly.

Exercise 0322   Hits: V

Target: Volley displacement control
Striking sequence: VR//

Description:
Located player in the line of serve held parallel backhand volleys to the mark on the back of the court. If the volleys are well made, will progress to the next cone but if it fails, repeat to do it correctly.

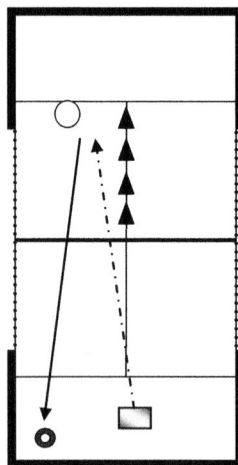

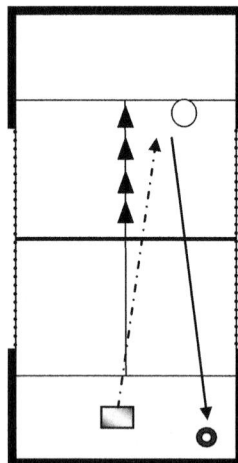

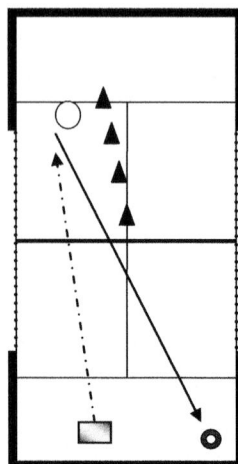

Exercise 0323   Hits: V

Target: Volley displacement control
Striking sequence: VD//

Description:
Located player in the line of serve held parallel forehand volleys to the mark on the back of the court. If the volleys are well made, will progress to the next cone but if it fails, repeat to do it correctly.

Exercise 0324   Hits: V

Target: Volley displacement control
Striking sequence: VDX

Description:
Located player in the line of serve, held crossed over forehand volleys to the mark on the back of the court. If the volleys are well made, will progress to the next cone but if it fails, repeat to do it correctly.

Exercise 0325   Hits: V

Target: Volley displacement control
Striking sequence: VRX

Description:
Located player in the line of serve, held crossed over backhand volleys to the mark on the back of the court. If the volleys are well made, will progress to the next cone but if it fails, repeat to do it correctly.

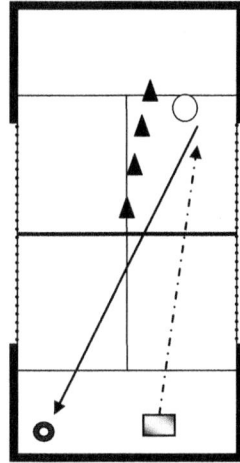

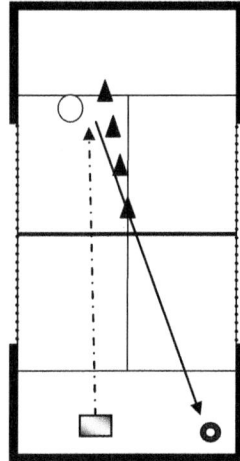

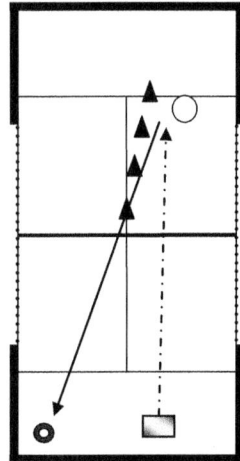

Exercise 0326   Hits: V

Target: Volley displacement control
Striking sequence: VRX

Description:
Located player in the line of serve, held crossed over backhand volleys to the mark on the back of the court. If the volleys are well made, will progress to the next cone but if it fails, repeat to do it correctly.

Exercise 0327   Hits: V

Target: Volley displacement control
Striking sequence: VDX

Description:
Located player in the line of serve, held crossed over forehand volleys to the mark on the back of the court. If the volleys are well made, will progress to the next cone but if it fails, repeat to do it correctly.

EXERCISES OF LOB

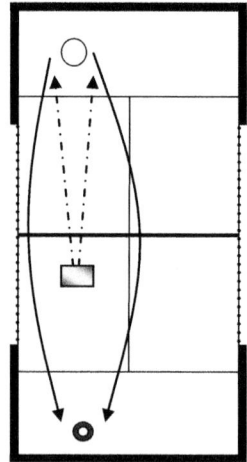

Exercise 0328   Hits: G

Target: Control lob without rebound
Striking sequence: GD // - GR//

Description:
Set the player at the bottom of the court, made parallel forehand lobs and parallel backhand lobs to the mark on the bottom of the court.
After 10 balls is changed player.

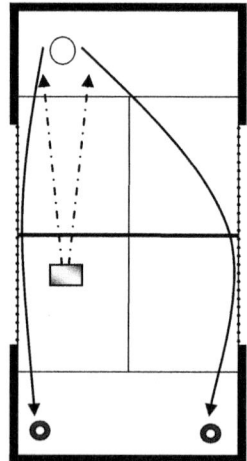

Exercise 0329   Hits: G

Target: Control lob without rebound
Striking sequence: GD // - GRX

Description:
Set the player at the bottom of the court, made parallel forehand lobs and crossed over backhand lobs to the mark on the bottom of the court.
After 10 balls is changed player.

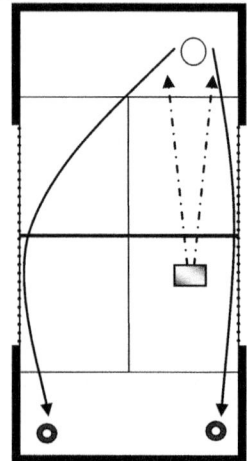

Exercise 0330   Hits: G

Target: Control lob without rebound
Striking sequence: GD X – GR//

Description:
Set the player at the bottom of the court, made crossed over forehand lobs and parallel backhand lobs to the mark on the bottom of the court.
After 10 balls is changed player.

Exercise 0331   Hits: SF – G

Target: Control lob with and without rebound
Striking sequence: GRX – GRX

Description:
Located player at the bottom of the court, made crossed over backhand lobs with and without bounce to the mark on the bottom of the court.
After 10 balls is changed player.

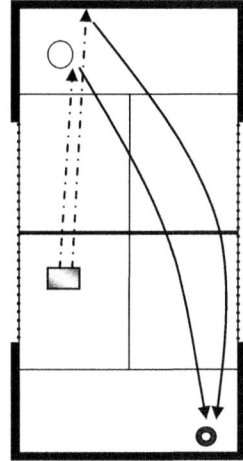

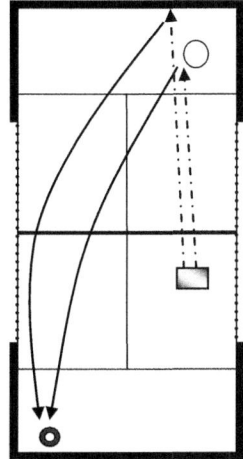

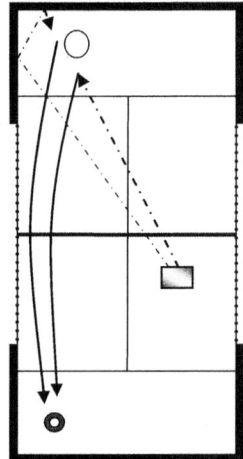

Exercise 0332   Hits: SF – G

Target: Control lob with and without rebound
Striking sequence: GDX – GDX

Description:
Located player at the bottom of the court, made crossed over forehand lobs with and without bounce to the mark on the bottom of the court.
After 10 balls is changed player.

Exercise 0333   Hits: SDP – G

Target: Control lob with and without rebound
Striking sequence: GD// – GD//

Description:
Located player at the bottom of the court, made parallel forehand lobs without rebound and with rebound after two walls to the mark on the bottom of the court.
After 10 balls is changed player.

Exercise 0334   Hits: SDP – G

Target: Control lob with and without rebound
Striking sequence: GR//– GR//

Description:
Located player at the bottom of the court, made parallel backhand lobs without rebound and with rebound after two walls to the mark on the bottom of the court.
After 10 balls is changed player.

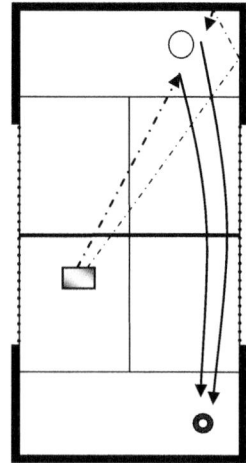

Exercise 0335   Hits: SF – SDP – G

Target: Control lob with rebound
Striking sequence: GD// – GRX

Description:
Located player at the bottom of the court, made parallel forehand lobs after double wall rebound and crossed over backhand lobs after rebound in the bottom wall to the marks at the bottom of the court.
After 10 balls is changed player.

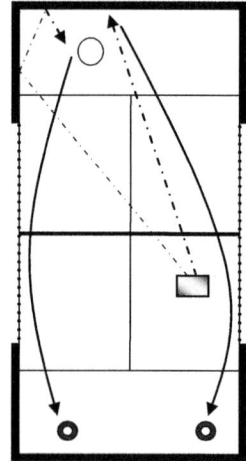

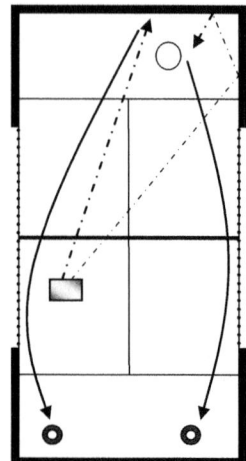

Exercise 0336   Hits: SF – SDP – G

Target: Control lob with rebound
Striking sequence: GR// – GDX

Description:
Located player at the bottom of the court, made parallel backhand lobs after double wall rebound and crossed over forehand lobs after rebound in the bottom wall to the marks at the bottom of the court.
After 10 balls is changed player.

Exercise 0337   Hits: SDP – G

Target: Control lob with rebound
Striking sequence: GRX

Description:
Located players at the bottom of the court, made crossed over backhand lobs after double bounce in the wall to the mark on the bottom of the court and return to the row.

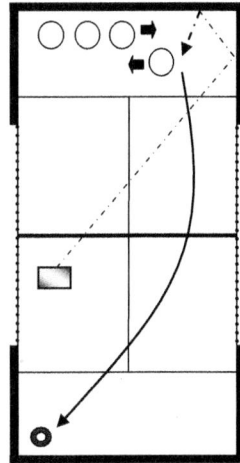

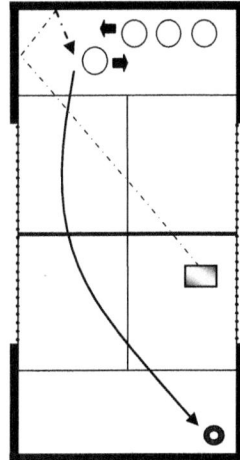

Exercise 0338   Hits: SDP – G

Target: Control lob with rebound
Striking sequence: GDX

Description:
Located players at the bottom of the court, made crossed over forehand lobs after double bounce in the wall to the mark on the bottom of the court and return to the row.

Exercise 0339   Hits: G

Target: Lobs control
Striking sequence: GD// – GRX

Description:
Set the player at the bottom of the court, made parallels forehand lobs and crossed over backhand lobs above the string located between the peaks of the bottom of the court.
After 10 balls is changed player.

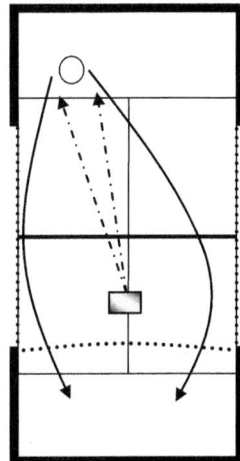

Exercise 0340   Hits: G

Target: Lobs control
Striking sequence: GDX – GR//

Description:
Set the player at the bottom of the court, made parallels backhand lobs and crossed over forehand lobs above the string located between the peaks of the bottom of the court.
After 10 balls is changed player.

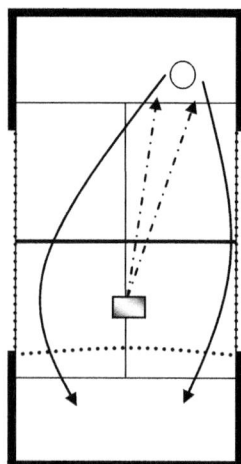

EXERCISES DE SERVE

Exercise 0341   Hits: Sq

Target: Different service areas
Striking sequence: Serve

Description:
Players located on the back of the court, held serves to several targets in which they alternate speed and type of stroke, ranging from flat, topspin and cut.
The players are switching sides every 10 balls.

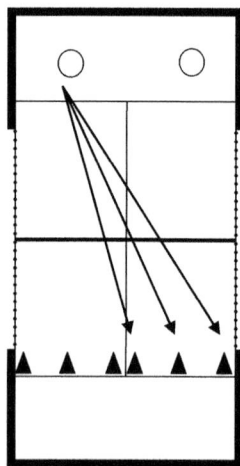

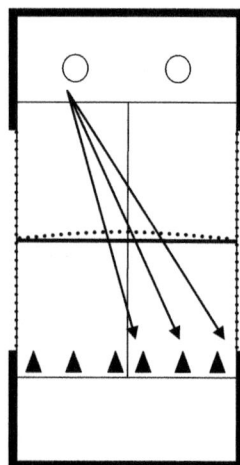

Exercise 0342   Hits: Sq

Target: Service areas with different height limit
Striking sequence: Serve

Description:
Players located on the back of the court, held serves to several targets in which they alternate speed and type of stroke, ranging from flat, topspin and cut, with height limitation imposed by the string that is on the net.
The players are switching sides every 10 balls.

Exercise 0343   Hits: Sq

Target: Service to distinct zones across the hoops
Striking sequence: Serve

Description:
Players located on the back of the court, held serves through the rings will alternate on the speed and type of stroke, ranging from flat, topspin and cut.
The players are switching sides every 10 balls.

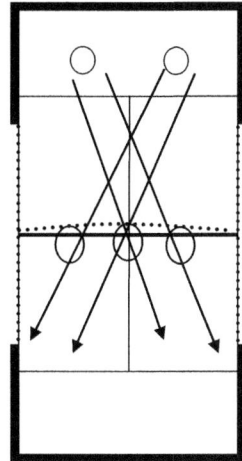

EXERCISES OF VOLLEY TRAY (BD)

Exercise 0344   Hits: Bd

Target: Volley Tray (Bd) from different positions
Striking sequence: Bd// - BdX

Description:
Players located in two rows near the net, hold a parallel volley tray and change row for a crossed over volley tray, with the target of the marked area in the corner of the court.

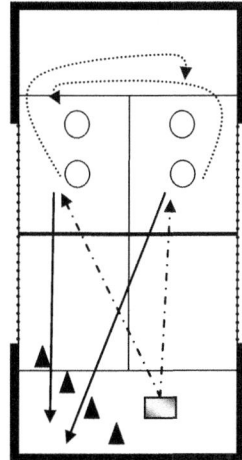

Exercise 0345   Hits: Bd

Target: Volley Tray (Bd) from different positions
Striking sequence: Bd// - BdX

Description:
Players located in two rows near the net, hold a parallel volley tray and change row for a crossed over volley tray, with the target of the marked area in the corner of the court.

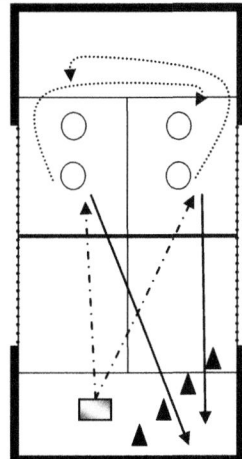

Exercise 0346   Hits: Bd

Target: Reaction to a situation
Striking sequence: BdX

Description:
Player lying face down on half court, he stands and try to get a lob to make a crossed over volley tray (Bd). After each recovery, again lie next to the cone.
After 5 balls you change player.

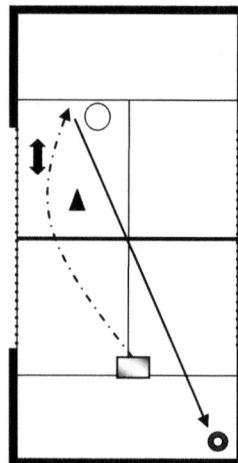

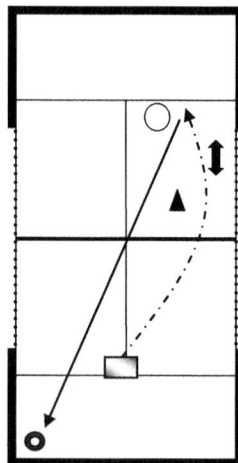

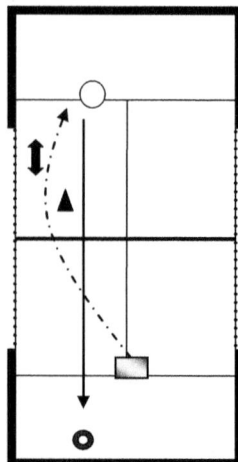

Exercise 0347   Hits: Bd

Target: Reaction to a situation
Striking sequence: BdX

Description:
Player lying face down on half court, he stands and try to get a lob to make a crossed over volley tray (Bd). After each recovery, again lie next to the cone.
After 5 balls you change player.

Exercise 0348   Hits: Bd

Target: Reaction to a situation
Striking sequence: Bd//

Description:
Player lying face down on half court, he stands and tries to get a lob to make a parallel volley tray (Bd). After each recovery, again lie next to the cone.
After 5 balls you change player.

Exercise 0349   Hits: Bd

Target: Reaction to a situation
Striking sequence: Bd//

Description:
Player lying face down on half court, he stands and tries to get a lob to make a parallel volley tray (Bd). After each recovery, again lie next to the cone.
After 5 balls you change player.

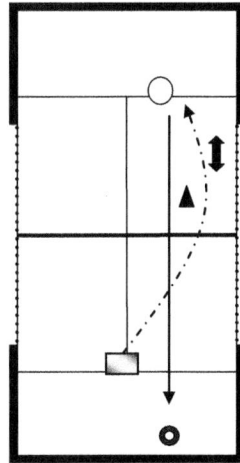

Exercise 0350   Hits: Bd

Target: Volley Tray (Bd) control to different targets
Striking sequence: Bd// – Bd middle – BdX

Description:
Set the player near the net, working 3 types of volley tray. If this comfortable attacks with slow to middle or heavy crossed over volley tray, if this is uncomfortable defend with a parallel volley tray.
After 12 balls is changed player.

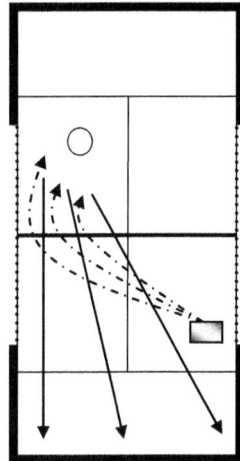

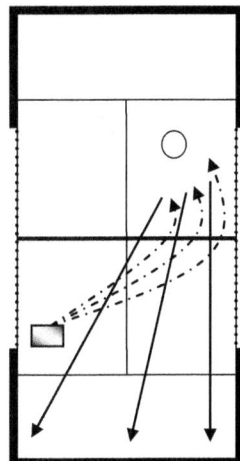

Exercise 0351   Hits: Bd

Target: Volley Tray (Bd) control to different targets
Striking sequence: Bd// – Bd middle – BdX

Description:
Set the player near the net, working 3 types of volley tray. If this comfortable volley tray attacks with strong parallel or crossed over. If you are uncomfortable defends with slow volley tray to the middle.
After 12 balls is changed player.

Exercise 0352   Hits: Bd

Target: Learning assembling the Volley Tray (Bd)
Striking sequence: Bd

Description:
Set the player with his back against the wall in the background, made volley trays. He sticks his back to the wall so as not to overdo the armed coup. When you advance to master the net.
It can be done from the other side to practice all angles of striking.

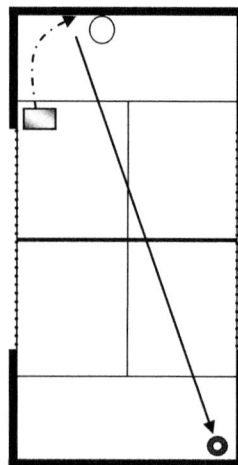

Exercise 0353   Hits: Bd

Target: Learning Volley Tray (Bd)
Striking sequence: Bd//

Description:
Located half-court player at the height of the cones, made a slow parallel volley tray (Bd) to monitor in each cone. With this exercise will begin to correctly assemble the volley tray. The technique of striking work, not force or effect.
After 10 balls is changed player.

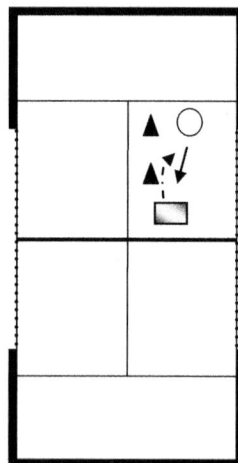

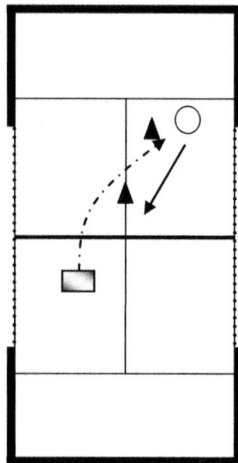

Exercise 0354   Hits: Bd

Target: Learning Volley Tray (Bd)
Striking sequence: BdX

Description:
Located half-court player at the height of the cones, made a slow crossed over volley Tray (Bd) to monitor in each cone. With this exercise will begin to correctly assemble the volley tray. The technique of striking work, not force or effect.
After 10 balls is changed player.

Exercise 0355   Hits: Bd

Target: Control Volley Tray (Bd) at different heights
Striking sequence: Bd// – Bd// - Bd//

Description:
Located player in the line of serve, made three parallel volley trays to the height of each cone. If done well progress to the next cone, but if it fails in some cone, with repeated until done correctly.
After 12 balls is changed player.

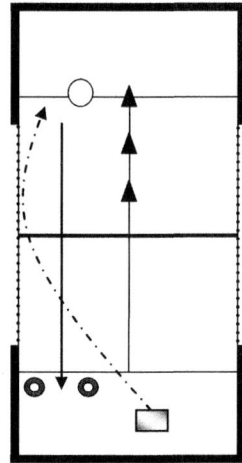

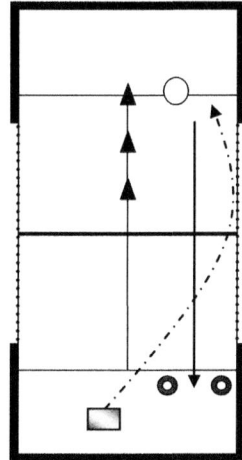

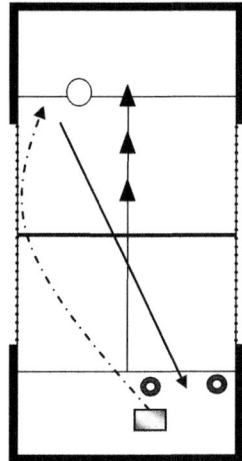

Exercise 0356   Hits: Bd

Target: Control Volley Tray (Bd) at different heights
Striking sequence: Bd// – Bd// - Bd//

Description:
Located player in the line of serve, made three parallel volley trays to the height of each cone. If done well progress to the next cone, but if it fails in some cone, with repeated until done correctly.
After 12 balls is changed player.

Exercise 0357   Hits: Bd

Target: Control Volley Tray (Bd) at different heights
Striking sequence: BdX – BdX - BdX

Description:
Located player in the line of serve, made three crossed over volley trays to the height of each cone. If done well progress to the next cone, but if it fails in some cone, with repeated until done correctly.
After 12 balls is changed player.

Exercise 0358   Hits: Bd

Target: Control Volley Tray (Bd) at different heights
Striking sequence: BdX – BdX - BdX

Description:
Located player in the line of serve, made three crossed over volley trays to the height of each cone. If done well progress to the next cone, but if it fails in some cone, with repeated until done correctly.
After 12 balls is changed player.

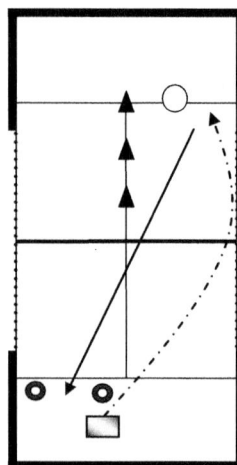

Exercise 0359   Hits: Bd

Target: Control displacement Volley Tray (Bd)
Striking sequence: Bd// - Bd//

Description:
Located players near the net, perform parallel volley trays at the bottom of the court. After each stroke, the marks will surround ahead to return to make a volley tray.
After 10 balls position players alternates.

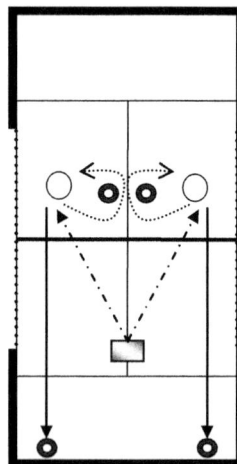

Exercise 0360   Hits: Bd

Target: Control displacement Volley Tray (Bd)
Striking sequence: BdX - BdX

Description:
Located players near the net, perform cross over volley tray (Bd). After each stroke, the marks will surround ahead to return to make a volley tray.
After 10 balls position players alternates.

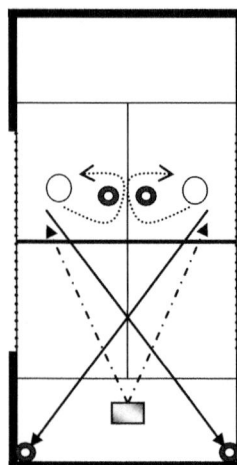

Exercise 0361   Hits: Bd

Target: Control displacement Volley Tray (Bd)
Striking sequence: Bd// - Bd//

Description:
Located players near the net, perform parallel volley trays. After each stroke, they will surround the brands to return to make a volley tray.
After 10 balls position players alternates.

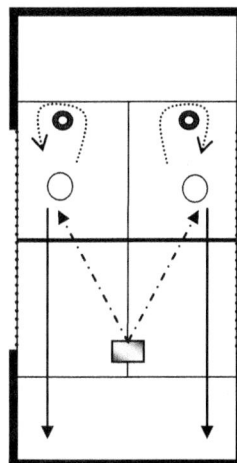

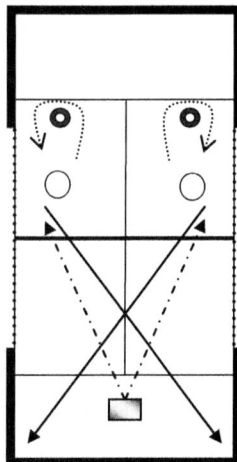

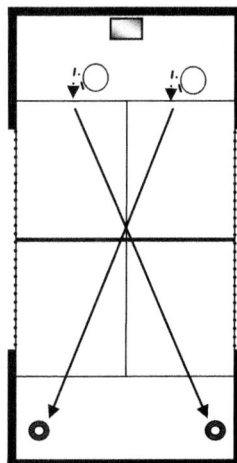

Exercise 0362   Hits: Bd

Target: Control displacement Volley Tray (Bd)
Striking sequence: BdX - BdX

Description:
Located players near the net, perform crossed over volley tray (Bd). After each stroke, they will surround the brands to return to make a volley tray.
After 10 balls position players alternates.

Exercise 0363   Hits: Bd

Target: Learning Volley Tray (Bd)
Striking sequence: BdX

Description:
Located player on the line of serve, catch a ball and bounce hard on the ground to have much bounce. At the height corresponding will hold a crossed over volley tray to the marks at the bottom of the court.
After 10 balls position players alternates.

Exercise 0364   Hits: Bd

Target: Learning Volley Tray (Bd)
Striking sequence: Bd//

Description:
Located player on the line of serve, catch a ball and bounce hard on the ground to have much bounce. At the height corresponding will hold a parallel volley tray to the marks at the bottom of the court.
After 10 balls position players alternates.

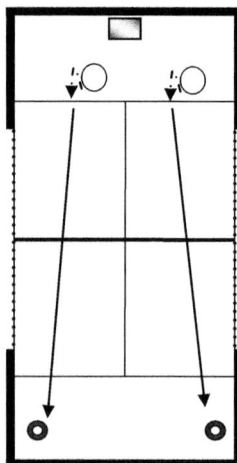

Exercise 0365   Hits: Bd

Target: Learning Volley Tray (Bd)
Striking sequence: BdX

Description:
Located player in the middle of the court, catch a ball and bounce hard on the ground to have much bounce. At the height corresponding will hold a crossed over volley tray to the grid.
After 10 balls position players alternates.

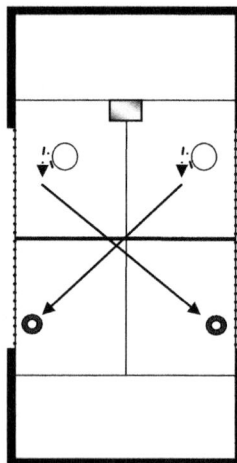

Exercise 0366   Hits: Bd

Target: Learning Volley Tray (Bd)
Striking sequence: Bd//

Description:
Located player in the middle of the court, catch a ball and bounce hard on the ground to have much bounce. At the height corresponding will hold a parallel volley tray to the grid.
After 10 balls position players alternates.

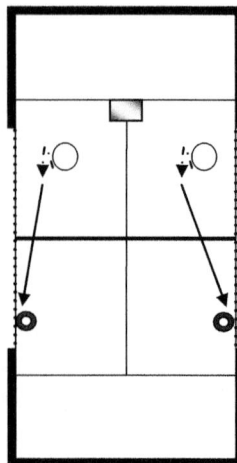

Exercise 0367   Hits: Bd

Target: Volley Tray (Bd) control
Striking sequence: BdX

Description:
Set the player near the net, hold a crossed over volley tray to the mark on the bottom near the wall, to the lobs launched by the monitor.
After the volley tray, the player returns to the row.

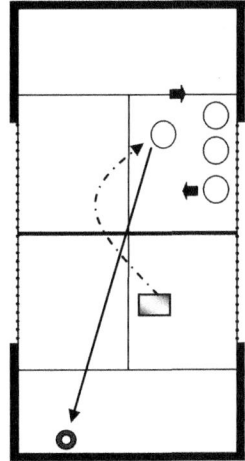

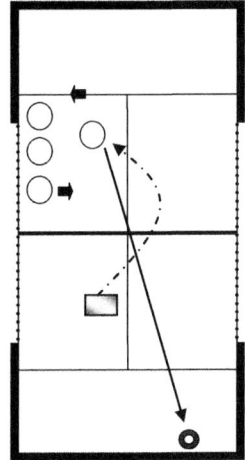

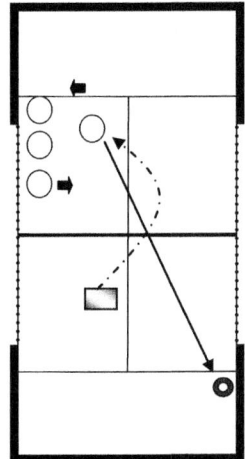

Exercise 0368   Hits: Bd

Target: Volley Tray (Bd) control
Striking sequence: BdX

Description:
Set the player near the net, hold a crossed over volley tray to the mark on the bottom near the wall, to the lobs launched by the monitor.
After the volley tray, the player returns to the row.

Exercise 0369   Hits: Bd

Target: Volley Tray (Bd) control
Striking sequence: BdX

Description:
Set the player near the net, hold a crossed over volley tray to the mark on the bottom near the wall, to the lobs launched by the monitor.
After the volley tray, the player returns to the row.

Exercise 0370   Hits: Bd

Target: Volley Tray (Bd) control
Striking sequence: BdX

Description:
Set the player near the net, hold a crossed over volley tray to the mark on the bottom near the wall, to the lobs launched by the monitor.
After the volley tray, the player returns to the row.

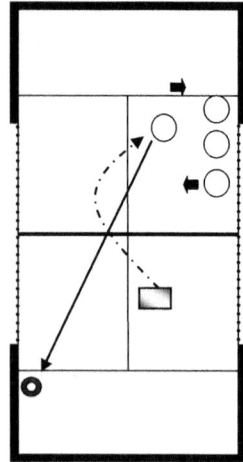

Exercise 0371   Hits: Bd

Target: Volley Tray (Bd) control
Striking sequence: Bd in the middle - BdX

Description:
Located player near the net, hold a volley tray in the middle and another short crossed over volley tray with the target of the marks on the court, to the lobs launched by the monitor.
After the volley trays, the player returns to the row.

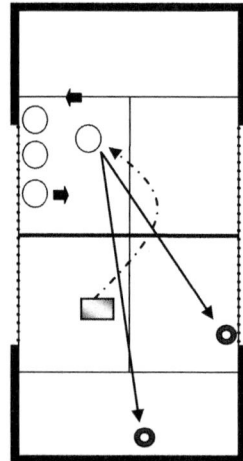

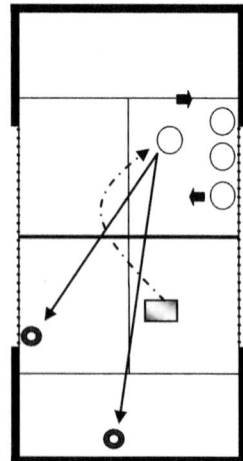

Exercise 0372   Hits: Bd

Target: Volley Tray (Bd) control
Striking sequence: Bd in the middle - BdX

Description:
Located player near the net, hold a volley tray in the middle and another short crossed over volley tray with the target of the marks on the court, to the lobs launched by the monitor.
After the volley trays, the player returns to the row.

Exercise 0373   Hits: Bd

Target: Volley Tray (Bd) control
Striking sequence: Bd// - BdX

Description:
Set the player near the net, hold a parallel volley tray and another crossed over volley tray to the target of the marks on the court, to the lobs launched by the monitor. After the volley trays, the player returns to the row.

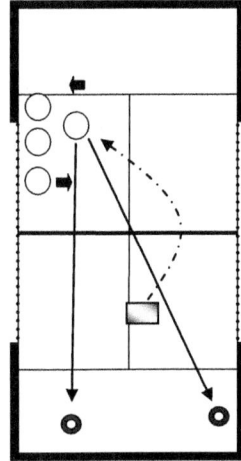

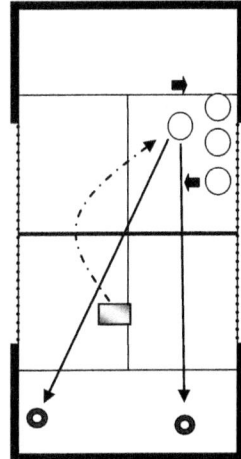

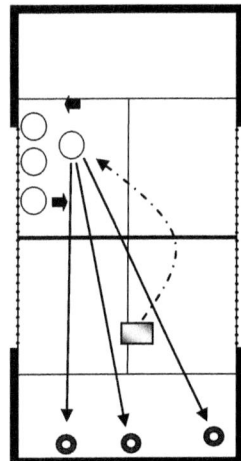

Exercise 0374   Hits: Bd

Target: Volley Tray (Bd) control
Striking sequence: Bd// - BdX

Description:
Set the player near the net, hold a parallel volley tray and another crossed over volley tray to the target of the marks on the court, to the lobs launched by the monitor. After the volley trays, the player returns to the row.

Exercise 0375   Hits: Bd

Target: Volley Tray (Bd) control
Striking sequence: Bd// - Bd in the middle - BdX

Description:
Set the player near the net, hold a parallel volley tray, a volley tray to the middle and a crossed over volley tray to the target of the marks on the court, to the lobs launched by the monitor.
After the volley trays, the player returns to the row.

Exercise 0376   Hits: Bd

Target: Volley Tray (Bd) control
Striking sequence: Bd// - Bd in the middle - BdX

Description:
Set the player near the net, hold a parallel volley tray, a volley tray to the middle and a crossed over volley tray to the target of the marks on the court, to the lobs launched by the monitor.
After the volley trays, the player returns to the row.

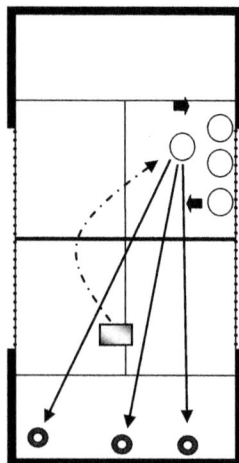

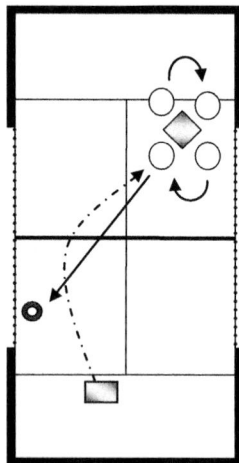

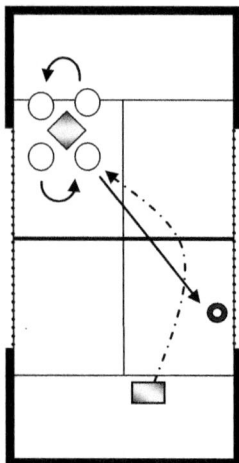

Exercise 0377   Hits: Bd

Target: Volley Tray (Bd) control
Striking sequence: BdX

Description:
Set the player near the net, made a crossed over volley tray (Bd) to the grid to the lobs launched by the monitor and return to the line, with the target of the mark on the court.
After the volley trays, the player returns to the row.

Exercise 0378   Hits: Bd

Target: Volley Tray (Bd) control
Striking sequence: BdX

Description:
Set the player near the net, made a crossed over volley tray (Bd) to the grid to the lobs launched by the monitor and return to the line, with the target of the mark on the court.
After the volley trays, the player returns to the row.

Exercise 0379   Hits: Bd

Target: Volley Tray (Bd) control
Striking sequence: BdX

Description:
Set the player near the net, made a crossed over volley tray (Bd) to the grid to the lobs launched by the monitor and return to the line, with the target of the mark on the court.
After the volley trays, the player returns to the row.

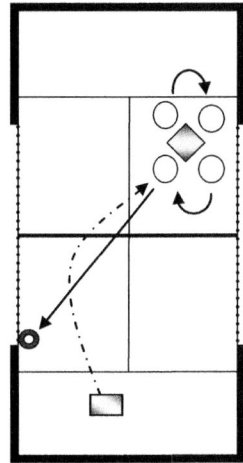

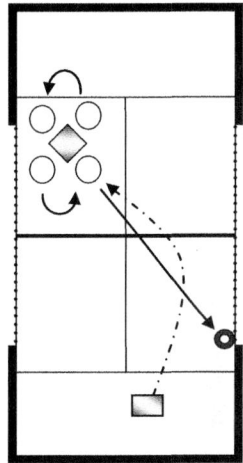

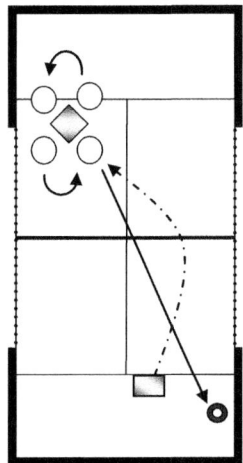

Exercise 0380   Hits: Bd

Target: Volley Tray (Bd) control
Striking sequence: BdX

Description:
Set the player near the net, made a crossed over volley tray (Bd) to the grid to the lobs launched by the monitor and return to the line, with the target of the mark on the court.
After the volley trays, the player returns to the row.

Exercise 0381   Hits: Bd

Target: Volley Tray (Bd) control
Striking sequence: BdX

Description:
Set the player near the net, made a crossed over volley tray (Bd) to the grid to the lobs launched by the monitor and return to the line, with the target of the mark on the court.
After the volley trays, the player returns to the row.

Exercise 0382   Hits: Bd

Target: Volley Tray (Bd) control
Striking sequence: BdX

Description:
Set the player near the net, made a crossed over volley tray (Bd) to the grid to the lobs launched by the monitor and return to the line, with the target of the mark on the court.
After the volley trays, the player returns to the row.

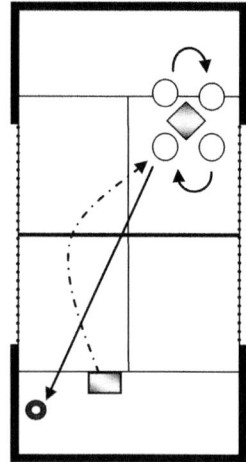

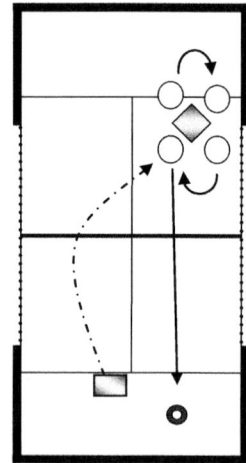

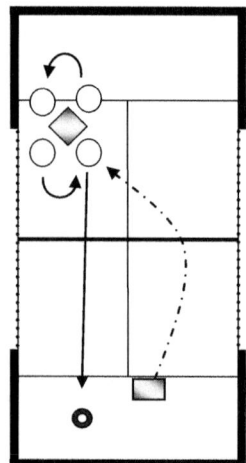

Exercise 0383   Hits: Bd

Target: Volley Tray (Bd) control
Striking sequence: Bd//

Description:
Set the player near the net, made a parallel volley tray (Bd) to the grid to the lobs launched by the monitor and return to the line, with the target of the mark on the court.
After the volley trays, the player returns to the row.

Exercise 0384   Hits: Bd

Target: Volley Tray (Bd) control
Striking sequence: Bd//

Description:
Set the player near the net, made a parallel volley tray (Bd) to the grid to the lobs launched by the monitor and return to the line, with the target of the mark on the court.
After the volley trays, the player returns to the row.

Exercise 0385   Hits: Bd

Target: Volley Tray (Bd) control
Striking sequence: Bd// - net – Bd//

Description:
Set the player near the net, hold a parallel volley tray to the mark on the bottom of the court, touch the net and will repeat the exercise, to the lobs launched by the monitor.
After 10 balls is changed player.

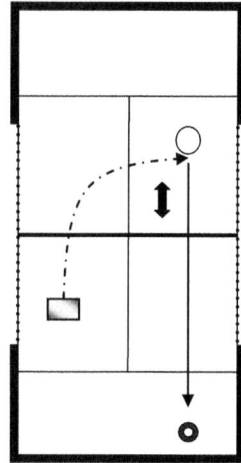

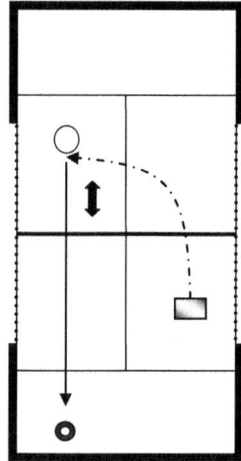

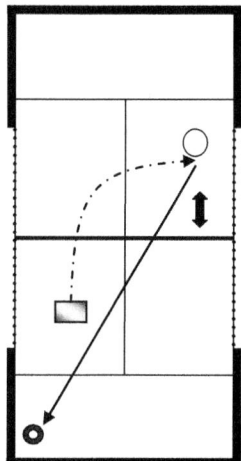

Exercise 0386   Hits: Bd

Target: Volley Tray (Bd) control
Striking sequence: Bd// - net – Bd//

Description:
Set the player near the net, hold a parallel volley tray to the mark on the bottom of the court, touch the net and will repeat the exercise, to the lobs launched by the monitor.
After 10 balls is changed player.

Exercise 0387   Hits: Bd

Target: Volley Tray (Bd) control
Striking sequence: BdX - net – BdX

Description:
Set the player near the net, hold a crossed over volley tray to the mark on the bottom of the court, touch the net and will repeat the exercise, to the lobs launched by the monitor.
After 10 balls is changed player.

Exercise 0388   Hits: Bd

Target: Volley Tray (Bd) control
Striking sequence: BdX - net – BdX

Description:
Set the player near the net, hold a crossed over volley tray to the mark on the bottom of the court, touch the net and will repeat the exercise, to the lobs launched by the monitor.
After 10 balls is changed player.

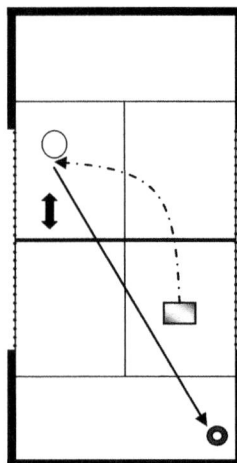

Exercise 0389   Hits: Bd

Target: Volley Tray (Bd) control
Striking sequence: Bd// - net – Bd middle – net – Bd// - net

Description:
Set the player near the net, hold a parallel volley tray, a volley tray to the middle and a crossed over volley tray to the target of the marks on the court, to the lobs launched by the monitor. After each volley tray, the player touches the net and return to the volley tray area.
After 12 balls is changed player.

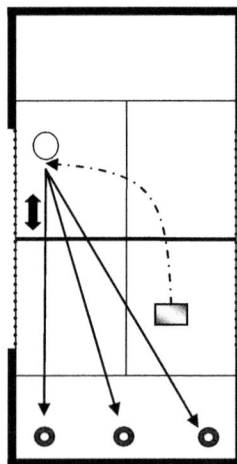

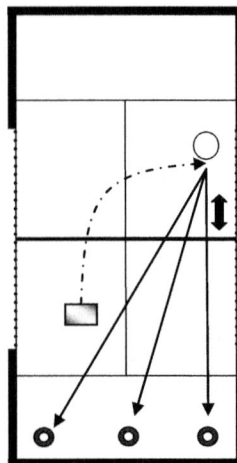

Exercise 0390   Hits: Bd

Target: Volley Tray (Bd) control
Striking sequence: Bd// - net – Bd middle – net – Bd// - net

Description:
Set the player near the net, hold a parallel volley tray, a volley tray to the middle and a crossed over volley tray to the target of the marks on the court, to the lobs launched by the monitor. After each volley tray, the player touches the net and return to the volley tray area.
After 12 balls is changed player.

Exercise 0391   Hits: Bd

Target: Volley Tray (Bd) control
Striking sequence: BdX

Description:
Located the player near the net, held a crossed over volley tray (Bd) to the mark on the peak and touch the cone, to the lobs launched by the monitor. After each volley tray, the player touches the cone and return to the volley tray area.
After 12 balls is changed player.

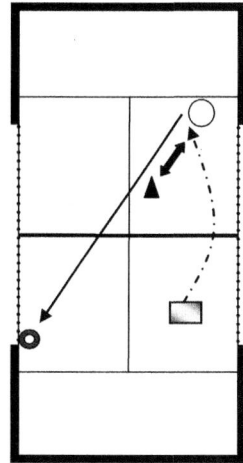

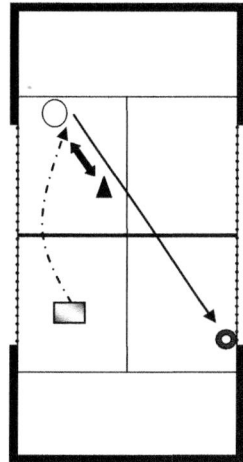

Exercise 0392   Hits: Bd

Target: Volley Tray (Bd) control
Striking sequence: BdX

Description:
Located the player near the net, held a crossed over volley tray (Bd) to the mark on the peak and touch the cone, to the lobs launched by the monitor. After each volley tray, the player touches the cone and return to the volley tray area.
After 12 balls is changed player.

Exercise 0393   Hits: Bd

Target: Volley Tray (Bd) control
Striking sequence: BdX – Bd//

Description:
Located player near the net, hold a crossed over volley tray, pass in front of the cone and make a parallel volley tray (Bd) with the target of the marks at the bottom of the court.
After 10 balls is changed player.

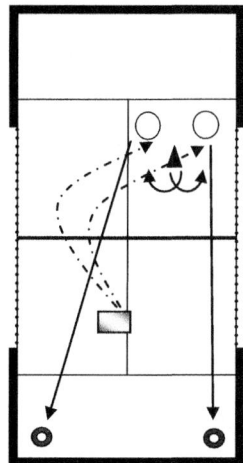

Exercise 0394   Hits: Bd

Target: Volley Tray (Bd) control
Striking sequence: BdX – Bd//

Description:
Located player near the net, hold a crossed over volley tray, pass in front of the cone and make a parallel volley tray (Bd) with the target of the marks at the bottom of the court.
After 10 balls is changed player.

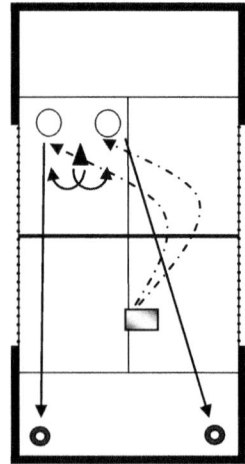

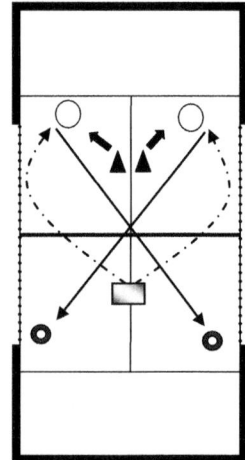

Exercise 0395   Hits: Bd

Target: Volley Tray (Bd) control
Striking sequence: BdX - BdX

Description:
Located player near the net, hold a crossed over volley tray, pass in front of the cone and make another crossed over volley tray, with the target of the marks on the peaks of the court. After each volley tray, the player touches the cone and return to the volley tray area.

After 10 balls is changed player.

EXERCISES OF SHOT

Exercise 0396   Hits: Rm

Target: Shot control
Striking sequence: RmX

Description:
Set the player near the net, hits a crossed over shot to the mark on the bottom of the court.
After the shot, the player returns to the row.

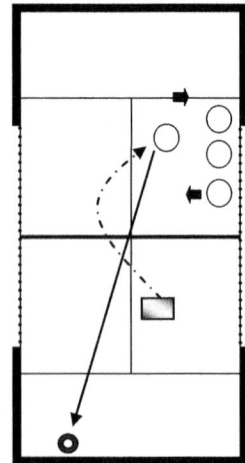

Exercise 0397   Hits: Rm

Target: Shot control
Striking sequence: RmX

Description:
Set the player near the net, hits a crossed over shot to the mark on the bottom of the court.
After the shot, the player returns to the row.

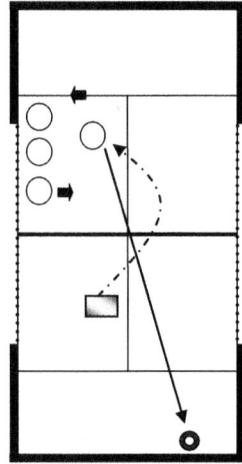

Exercise 0398   Hits: Rm

Target: Shot control
Striking sequence: RmX

Description:
Set the player near the net, hits a crossed over shot to the mark on the bottom of the court near the wall.
After the shot, the player returns to the row.
Then you can do on the other side.

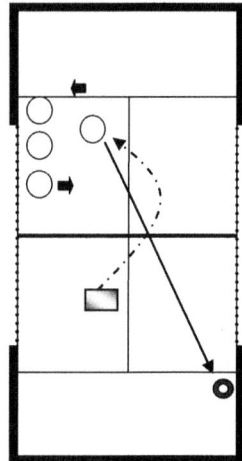

Exercise 0399   Hits: Rm

Target: Shot control
Striking sequence: Shot

Description:
Located two players at the bottom of the court and made parallel lobs, the other two in the net made crossed over shots. The exercise will be done with a single ball.
After 2' position players alternates.
If the exercise is mastered it can be done with two balls.

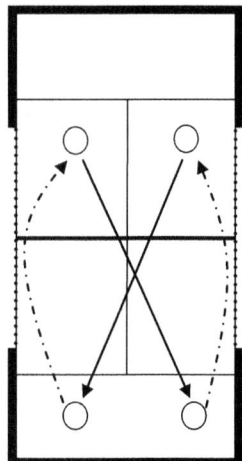

Exercise 0400   Hits: Rm

Target: Shot control
Striking sequence: RmX – Rm middle

Description:
Set the player near the net, hits a parallel shot to the middle and another crossed over shot, with the target of the marks on the court.
After the shots, the player will return to the row.

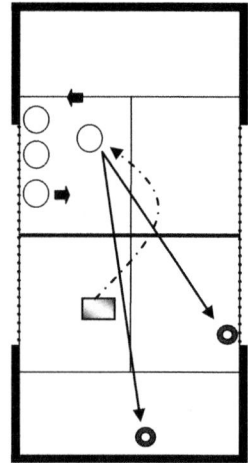

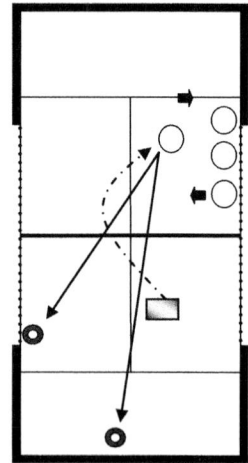

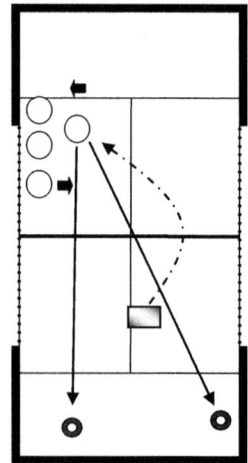

Exercise 0401   Hits: Rm

Target: Shot control
Striking sequence: RmX – Rm middle

Description:
Set the player near the net, hits a parallel shot to the middle and another crossed over shot, with the target of the marks on the court.
After the shots, the player will return to the row.

Exercise 0402   Hits: Rm

Target: Shot control
Striking sequence: Rm// - RmX

Description:
Set the player near the net, hits a parallel shot and another crossed over shot, with the target of the marks on the court.
After the shots, the player will return to the row.

Exercise 0403   Hits: Rm

Target: Shot control
Striking sequence: Rm// - RmX

Description:
Set the player near the net, hits a parallel shot and another crossed over shot, with the target of the marks on the court.
After the shots, the player will return to the row.

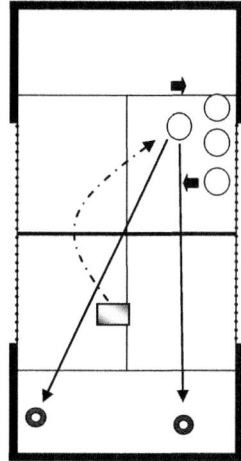

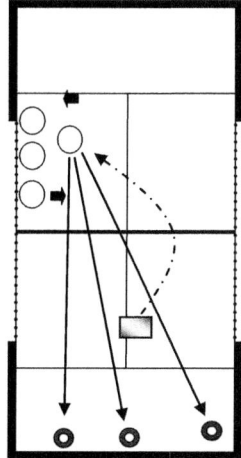

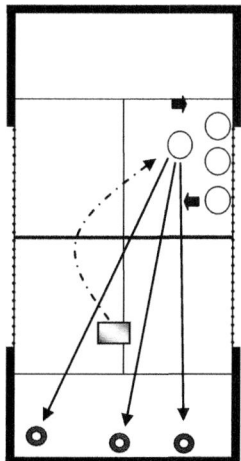

Exercise 0404   Hits: Rm

Target: Shot control
Striking sequence: Rm// - Rm middle - RmX

Description:
Set the player near the net, hits a parallel shot, another shot to the middle and another crossed over shot, with the target of the marks on the court.
After the shots, the player will return to the row.

Exercise 0405   Hits: Rm

Target: Shot control
Striking sequence: Rm// - Rm middle - RmX

Description:
Set the player near the net, hits a parallel shot, another shot to the middle and another crossed over shot, with the target of the marks on the court.
After the shots, the player will return to the row.

151

Exercise 0406   Hits: Rm

Target: Shot control
Striking sequence: RmX

Description:
Set the player near the net, makes a shot to the grid and return to the row, with the target of the mark on the court.

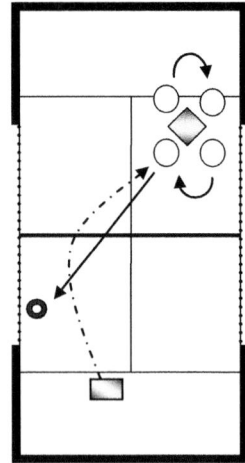

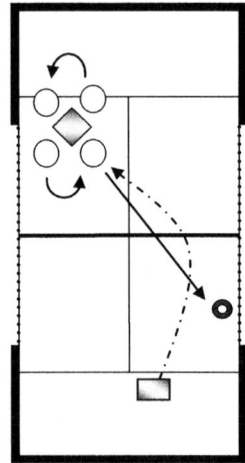

Exercise 0407   Hits: Rm

Target: Shot control
Striking sequence: RmX

Description:
Set the player near the net, makes a shot to the grid and return to the row, with the target of the mark on the court.

Exercise 0408   Hits: Rm

Target: Shot control
Striking sequence: RmX

Description:
Set the player near the net, makes a shot to the peak and return to the row, with the target of the mark on the court.

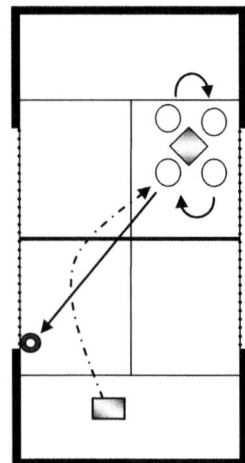

Exercise 0409   Hits: Rm

Target: Shot control
Striking sequence: RmX

Description:
Set the player near the net, makes a shot to the peak and return to the row, with the target of the mark on the court.

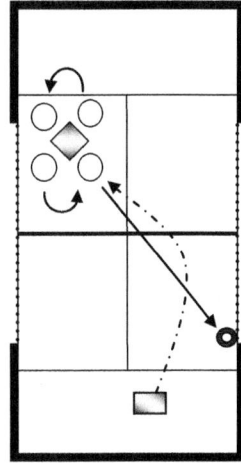

Exercise 0410   Hits: Rm

Target: Shot control
Striking sequence: RmX

Description:
Set the player near the net, makes a shot to the side wall and return to the row, with the target of the mark on the court.

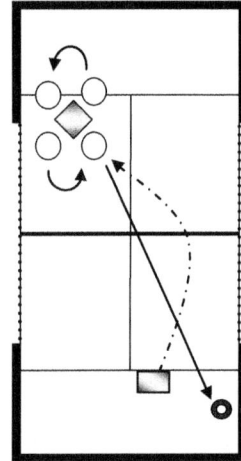

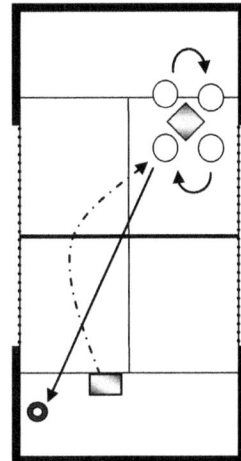

Exercise 0411   Hits: Rm

Target: Shot control
Striking sequence: RmX

Description:
Set the player near the net, makes a shot to the side wall and return to the row, with the target of the mark on the court.

Exercise 0412   Hits: Rm

Target: Shot control
Striking sequence: RmX

Description:
Set the player near the net, makes a shot to the bottom wall and return to the row, with the target of the mark on the court.

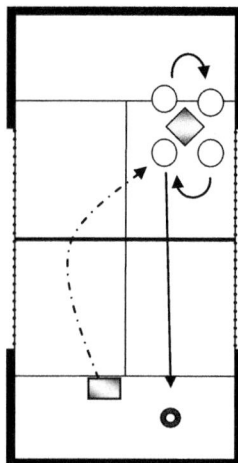

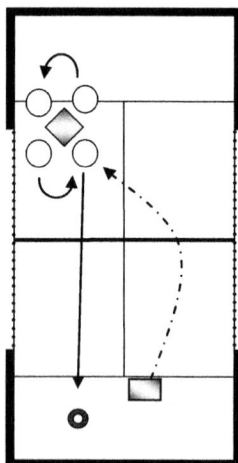

Exercise 0413   Hits: Rm

Target: Shot control
Striking sequence: RmX

Description:
Set the player near the net, makes a shot to the bottom wall and return to the row, with the target of the mark on the court.

Exercise 0414   Hits: Rm

Target: Shot control
Striking sequence: Rm//

Description:
Set the player near the net, hits a parallel shot to the bottom wall and touch the net, with the target of the mark on the bottom of the court.
After 10 balls is changed player.

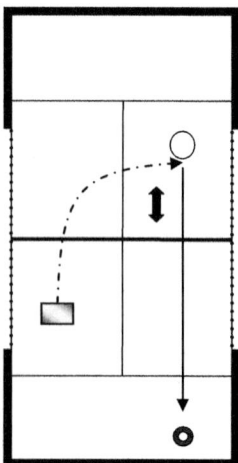

Exercise 0415   Hits: Rm

Target: Shot control
Striking sequence: Rm//

Description:
Set the player near the net, hits a parallel shot to the bottom wall and touch the net, with the target of the mark on the bottom of the court.
After 10 balls is changed player.

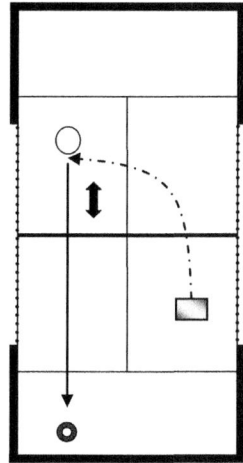

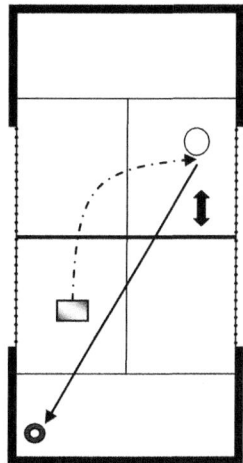

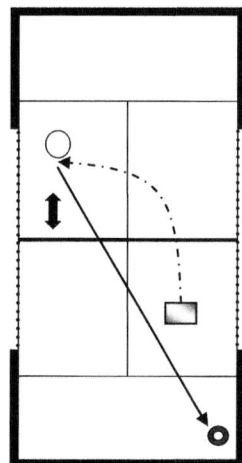

Exercise 0416   Hits: Rm

Target: Shot control
Striking sequence: RmX

Description:
Set the player near the net, hits a crossed over shot to the bottom wall and touch the net, with the target of the mark on the bottom of the court.
After 10 balls is changed player.

Exercise 0417   Hits: Rm

Target: Shot control
Striking sequence: RmX

Description:
Set the player near the net, hits a crossed over shot to the bottom wall and touch the net, with the target of the mark on the bottom of the court.
After 10 balls is changed player.

Exercise 0418   Hits: Rm

Target: Shot control
Striking sequence: Rm// - Rm middle - RmX

Description:
Located player near the net, made parallel shots, shots to the middle and crossed over shots, to the lobs launched by the monitor. After each shot, the player touches the net and return to the shot area.
After 12 balls is changed player.

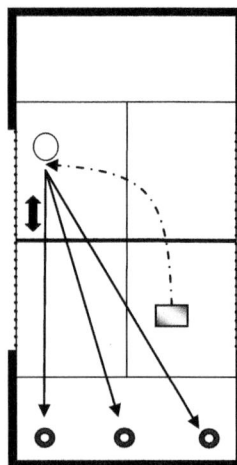

Exercise 0419   Hits: Rm

Target: Shot control
Striking sequence: Rm// - Rm middle - RmX

Description:
Located player near the net, made parallel shots, shots to the middle and crossed over shots, to the lobs launched by the monitor. After each shot, the player touches the net and return to the shot area.
After 12 balls is changed player.

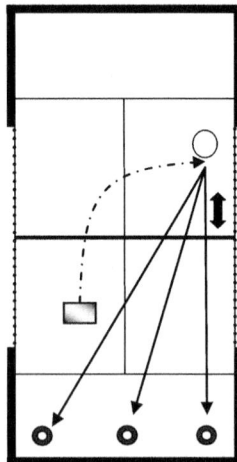

Exercise 0420   Hits: Rm

Target: Shot control
Striking sequence: RmX

Description:
Set the player near the net, hits a crossed over shot to the peak and touch the cone, to the lobs launched by the monitor.
After 10 balls is changed player.

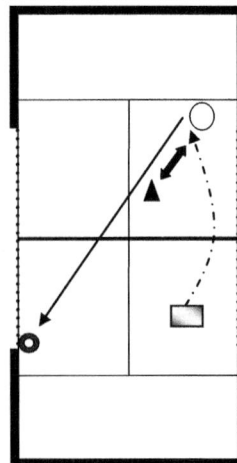

Exercise 0421   Hits: Rm

Target: Shot control
Striking sequence: RmX

Description:
Set the player near the net, hits a crossed over shot to the peak and touch the cone, to the lobs launched by the monitor.
After 10 balls is changed player.

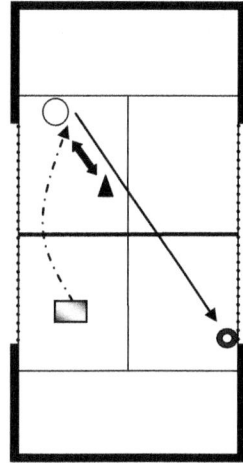

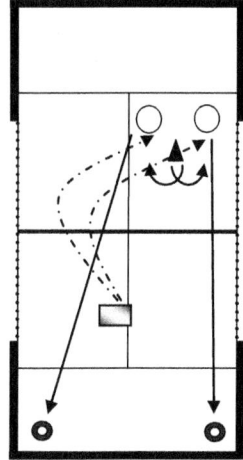

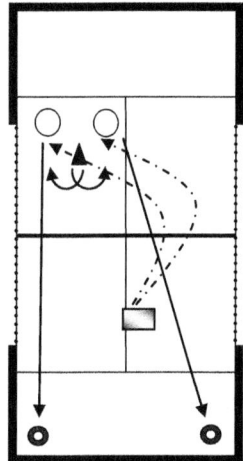

Exercise 0422   Hits: Rm

Target: Shot control
Striking sequence: RmX – Rm//

Description:
Set the player near the net, hits a crossed over shot, pass in front of the cone and hits a parallel shot to the lobs launched by the monitor with the target of the marks on the court.
After 10 balls is changed player.

Exercise 0423   Hits: Rm

Target: Shot control
Striking sequence: RmX – Rm//

Description:
Set the player near the net, hits a crossed over shot, pass in front of the cone and hits a parallel shot to the lobs launched by the monitor with the target of the marks on the court.
After 10 balls is changed player.

Exercise 0424   Hits: Rm

Target: Shot control
Striking sequence: RmX – RmX

Description:
Located two players near the net, hits a crossed over shot and touch the cone of the middle with the target of the marks on the court.
After 10 balls position players alternates.

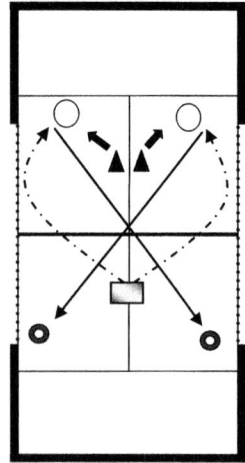

Exercise 0425   Hits: Rm

Target: Shot control
Striking sequence: Rm

Description:
Located two players at the bottom of the court and one on the net, the player of the net alternate parallel shots and crossed over shots in the half-court to the lobs launched by the monitor.
After 10 shots position players alternates.

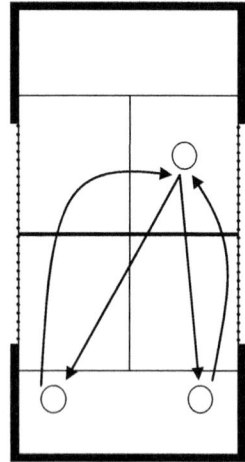

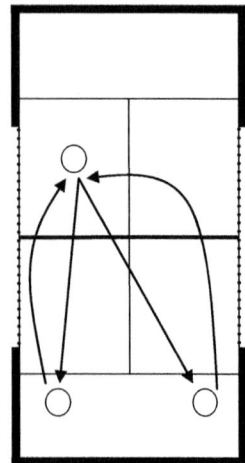

Exercise 0426   Hits: Rm

Target: Shot control
Striking sequence: Rm

Description:
Located two players at the bottom of the court and one on the net, the player of the net alternate parallel shots and crossed over shots in the half-court to the lobs launched by the monitor.
After 10 shots position players alternates.

Exercise 0427   Hits: Rm

Target: Shot control
Striking sequence: Rm

Description:
Located two players at the bottom of the court and one on the net, the player of the net alternate deep parallel shots and deep crossed over shots in the half-court to the lobs launched by the monitor.

After 10 shots position players alternates.

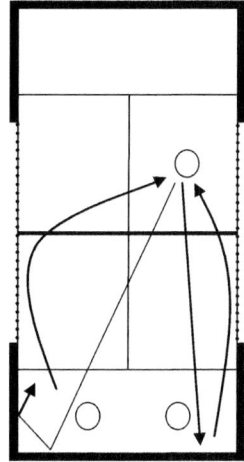

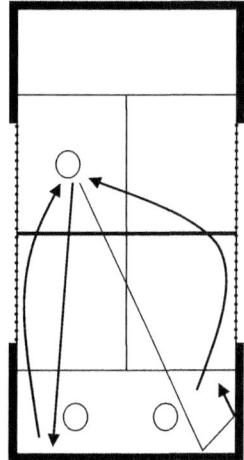

Exercise 0428   Hits: Rm

Target: Shot control
Striking sequence: Rm

Description:
Located two players at the bottom of the court and one on the net, the player of the net alternate deep parallel shots and deep crossed over shots in the half-court to the lobs launched by the monitor.

After 10 shots position players alternates.

Exercise 0429   Hits: Rm

Target: Shot control
Striking sequence: Shot

Description:
Located two players at the bottom of the court and two in the net, players court background made crossed over lobs and the net made shot parallels. The exercise will be done with a single ball.
After 2' position players alternates.
If mastered it can be done with two balls.

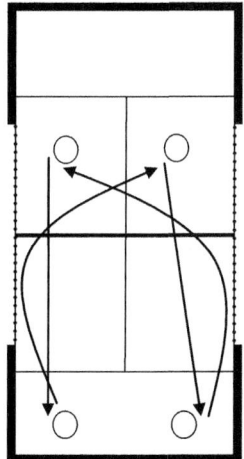

Exercise 0430   Hits: Rm

Target: Shot control
Striking sequence: Shot

Description:
Placed four players on the line of serve, two players made parallel lobs and other made parallel shots. The exercise will take place with two balls.
After 2 'position players alternates.

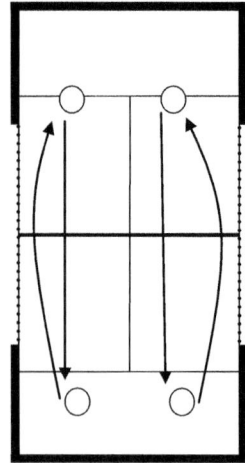

Exercise 0431   Hits: Rm

Target: Shot from different positions
Striking sequence: Rm// - RmX

Description:
Players located in two rows near the net, perform a parallel shot and change row for a crossed over, with the target of the marked area in the corner.

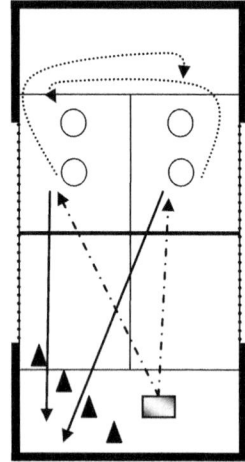

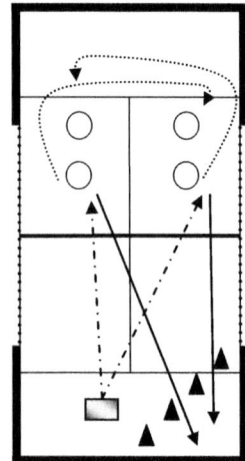

Exercise 0432   Hits: Rm

Target: Shot from different positions
Striking sequence: Rm// - RmX

Description:
Players located in two rows near the net, perform a parallel shot and change row for a crossed over, with the target of the marked area in the corner.

Exercise 0433   Hits: G – Rm

Target: Shot & Protection
Striking sequence: GX - RmX

Description:
Faced two players on crossed over, the attacking player will always do crossed over shot and the player will defend with crossed over lobs.
After 10 balls position players alternates.

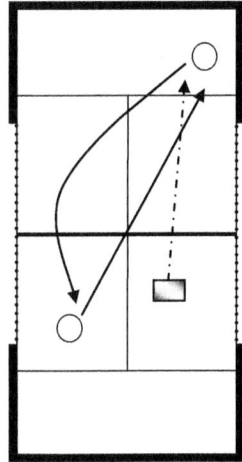

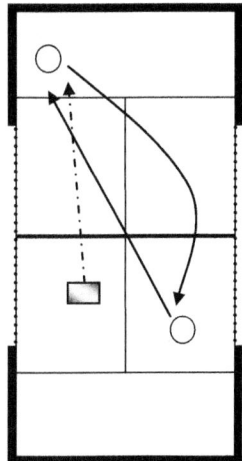

Exercise 0434   Hits: Gb – Rm

Target: Shot & Protection
Striking sequence: GX - RmX

Description:
Faced two players on crossed over, the attacking player will always do crossed over shot and the player will defend with crossed over lobs.
After 10 balls position players alternates.

Exercise 0435   Hits: Rm

Target: Left shot
Striking sequence: Shot and left

Description:
Set the player near the net, the ball is thrown and hits a parallel shot to his wall and trying to make a left turn.
With this we practice the shot and left.

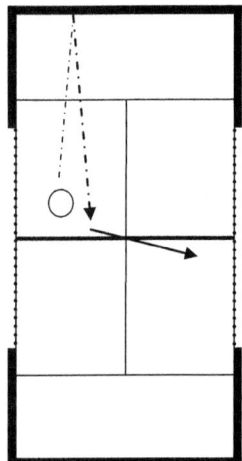

Exercise 0436   Hits: Rm

Target: Left shot
Striking sequence: Shot and left

Description:
Set the player near the net, the ball is thrown and hits a parallel shot to his wall and trying to make a left turn.
With this we practice the shot and left.

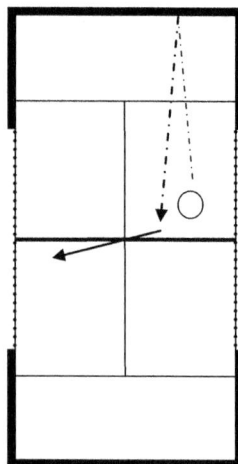

Exercise 0437   Hits: Rm

Target: Learning the shot
Striking sequence: Rm//

Description:
Located player near the net, catch a ball and bounce hard on the ground to have much bounce. At the height corresponding perform a parallel shot to the mark on the bottom of the court.
After 10 balls position players alternates.

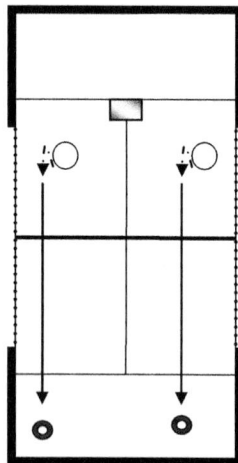

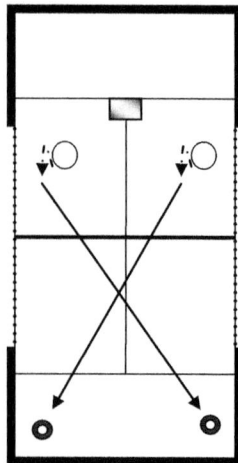

Exercise 0438   Hits: Rm

Target: Learning the shot
Striking sequence: RmX

Description:
Located player near the net, catch a ball and bounce hard on the ground to have much bounce. At the height corresponding perform a crossed over shot to the mark on the bottom of the court.
After 10 balls position players alternates.

162

EXERCISES COMBINATION: FOREHAND, BACKHAND, WALL

Exercise 0439   Hits: SF

Target: Control of scrimmage between 3 players with rebound

Striking sequence: SFD – SFR

Description:
Control of scrimmage between three players that hit forehand or backhand after rebound in background wall.
The top player will make a striking parallel and the second hit a crossed over after rebound.
Players down, one striking held in parallel and the other in crossed over, even after rebound.
After 2 ' position players alternates.

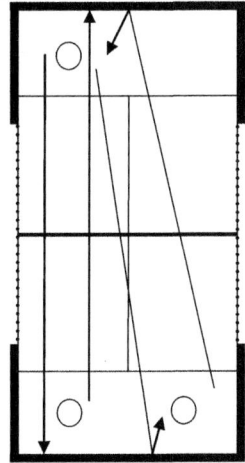

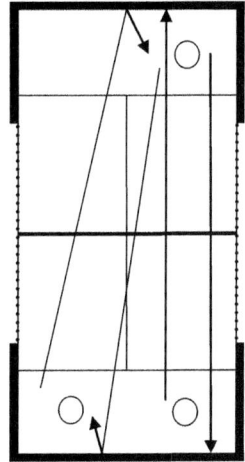

Exercise 0440   Hits: SF

Target: Control of scrimmage between 3 players with rebound

Striking sequence: SFD – SFR

Description:
Control of scrimmage between three players that hit forehand or backhand after rebound in background wall.
The top player will make a striking parallel and the second hit a crossed over after rebound.
Players down, one striking held in parallel and the other in crossed over, even after rebound.
After 2 ' position players alternates.

Exercise 0441   Hits: D – SL – G

Target: Control several hits displacement

Striking sequence: DX - GD// - SLDX

Description:
Set the player at the bottom of the court, hits a crossed over forehand, a forehand lob from the center and a crossed over forehand side wall out, to the marks at the bottom of the court.
The player waits for his partner perform the hit lob to return to the row.

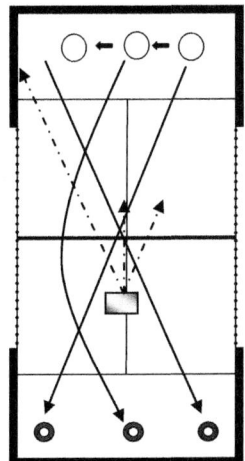

Exercise 0442   Hits: R – SL – G

Target: Control several hits displacement
Striking sequence: RX - GR// - SLRX

Description:
Set the player at the bottom of the court, hits a crossed over backhand, a backhand lob from the center and a crossed over backhand side wall out, to the marks at the bottom of the court.
The player waits for his partner perform the hit lob to return to the row.

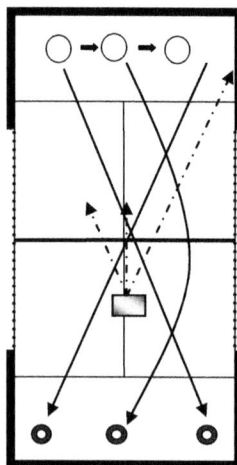

Exercise 0443   Hits: D – SL – G

Target: Control several hits displacement
Striking sequence: D// - GD// - SLD//

Description:
Set the player at the bottom of the court, hits a parallel forehand, a forehand lob from the center and a parallel forehand side wall out, to the marks at the bottom of the court.
The player waits for his partner perform the hit lob to return to the row.

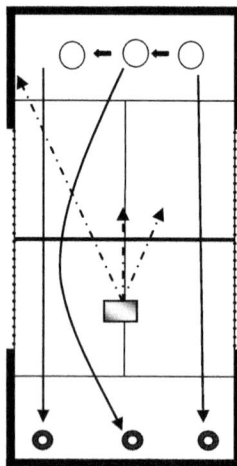

Exercise 0444   Hits: R – SL – G

Target: Control several hits displacement
Striking sequence: R// - GR// - SLR//

Description:
Set the player at the bottom of the court, hits a parallel backhand, a backhand lob from the center and a parallel backhand side wall out, to the marks at the bottom of the court.
The player waits for his partner perform the hit lob to return to the row.

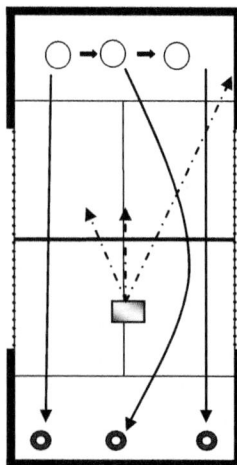

Exercise 0445   Hits: D – SL – G

Target: Control several hits displacement
Striking sequence: D// - GDX - SLDX

Description:
Set the player at the bottom of the court, hits a parallel forehand, a forehand lob from the center and a crossed over forehand side wall out, to the marks at the bottom of the court.
The player waits for his partner perform the hit lob to return to the row.

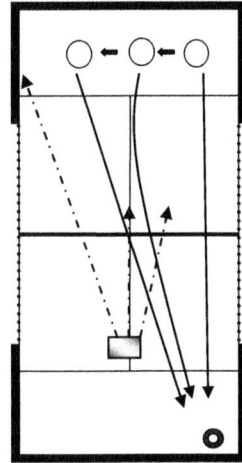

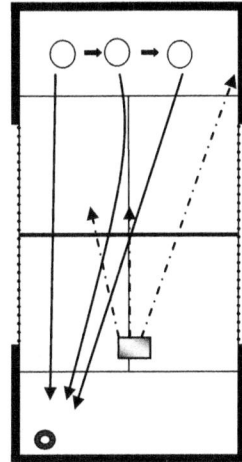

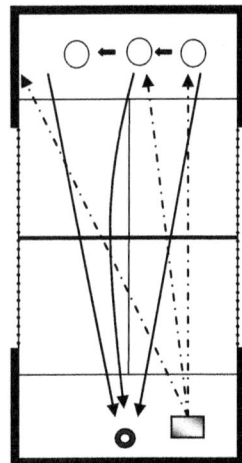

Exercise 0446   Hits: R – SL – G

Target: Control several hits displacement
Striking sequence: R// - GRX - SLRX

Description:
Set the player at the bottom of the court, hits a parallel backhand, a backhand lob from the center and a crossed over backhand side wall out, to the marks at the bottom of the court.
The player waits for his partner perform the hit lob to return to the row.

Exercise 0447   Hits: D – SL – G

Target: Control several hits displacement
Striking sequence: D middle – GD// - SLD middle

Description:
Set the player at the bottom of the court, hits a crossed over forehand, a forehand lob from the center and a crossed over forehand side wall out, to the marks at the bottom of the court.
The player waits for his partner perform the hit lob to return to the row.

Exercise 0448   Hits: R – SL – G

Target: Control several hits displacement
Striking sequence: R middle – GR// - SLR middle

Description:
Set the player at the bottom of the court, hits a crossed over backhand, a backhand lob from the center and a crossed over backhand side wall out, to the marks at the bottom of the court.
The player waits for his partner perform the hit lob to return to the row.

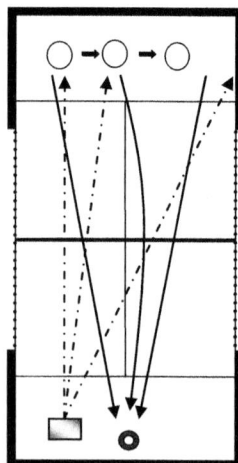

Exercise 0449   Hits: D – SL – G

Target: Control several hits displacement
Striking sequence: DX– GDX – SLD//

Description:
Set the player at the bottom of the court, hits a crossed over forehand, a forehand lob from the center and a parallel forehand side wall out, to the marks at the bottom of the court.
The player waits for his partner perform the hit lob to return to the row.

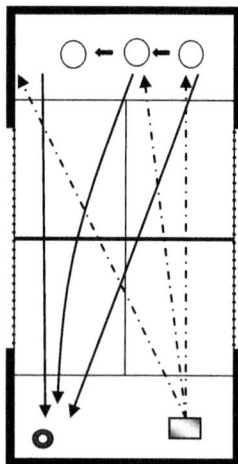

Exercise 0450   Hits: R – SL – G

Target: Control several hits displacement
Striking sequence: RX– GRX – SLR//

Description:
Set the player at the bottom of the court, hits a crossed over backhand, a backhand lob from the center and a parallel backhand side wall out, to the marks at the bottom of the court.
The player waits for his partner perform the hit lob to return to the row.

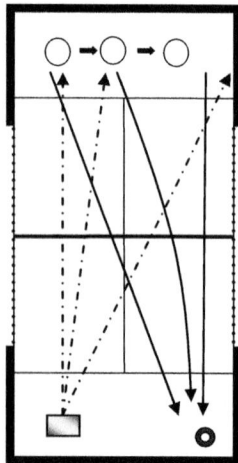

Exercise 0451   Hits: D – SF – SL

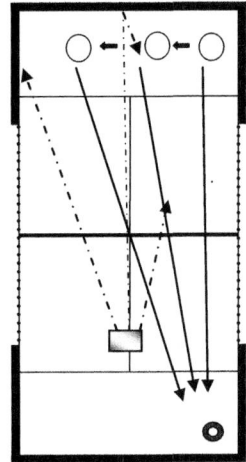

Target: Alternate moving forehand hits
Striking sequence: D// - SFDX - SLDX

Description:
Set the player at the bottom of the court, hits a parallel forehand, a crossed over forehand output background and a crossed over forehand side wall out, with the target of the marks at the bottom of the court.
The players, after the last blow, wait for the next player to make the SFD to cross and return to the row.

Exercise 0452   Hits: R – SF – SL

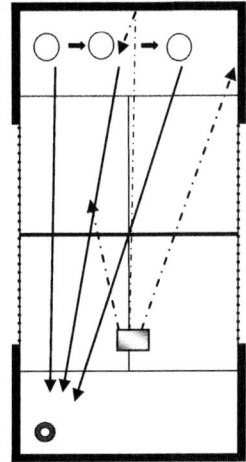

Target: Alternate moving backhand hits
Striking sequence: R// - SFRX - SLRX

Description:
Set the player at the bottom of the court, hits a parallel backhand, a crossed over backhand output background and a crossed over backhand side wall out, with the target of the marks at the bottom of the court.
The players, after the last blow, wait for the next player to make the SFR to cross and return to the row.

Exercise 0453   Hits: D – SF – SL

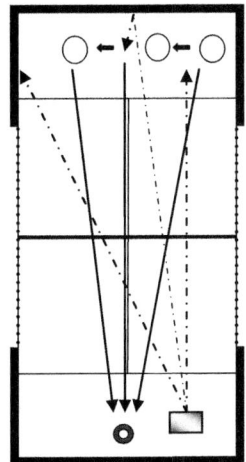

Target: Alternate moving forehand hits
Striking sequence: D - SFD - SLD

Description:
Set the player at the bottom of the court, hits a forehand, a forehand out background and a crossed over forehand side wall out, all the media, with the target of the marks at the bottom of the court.
The players, after the last blow, wait for the next player to make the SFD to cross and return to the row.

Exercise 0454   Hits: R – SF – SL

Target: Alternate moving backhand hits
Striking sequence: R - SFR - SLR

Description:
Set the player at the bottom of the court, hits a backhand, a bottom outlet and a crossed over backhand side wall out, all the media, with the target of the marks at the bottom of the court.
The players, after the last blow, wait for the next player to make the SFR to cross and return to the row.

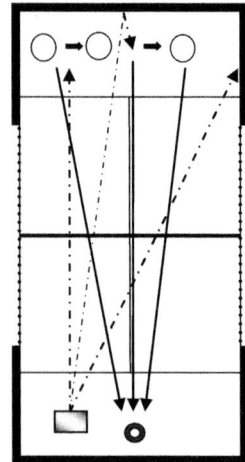

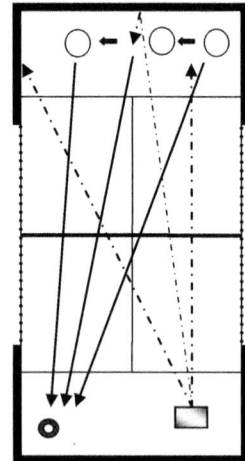

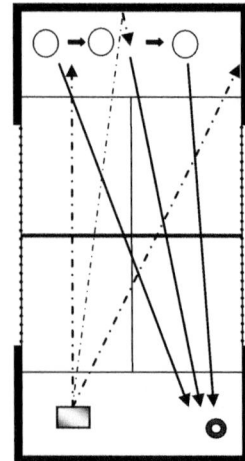

Exercise 0455   Hits: D – SF – SL

Target: Alternate moving Forehand hits
Striking sequence: DX - SFDX – SLD//

Description:
Set the player at the bottom of the court, hits a crossed over forehand, a forehand out background and a parallel forehand side wall out, with the target of the marks at the bottom of the court.
The players, after the last blow, wait for the next player to make the SFR to cross and return to the row.

Exercise 0456   Hits: R – SF – SL

Target: Alternate moving Backhand hits
Striking sequence: RX - SFRX – SLR//

Description:
Set the player at the bottom of the court, hits a crossed over backhand, a bottom outlet and a parallel backhand side wall out, with the target of the marks at the bottom of the court.
The players, after the last blow, wait for the next player to make the SFR to cross and return to the row.

Exercise 0457   Hits: D – SF

Target: Background output control
Striking sequence: SFD – D o R o Cadete

Description:
Set the player at the bottom of the court, makes a soft forehand out background over the bar and again hitting forehand, backhand or cadet after the bounce.
Important control in the first blow to facilitate second.

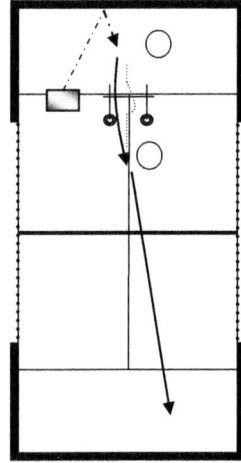

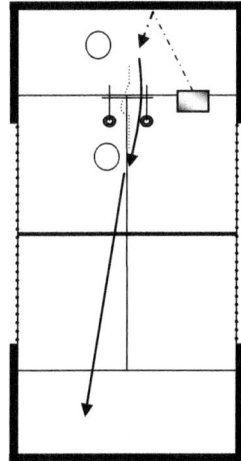

Exercise 0458   Hits: R – SF

Target: Background output control
Striking sequence: SFR – D o R o Cadete

Description:
Set the player at the bottom of the court, makes a soft bottom outlet over the bar and again hitting forehand, backhand or cadet after the bounce.
Important control in the first blow to facilitate second.

Exercise 0459   Hits: R – SF

Target: Mechanization of movement
Striking sequence: SFD - R

Description:
Set the player at the bottom of the court, takes an exercise to machine movements. The monitor will throw balls with the hand for forehand out background and backhand stroke.
After 10 balls is changed player.
Then it is made from the other side.

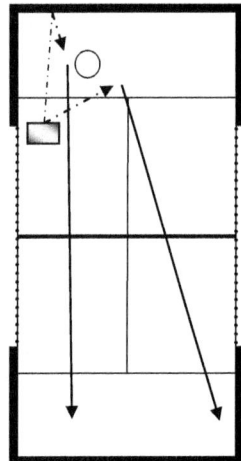

Exercise 0460   Hits: D – SF

Target: Mechanization of movement
Striking sequence: SFD - D

Description:
Set the player at the bottom of the court, takes an exercise to machine movements out background and the importance of returning to the line of serve after every shot. After 5 balls, will go up to the net to hit a short ball with a forehand.
Then you can do from the other side and changing the output side exit background or double wall outlet.

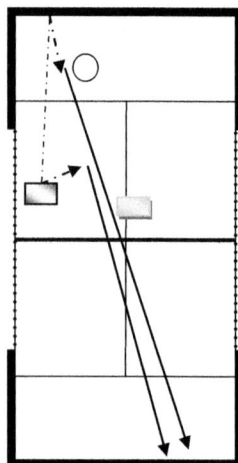

Exercise 0461   Hits: D – R – SF

Target: Different ball speeds
Striking sequence: D – R – SFD – SFR

Description:
Set the player at the bottom of the court, made different hits, both forehand as backhand, depending on the speed and location of impact of the ball:
.- If it comes easy and slow, will make a lob
.- If it comes hard or difficult, it hit hard for the volley of opposites.
.- If it hits high wall, attack or perform lob, and if you come down, try to lob bending well knees.
After 12 balls is changed player.

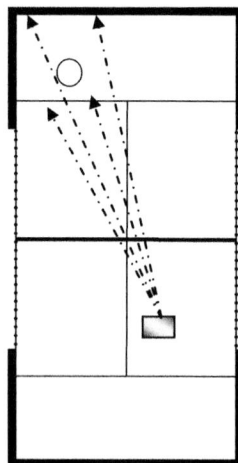

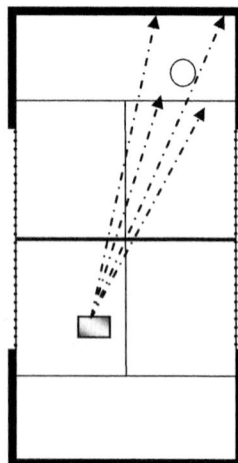

Exercise 0462   Hits: D – R – SF

Target: Different ball speeds
Striking sequence: D – R – SFD – SFR

Description:
Set the player at the bottom of the court, made different hits, both forehand as backhand, depending on the speed and location of impact of the ball:
.- If it comes easy and slow, will make a lob
.- If it comes hard or difficult, it hit hard for the volley of opposites.
.- If it hits high wall, attack or perform lob, and if you come down, try to lob bending well knees.
After 12 balls is changed player.

EXERCISES COMBINATION: FOREHAND, BACKHAND,

Exercise 0463   Hits: D – R – G

Target: Combination hits with 4 players
Striking sequence: G// – DX o RX

Description:
Placed four players in the bottom of the court, two players below made hits crossed over forehand or crossed over backhand, and the other players will made parallel lobs.
If the exercise is mastered, you can try with two balls at once.
After 2' position players alternates.

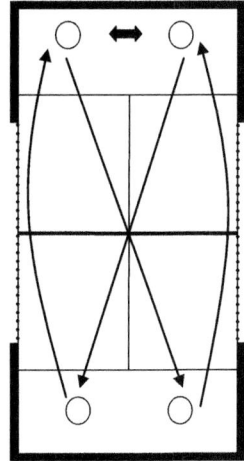

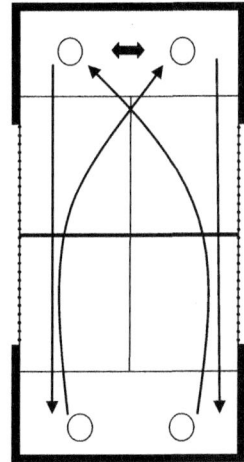

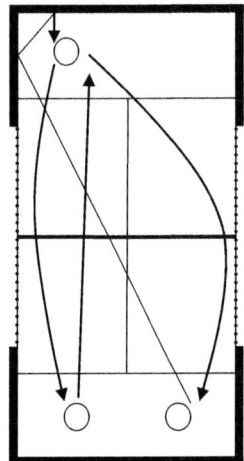

Exercise 0464   Hits: D – R – G

Target: Combination hits with 4 players
Striking sequence: GX – D// o R//

Description:
Placed four players in the bottom of the court, two players below made hits parallel forehand or parallel backhand, and the other players will made crossed over lobs.
If the exercise is mastered, you can try with two balls at once.
After 2' position players alternates.

Exercise 0465   Hits: D – R – G

Target: Combination hits with 3 players
Striking sequence: GX o G// – D// o DX / R// o RX

Description:
Located three players in the bottom of the court, single player alternate parallel forehand lobs or crossed over backhand lobs to the other players who made frees hits from the bottom of the track to the single player.
After 2' position players alternates.

Exercise 0466   Hits: D – R – G

Target: Combination hits with 3 players
Striking sequence: GX o G// – D// o DX / R// o RX

Description:
Located three players in the bottom of the court, single player alternate parallel backhand lobs or crossed over forehand lobs to the other players who made frees hits from the bottom of the track to the single player.
After 2' position players alternates.

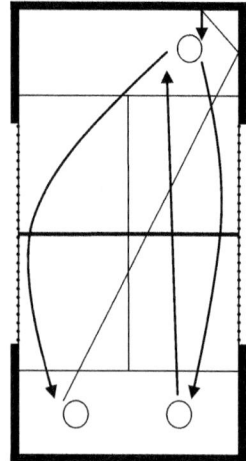

Exercise 0467   Hits: D – R – G

Target: Combination hits with 4 players
Striking sequence: GX o G// – DX o R//

Description:
Placed four players in the bottom of the court, one of the top players perform crossed over lob and the other in the bottom performs crossed over hits. One of those below performs lobs parallels and the other parallel hits.
If the exercise is mastered you can try with two balls at once.
After 2' position players alternates.

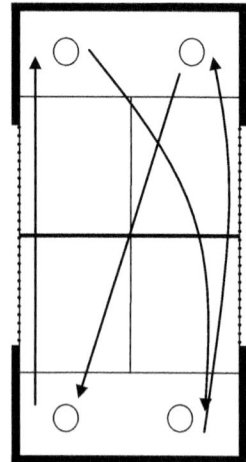

Exercise 0468   Hits: D – R – G

Target: Combination hits with 4 players
Striking sequence: GX o G// – DX o R//

Description:
Placed four players in the bottom of the court, one of the top players perform parallel lob and the other in the bottom perform parallel hits. One of those below performs lobs crossed over and the other crossed over hits.
If the exercise is mastered you can try with two balls at once.
After 2' position players alternates.

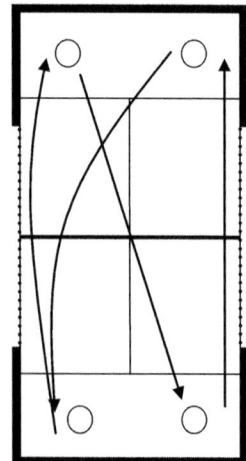

Exercise 0469   Hits: D – G

Target: Controlling multiple hits with displacement
Striking sequence: D// - GD// - D//

Description:
Set the player at the bottom of the court, performed parallel forehand, a forehand lob from the center and a parallel forehand, to the marks at the bottom of the court.
The player waits for his partner perform the hit lob to return to the row.

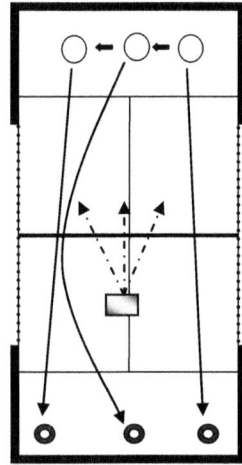

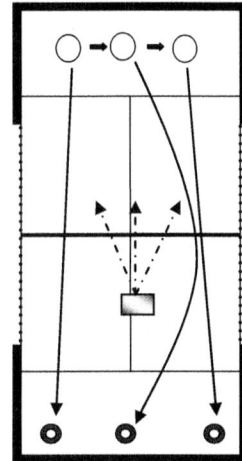

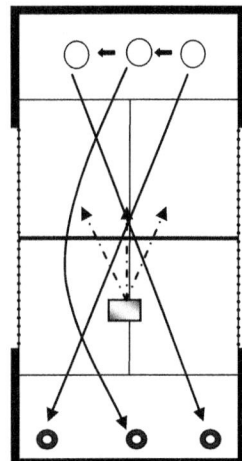

Exercise 0470   Hits: R – G

Target: Controlling multiple hits with displacement
Striking sequence: R// - GR// - R//

Description:
Set the player at the bottom of the court, performed parallel backhand, a backhand lob from the center and a parallel backhand, to the marks at the bottom of the court.
The player waits for his partner perform the hit lob to return to the row.

Exercise 0471   Hits: D – G

Target: Controlling Multiple hits with displacement
Striking sequence: DX - GD// - DX

Description:
Set the player at the bottom of the court, performed crossed over forehand, a forehand lob from the center and a crossed over forehand, to the marks at the bottom of the court.
The player waits for his partner perform the hit lob to return to the row.

Exercise 0472   Hits: R – G

Target: Control several hits displacement
Striking sequence: RX - GR// - RX

Description:
Set the player at the bottom of the court, performed crossed over backhand, a backhand lob from the center and a crossed over backhand, to the marks at the bottom of the court.
The player waits for his partner perform the hit lob to return to the row.

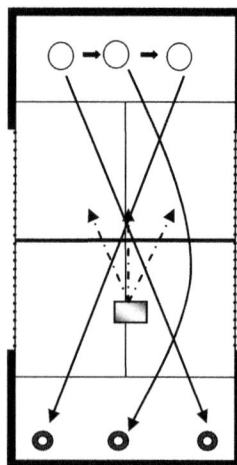

EXERCISES COMBINATION: FOREHAND, BACKHAND,

Exercise 0473   Hits: D – R – V

Target: Volleys control and defense
Striking sequence: VDX – DX o RX – VRX

Description:
Faced two players on crossed over, one on the net and another in defense, the bottom player plays a ball in the middle and the following next to his partner perform volleys against him.
After 2' position players alternates.

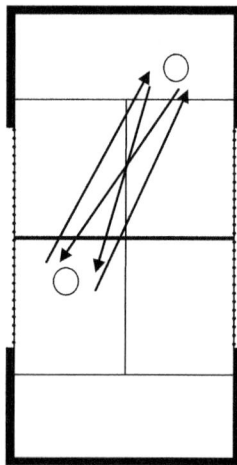

Exercise 0474   Hits: D – R – V

Target: Volleys control and defense
Striking sequence: VDX – DX o RX – VRX

Description:
Faced two players on crossed over, one on the net and another in defense, the bottom player plays a ball in the middle and the following next to his partner perform volleys against him.
After 2'position players alternates.

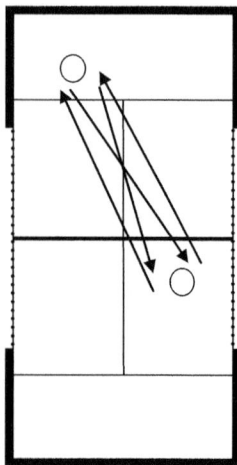

Exercise 0475   Hits: D – R – V

Target: Volleys control and defense
Striking sequence: VD// – D// o R// – VR//

Description:
Located two players in parallel, one in the net and another in defense, the defending player made forehand or backhand to the player in the net.
After 2'position players alternates.

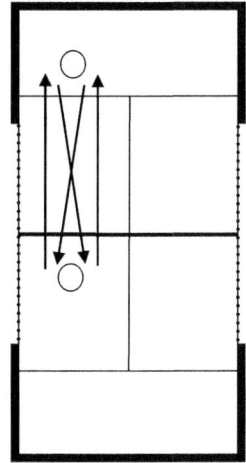

Exercise 0476   Hits: D – R – V

Target: Alternate moving hits
Striking sequence: DX – RX – VDX – VRX

Description:
Set the player at the bottom of the court, hits a crossed over forehand and a crossed over backhand, go up to the net and perform a crossed over forehand volley and a crossed over backhand volley, to the square target marked on the corner.
After 12 balls is changed player.

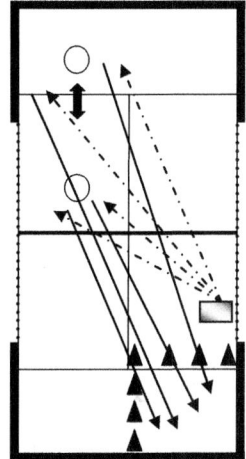

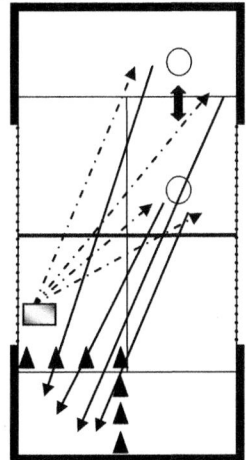

Exercise 0477   Hits: D – R – V

Target: Alternate moving hits
Striking sequence: DX – RX – VDX – VRX

Description:
Set the player at the bottom of the court, hits a crossed over forehand and a crossed over backhand, go up to the net and perform a crossed over forehand volley and a crossed over backhand volley, to the square target marked on the corner.
After 12 balls is changed player.

Exercise 0478   Hits: D – R – V

Target: Alternate moving hits
Striking sequence: DX – RX – VDX – VRX

Description:
A player works with the monitor to finish the ball trolley. It located on the bottom of the court, made a crossed over forehand and a crossed over backhand, go up to the net and perform a crosses over forehand volley and a crossed over backhand volley, returning back to the starting position. The target will be the square marked in the corner. The other two players made ball control, one from the bottom and the other on the volley.
Upon completion of the ball trolley, the position of the players alternate.

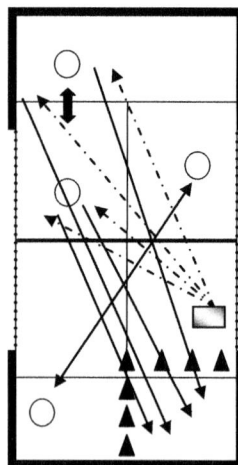

Exercise 0479   Hits: D – R – V

Target: Alternate moving hits
Striking sequence: DX – RX – VDX – VRX

Description:
A player works with the monitor to finish the ball trolley. It located on the bottom of the court, made a crossed over forehand and a crossed over backhand, go up to the net and perform a crosses over forehand volley and a crossed over backhand volley, returning back to the starting position. The target will be the square marked in the corner. The other two players made ball control, one from the bottom and the other on the volley.
Upon completion of the ball trolley, the position of the players alternate.

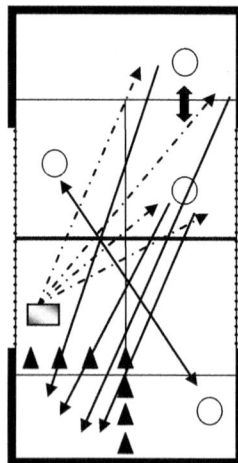

Exercise 0480   Hits: R – V

Target: Volleys control
Striking sequence: RX – V//

Description:
Located two players at the bottom of the court and one on the net, players perform crossed over backhand background out the player who is on the net. After each stroke, the player will touch the cone next to them. The player on the net, held parallel volleys to the cones back of the court, as both forehand and backhand.
After 20 balls position players alternates.

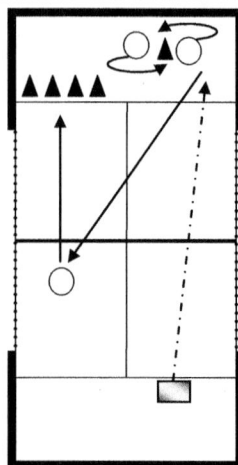

Exercise 0481   Hits: D – V

Target: Volleys control
Striking sequence: DX – V//

Description:
Located two players at the bottom of the court and one on the net, players perform crossed over forehand background out the player who is on the net. After each stroke, the player will touch the cone next to them. The player on the net, held parallel volleys to the cones back of the court, as both forehand and backhand.
After 20 balls position players alternates.

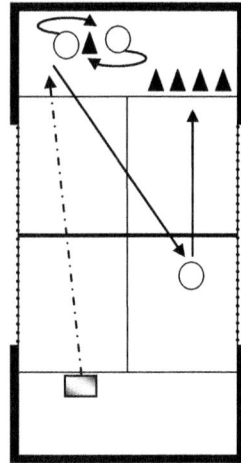

Exercise 0482   Hits: D – V

Target: Rise to the net with short ball
Striking sequence: Bola short DX - VDX

Description:
Set the player to the peak height, hit a short ball without bounce, making a crossed over forehand, go up to the net to make a crossed over forehand volley, with the target of the mark on the bottom of the court.

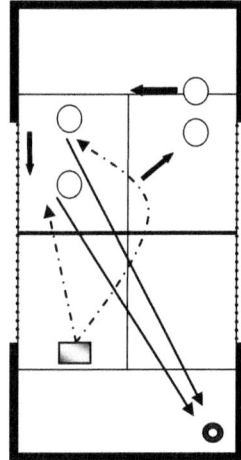

Exercise 0483   Hits: R – V

Target: Rise to the net with short ball
Striking sequence: Bola short RX - VRX

Description:
Set the player to the peak height, hits a short ball without bounce, making a crossed over backhand, go up to the net to make a crossed over backhand volley, with the target of the mark on the bottom of the court.

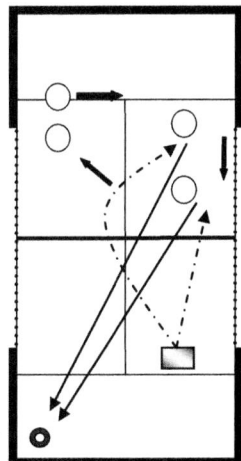

Exercise 0484   Hits: D – V

Target: Combination of hits
Striking sequence: Low ball DX deep - VDX – VDX

Description:
Set the player to the peak height, hits a deep crossed over forehand to a low ball which will rise and make a power crossed over forehand volley and a slow crossed over forehand volley to the grid.
After 12 balls is changed player.

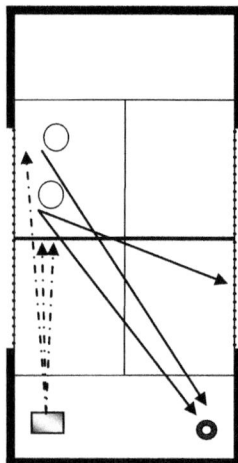

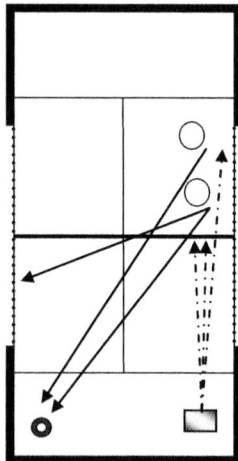

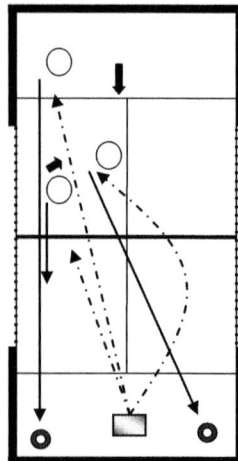

Exercise 0485   Hits: R – V

Target: Combination of hits
Striking sequence: Low ball RX deep - VRX – VRX

Description:
Set the player to the peak height, hits a deep crossed over backhand to a low ball which will rise and make a power crossed over backhand volley and a slow crossed over backhand volley to the grid.
After 12 balls is changed player.

Exercise 0486   Hits: D – R – V

Target: Combination of hits
Striking sequence: D// - VD short // - RX

Description:
Set the player at the bottom of the court, hits a parallel forehand, rise to the net for a short ball with a parallel forehand volley and delay to make a crossed over backhand.
After 12 balls is changed player.

Exercise 0487   Hits: R – V

Target: Combination of hits
Striking sequence: R// - VR short // - RX

Description:
Set the player at the bottom of the court, hits a parallel backhand, rise to the net for a short ball with a parallel backhand volley and delay to make a crossed over backhand.
After 12 balls is changed player.

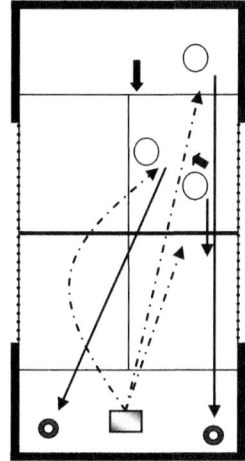

Exercise 0488   Hits: D – V

Target: Combination of hits
Striking sequence: Short ball D – 2VR// - VRX

Description:
Located half-court player, climbs the short ball with a forehand approach to the middle, makes two parallel backhand volleys and a crossed over backhand volley and continue with the monitor to finish the point.

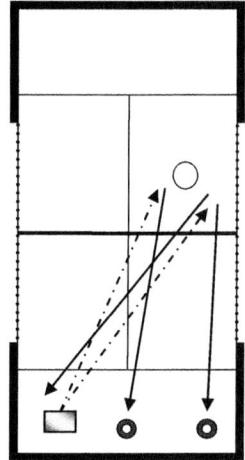

Exercise 0489   Hits: R – V

Target: Combination of hits
Striking sequence: Short ball R – 2VD// - VDX

Description:
Located half-court player, climbs the short ball with a backhand approach to the middle, makes two parallel forehand volleys and a crossed over forehand volley and continue with the monitor to finish the point.

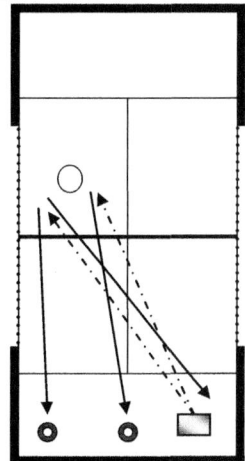

Exercise 0490   Hits: D – V

Target: Combination of hits and displacements
Striking sequence: DX – VDX – Disp. Lateral – Disp. back

Description:
Set the player at the bottom of the court, executes a crossed over forehand and go up to the net for a crossed over forehand volley, with the target of the mark on the back of the court. Then he will move sideways to the cone at the grid and back up laterally toward the cone at the bottom of the court.

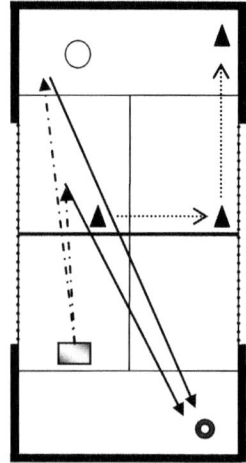

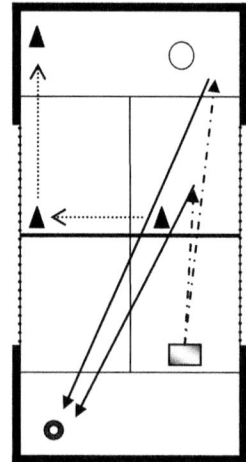

Exercise 0491   Hits: R – V

Target: Combination of hits and displacements
Striking sequence: RX – VRX – Disp. Lateral – Disp. back

Description:
Set the player at the bottom of the court, executes a crossed over backhand and go up to the net for a crossed over backhand volley, with the target of the mark on the back of the court. Then he will move sideways to the cone at the grid and back up laterally toward the cone at the bottom of the court.

Exercise 0492   Hits: D – V

Target: Combination of hits
Striking sequence: D middle – VD middle

Description:
Set the player at the bottom of the court, hits a forehand and rise to the net for a forehand volley, with the target of the string located in the middle of the court.
With this exercise work hits approach to consolidate our position in the net.

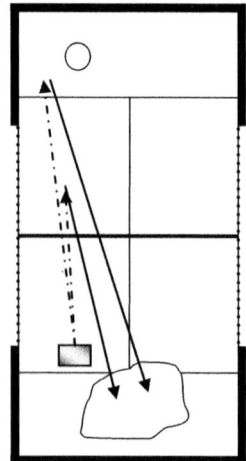

Exercise 0493   Hits: R – V

Target: Combination of hits
Striking sequence: R middle – VR middle

Description:
Set the player at the bottom of the court, hits a backhand and rise to the net for a backhand volley, with the target of the string located in the middle of the court.
With this exercise work hits approach to consolidate our position in the net.

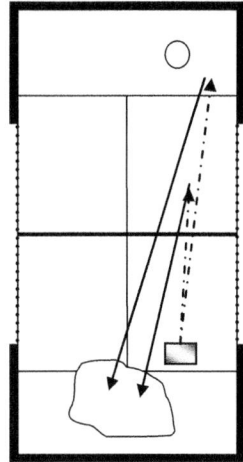

Exercise 0494   Hits: D – V

Target: Combination of hits
Striking sequence: 8 on cones – DX - VDX

Description:
Located the player near the cones located at the bottom of the court, held on 8 and run them to make a crossed over forehand and a crossed over forehand volley, with target of the mark on the back of the court.
He repeated the exercise after 10 balls and change of player.

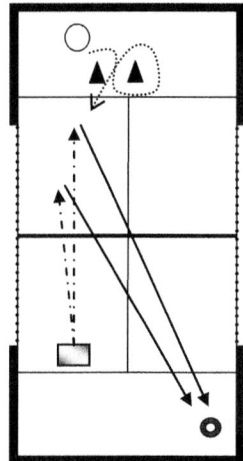

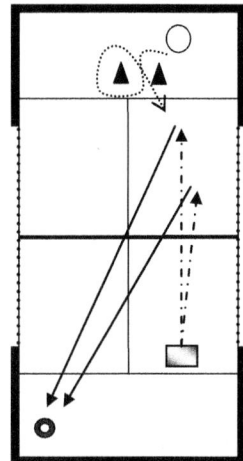

Exercise 0495   Hits: R – V

Target: Combination of hits
Striking sequence: 8 on cones – RX - VRX

Description:
Located the player near the cones located at the bottom of the court, held on 8 and run them to make a crossed over backhand and a crossed over backhand volley, with target of the mark on the back of the court.
He repeated the exercise after 10 balls and change of player.

EXERCISES COMBINATION: FOREHAND, BACKHAND, SHOT/ VOLLEY TRAY (BD)

Exercise 0496   Hits: R – Rm

Target: Combination of hits
Striking sequence: R// – RmX

Description:
Having more than 2 players on the court, we work in 3 positions. In the first he will made a parallel backhand, in another crossed over shot and the next rest. In each position we will hit two balls.

Exercise 0497   Hits: D – Rm

Target: Combination of hits
Striking sequence: D// – RmX

Description:
Having more than 2 players on the court, we work in 3 positions. In the first he will made a parallel forehand, in another crossed over shot and the next rest. In each position we will hit two balls.

Exercise 0498   Hits: R – Rm

Target: Reaction to a situation
Striking sequence: RX – Rm//

Description:
Set the player at the bottom of the court, hits a crossed over backhand and he will rise running to the net to smash a strong parallel.

Exercise 0499   Hits: D – Rm

Target: Reaction to a situation
Striking sequence: DX – Rm//

Description:
Set the player at the bottom of the court, hits a crossed over forehand and he will rise running to the net to smash a strong parallel.

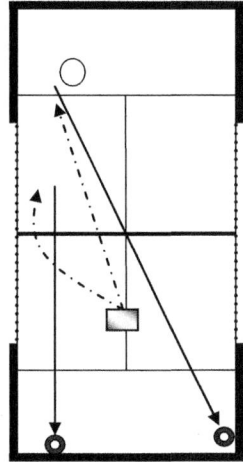

Exercise 0500   Hits: D – R – Rm

Target: Control ball from the bottom of the court
Striking sequence: DX – R// - DX – R// - Rm//

Description:
Set the player at the bottom of the court, try all the balls reach the bottom of the opposite court. It will perform the following hits: crossed over forehand, parallel backhand, crossed over forehand, parallel backhand and then climb to the net and do a parallel shot.

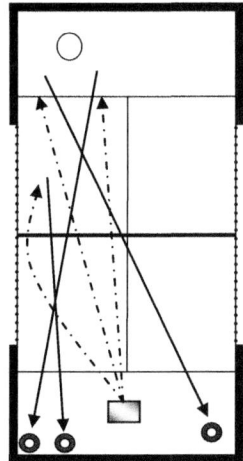

Exercise 0501   Hits: D – R – Rm

Target: Ball Control desde el fondo de la court
Striking sequence: D// – RX – D// – RX - Rm//

Description:
Set the player at the bottom of the court, try all the balls reach the bottom of the opposite court. It will perform the following hits: crossed over backhand, parallel forehand, crossed over backhand, parallel forehand and then climb to the net and do a parallel shot.

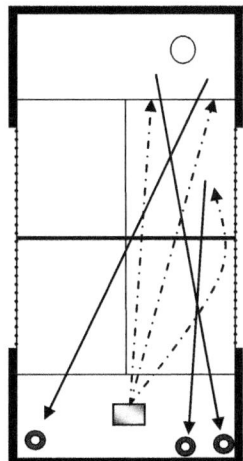

EXERCISES COMBINATION: LOB, SHOT / VOLLEY TRAY

Exercise 0502   Hits: G – Bd

Target: Lob and Volley Tray (Bd)
Striking sequence: GRX - BdX

Description:
With two players on the court, we will work in two different positions. In the first we perform a crossed over backhand lob from the back of the court and in the other position perform a crossed over volley tray, with the target of the marks on the corners of the court.
After 20 balls position players alternates.

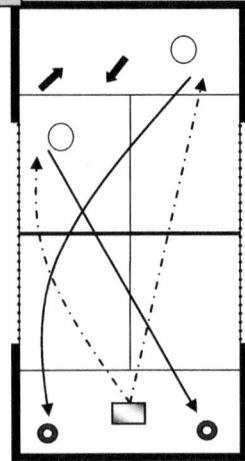

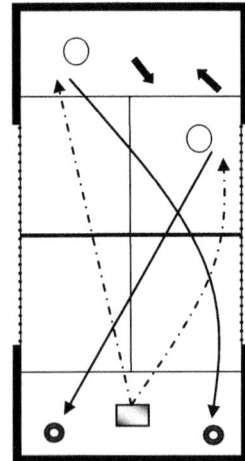

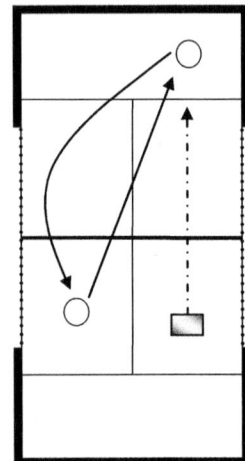

Exercise 0503   Hits: G – Bd

Target: Lob and Volley Tray (Bd)
Striking sequence: GDX - BdX

Description:
With two players on the court, we will work in two different positions. In the first we perform a crossed over forehand lob from the back of the court and in the other position perform a crossed over volley tray, with the target of the marks on the corners of the court.
After 20 balls position players alternates.

Exercise 0504   Hits: G – Rm

Target: Alternate hits moving
Striking sequence: GX – RmX

Description:
With two players in crossed over, the player who is in the back of the court held crossed over lobs to allow the crossed over shot of his partner. The game continues until the end point.
After 20 balls position players alternates.

Exercise 0505   Hits: G – Rm

Target: Alternate hits moving
Striking sequence: GX – RmX

Description:
With two players in crossed over, the player who is in the back of the court held crossed over lobs to allow the crossed over shot of his partner. The game continues until the end point.
After 20 balls position players alternates.

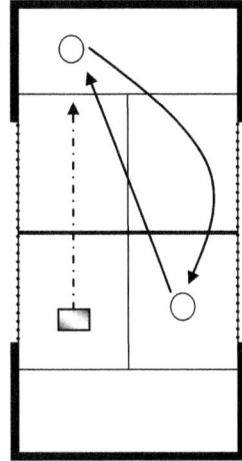

Exercise 0506   Hits: G – Dev. Rm

Target: Reaction to a situation
Striking sequence: GD – Dev. Rm

Description:
Set the player at the bottom of the court, hits a forehand lob and he will dodge the shot of the monito to get the ball and return it.
After 10 balls is changed player.

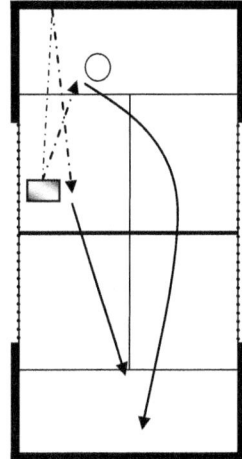

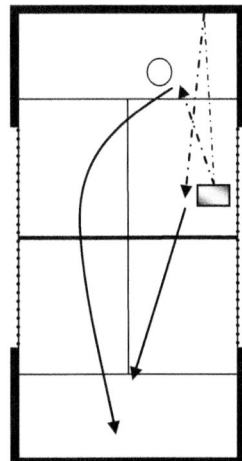

Exercise 0507   Hits: G – Dev. Rm

Target: Reaction to a situation
Striking sequence: GR – Dev. Rm

Description:
Set the player at the bottom of the court, hits a backhand lob and he will dodge the shot of the monito to get the ball and return it.
After 10 balls is changed player.

EXERCISES COMBINATION: FOREHAND, BACKHAND, WALL, VOLLEY

Exercise 0508   Hits: SF – G – V

Target: Combination of hits with movement
Striking sequence: GR// – VD middle – Down Wall X

Description:
From the starting position is moved to the opposite corner to make a parallel backhand lob, then you will go running to the net and perform a forehand volley to the middle and be delayed for a crossed over forehand drop wall, with the target of marks on the back of the court.

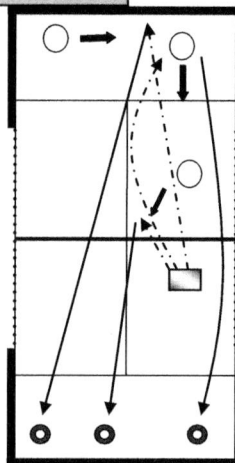

Exercise 0509   Hits: SF – G – V

Target: Combination of hits with movement
Striking sequence: Lob D// – VR middle – Down Wall X

Description:
From the starting position is moved to the opposite corner to make a parallel forehand lob, then you will go running to the net and perform a backhand volley to the middle and be delayed for a crossed over backhand drop wall, with the target of marks on the back of the court.

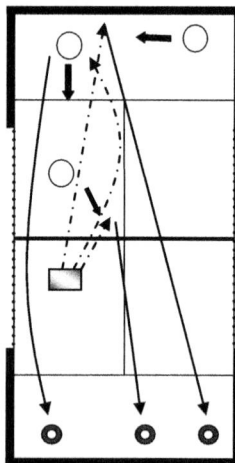

Exercise 0510   Hits: SF – G – V

Target: Combination of hits with effort
Striking sequence: GDX – VR middle – VD// – BFDX

Description:
Set the player at the bottom of the court, hits a crossed over forehand lob to the net to go up and make a backhand volley from the middle and a forehand volley into the corner and slow enough to make a crossed over forehand drop wall, with the target of the marks on the back of the court.

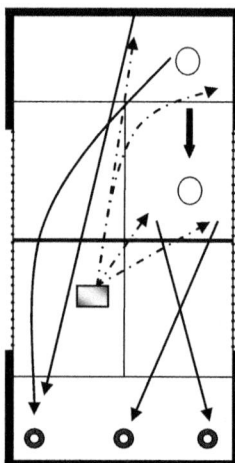

Exercise 0511   Hits: SF – G – V

Target: Combination of hits with effort
Striking sequence: GRX – VD middle – VR// – BFRX

Description:
Set the player at the bottom of the court, hits a crossed over backhand lob to the net to go up and make a forehand volley from the middle and a backhand volley into the corner and slow enough to make a crossed over backhand drop wall, with the target of the marks on the back of the court.

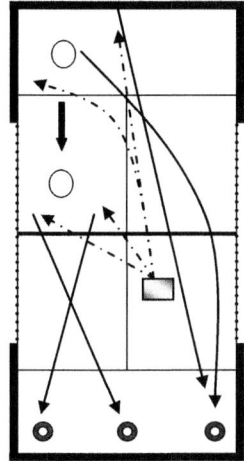

Exercise 0512   Hits: D – SF – V

Target: Combination of hits
Striking sequence: Low ball D// deep - VR// - SFD//

Description:
Set the player to the height of the peak, hits a deep parallel forehand to a low ball which will go up and make a parallel backhand volley. Then they drop to the backcourt to return a parallel forehand output.
After 12 balls is changed player.

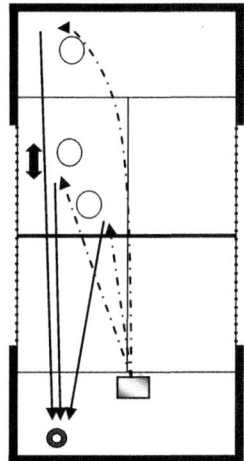

Exercise 0513   Hits: R – SF – V

Target: Combination of hits
Striking sequence: Low ball R// deep - VD// - SFR//

Description:
Set the player to the height of the peak, hits a deep parallel backhand to a low ball which will go up and make a parallel forehand volley. Then they drop to the backcourt to return a parallel backhand output.
After 12 balls is changed player.

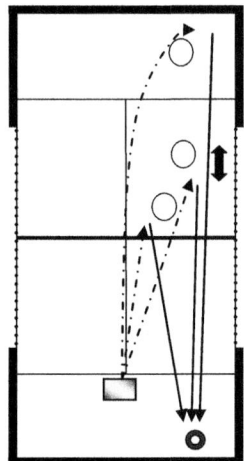

Exercise 0514   Hits: D – SF – V

Target: Combination of hits
Striking sequence: Low ball DX deep – VDX – SFDX

Description:
Set the player to the height of the peak, hits a deep crossed over forehand to a low ball with which he will go up and make a power crossed over forehand volley and drop to the backcourt to make a crossed over forehand output.
After 12 balls is changed player.

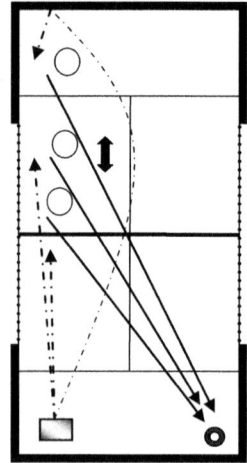

Exercise 0515   Hits: R – SF – V

Target: Combination of hits
Striking sequence: Low ball RX deep – VRX – SFRX

Description:
Set the player to the height of the peak, hits a deep crossed over backhand to a low ball with which he will go up and make a power crossed over backhand volley and drop to the backcourt to make a crossed over backhand output.
After 12 balls is changed player.

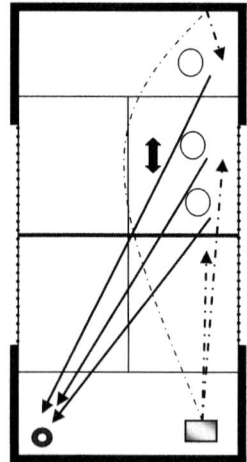

Exercise 0516   Hits: R – SL – V

Target: Combination of hits
Striking sequence: RX – SLDX – VRX

Description:
Set the player at the bottom of the court, hits a backhand and a crossed over forehand output side with which rise to the net and end up with a crossed over backhand volley, with the brand target fund the court.
After 12 balls is changed player.

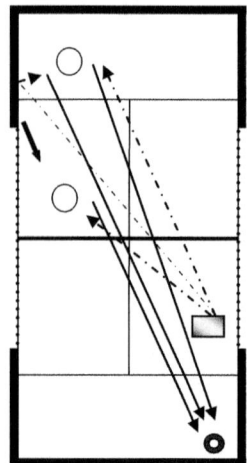

Exercise 0517   Hits: D – SL – V

Target: Combination of hits
Striking sequence: DX – SLRX – VDX

Description:
Set the player at the bottom of the court, hits a forehand and a crossed over backhand output side with which rise to the net and end up with a crossed over forehand volley, with the brand target fund the court.
After 12 balls is changed player.

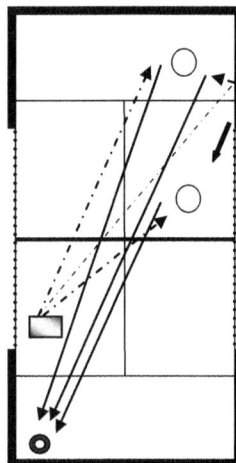

Exercise 0518   Hits: R – SF – V

Target: Combination of hits
Striking sequence: RX – SFD// - VR// - VDX

Description:
Set the player at the bottom of the court, hits a crossed over backhand to the mark on the corner of the court, a return parallel forehand output to the monitor to make a parallel backhand volley, the monitor will return to the player and finish with a crossed over forehand volley to the corner cross.

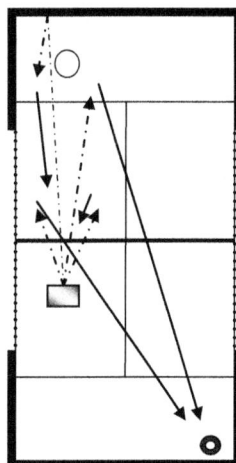

Exercise 0519   Hits: D – SF – V

Target: Combination of hits
Striking sequence: DX – SFR// - VD// - VRX

Description:
Set the player at the bottom of the court, hits a crossed over forehand to the mark on the corner of the court, a return parallel backhand output to the monitor to make a parallel forehand volley, the monitor will return to the player and finish with a crossed over backhand volley to the corner cross.

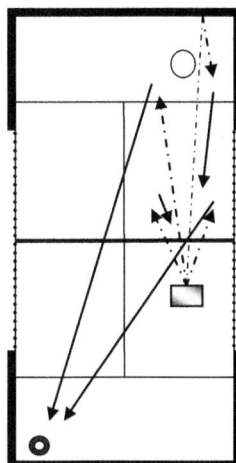

EXERCISES COMBINATION: FOREHAND, BACKHAND, WALL, SHOT

Exercise 0520   Hits: G – SF – Rm

Target: Combination of hits
Striking sequence: Rm// - G// - SF// – Rm//

Description:
Faced two players in parallel, a player takes a parallel shot, the other returned with a deep lob that he had topped perform a bottom outlet with her partner will continue with a shot and will continue the exercise.

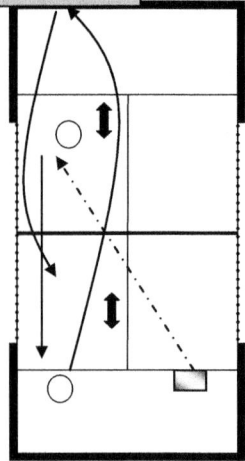

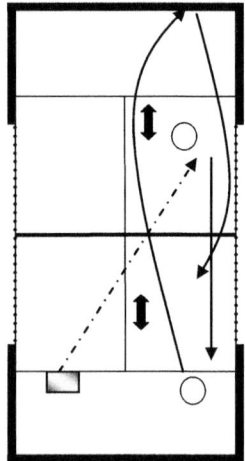

Exercise 0521   Hits: G – SF – Rm

Target: Combination of hits
Striking sequence: Rm// - G// - SF// – Rm//

Description:
Faced two players in parallel, a player takes a parallel shot, the other returned with a deep lob that he had topped perform a bottom outlet with her partner will continue with a shot and will continue the exercise.

EXERCISES COMBINATION: FOREHAND, BACKHAND, VOLLEY, SHOT

Exercise 0522   Hits: G – V – Rm

Target: Combination of hits with movement
Striking sequence: GDX – VR middle – RmX

Description:
From the starting position is moved to the opposite corner for a hit a crossed over forehand lob, then will go running to the net and perform a backhand volley to the middle and enough for a crossed over shot to the grid, to be delayed the target of the marks on the back of the court.

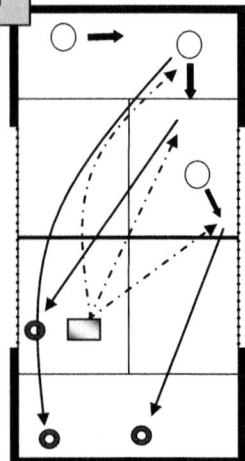

Exercise 0523   Hits: G – V – Rm

Target: Combination of hits with movement
Striking sequence: GRX – VD middle – RmX

Description:
From the starting position is moved to the opposite corner for a hit a crossed over backhand lob, then will go running to the net and perform a forehand volley to the middle and enough for a crossed over shot to the grid, to be delayed the target of the marks on the back of the court.

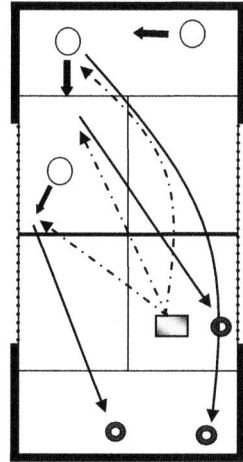

Exercise 0524   Hits: G – V – Rm

Target: Combination of hits with movement
Striking sequence: GD// – VDX short – RmX

Description:
From the starting position is moved to the opposite corner for a parallel forehand lob, then you will go running to the net and perform a short crossed over forehand volley and slow enough for a crossed over shot, with the target of brands located on the back of the court.

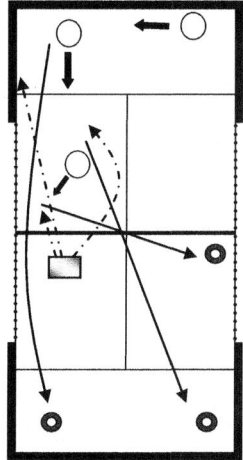

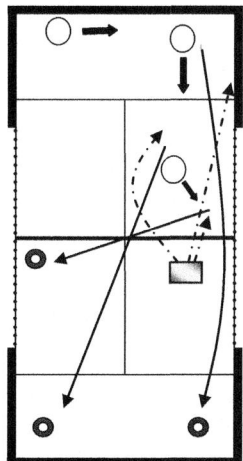

Exercise 0525   Hits: G – V – Rm

Target: Combination of hits with movement
Striking sequence: GR // – VRX short – RmX

Description:
From the starting position is moved to the opposite corner for a parallel backhand lob, then you will go running to the net and perform a short crossed over backhand volley and slow enough for a crossed over shot, with the target of brands located on the back of the court.

Exercise 0526   Hits: G – V

Target: Combination of hits with effort
Striking sequence: GR// - VD// - VR//

Description:
Set the player at the bottom of the court, executes a parallel backhand lob with that rise to the net and hit a parallel forehand volley and a parallel backhand volley with the target of the mark on the back of the court.
After 12 balls is changed player.

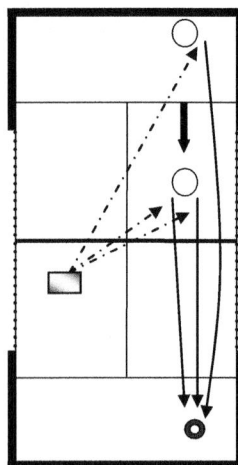

Exercise 0527   Hits: G – V

Target: Combination of hits with effort
Striking sequence: GD// - VD// - VR//

Description:
Set the player at the bottom of the court, executes a parallel forehand lob with that rise to the net and hit a parallel backhand volley and a parallel forehand volley with the target of the mark on the back of the court.
After 12 balls is changed player.

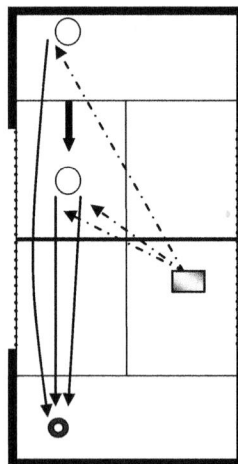

Exercise 0528   Hits: G – V – Rm

Target: Combination of hits with effort
Striking sequence: GRX – VR// - Rm// - VD//

Description:
Located player in the back of the court, perform a crossed over backhand lob with which it will go to the net and perform a parallel backhand volley, it will be delayed enough for a parallel shot and rise again to a parallel forehand volley with the target of the marks on the corners of the court.
After 12 balls you change player.

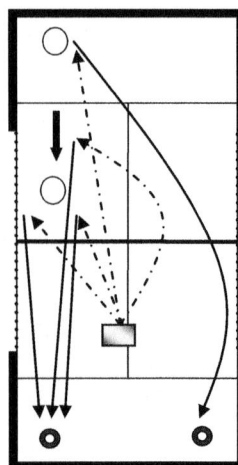

Exercise 0529   Hits: G – V – Rm

Target: Combination of hits with effort
Striking sequence: GDX – VD// - Rm// - VR//

Description:
Located player in the back of the court, perform a crossed over forehand lob with which it will go to the net and perform a parallel forehand volley, it will be delayed enough for a parallel shot and rise again to a parallel backhand volley with the target of the marks on the corners of the court.
After 12 balls you change player.

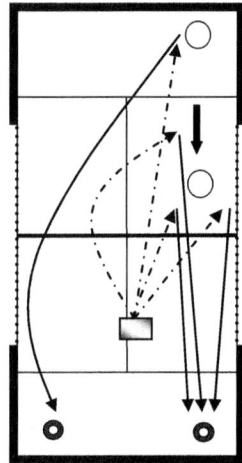

Exercise 0530   Hits: G – V – Rm

Target: Turn after rebound
Striking sequence: Turn – GDX – VR// - RmX

Description:
Set the player at the bottom of the court, make a turn to accompany the ball on its way to bounce back and side wall to make a crossed over forehand lob with which it will go to the net to make a parallel backhand volley and slow enough to make a crossed over shot to the grid, with the target of the marks on the court.
After 12 balls is changed player.

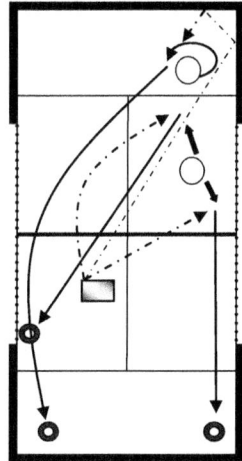

Exercise 0531   Hits: G – V – Rm

Target: Turn after rebound
Striking sequence: Turn – GRX – VD// - RmX

Description:
Set the player at the bottom of the court, make a turn to accompany the ball on its way to bounce back and side wall to make a crossed over backhand lob with which it will go to the net to make a parallel forehand volley and slow enough to make a crossed over shot to the grid, with the target of the marks on the court.
After 12 balls is changed player.

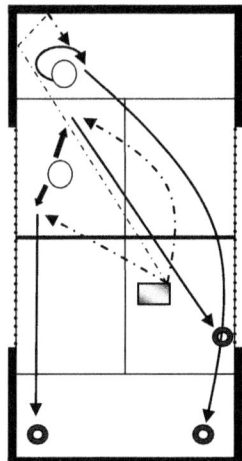

Exercise 0532   Hits: D – R – V – Rm

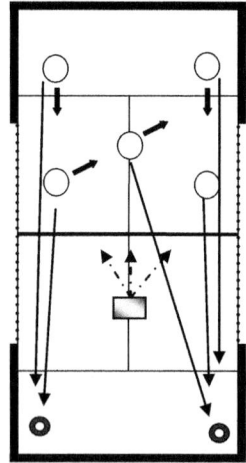

Target: Combination of hits with movement
Striking sequence: D// - VD// - RmX – R// - VR//

Description:
Set the player at the bottom of the court, he will combine moving a parallel forehand, a parallel forehand volley, a crossed over shot, a parallel backhand and a parallel backhand volley with the target of the marks on the court.
After 10 balls is changed player.

Exercise 0533   Hits: D – R – V – Rm

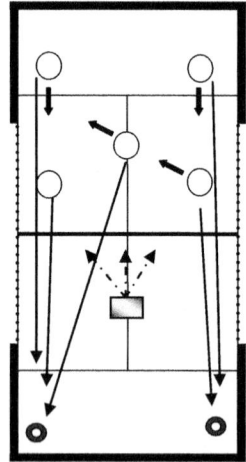

Target: Combination of hits with movement
Striking sequence: R// - VR// - RmX – D// - VD//

Description:
Set the player at the bottom of the court, he will combine moving a parallel backhand, a parallel backhand volley, a crossed over shot, a parallel forehand and a parallel forehand volley with the target of the marks on the court.
After 10 balls is changed player.

Exercise 0534   Hits: D – R – V – Rm

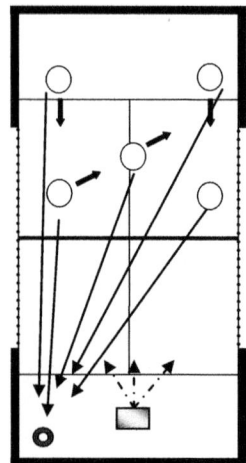

Target: Combination of hits with movement
Striking sequence: D// - VD// - RmX – RX – VRX

Description:
Set the player at the bottom of the court, he will combine moving a parallel forehand, a parallel forehand volley, a crossed over shot, a crossed over backhand and a crossed over backhand volley, with the target of the mark on the bottom of the court.
After 10 balls is changed player.

Exercise 0535   Hits: D – R – V – Rm

Target: Combination of hits with movement
Striking sequence: R// - VR// - RmX – DX – VDX

Description:
Set the player at the bottom of the court, he will combine moving a parallel backhand, a parallel backhand volley, a crossed over shot, a crossed over forehand and a crossed over forehand volley, with the target of the mark on the bottom of the court.
After 10 balls is changed player.

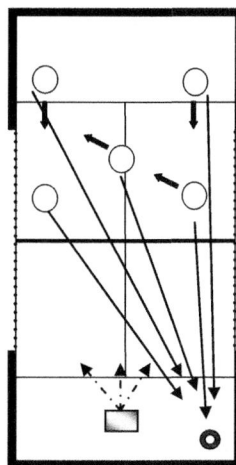

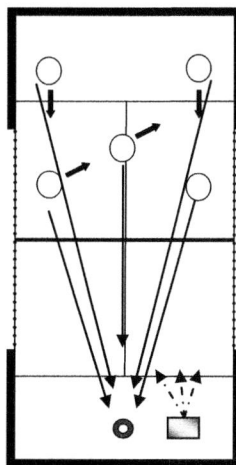

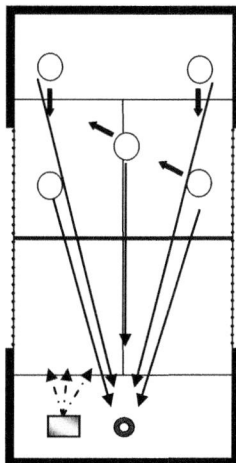

Exercise 0536   Hits: D – R – V – Rm

Target: Combination of hits with movement
Striking sequence: D - VD - Rm – R – VR

Description:
Set the player at the bottom of the court, he will combine moving a forehand, a volley forehand, a shot, a backhand and a backhand volley, all to the middle, with the target of the mark on the back of the court.
After 10 balls is changed player.

Exercise 0537   Hits: D – R – V – Rm

Target: Combination of hits with movement
Striking sequence: R - VR - Rm – D – VD

Description:
Set the player at the bottom of the court, he will combine moving a backhand, a volley backhand, a shot, a forehand and a forehand volley, all to the middle, with the target of the mark on the back of the court.
After 10 balls is changed player.

Exercise 0538   Hits: D – R – V – Rm

Target: Combination of hits with movement
Striking sequence: DX - VDX - RmX – R// – VR//

Description:
Set the player at the bottom of the court, he will combine moving a crossed over forehand, a crossed over forehand volley, a crossed over shot, a parallel backhand and a parallel backhand volley with the target of the mark on the back of the court.
After 10 balls is changed player.

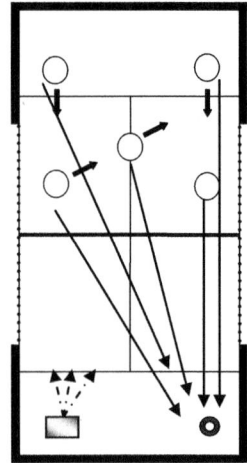

Exercise 0539   Hits: D – R – V – Rm

Target: Combination of hits with movement
Striking sequence: RX - VRX - RmX – D// – VD//

Description:
Set the player at the bottom of the court, he will combine moving a crossed over backhand, a crossed over backhand volley, a crossed over shot, a parallel forehand and a parallel forehand volley with the target of the mark on the back of the court.
After 10 balls is changed player.

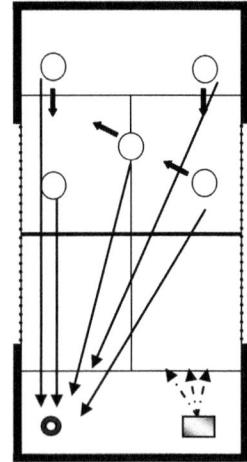

Exercise 0540   Hits: D – V – Rm

Target: Combination of hits with movement
Striking sequence: DX – VDX – RmX

Description:
Set the player at the bottom of the court, he will combine moving a crossed over forehand, a crossed over forehand volley and a crossed over shot, with the target of the mark on the back of the court.
After 12 balls is changed player.

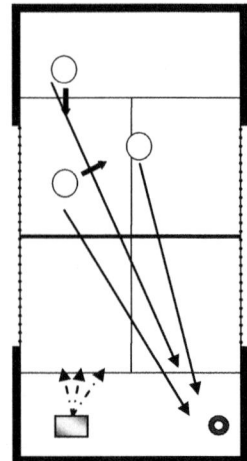

Exercise 0541   Hits: R – V – Rm

Target: Combination of hits with movement
Striking sequence: RX – VRX – RmX

Description:
Set the player at the bottom of the court, he will combine moving a crossed over backhand, a crossed over backhand volley and a crossed over shot, with the target of the mark on the back of the court.
After 12 balls is changed player.

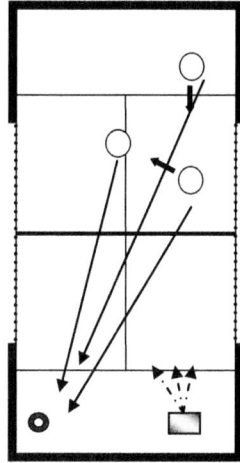

Exercise 0542   Hits: D – V – Rm

Target: Combination of hits with movement
Striking sequence: D – VD – Rm

Description:
Set the player at the bottom of the court, he will combine moving a forehand, a forehand volley and a shot, all to the middle, with the target of the mark on the back of the court.
After 12 balls is changed player.

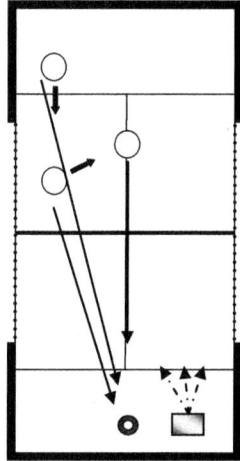

Exercise 0543   Hits: R – V – Rm

Target: Combination of hits with movement
Striking sequence: R – VR - Rm

Description:
Set the player at the bottom of the court, he will combine moving a forehand, a forehand volley and a shot, all to the middle, with the target of the mark on the back of the court.
After 12 balls is changed player.

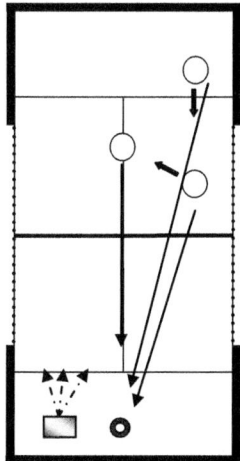

Exercise 0544   Hits: D – V – Rm

Target: Combination of hits with movement
Striking sequence: D// – VD// - Rm//

Description:
Set the player at the bottom of the court, he will combine moving a parallel forehand, a parallel forehand volley and a parallel shot, with the target of the mark on the back of the court.
After 12 balls is changed player.

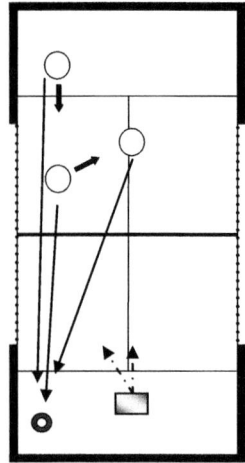

Exercise 0545   Hits: R – V – Rm

Target: Combination of hits with movement
Striking sequence: R// – VR// - Rm//

Description:
Set the player at the bottom of the court, he will combine moving a parallel backhand, a parallel backhand volley and a parallel shot, with the target of the mark on the back of the court.
After 12 balls is changed player.

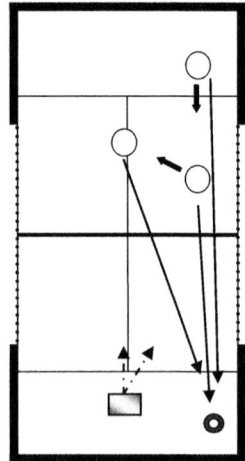

Exercise 0546   Hits: D – R – V – Rm

Target: Defense rise to the net and attack
Striking sequence: D – R – GD – V – Rm

Description:
Set the player at the bottom of the court, the monitor will throw 10 balls to defend the corner. The ball goes to lob tenth performs a volley and approach shot, all with striking free to the area they want. Forehand, backhand, forehand lob, volley and shot.

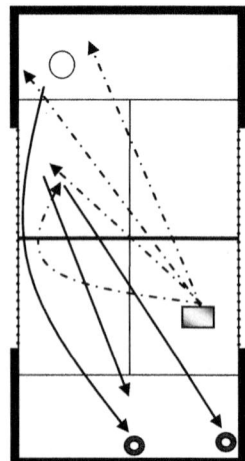

Exercise 0547   Hits: D – R – V – Rm

Target: Defense rise to the net and attack
Striking sequence: D – R – GD – V – Rm

Description:
Set the player at the bottom of the court, the monitor will throw 10 balls to defend the corner. The ball goes to lob tenth performs a volley and approach shot, all with striking free to the area they want. Forehand, backhand, forehand lob, volley and shot.

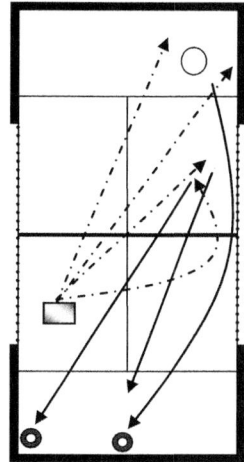

Exercise 0548   Hits: D – R – V – Rm

Target: Combination of hits
Striking sequence: D// – R// – VD// - VR// – Rm//

Description:
Set the player at the bottom of the court, held a parallel forehand and a parallel backhand with that rise to the net to make a parallel forehand volley and a parallel backhand volley, and end with a shot parallel, with the target of the marks on the back of the court.

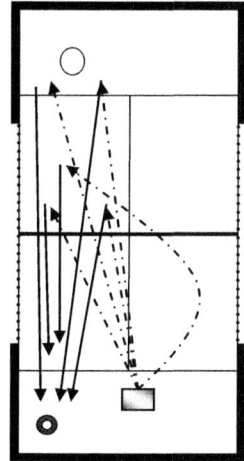

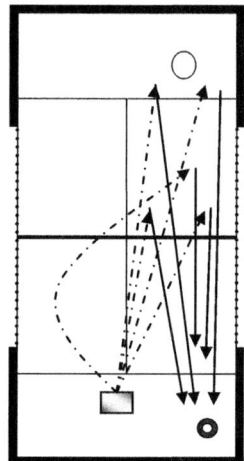

Exercise 0549   Hits: D – R – V – Rm

Target: Combination of hits
Striking sequence: D// – R// – VD// - VR// – Rm//

Description:
Set the player at the bottom of the court, held a parallel forehand and parallel backhand with that rise to the net to make a parallel forehand volley and a parallel backhand volley, and end with a shot parallel, with the target of the marks on the back of the court.

Exercise 0550   Hits: D – R – V – Rm

Target: Combination of hits
Striking sequence: DX – RX – VDX - VRX – RmX

Description:
Set the player at the bottom of the court, perform a crossed over forehand and a crossed over backhand with that rise to the net to make a crossed over forehand volley, a crossed over backhand volley and end with a crossed over shot, with the target of the mark on the back of the court.

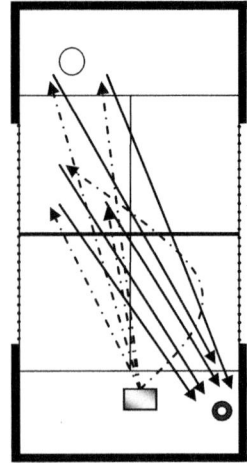

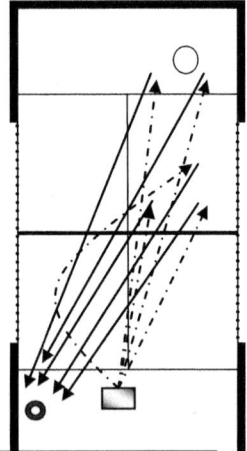

Exercise 0551   Hits: D – R – V – Rm

Target: Combination of hits
Striking sequence: DX – RX – VDX - VRX – RmX

Description:
Set the player at the bottom of the court, perform a crossed over forehand and a crossed over backhand with that rise to the net to make a crossed over forehand volley, a crossed over backhand volley and end with a crossed over shot, with the target of the mark on the back of the court.

EXERCISES COMBINATION: FOREHAND, BACKHAND, VOLLEY, VOLLEY TRAY

Exercise 0552   Hits: D – R – V – Bd

Target: Defense rise to the net and attack
Striking sequence: D – R – V – Bd

Description:
Set the player at the bottom of the court, the monitor will throw 10 balls to defend the corner. The tenth ball goes to a backhand lob, makes a volley approach and a volley tray, all with striking free to the area they want.

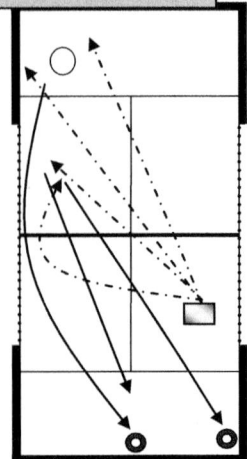

Exercise 0553   Hits: D – R – V – Bd

Target: Defense rise to the net and attack
Striking sequence: D – R – V – Bd

Description:
Set the player at the bottom of the court, the monitor will throw 10 balls to defend the corner. The tenth ball goes to a forehand lob, makes a volley approach and a volley tray, all with striking free to the area they want.

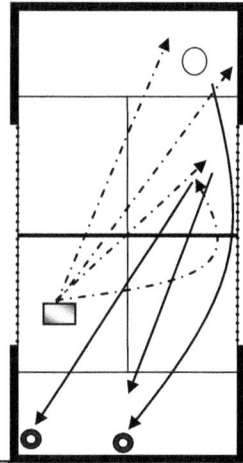

EXERCISES COMBINATION: WALL, LOB, VOLLEY

Exercise 0554   Hits: SF – G – V

Target: Combination of hits with movement
Striking sequence: GD// – VR middle – Down Wall RX

Description:
From the starting position, the player moves to the opposite corner for a parallel forehand lob, then will go running to the net and perform a backhand volley to the middle and be delayed for a drop wall with a crossed over backhand, with the target of the marks on the back of the court.

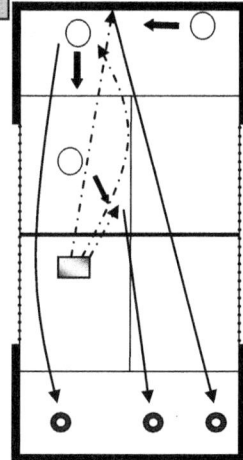

Exercise 0555   Hits: SF – G – V

Target: Combination of hits with movement
Striking sequence: GR// – VD middle – Down Wall DX

Description:
From the starting position, the player moves to the opposite corner for a parallel backhand lob, then will go running to the net and perform a forehand volley to the middle and be delayed for a drop wall with a crossed over forehand, with the target of the marks on the back of the court

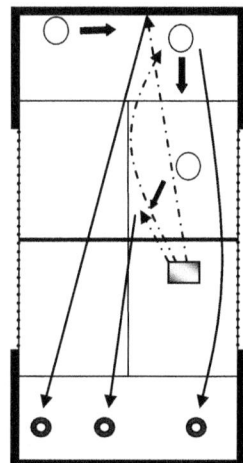

EXERCISES COMBINATION: WALL, LOB

Exercise 0556   Hits: CP – G

Target: Lob without bounce and against wall
Striking sequence: GD – GD – CPD

Description:
Located player on the bottom line, make two forehand lobs without bounce of the ball thrown by the monitor. Then he run crossed over the monitor to hit a forehand against wall.

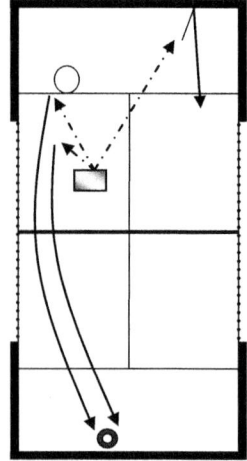

Exercise 0557   Hits: CP – G

Target: Lob without bounce y against wall
Striking sequence: GR – GR – CPR

Description:
Located player on the bottom line, make two backhand lobs without bounce of the ball thrown by the monitor. Then he run crossed over the monitor to hit a backhand against wall.

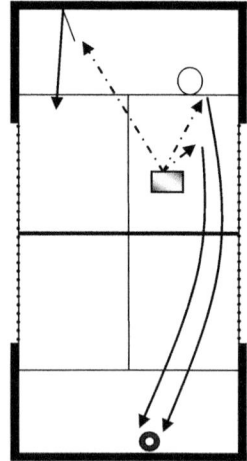

EXERCISES COMBINATION: WALL, VOLLEY

Exercise 0558   Hits: SF – V

Target: Background wall outlet – Ball control
Striking sequence: SFD// – VR// – SFDX

Description:
Control of scrimmageled between two players and the monitor.
After bouncing on the bottom wall of a ball thrown in crossed over by the monitor, the defending player hit a parallel forehand your partner to perform a parallel backhand volley to hit bounce off the wall in the background. The defending player, after the rebound, hit a crossed over forehand to the monitor, which will continue the exercise.
After 2' position players alternates.

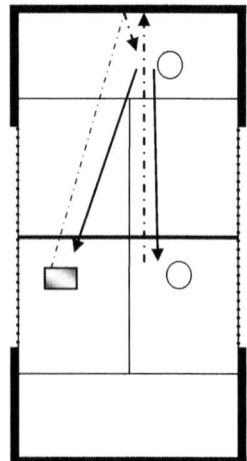

Exercise 0559   Hits: SF – V

Target: Background wall outlet – Ball control
Striking sequence: SFR// – VD// – SFRX

Description:
Control of scrimmageled between two players and the monitor.
After bouncing on the bottom wall of a ball thrown in crossed over by the monitor, the defending player hit a parallel backhand your partner to perform a parallel forehand volley to hit bounce off the wall in the background. The defending player, after the rebound, hit a crossed over backhand to the monitor, which will continue the exercise.
After 2' position players alternates.

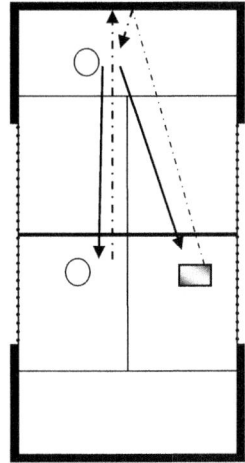

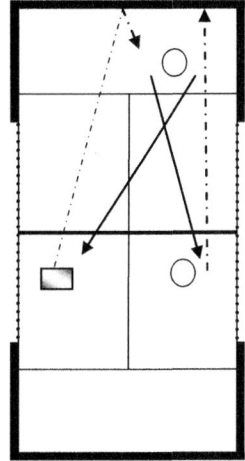

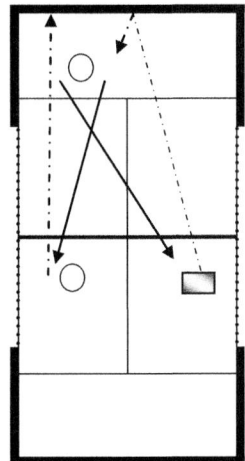

Exercise 0560   Hits: SF – V

Target: Background wall outlet – Ball control
Striking sequence: SFD// – VD// – SFRX

Description:
Control of scrimmageled between two players and the monitor.
After bouncing on the bottom wall of a ball thrown in crossed over by the monitor, the defending player hit a parallel forehand to your partner to perform a parallel forehand volley to hit bounce off the wall in the background. The defending player, after the rebound, strike a crossed over backhand to the monitor, which will continue the exercise.
After 2' position players alternates.

Exercise 0561   Hits: SF – V

Target: Background wall outlet – Ball control
Striking sequence: SFR// – VR// – SFDX

Description:
Control of scrimmageled between two players and the monitor.
After bouncing on the bottom wall of a ball thrown in crossed over by the monitor, the defending player hit a parallel forehand to your partner to perform a parallel forehand volley to hit bounce off the wall in the background. The defending player, after the rebound, strike a crossed over backhand to the monitor, which will continue the exercise.
After 2' position players alternates.

Exercise 0562   Hits: SF – V

Target: Background wall outlet – Ball control
Striking sequence: SFDX – VD// – SFRX

Description:
Control of scrimmageled between two players and the monitor.
After bouncing on the background wall a ball thrown in parallel by the monitor, the defending player will hit a crossed over forehand to his partner to perform a parallel forehand volley to hit bounce off the wall in the background. The defending player, after the rebound, hit a crossed over backhand to the monitor, which will continue the exercise.
After 2' position players alternates.

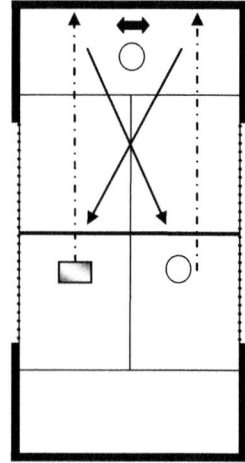

Exercise 0563   Hits: SF – V

Target: Output side wall against wall
Striking sequence: VDX – SLD CP

Description:
Set the player near the net, hold a crossed over forehand volley and run in crossed over to hit a crossed over that hitting first sidewall.
Then you can do on the other side, with a crossed over backhand volley and performed an output side against.

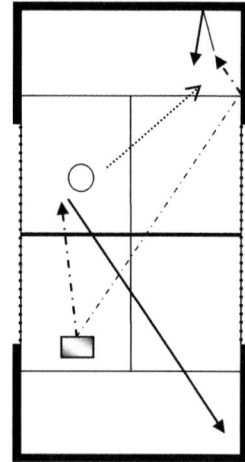

Exercise 0564   Hits: SF – V

Target: Background wall outlet – Ball control
Striking sequence: SFD// – VDX – SFR//

Description:
Control of scrimmageled between two players and the monitor.
After bouncing on the bottom wall of a ball thrown in crossed over by the monitor, the defending player of a parallel forehand hit of his partner to perform a crossed over forehand volley to reach bounce off the wall in the background. The defending player, after the rebound, hit a parallel backhand to the monitor, which will continue the exercise.
After 2' position players alternates.

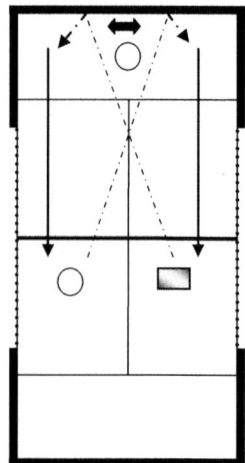

Exercise 0565   Hits: SF – V

Target: Background wall outlet – Ball control
Striking sequence: SFR// – VRX – SFD//

Description:
Control of scrimmageled between two players and the monitor.
After bouncing on the bottom wall of a ball thrown in crossed over by the monitor, the defending player of a parallel backhand hit of his partner to perform a crossed over backhand volley to reach bounce off the wall in the background. The defending player, after the rebound, hit a parallel forehand to the monitor, which will continue the exercise.
After 2' position players alternates.

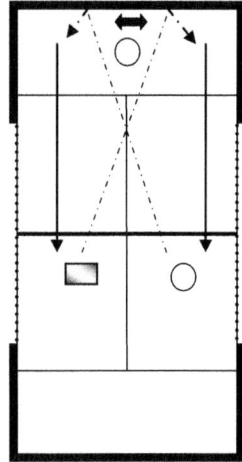

Exercise 0566   Hits: SF – V

Target: Control ball between three players
Striking sequence: V// deep – SF// - VX short – SFX

Description:
The player who is on the net will made a deep parallel volley to rebound in the bottom wall, which will be returned in parallel and then make a crossed over volley.
Once returned, the exercise continues.
After 2' position players alternates.
Then it is done from the opposite side.

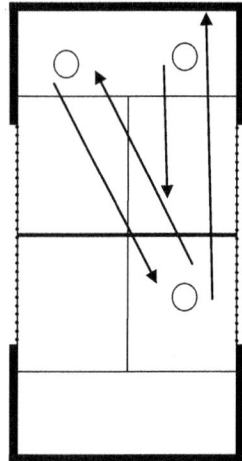

Exercise 0567   Hits: SL – SDP – V

Target: Defense with several hits
Striking sequence: SDPD – VD – Turn SDPR

Description:
Set the player at the bottom of the court, makes a double all output after bouncing, a forehand volley and turn to a double wall out of backhand after rebound in the side Wall and background.
After 12 balls is changed player.
Then you can do the opposite.

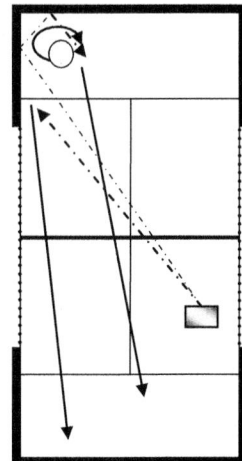

Exercise 0568   Hits: D – R – SF – V

Target: Control ball between three players
Striking sequence: Bola deep // - SF – X - VX

Description:
The player starts with a ball down deep parallel so that the player perform a parallel output line to answer a blow that crossed over to give us back volley and continue the exercise.
After 2' position players alternates.

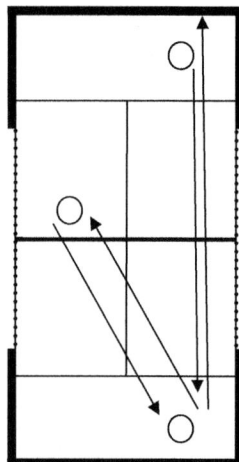

Exercise 0569   Hits: D – R – SF – V

Target: Lateral movement and striking
Striking sequence: Desp. Lateral – VRX – CPR

Description:
Located player in the back of the court, will enter it side-scrolling grid and cones to reach a crossed over backhand volley, then slow down and make a backhand against wall.
After 6 balls is changed player.
Then it is on the opposite side, making forehand volley and a forehand against wall.

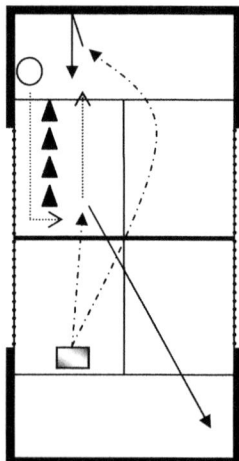

Exercise 0570   Hits: D – R – SF – V

Target: Control ball between four players
Striking sequence: D o R// - VX – D o R// - SF X

Description:
The player starts with a ball down parallel to the volley, responds with a crossed over volley, a parallel volley to the bottom and continue the exercise.
After 2'position players alternates.
Then it is done from the opposite side.

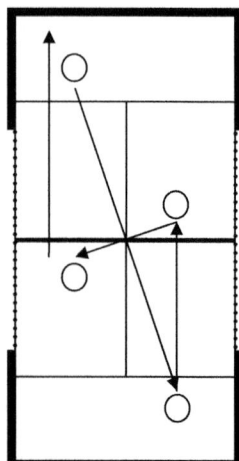

Exercise 0571   Hits: SF – V

Target: Bottom outlet leg below
Striking sequence: SFD – VDX

Description:
Set the player at the bottom of the court, makes a wall outlet back to the counter beneath the legs and a crossed over forehand volley.
After 10 balls is changed player.
Then it is on the other side with wall outlet below legs and crossed over backhand volley.

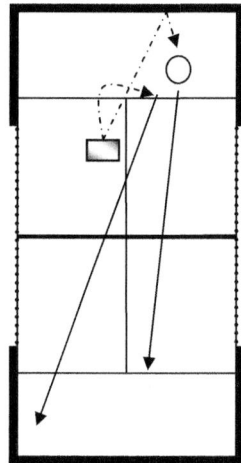

Exercise 0572   Hits: D – R – SF – V

Target: Control ball between four players
Striking sequence: V// - VX – SF// - SFX

Description:
The player in the net starts with a parallel volley, which responds with a crosses over volley, long parallel bottom outlet to bounce back and crossed over out to the volley and continue the exercise.
After 2' position players alternates.

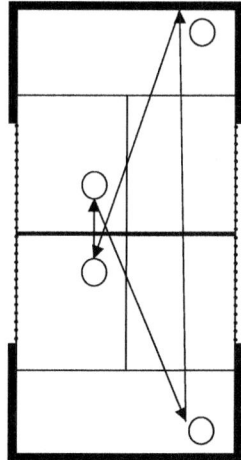

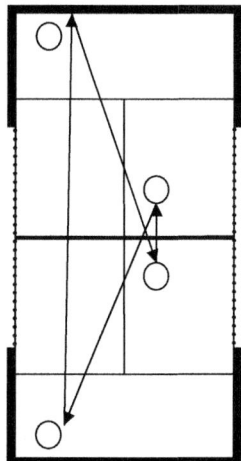

Exercise 0573   Hits: D – R – SF – V

Target: Control ball between four players
Striking sequence: V// - VX – SF// - SFX

Description:
The player in the net starts with a parallel volley, which responds with a crossed over volley, long parallel bottom outlet to bounce back and crossed over out to the volley and continue the exercise.
After 2' position players alternates.

Exercise 0574   Hits: SF – V

Target: Control ball between four players
Striking sequence: V// - SFD //

Description:
Set the player at the net, held a long parallel volley to rebound in the bottom wall, which is returned parallel forehand by his partner below and returns to the row. After 2' position players alternates.

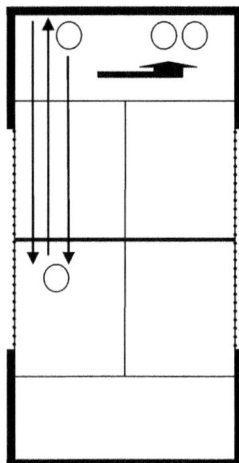

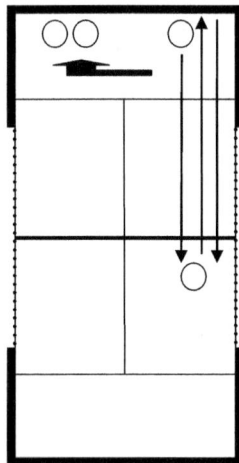

Exercise 0575   Hits: SF – V

Target: Control ball between four players
Striking sequence: V// - SFR //

Description:
Set the player at the net, held a long parallel volley to rebound in the bottom wall, which is returned parallel backhand by his partner below and returns to the row. After 2' position players alternates.

Exercise 0576   Hits: SF – V

Target: Volley rebound control
Striking sequence: V// – SF// – V// – SF//

Description:
Placed a player on the back of the court and the other on the net, the player of the bottom will perform two parallel outputs of the background and the other perform two parallel volleys. A third ball, the player on the bottom will rise and the net will fall to the bottom to start the exercise again.
Duration of exercise 2'

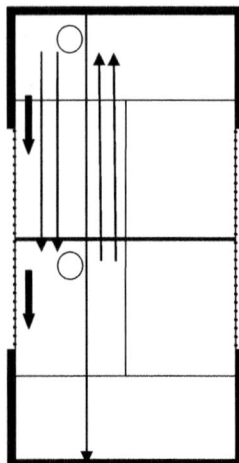

Exercise 0577   Hits: SL – V

Target: Volley rebound control
Striking sequence: VX – SLFX – VX – SLFX

Description:
Placed a player on the back of the court and the other on the net, the player of the bottom will perform two crossed over outputs of the background and the other perform two crossed over volleys. A third ball, the player on the bottom will rise and the net will fall to the bottom to start the exercise again.
Duration of exercise 2'

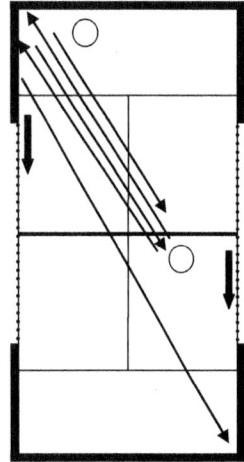

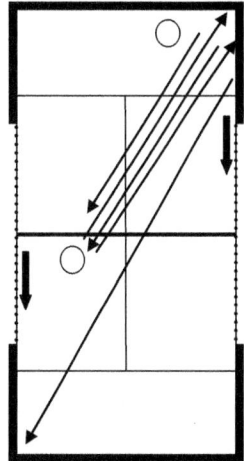

Exercise 0578   Hits: SL – V

Target: Volley rebound control
Striking sequence: VX – SLFX – VX – SLFX

Description:
Placed a player on the back of the court and the other on the net, the player of the bottom will perform two crossed over outputs of the background and the other perform two crossed over volleys. A third ball, the player on the bottom will rise and the net will fall to the bottom to start the exercise again.
Duration of exercise 2'

Exercise 0579   Hits: SF – V

Target: Rebound control and volley moving
Striking sequence: V// – SFDX – V// – SFRX

Description:
Located a player on the bottom of the court and two in the net, the player end of the court responds after blow bounce crossed over to the parallel volleys of players located the net.
After 2' position players alternates.

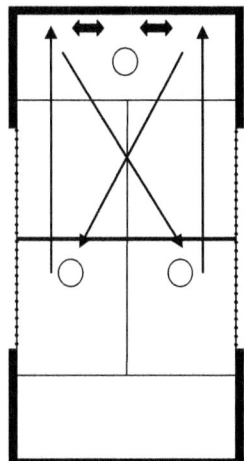

Exercise 0580   Hits: SF – V

Target: Rebound control and volley moving
Striking sequence: VX – SFD// – VX – SFR//

Description:
Located a player on the bottom of the court and two in the net, the player end of the court responds after blow bounce parallel to the crossed over volleys of players located the net.
After 2' position players alternates.

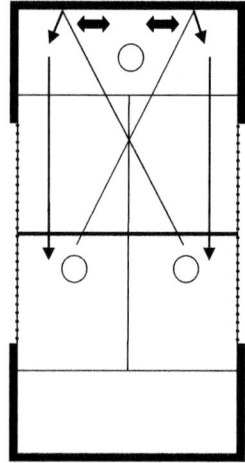

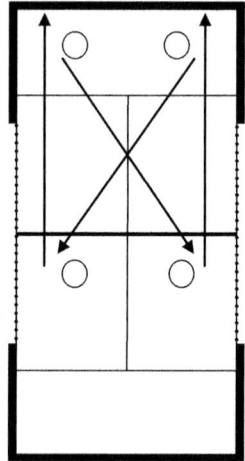

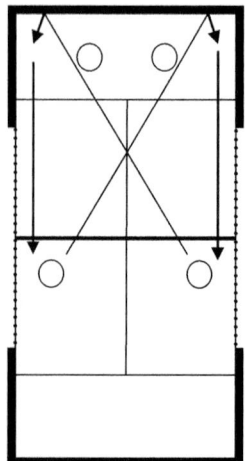

Exercise 0581   Hits: SF – V

Target: Rebound control and volley moving
Striking sequence: V// – SFDX – V// – SFRX

Description:
Located two players the bottom of the court and two in the net, players respond background court after bounce hits crossed overs to parallel volleys of players located the net.
After 2' position players alternates.

Exercise 0582   Hits: SF – V

Target: Volley rebound control
Striking sequence: SFD// – VX – SFR// – VX

Description:
Located two players the bottom of the court and two in the net, players respond background court after bounce hits parallel volleys to players located crossed over the net.
After 2' position players alternates.

Exercise 0583   Hits: G – V

Target: Combination of hits with movement
Striking sequence: GRX – VD// - VR//

Description:
From the starting position, the player moves to the opposite corner for a backhand lob to bounce crossed over after double wall, will go running to the net and perform a parallel forehand volley and a parallel backhand volley with the target of the marks on the back of the court.
After 10 balls is changed player.

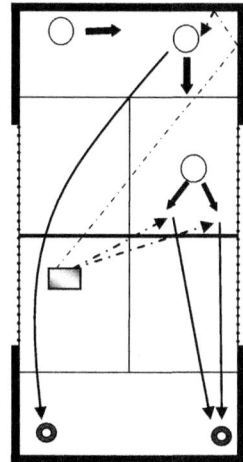

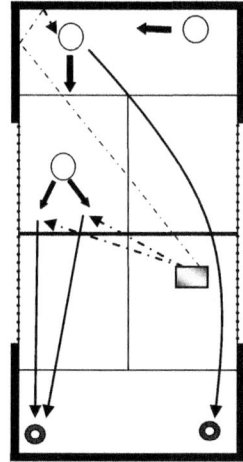

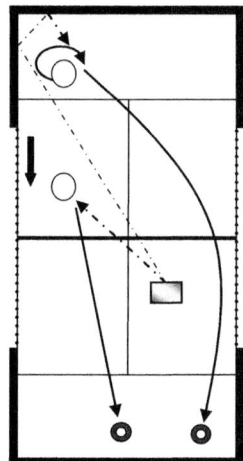

Exercise 0584   Hits: G – V

Target: Combination of hits with movement
Striking sequence: GDX – VD// - VR//

Description:
From the starting position, the player moves to the opposite corner for a backhand lob to bounce crossed over after double wall, will go running to the net and perform a parallel forehand volley and a parallel backhand volley with the target of the marks on the back of the court.
After 10 balls is changed player.

Exercise 0585   Hits: G – V

Target: Turn after rebound
Striking sequence: Turn – GRX – VD middle

Description:
Located in the back of the court, the player takes a turn accompanying the ball bounce on its way side and bottom wall, perform a crossed over backhand lob and rise to the net to make a forehand volley from the middle, with the target of the marks on the back of the court.
After 10 balls is changed player.

Exercise 0586   Hits: G – V

Target: Turn after rebound
Striking sequence: Turn – GDX – VR middle

Description:
Located in the back of the court, the player takes a turn accompanying the ball bounce on its way side and bottom wall, perform a crossed over forehand lob and rise to the net to make a backhand volley from the middle, with the target of the marks on the back of the court.
After 10 balls is changed player.

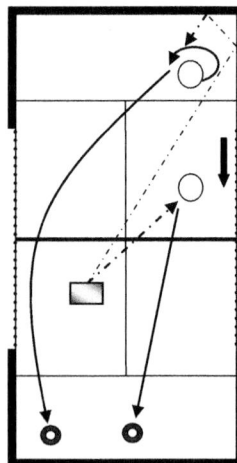

Exercise 0587   Hits: G – V

Target: Turn after rebound
Striking sequence: Turn – GRX – VD// - VR//

Description:
Located in the back of the court, the player takes a turn accompanying the ball bounce on its way side and bottom wall, perform a crossed over backhand lob and rise to the net for a parallel forehand volley and a parallel backhand volley, with the target of the marks on the back of the court.
After 12 balls is changed player.

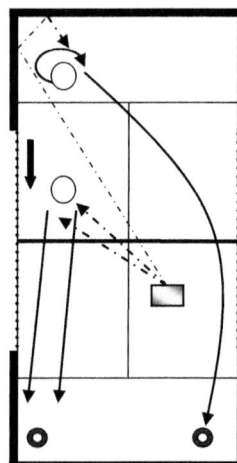

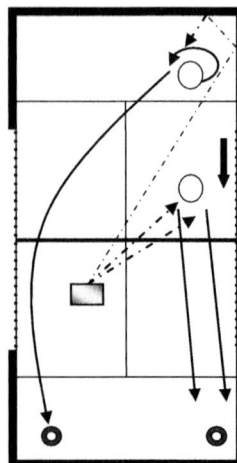

Exercise 0588   Hits: G – V

Target: Turn after rebound
Striking sequence: Turn – GDX – VR// - VD//

Description:
Located in the back of the court, the player takes a turn accompanying the ball bounce on its way side and bottom wall, perform a crossed over forehand lob and rise to the net for a parallel forehand volley and a parallel backhand volley, with the target of the marks on the back of the court.
After 12 balls is changed player.

Exercise 0589   Hits: G – V

Target: Turn after rebound
Striking sequence: Turn – GD// – VR middle – VD//

Description:
Located in the back of the court, the player takes a turn accompanying the ball bounce on its way side and bottom wall, perform a parallel forehand lob and rise to the net to make a backhand volley to the middle and a forehand volley to the corner, with the target of the marks on the back of the court.
After 12 balls is changed player.

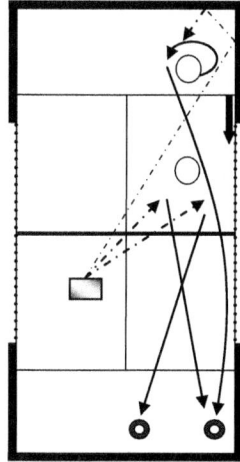

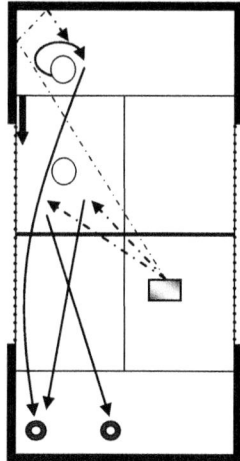

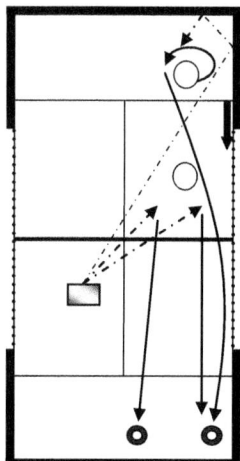

Exercise 0590   Hits: G – V

Target: Turn after rebound
Striking sequence: Turn – GR// – VD middle – VR//

Description:
Located in the back of the court, the player takes a turn accompanying the ball bounce on its way side and bottom wall, perform a parallel handback lob and rise to the net to make a forehand volley to the middle and a backhand volley to the corner, with the target of the marks on the back of the court.
After 12 balls is changed player.

Exercise 0591   Hits: G – V

Target: Turn after rebound
Striking sequence: Turn – GD// – VR// – VD//

Description:
Located in the back of the court, the player takes a turn accompanying the ball bounce on its way side and bottom wall, perform a parallel forehand lob and rise to the net to make a parallel backhand volley and a parallel forehand volley, with the target of the marks on the back of the court.
After 12 balls is changed player.

Exercise 0592   Hits: G – V

Target: Turn after rebound
Striking sequence: Turn – GR// – VD// – VR//

Description:
Located in the back of the court, the player takes a turn accompanying the ball bounce on its way side and bottom wall, perform a parallel backhand lob and rise to the net to make a parallel forehand volley and a parallel backhand volley, with the target of the marks on the back of the court.
After 12 balls is changed player.

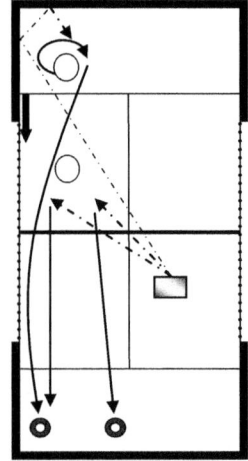

Exercise 0593   Hits: SF – V

Target: Combination of hits
Striking sequence: SFDX – VR//

Description:
Taking more than 2 players on court, we work in 3 positions. In the first we hit a crossed over forehand background, in another parallel backhand volley and the next rest.
After 2 balls the position of the players alternate.

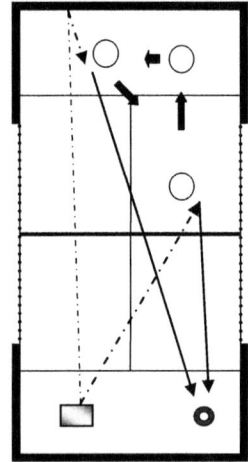

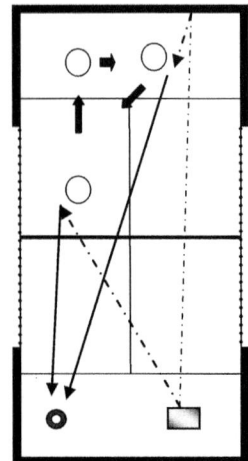

Exercise 0594   Hits: SF – V

Target: Combination of hits
Striking sequence: SFRX – VD//

Description:
Taking more than 2 players on court, we work in 3 positions. In the first we hit a crossed over backhand background, in another a parallel forehand volley and the next rest.
After 2 balls the position of the players alternate.

Exercise 0595   Hits: SL – V

Target: Combination of hits
Striking sequence: SLD// – VRX

Description:
Taking more than 2 players on court, we work in 3 positions. In the first he will make a parallel forehand output side wall, in another a crossed over backhand volley and the next rest.
After 2 balls the position of the players alternate.

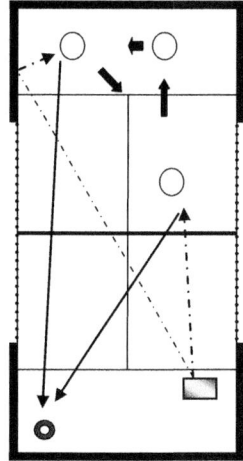

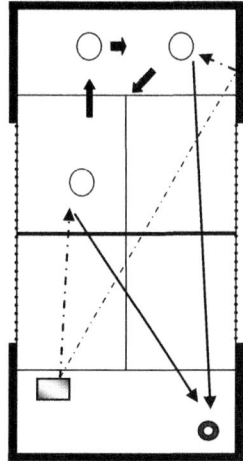

Exercise 0596   Hits: SL – V

Target: Combination of hits
Striking sequence: SLR// – VDX

Description:
Taking more than 2 players on court, we work in 3 positions. In the first he will make a parallel backhand output side wall, in another a crossed over forehand volley and the next rest.
After 2 balls the position of the players alternate.

Exercise 0597   Hits: SL – V

Target: Volleys control
Striking sequence: SLRX – V//

Description:
Located two players at the bottom of the court and one in the net, player's background made crossed over backhand side out against the player who is on the net. After each stroke, you will surround the cone is with them. The player of the net, held parallel volleys to the cones background court, as both forehand and backhand.
After 20 balls position players alternates.

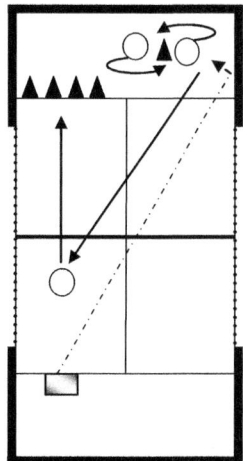

Exercise 0598   Hits: SL – V

Target: Volleys control
Striking sequence: SLDX – V//

Description:
Located two players at the bottom of the court and one in the net, player's background made crossed over forehand side out against the player who is on the net. After each stroke, you will surround the cone is with them. The player of the net, held parallel volleys to the cones background court, as both forehand and backhand.
After 20 balls position players alternates.

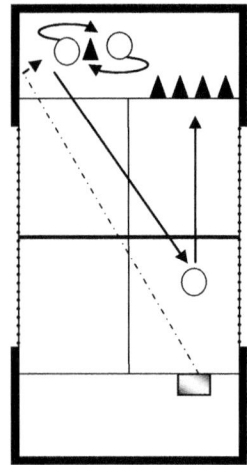

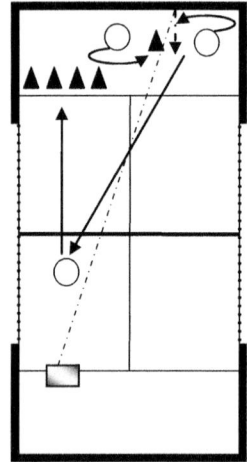

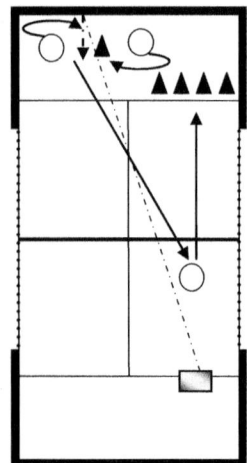

Exercise 0599   Hits: SF – V

Target: Volleys control
Striking sequence: SFDX – V//

Description:
Located two players at the bottom of the court and one in the net, player's background made crossed over forehand side out against the player who is on the net. After each stroke, you will surround the cone is with them. The player of the net, held parallel volleys to the cones background court, as both forehand and backhand.
After 20 balls position players alternates.

Exercise 0600   Hits: SF – V

Target: Volleys control
Striking sequence: SFRX – V//

Description:
Located two players at the bottom of the court and one in the net, player's background made crossed over backhand side out against the player who is on the net. After each stroke, you will surround the cone is with them. The player of the net, held parallel volleys to the cones background court, as both forehand and backhand.
After 20 balls position players alternates.

Exercise 0601   Hits: SF – V

Target: Combination of hits
Striking sequence: SFDX – VDX

Description:
Set the player at the bottom of the court, makes a forehand out background, rise to the net and make a crossed over forehand volley, with the target of the mark on the back of the court.
After 10 balls is changed player.

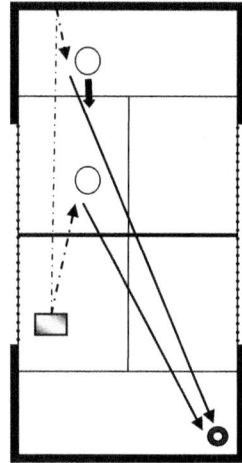

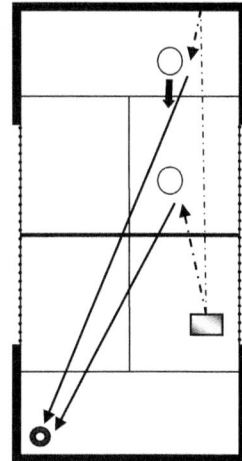

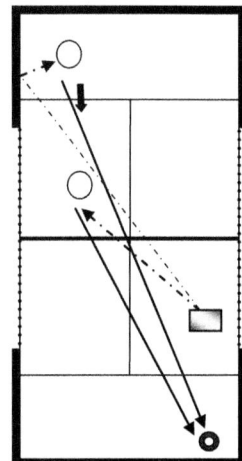

Exercise 0602   Hits: SF – V

Target: Combination of hits
Striking sequence: SFRX – VRX//

Description:
Set the player at the bottom of the court, makes a bottom outlet, rise to the net and make a crossed over backhand volley, with the target of the mark on the back of the court.
After 10 balls is changed player.

Exercise 0603   Hits: SL – V

Target: Combination of hits
Striking sequence: SLDX – VDX

Description:
Set the player at the bottom of the court, makes a crossed over forehand output side with which he will go to the net and perform a crossed over forehand volley, with the target of the mark on the back of the court.
After 10 balls is changed player.

Exercise 0604   Hits: SL – V

Target: Combination of hits
Striking sequence: SLRX – VRX

Description:
Set the player at the bottom of the court, makes a crossed over backhand output side with which he will go to the net and perform a crossed over backhand volley, with the target of the mark on the back of the court.
After 10 balls is changed player.

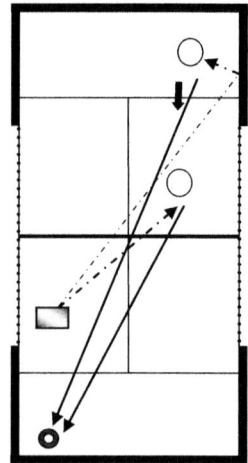

Exercise 0605   Hits: CP – V

Target: Combination of hits and against Wall parallel
Striking sequence: VDX – VRX – CPD//

Description:
Located a player near the net, hold a crossed over forehand volley and a crossed over backhand volley, and then go down to make a parallel forehand against wall with the target of the mark on the back of the court.
After 12 balls is changed player.

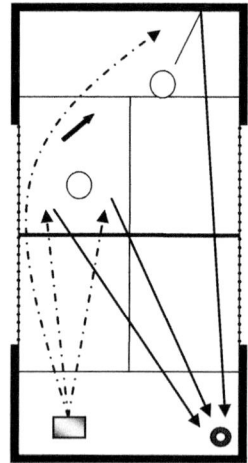

Exercise 0606   Hits: CP – V

Target: Combination of hits and parallel against wall
Striking sequence: VDX – VRX – CPR//

Description:
Located a player near the net, hold a crossed over backhand volley and a crossed over forehand volley, and then go down to make a parallel backhand against wall with the target of the mark on the back of the court.
After 12 balls is changed player.

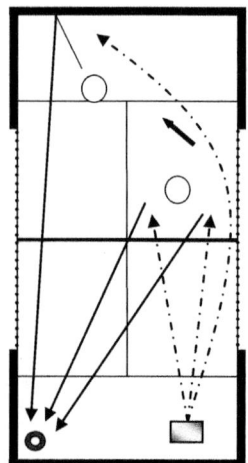

Exercise 0607   Hits: CP – V

Target: Combination of hits and parallel against wall
Striking sequence: VD// – VR// – CPDX

Description:
Located a player near the net, perform a parallel forehand volley and a parallel backhand volley, then crossed over to go down to make a crossed over forehand against wall, with the target of the mark on the back of the court.
After 12 balls is changed player.

Exercise 0608   Hits: CP – V

Target: Combination of hits and parallel against wall
Striking sequence: VD// – VR// – CPRX

Description:
Located a player near the net, perform a parallel forehand volley and a parallel backhand volley, then crossed over to go down to make a crossed over backhand against wall, with the target of the mark on the back of the court.
After 12 balls is changed player.

Exercise 0609   Hits: SF – V

Target: Combination of strokes moving
Striking sequence: SFDX – 3VRX - SFRX

Description:
Set the player at the bottom of the court, makes a crossed over forehand bottom outlet to the monitor, rise to the return of this and make 3 crossed over backhand volleys. Then he crossed over to lower in after rebound, make an exit background crossed over backhand, with the target of the marks on the back of the court.

Exercise 0610   Hits: SF – V

Target: Combination of strokes moving
Striking sequence: SFRX – 3VDX – SFDX

Description:
Set the player at the bottom of the court, makes a crossed over forehand bottom outlet to the monitor, rise to the return of this and make 3 crossed over backhand volleys. Then he crossed over to lower in after rebound, make an exit background crossed over backhand, with the target of the marks on the back of the court.

Exercise 0611   Hits: SF – SL – V

Target: Combination of strokes moving
Striking sequence: SF-SL-SF-SL-VD-VR-VD-VR

Description:
Combination of a player hits frees located in the back of the court to carry out the following series: exit background backhand, forehand side exit, exit background backhand, forehand side exit, go up to the net and perform one forehand volley, a backhand volley, a forehand volley and a backhand volley, after which the fund will repeat the exercise.
After 16 balls is changed player.

Exercise 0612   Hits: SF – SL – V

Target: Combination of strokes moving
Striking sequence: SF-SL-SF-SL-VD-VR-VD-VR

Description:
Combination of a player hits frees located in the back of the court to carry out the following series: background out forehand, backhand output side, bottom outlet of forehand, backhand side exit, go up to the net and perform one forehand volley, a backhand volley, a forehand volley and a backhand volley, after which the fund will repeat the exercise.
After 16 balls is changed player.

Exercise 0613   Hits: SF – V

Target: Combination of hits
Striking sequence: Combination volleys and SF in parallel

Description:
Placed a player on the net and one in the back of the court, the player in the net hit a deep parallel volley so that there will rebound to their bottom line to bottom outlet against parallel parallel. Player hits volley and return to his bottom line.
Duration of exercise 2'

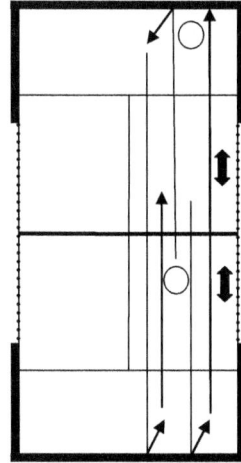

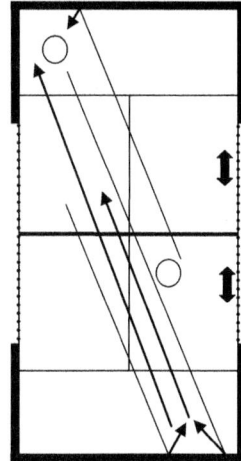

Exercise 0614   Hits: SF – V

Target: Combination of hits
Striking sequence: Combination volleys and SF in crossed over

Description:
Placed a player on the net and one in the back of the court, the player in the net hit a deep crossed over volley so that there will rebound to their bottom line to bottom outlet against crossed over parallel. Player hits volley and return to his bottom line.
Duration of exercise 2'

Exercise 0615   Hits: SF – SL – V

Target: Combination of hits
Striking sequence: SFD – SLD – Turn SFD – VRX

Description:
Set the player at the bottom of the court, made an exit beatings free background forehand, a turn for background exit forehand, rise to the net and end up with a crossed over backhand volley.

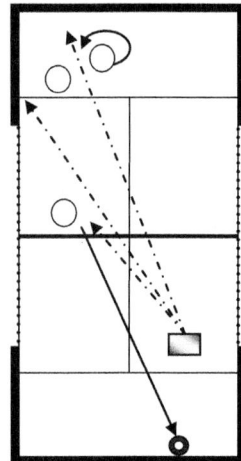

Exercise 0616   Hits: SF – SL – V

Target: Combination of hits
Striking sequence: SFR – SLR - Turn SFR – VD//

Description:
Set the player at the bottom of the court, made an exit beatings free background forehand, a turn for background exit forehand, rise to the net and end up with a crossed over backhand volley.

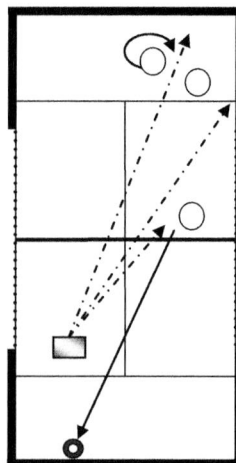

Exercise 0617   Hits: SF – SL – V

Target: Combination of hits
Striking sequence: SFD – SLD - Turn SFD – VR//

Description:
Set the player at the bottom of the court, makes a forehand out background, forehand output side a turn for bottom outlet of forehand and rise to the net to finish with a parallel backhand volley.

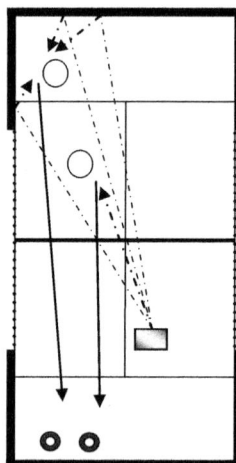

Exercise 0618   Hits: SF – SL – V

Target: Combination of hits
Striking sequence: SFR – SLR - Turn SFR – VD

Description:
Set the player at the bottom of the court, makes a bottom outlet, backhand output side a turn for bottom outlet of backhand and rise to the net to finish with a parallel forehand volley.

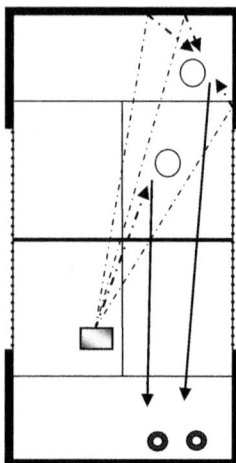

Exercise 0619   Hits: CP – V

Target: Control volleys and against wall
Striking sequence: VR – VR – VR - CPD

Description:
Set the player near the net, perform a backhand volley in the middle of the court and return to the grid to touch the cone, repeated twice more and after the last, touch cone and run at the corner for a parallel forehand against wall.
After 12 balls is changed player.

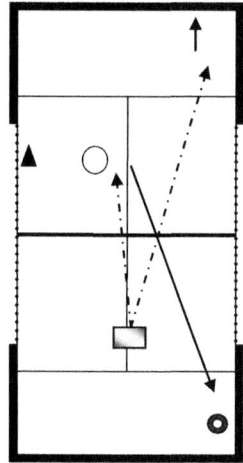

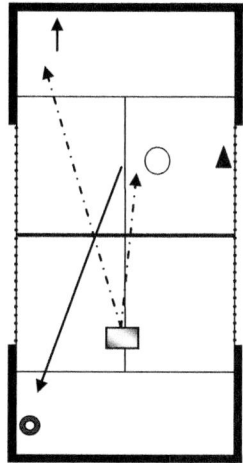

Exercise 0620   Hits: CP – V

Target: Control volleys and against wall
Striking sequence: VD – VD – VD - CPR

Description:
Set the player near the net, perform a forehand volley in the middle of the court and return to the grid to touch the cone, repeated twice more and after the last, touch cone and run at the corner for a parallel backhand against wall.
After 12 balls is changed player.

Exercise 0621   Hits: CP – V

Target: Volleys control, cadete and against wall
Striking sequence: VR - VD - Cadete - VD - CP

Description:
Exercise round. The player of the turning upside position hits always volleys to the right hand monitor. In this way we ensure that pupils find the angle of the grid. We throw the ball to the grid side drive, so burdensome. Now we add cadet as a last resort, because sometimes very open to get to the grid faster opponents try to play the middle, we return to parallel forehand volley and we go back to against wall.

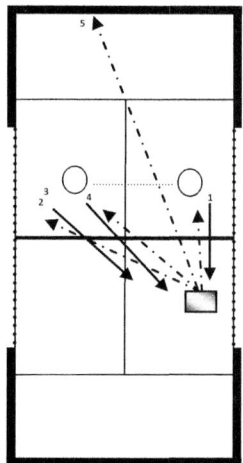

Exercise 0622   Hits: CP – V

Target: Cadete against wall and let
Striking sequence: Cadete CPD – VR – Let

Description:
Set the player at the bottom of the court, make a forehand cadet against wall, then a background backhand volley to get the shot on net and return to the starting position with frontal displacements to pull another cadet and start the exercise.
We must be very well trained and it is a very complicated exercise.

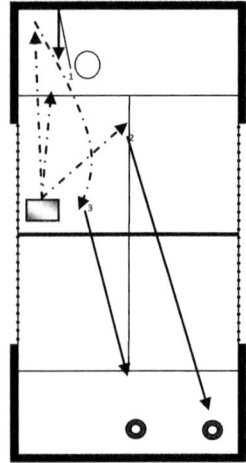

Exercise 0623   Hits: CP – V

Target: Cadete against wall and let
Striking sequence: Cadete CPR – VD - Let

Description:
Set the player at the bottom of the court, make a backhand cadet against wall, then a background forehand volley to get the shot on net and return to the starting position with frontal displacements to pull another cadet and start the exercise.
We must be very well trained and it is a very complicated exercise.

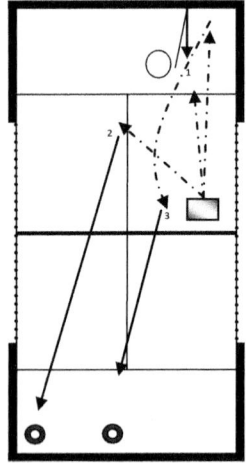

Exercise 0624   Hits: SF – V

Target: Chiquita and recovery
Striking sequence: Crossed over chiquita and volley

Description:
Located a player in the position of defense and another near the net, the player end of the court will begin with a wall outlet of crossed over backhand chiquita to the grid and try to take the net with it.
The player works in background reaching to the middle backhand volley or volley arrive so downloading parallel drive, returning the player to the net, alternating the middle and crossed over.
After 20 balls position players alternates.

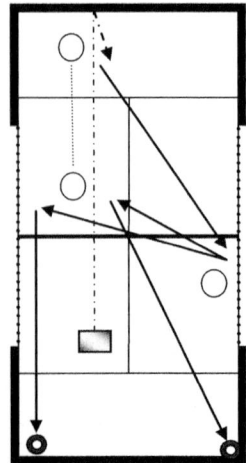

Exercise 0625   Hits: SF – V

Target: Chiquita and recovery
Striking sequence: Crossed over chiquita and volley

Description:
Located a player in the position of defense and another near the net, the player end of the court will begin with a wall outlet of crossed over forehand chiquita to the grid and try to take the net with it.
The player works in background reaching to the middle forehand volley or volley arrive so downloading parallel drive, returning the player to the net, alternating the middle and crossed over.
After 20 balls position players alternates.

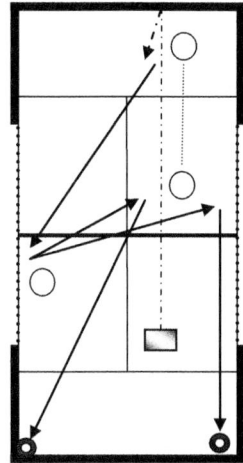

Exercise 0626   Hits: CP – V

Target: Displacement volley
Striking sequence: VRX x3 – CPD//

Description:
Set the player near the net, made three crossed over backhand volleys treading black cone with the right foot at the time of striking. After hitting will play the white cone and repeat the exercise. After the third volley, we will run in crossed over for a parallel forehand against wall.

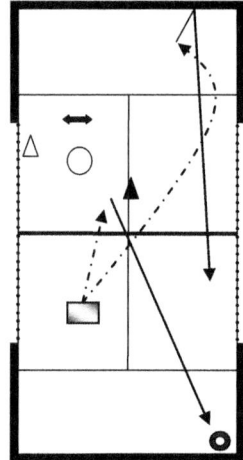

Exercise 0627   Hits: CP – V

Target: Displacement volley
Striking sequence: VDX x3 – CPR//

Description:
Set the player near the net, made three crossed over forehand volleys treading black cone with the right foot at the time of striking. After hitting will play the white cone and repeat the exercise. After the third volley, we will run in crossed over for a parallel backhand against wall.

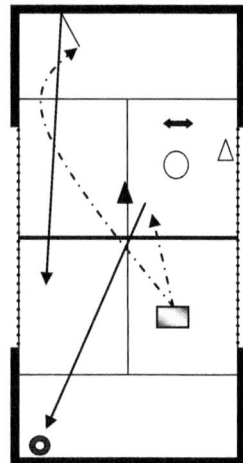

Exercise 0628   Hits: SDP – V

Target: Composite wall outlet - Progressions
Striking sequence: SDP with turn GD - VR

Description:
Set the player at the bottom of the court, hits a forehand lob with turn after the ball bounces on the bottom-side, then climb the net with a backhand volley, where more damage us they can do.
After 10 balls is changed player.

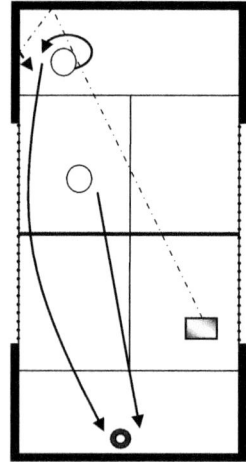

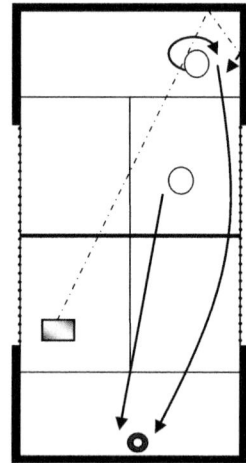

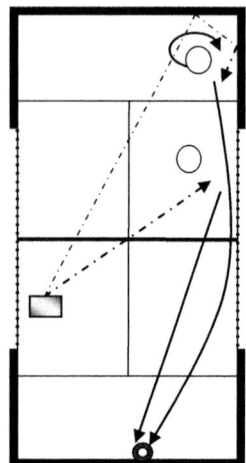

Exercise 0629   Hits: SDP – V

Target: Composite wall outlet - Progressions
Striking sequence: SDP with turn GR - VD

Description:
Set the player at the bottom of the court, hits a backhand lob with turn after the ball bounces on the bottom-side, then climb the net with a forehand volley, where more damage us they can do.
After 10 balls is changed player.

Exercise 0630   Hits: SDP – V

Target: Output forehand lob to turn
Striking sequence: SDP GR - VR

Description:
Located the player at the position of defense, makes a backhand composite output (2 walls opening) dating backhand lob from and going to the net to make a backhand volley to counter.
After 10 balls is changed player.

Exercise 0631   Hits: SDP – V

Target: Output forehand lob to turn
Striking sequence: SDP GD - VD

Description:
Located the player at the position of defense, makes a forehand composite output (2 walls opening) dating forehand lob from and going to the net to make a forehand volley to counter.
After 10 balls is changed player.

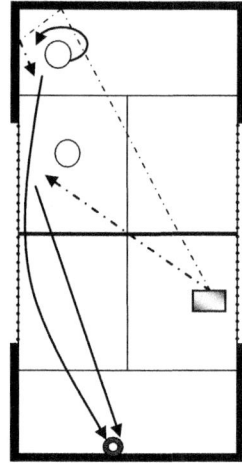

Exercise 0632   Hits: SF – V

Target: Ball Control
Striking sequence: SFD - VD

Description:
Set the player at the bottom of the court, monitor will launch the balls against the wall for the player to perform a soft bottom outlet forehand over the counter and without the ball bounce, hit a volley after having avoided the obstacle.

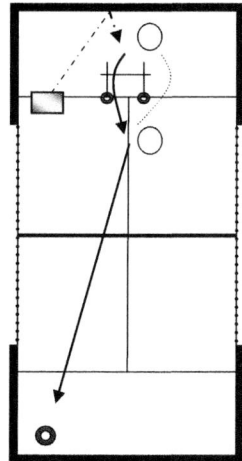

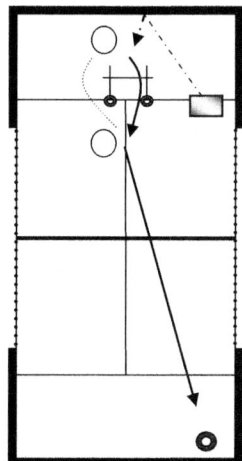

Exercise 0633   Hits: SF – V

Target: Ball Control
Striking sequence: SFR - VR

Description:
Set the player at the bottom of the court, monitor will launch the balls against the wall for the player to perform a soft bottom outlet backhand over the counter and without the ball bounce, hit a volley after having avoided the obstacle.

Exercise 0634   Hits: SF – CP – V

Target: Ball Control
Striking sequence: SFD – VR – CPR

Description:
Set the player at the bottom of the court, monitor will launch the balls against the wall for the player to perform a soft bottom outlet forehand over the counter and without the ball bounce, return it to the same place to avoid the obstacle to make a backhand against wall.

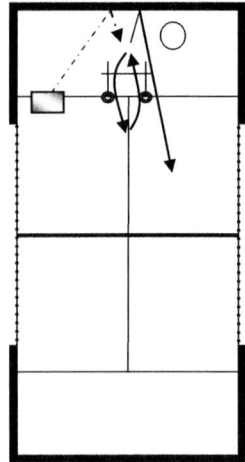

Exercise 0635   Hits: SF – CP – V

Target: Ball Control
Striking sequence: SFR – VD – CPD

Description:
Set the player at the bottom of the court, monitor will launch the balls against the wall for the player to perform a soft bottom outlet forehand over the counter and without the ball bounce, return it to the same place to avoid the obstacle to make a forehand against wall.

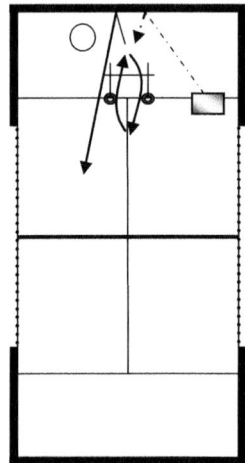

Exercise 0636   Hits: V

Target: Volley displacement
Striking sequence: Volley on each side of the cones – CPD//

Description:
Set the player at the bottom of the court, perform a volley on each side of the cones, progressing crossed over. After the last volley, he will go back and perform a parallel forehand against wall with the target of the mark on the back of the court.

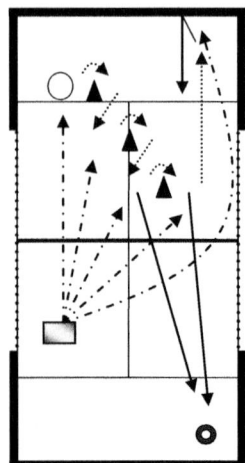

Exercise 0637   Hits: V

Target: Volley displacement
Striking sequence: Volley on each side of the cones – CPR//

Description:
Set the player at the bottom of the court, perform a volley on each side of the cones, progressing crossed over. After the last volley, he will go back and perform a parallel backhand against wall with the target of the mark on the back of the court.

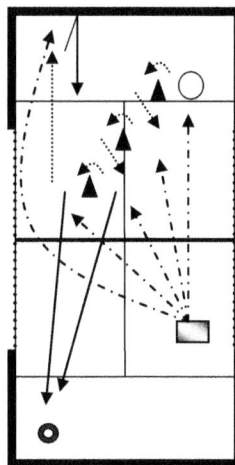

Exercise 0638   Hits: SF – V

Target: Combination of hits
Striking sequence: VDX – VR middle – SFRX – V//

Description:
Set the player near the net, hold a crossed over forehand volley and a backhand volley to the middle, then run crossed over to take an exit background crossed over backhand against the monitor, who will return the ball to the pupil to perform a parallel volley.

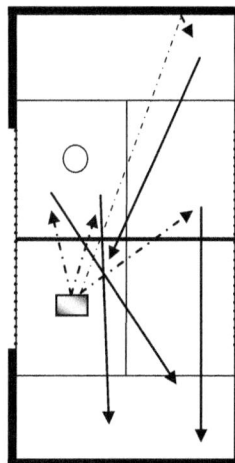

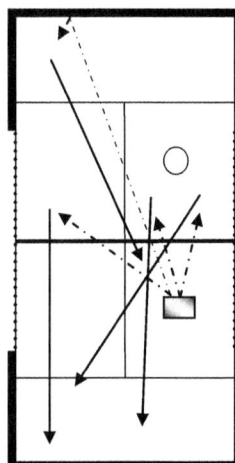

Exercise 0639   Hits: SF – V

Target: Combination of hits
Striking sequence: VRX – VD middle – SFDX – V//

Description:
Set the player near the net, hold a crossed over backhand volley and a forehand volley to the middle, then run crossed over to take an exit background crossed over forehand against the monitor, who will return the ball to the pupil to perform a parallel volley.

Exercise 0640   Hits: CP – V

Target: Volleys controls y against Wall
Striking sequence: VD// - CPD – VR// - CPR

Description:
Set the player near the net, perform a parallel forehand volley, run in the background to make a forehand against wall, rise in crossed over to make a parallel backhand volley and return to the back of the court to make a backhand against wall.

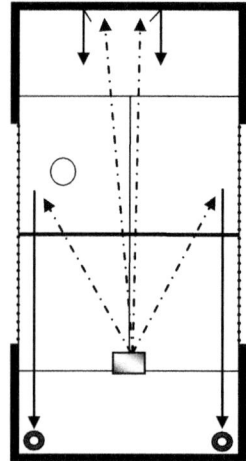

Exercise 0641   Hits: CP – V

Target: Volleys controls and against Wall
Striking sequence: VR// - CPR – VD// - CPD

Description:
Set the player near the net, perform a parallel backhand volley, run in the background to make a backhand against wall, rise in crossed over to make a parallel forehand volley and return to the back of the court to make a forehand against wall.

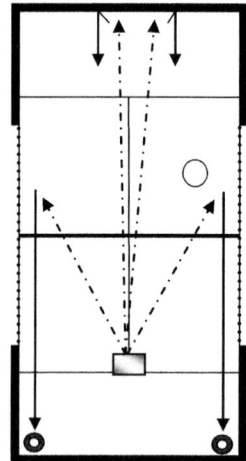

Exercise 0642   Hits: SF – V

Target: Defense volleys and Wall outlets
Striking sequence: VR// - SFDX

Description:
Set the player at the bottom of the court, held a parallel backhand volley from the bottom and an exit background crossed over forehand.
After 10 balls is changed player.

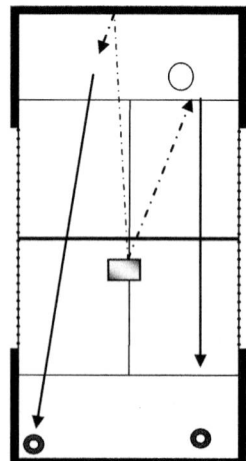

Exercise 0643   Hits: SF – V

Target: Defense volleys and Wall outlets
Striking sequence: VD// - SFRX

Description:
Set the player at the bottom of the court, held a parallel backhand volley from the bottom and an exit background crossed over forehand.
After 10 balls is changed player.

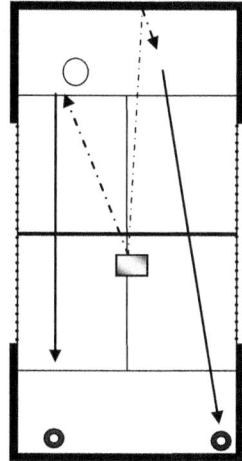

Exercise 0644   Hits: CP – V

Target: Defense situation
Striking sequence: VR - CPR

Description:
Set the player at the bottom of the court, the player goes to counter of backhand volley from the bottom but stays away from the side wall, so to regain the position must perform a backhand against wall.
After 10 balls position players alternates.

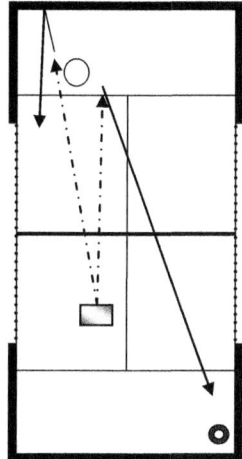

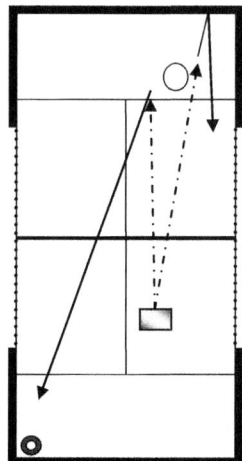

Exercise 0645   Hits: CP – V

Target: Defense situation
Striking sequence: VD - CPD

Description:
Set the player at the bottom of the court, the player goes to counter of forehand volley from the bottom but stays away from the side wall, so to regain the position must perform a forehand against wall.
After 10 balls position players alternates.

Exercise 0646   Hits: SL – V

Target: Reaction to a situation
Striking sequence: SLD// - VRX

Description:
Set the player's position defense makes an output side parallel forehand and run the middle to make an approximation crossed over backhand volley.
After 10 balls is changed player.

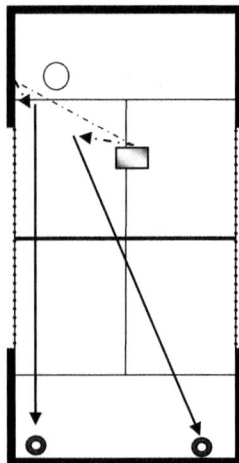

Exercise 0647   Hits: SL – V

Target: Reaction to a situation
Striking sequence: SLR// - VDX

Description:
Set the player's position defense makes an output side parallel backhand and run the middle to make an approximation crossed over forehand volley.
After 10 balls is changed player.

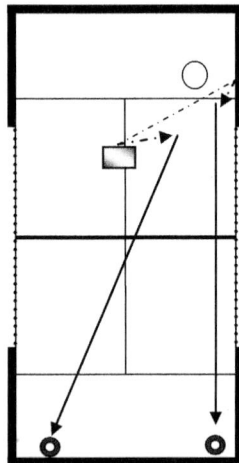

Exercise 0648   Hits: SF – V

Target: Reaction to a situation
Striking sequence: SFDX – VR//

Description:
Located players in the side of the court near the cone will be delayed in the back of the court to make an out background crossed over forehand and uploaded to the net to make a parallel backhand volley. Then they will return to the line.

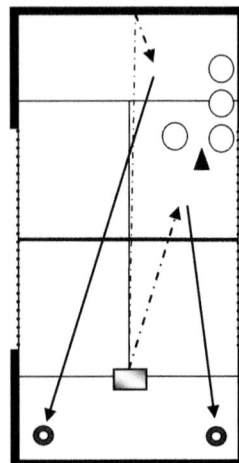

Exercise 0649   Hits: SF – V

Target: Reaction to a situation
Striking sequence: SFRX – VD//

Description:
Located players in the side of the court near the cone will be delayed in the back of the court to make an out background crossed over backhand and uploaded to the net to make a parallel forehand volley. Then they will return to the line.

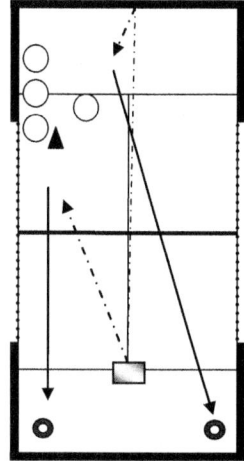

Exercise 0650   Hits: SF – V

Target: Special hits
Striking sequence: SFDX Chiquita – VRX

Description:
Located players in the side of the court near the cone will be delayed in the back of the court to make a petite out background crossed over forehand and go up to the net to close the middle with a crossed over backhand volley. Then they will return to the line.

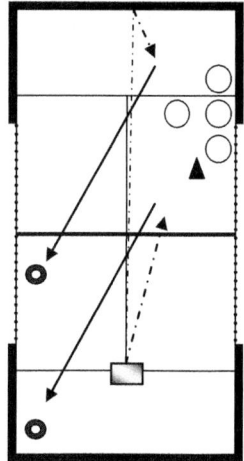

Exercise 0651   Hits: SF – V

Target: Special hits
Striking sequence: SFRX Chiquita – VDX

Description:
Located players in the side of the court near the cone will be delayed in the back of the court to make a petite out background crossed over backhand and go up to the net to close the middle with a crossed over forehand volley. Then they will return to the line.

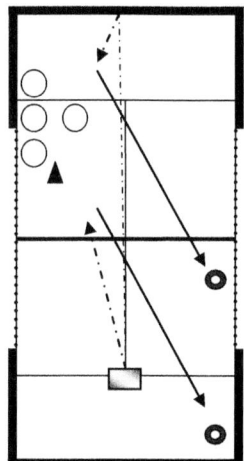

Exercise 0652   Hits: SF – Rm

Target: Reaction to a situation
Striking sequence: SFDG – SFD – Return Rm

Description:
Set the player at the bottom of the court, hits an outlet with forehand lob, a forehand attack of a high ball from a ball of bottom wall and run at the net to make a return of a parallel shot.

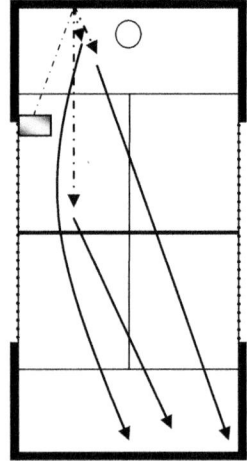

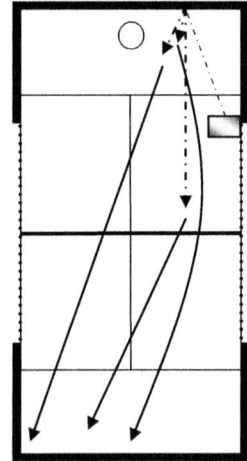

Exercise 0653   Hits: SF – Rm

Target: Reaction to a situation
Striking sequence: SFGR – SFR – Return Rm

Description:
Set the player at the bottom of the court, hits an outlet with backhand lob, a backhand attack of a high ball from a ball of bottom wall and run at the net to make a return of a parallel shot.

Exercise 0654   Hits: CP – V – Rm

Target: Hits variation displacement
Striking sequence: VDX x3 – CPR// – Rm//

Description:
Set the player near the net, made three crossed over forehand volleys treading black cone with the left foot at the time of striking. After hitting will play the white cone and repeat the exercise. After the third volley, will run in crossed over for a parallel backhand against wall after which it will go to the net to make a parallel shot.

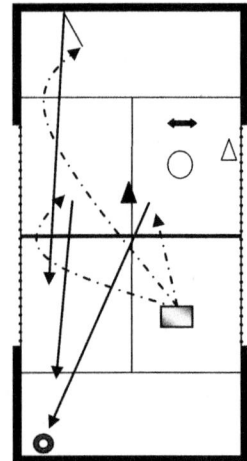

Exercise 0655   Hits: CP – V – Rm

Target: Hits variation displacement
Striking sequence: VRX x3 – CPD// – Rm//

Description:
Set the player near the net, made three crossed over backhand volleys treading black cone with the left foot at the time of striking. After hitting will play the white cone and repeat the exercise. After the third volley, will run in crossed over for a parallel forehand against wall after which it will go to the net to make a parallel shot.

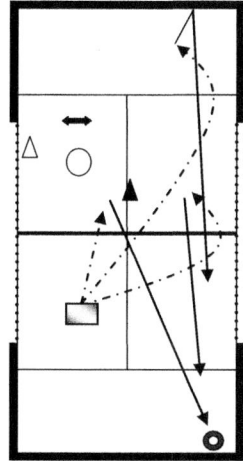

Exercise 0656   Hits: SF – V

Target: Volleys control
Striking sequence: SFRX – V//

Description:
Located two players at the bottom of the court and another near the net, players made out background crossed over backhand against the player in the net. After each stroke, the cone will play next to them. The player in the net hits parallel volleys to the cones background court, as both forehand and backhand.
After 20 balls position players alternates.

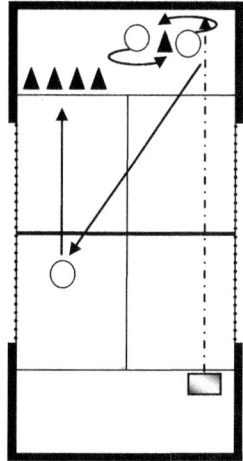

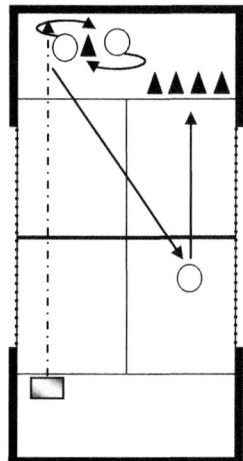

Exercise 0657   Hits: SF – V

Target: Volleys control
Striking sequence: SFDX – V//

Description:
Located two players at the bottom of the court and another near the net, players made out background crossed over forehand against the player in the net. After each stroke, the cone will play next to them. The player in the net hits parallel volleys to the cones background court, as both forehand and backhand.
After 20 balls position players alternates.

EXERCISES COMBINATION: WALL, SHOT

Exercise 0658   Hits: CP – Rm

Target: Reaction to a situation
Striking sequence: CPX - RmX

Description:
Set the player near the net, recovered with a forehand against wall of a ball through the middle with little bounce in the wall and runs forward to a strong shot, with the target of the mark on the court.
After 10 balls is changed player.

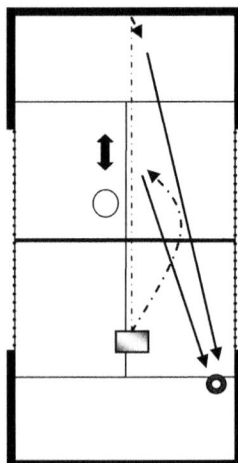

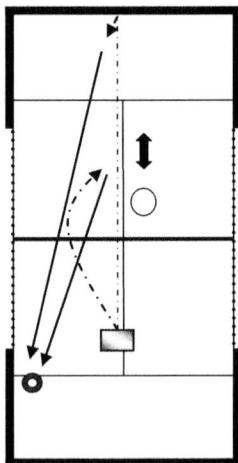

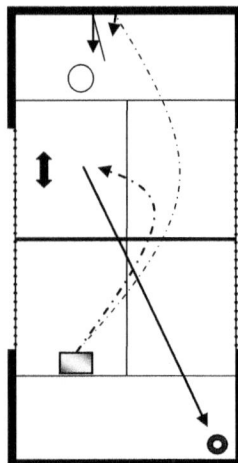

Exercise 0659   Hits: CP – Rm

Target: Reaction to a situation
Striking sequence: CPX - RmX

Description:
Set the player near the net, recovered with a backhand against wall of a ball through the middle with little bounce in the wall and runs forward to a strong shot, with the target of the mark on the court.
After 10 balls is changed player.

Exercise 0660   Hits: CP – Rm

Target: Reaction to a situation
Striking sequence: CPD - RmX

Description:
Set the player at the bottom of the court with a knee recovers a ball forehand against wall and runs forward to take a shot crossed over. After each shot, returns to stand with one knee on the ground in the starting position.
After 10 balls is changed player.

Exercise 0661   Hits: CP – Rm

Target: Reaction to a situation
Striking sequence: CPR - RmX

Description:
Set the player at the bottom of the court with a knee recovers a ball backhand against wall and runs forward to take a shot crossed over. After each shot, returns to stand with one knee on the ground in the starting position.
After 10 balls is changed player.

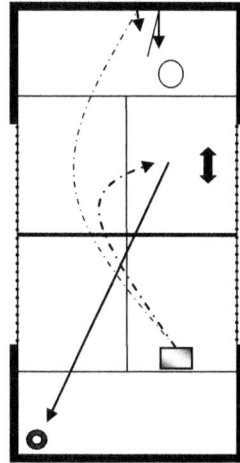

Exercise 0662   Hits: SF – SL – Rm

Target: Anticipate hits
Striking sequence: SFR – SLD – Return of Rm

Description:
Set the player at the bottom of the court, the monitor will launch balls from close to the players to make an exit background backhand and forehand. After the monitor will perform a shot to anticipate what players to return the ball before it touches the ground or exceed the net.

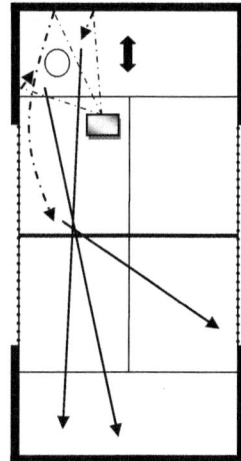

Exercise 0663   Hits: SF – SL – Rm

Target: Anticipate hits
Striking sequence: SFD – SLR – Return of Rm

Description:
Set the player at the bottom of the court, the monitor will launch balls from close to the players to make an exit background backhand and forehand. After the monitor will perform a shot to anticipate what players to return the ball before it touches the ground or exceed the net.

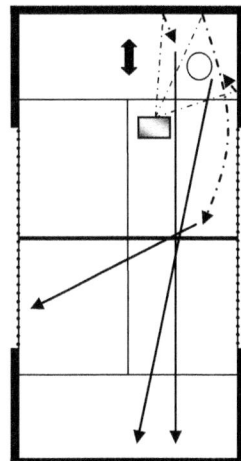

Exercise 0664   Hits: SF – SL – Rm

Target: Reaction to a situation
Striking sequence: SFR – SLD – SFD – Rm //

Description:
Set the player at the bottom of the court, made an exit frees striking background backhand, one forehand side exit, a side out forehand background, rise to the net and end with a power parallel shot.

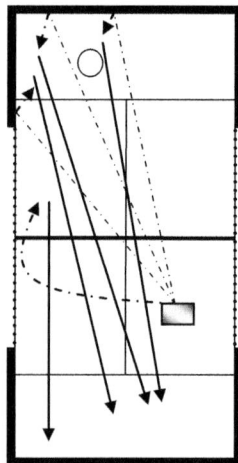

Exercise 0665   Hits: SF – SL – Rm

Target: Reaction to a situation
Striking sequence: SFD – SLR – SFR – Rm//

Description:
Set the player at the bottom of the court, made an exit frees striking background forehand, one backhand side exit, a side out backhand background, rise to the net and end with a power parallel shot.

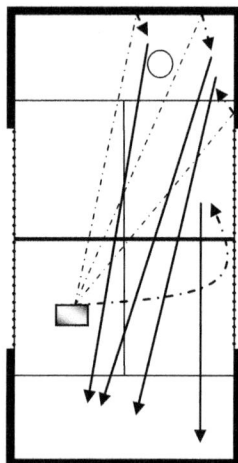

Exercise 0666   Hits: SF – SL – Rm

Target: Reaction to a situation
Striking sequence: SFR – SLD – SFD – RmX

Description:
Set the player at the bottom of the court, made a backhand bottom outlet, forehand output side and forehand bottom outlet with that rise to the net to finish with a crossed over shot.

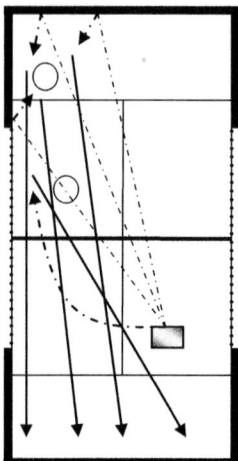

Exercise 0667   Hits: SF – SL – Rm

Target: Reaction to a situation
Striking sequence: SFD – SLR – SFR – RmX

Description:
Set the player at the bottom of the court, made a forehand bottom outlet, backhand output side and backhand bottom outlet with that rise to the net to finish with a crossed over shot.

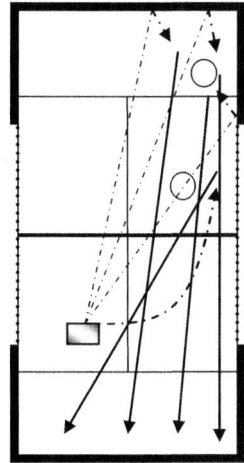

Exercise 0668   Hits: SF – SL – Rm

Target: Reaction to a situation
Striking sequence: SFR – SLD – Return Rm

Description:
Set the player at the bottom of the court, made a bottom outlet, a forehand output side and run at the net to try to return a parallel shot parallel of the monitor before the ball exceed the net.

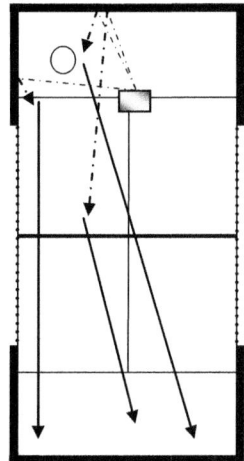

Exercise 0669   Hits: SF – SL – Rm

Target: Reaction to a situation
Striking sequence: SFD – SLR – Return Rm

Description:
Set the player at the bottom of the court, made a bottom outlet, a backhand output side and run at the net to try to return a parallel shot parallel of the monitor before the ball exceed the net.

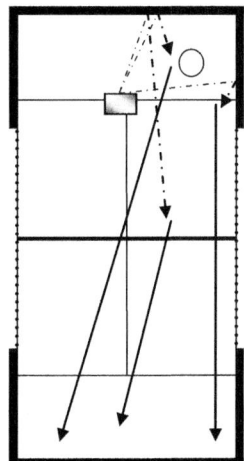

EXERCISES COMBINATION: WALL, VOLLEY TRAY

Exercise 0670   Hits: SF – Bd

Target: Blocking Volley Tray (Bd)
Striking sequence: SFR GX – BdX - Blocking

Description:
Faced two players on crossed over, one at the back of the court and the other near the net, the player end of the court made an bottom outlet with a crossed over backhand lob and go up to the net to block the crossed over volley tray (Bd) that your partner has done. The player taking the volley tray, hits volley to toggle the middle and volley trays to the grid.
After 20 balls position players alternates.

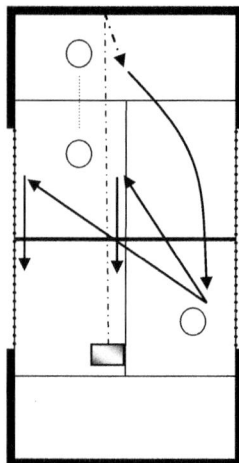

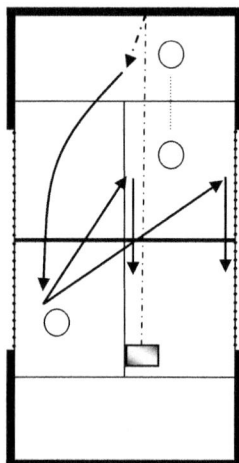

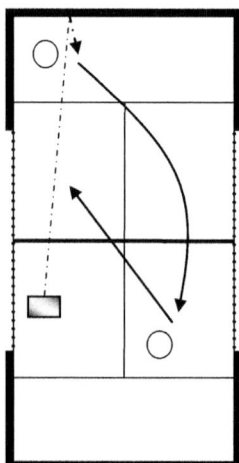

Exercise 0671   Hits: SF – Bd

Target: Blocking Volley Tray (Bd)
Striking sequence: SFD GX – BdX - Blocking

Description:
Faced two players on crossed over, one at the back of the court and the other near the net, the player end of the court made an bottom outlet with a crossed over forehand lob and go up to the net to block the crossed over volley tray (Bd) that your partner has done. The player taking the volley tray, hits volley to toggle the middle and volley trays to the grid.
After 20 balls position players alternates.

Exercise 0672   Hits: SF – Bd

Target: Match situation
Striking sequence: SFR GX – BdX – Blocking

Description:
Faced two players on crossed over, one at the back of the court and the other near the net, the player end of the court made an crossed over backhand lob bottom outlet and rise to block the crossed over volley tray that you will pull his partner. They continue to play until the point is finished.
After 20 balls position players alternates.

Exercise 0673   Hits: SL – Bd

Target: Match situation

Striking sequence: SL CPD - BDX

Description:

Set the player at the bottom of the court, it will pass the ball under his legs to hit in the side wall, after which it will turn and perform a forehand against wall. Then he will go for a crossed over volley tray (Bd).

The player will return to the starting position and after 10 balls change of player. Then you can do on the other side.

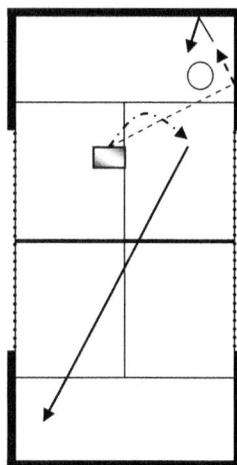

EXERCISES COMBINATION: WALL, VOLLEY, SHOT

Exercise 0674   Hits: SF – G – Rm

Target: Defending, passing attack and recover the net

Striking sequence: Chiquita – Let – G – G – Rm

Description:

Located in the back of the court, player plays the ball from the petite background crossed over backhand, looking anticipate chopping the ball over the player to drive and win the net. Drive player that was passed over, it reaches the bottom and load the player parallel backhand lob and that's where your partner is going to smash block player to retake the lost position before attack.

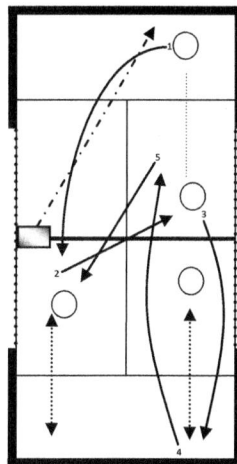

Exercise 0675   Hits: SF – V – Rm

Target: Combination of hits with movement

Striking sequence: RmX – VD// - Down Wall R center

Description:

Located players close to the net, they perform a crossed over shot, go up to the net and perform a parallel forehand volley and slow enough to make a backhand drop wall to the center, with the target of the marks on the background court. Once the three hits, they will return to the line.

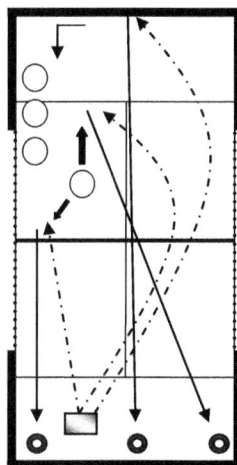

Exercise 0676   Hits: SF – V – Rm

Target: Combination of hits with movement
Striking sequence: RmX – VR// - Down Wall D center

Description:
Located players close to the net, they perform a crossed over shot, go up to the net and perform a parallel backhand volley and slow enough to make a forehand drop wall to the center, with the target of the marks on the background court. Once the three hits, they will return to the line.

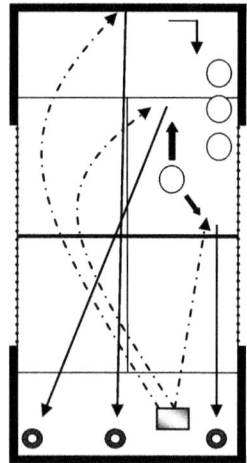

Exercise 0677   Hits: SF – V – Rm

Target: Combination of hits with movement
Striking sequence: Down Wall DX – VD middle – Rm//

Description:
Located players near the net are delayed for a crossed over forehand drop wall with angle and short, uploaded to the net and perform a forehand volley from the middle and slow to finish with a parallel shot, with the target of the marks on the back of the court. Once the three hits, they will return to the line.

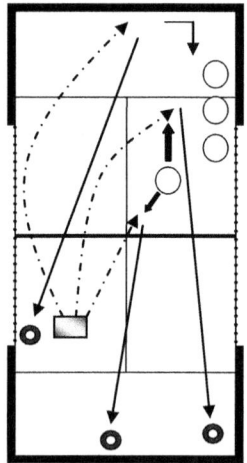

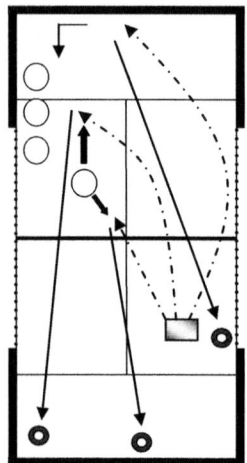

Exercise 0678   Hits: SF – V – Rm

Target: Combination of hits with movement
Striking sequence: Down Wall RX – VR middle – Rm//

Description:
Located players near the net are delayed for a crossed over backhand drop wall with angle and short, uploaded to the net and perform a backhand volley from the middle and slow to finish with a parallel shot, with the target of the marks on the back of the court. Once the three hits, they will return to the line.

Exercise 0679   Hits: SF – V – Rm

Target: Combination of hits with effort
Striking sequence: RmX – VR – VD – Down Wall D

Description:
Located in the middle player of the court, hits a crossed over shot to the peak and rise to the net to make a backhand volley into the corner and a strong forehand volley to the middle, and will be delayed all enough to make a drop in center with the target of the marks on the corners of the court.
After 12 balls is changed player.

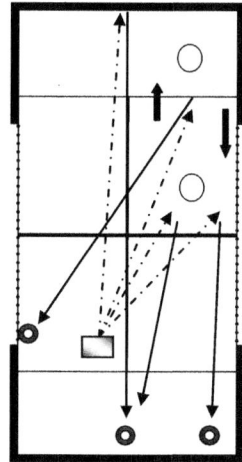

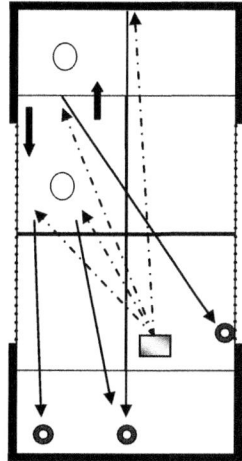

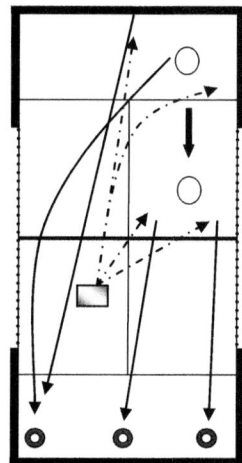

Exercise 0680   Hits: SF – V – Rm

Target: Combination of hits with effort
Striking sequence: RmX – VR – VD – Down Wall R

Description:
Located in the middle player of the court, hits a crossed over shot to the peak and rise to the net to make a forehand volley into the corner and a strong backhand volley to the middle, and will be delayed all enough to make a drop in center with the target of the marks on the corners of the court.
After 12 balls is changed player.

Exercise 0681   Hits: SF – V – Rm

Target: Combination of hits with effort
Striking sequence: GDX – VR – RmX – VD - BFDX

Description:
Set the player at the bottom of the court, hits a crossed over forehand lob to get on the net and make a backhand volley into the corner, it will be delayed enough for a crossed over shot, up to the net and perform a forehand volley to the middle and will be delayed for a crossed over forehand drop background wall, with the target of the marks on the corners of the court.
After 12 balls is changed player.

Exercise 0682   Hits: SF – V – Rm

Target: Combination of hits with effort
Striking sequence: GRX – VD – RmX – VR – BFRX

Description:
Set the player at the bottom of the court, hits a crossed over backhand lob to get on the net and make a forehand volley into the corner, it will be delayed enough for a crossed over shot, up to the net and perform a backhand volley to the middle and will be delayed for a crossed over backhand drop background wall, with the target of the marks on the corners of the court.
After 12 balls is changed player.

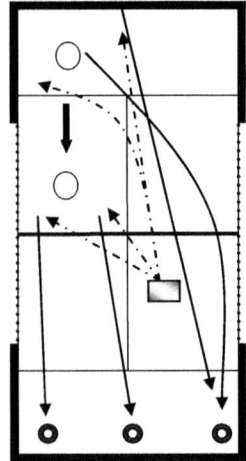

Exercise 0683   Hits: SL – V – Rm

Target: Combination of hits
Striking sequence: SFDX – VDX - RmX

Description:
Set the player at the bottom of the court, perform a crossed over forehand background out with which uploaded to the net, perform a crossed over forehand volley and a crossed over shot, with the target of the marks on the corners of the court.
After 12 balls is changed player.

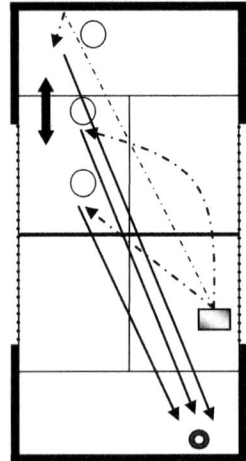

Exercise 0684   Hits: SL – V – Rm

Target: Combination of hits
Striking sequence: SFRX – VRX – RmX

Description:
Set the player at the bottom of the court, perform a crossed over backhand background out with which uploaded to the net, perform a crossed over backhand volley and a crossed over shot, with the target of the marks on the corners of the court.
After 12 balls is changed player.

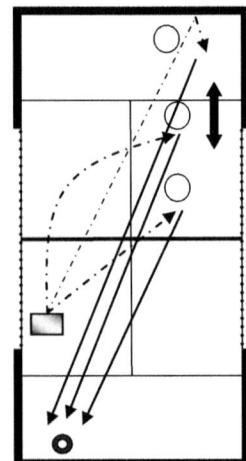

Exercise 0685   Hits: SF – V – Rm

Target: Combination of hits
Striking sequence: 2 VDX – 3 VRX – RmX – SFRG//

Description:
Set the player near the net, make two crossed over forehand volleys, three crossed over backhand volleys and a crossed over shot, lower the opposite corner and then rebound in the bottom wall to make a parallel backhand lob, with the target of the mark on the back of the court.

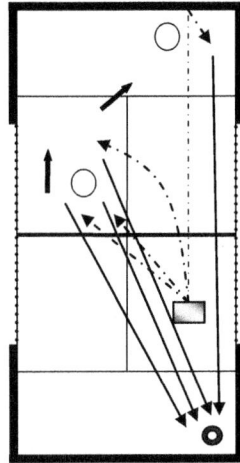

Exercise 0686   Hits: SF – V – Rm

Target: Combination of hits
Striking sequence: 2 VRX – 3 VDX – RmX – SFDG//

Description:
Set the player near the net, make two crossed over backhand volleys, three crossed over forehand volleys and a crossed over shot, lower the opposite corner and then rebound in the bottom wall to make a parallel forehand lob, with the target of the mark on the back of the court.

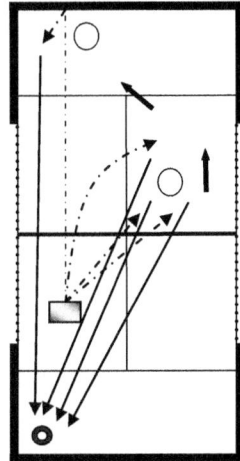

Exercise 0687   Hits: SF – V – Rm

Target: Combination of hits
Striking sequence: VD// - VR// - Rm// - SFRGX

Description:
Set the player near the net, perform a parallel forehand volley, a parallel backhand volley and a parallel shot, go down the opposite corner and then rebound in the bottom wall to make a crossed over backhand lob, with the target of the mark on the back of the court.
After 12 balls is changed player.

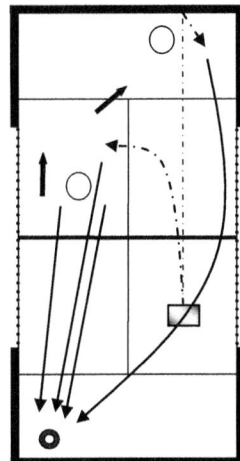

Exercise 0688   Hits: SF – V – Rm

Target: Combination of hits
Striking sequence: VD// - VR// - Rm// - SFDGX

Description:
Set the player near the net, perform a parallel backhand volley, a parallel forehand volley and a parallel shot, go down the opposite corner and then rebound in the bottom wall to make a crossed over forehand lob, with the target of the mark on the back of the court.
After 12 balls is changed player.

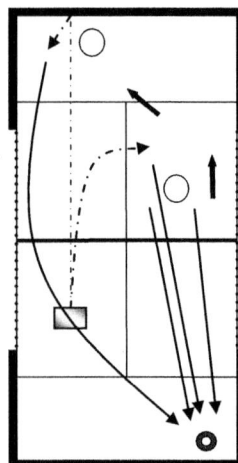

Exercise 0689   Hits: SF – V – Rm

Target: Defense hits and attack
Striking sequence: SFRX – VR// - Rm//

Description:
Set the player at the bottom of the court, the monitor will perform a parallel shot to what the player will return with a crossed over backhand output background , go up to the net on the opposite side and make a parallel backhand volley and a parallel shot with the target of the mark on the back of the court.
After 12 balls is changed player.

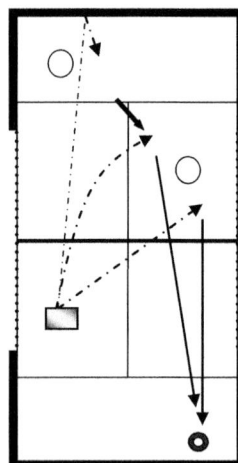

Exercise 0690   Hits: SF – V – Rm

Target: Defense hits and attack
Striking sequence: SFDX – VD// - Rm//

Description:
Set the player at the bottom of the court, the monitor will perform a parallel shot to what the player will return with a crossed over backhand output background , go up to the net on the opposite side and make a parallel backhand volley and a parallel shot with the target of the mark on the back of the court.
After 12 balls is changed player.

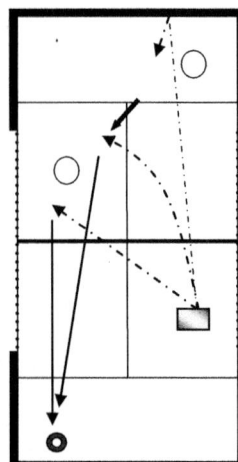

Exercise 0691   Hits: SF – V – Rm

Target: Defense hits and attack
Striking sequence: SFRX – VD// - RmX

Description:
Set the player at the bottom of the court, the monitor will perform a parallel shot to what the player will return with a crossed over backhand output background, rise to the net on the opposite side and make a parallel forehand volley and a crossed over shot with the target of the marks on the back of the court.
After 12 balls is changed player.

Exercise 0692   Hits: SF – V – Rm

Target: Defense hits and attack
Striking sequence: SFDX – VR// - RmX

Description:
Set the player at the bottom of the court, the monitor will perform a parallel shot to what the player will return with a crossed over forehand output background, rise to the net on the opposite side and make a parallel backhand volley and a crossed over shot with the target of the marks on the back of the court.
After 12 balls is changed player.

Exercise 0693   Hits: SF – V – Rm

Target: Combination of hits
Striking sequence: SFRX – VDX – RmX – SFR//

Description:
Set the player at the bottom of the court, makes an crossed over backhand output background, rise to the net and make a crossed over forehand volley and a crossed over shot, then go down in crossed over and then rebound in the background wall hitting parallel backhand with the target of the mark on the back of the court.
After 12 balls is changed player.

Exercise 0694   Hits: SF – V – Rm

Target: Combination of hits
Striking sequence: SFDX – VRX – RmX – SFD//

Description:
Set the player at the bottom of the court, makes an crossed over forehand output background, rise to the net and make a crossed over backhand volley and a crossed over shot, then go down in crossed over and then rebound in the background wall hitting parallel forehand with the target of the mark on the back of the court.
After 12 balls is changed player.

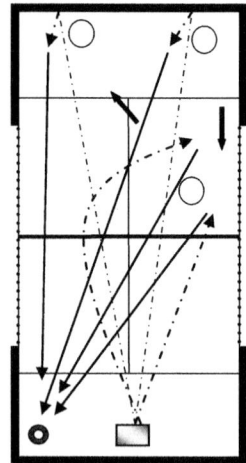

Exercise 0695   Hits: SL – SF – V – Rm

Target: Combination of hits
Striking sequence: SLDX – Turn SFDX – VD// - Rm//

Description:
Set the player at the bottom of the court, makes an crossed over forehand output side and turn for a crossed over forehand output background, rise to the net to make a parallel forehand volley and end with a power parallel shot, with the target of the marks on the back of the court.
After 12 balls is changed player.

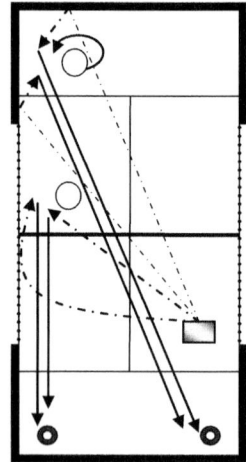

Exercise 0696   Hits: SL – SF – V – Rm

Target: Combination of hits
Striking sequence: SLRX – Turn SFRX – VR// - Rm//

Description:
Set the player at the bottom of the court, makes an crossed over backhand output side and turn for a crossed over backhand output background, rise to the net to make a parallel backhand volley and end with a power parallel shot, with the target of the marks on the back of the court.
After 12 balls is changed player.

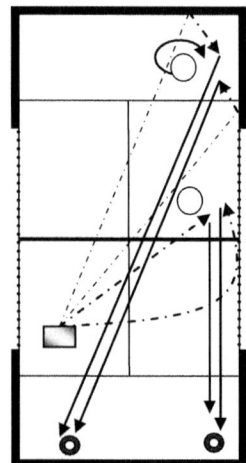

Exercise 0697   Hits: D – V – Rm

Target: Combination of hits
Striking sequence: Output grid D// – VR// - Rm //

Description:
Set the player near the net, retrieves a ball to the grid of parallel forehand, recover the position with a parallel backhand volley and end with a power parallel shot.
After 12 balls is changed player.

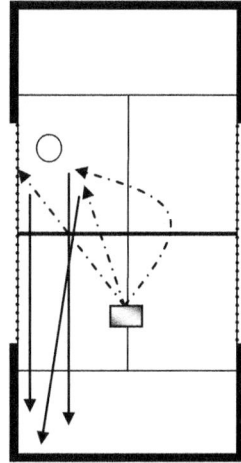

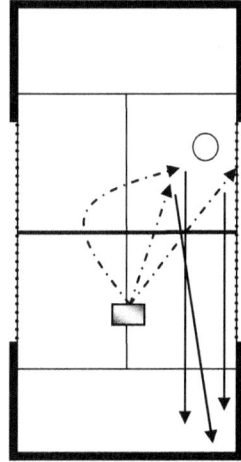

Exercise 0698   Hits: R – V – Rm

Target: Combination of hits
Striking sequence: Output grid R// – VD// - Rm//

Description:
Set the player near the net, retrieves a ball to the grid of parallel backhand, recover the position with a parallel forehand volley and end with a power parallel shot.
After 12 balls is changed player.

Exercise 0699   Hits: D – V – Rm

Target: Combination of hits
Striking sequence: Grid D – VR// - RmX

Description:
Located player near the net, recovering from a forehand on the grid, close the middle with a parallel backhand volley and end with a crossed over shot, with the target marks the bottom of the court.
After 12 balls you change player.

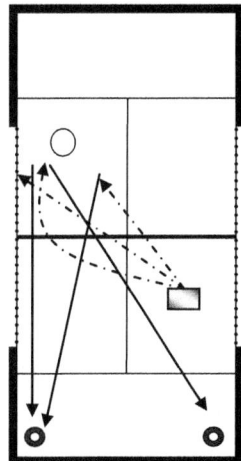

Exercise 0700   Hits: R – V – Rm

Target: Combination of hits
Striking sequence: Grid R – VD// - RmX

Description:
Located player near the net, recovering from a backhand on the grid, close the middle with a parallel forehand volley and end with a crossed over shot, with the target marks the bottom of the court.
After 12 balls you change player.

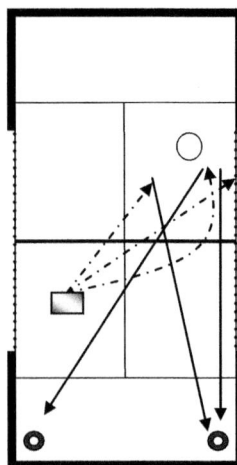

Exercise 0701   Hits: SF – SL – V – Rm

Target: Combination of hits
Striking sequence: SLD – Turn SFD – VR// - Rm//

Description:
Set the player at the bottom of the court, makes a forehand side exit, a turn for a forehand output background with which it will go to a backhand volley and end with a shot parallel, with the target of marks background of the court.
After 12 balls is changed player.

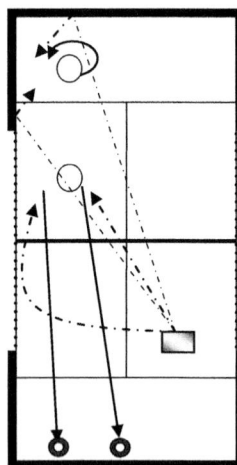

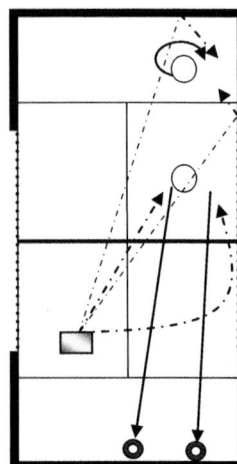

Exercise 0702   Hits: SF – SL – V – Rm

Target: Combination of hits
Striking sequence: SLR – Turn SFR – VD// - Rm//

Description:
Set the player at the bottom of the court, makes a backhand side exit, a turn for a backhand output background with which it will go to a forehand volley and end with a shot parallel, with the target of marks background of the court.
After 12 balls is changed player

Exercise 0703   Hits: V – Rm

Target: Ball control and speed
Striking sequence: VD – CP – Cadete Rm

Description:
Let cloning is not an exercise in real game situation. Exercise dynamic and ball control, working speed against wall and ball control in cadet with the same shot. Forehand volley in the middle, to go back against wall after striking the side wall, the net recovery and then make high cadet bounce to make a shot.

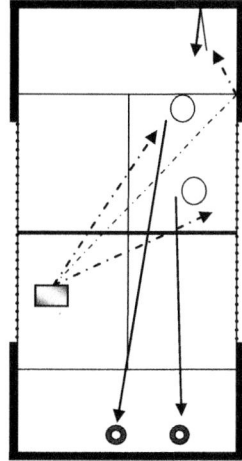

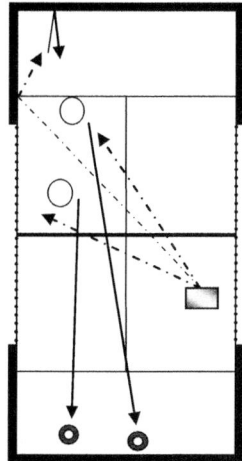

Exercise 0704   Hits: V – Rm

Target: Ball control and speed
Striking sequence: VR – CP – Cadete Rm

Description:
Let cloning is not an exercise in real game situation. Exercise dynamic and ball control, working speed against wall and ball control in cadet with the same shot. Backhand volley in the middle, to go back against wall after striking the side wall, the net recovery and then make high cadet bounce to make a shot.

Exercise 0705   Hits: SF – V – Rm

Target: Technical Physical Exercise
Striking sequence: Jump – VRx3 – SF GD – Jump – Rm//

Description:
Set the player at the bottom of the court, near the fence, begins with a jump fence, we crossed displacement over 3 backhand volleys, back to the bottom wall to dating background wall with forehand lob, fence jump shot again and ended with defining parallel.

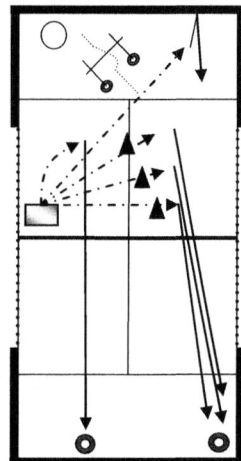

Exercise 0706   Hits: SF – V – Rm

Target: Technical Physical Exercise
Striking sequence: Jump – VDx3 – SF GR – Jump – Rm//

Description:
Set the player at the bottom of the court, near the fence, begins with a jump fence, we crossed displacement over 3 forehand volleys, back to the bottom wall to dating background wall with backhand lob, fence jump shot again and ended with defining parallel.

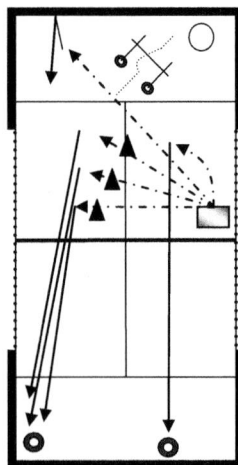

Exercise 0707   Hits: CP – V – Rm

Target: Combination of hits with movement
Striking sequence: VRX x3 – CPD – Rm//

Description:
Set the player near the net, made three crossed over backhand volleys treading black cone with the right foot at the time of striking. After hitting will play the white cone and repeat the exercise. After the third volley, will run in crossed over for a forehand against wall from behind which will go up to the net to make a parallel shot, with the target of the mark on the back of the court.
After 10 balls is changed player.

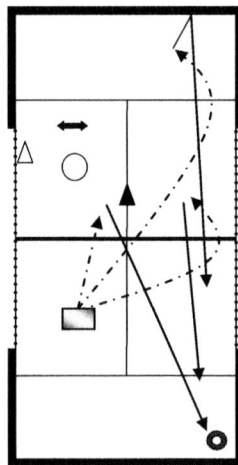

Exercise 0708   Hits: CP – V – Rm

Target: Combination of hits with movement
Striking sequence: VDX x3 – CPR – Rm//

Description:
Set the player near the net, made three crossed over forehand volleys treading black cone with the right foot at the time of striking. After hitting will play the white cone and repeat the exercise. After the third volley, will run in crossed over for a backhand against wall from behind which will go up to the net to make a parallel shot, with the target of the mark on the back of the court.
After 10 balls is changed player.

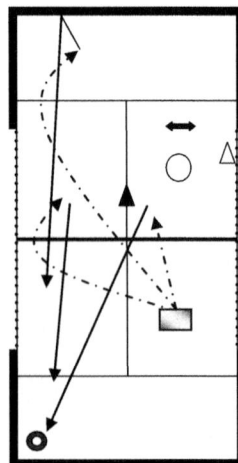

Exercise 0709   Hits: SF – SL – V – Rm

Target: Work on the Backhand
Striking sequence: VR// – SFD// – SLR// – Rm//

Description:
Exercise for the backhand player. We went flying parallel backhand background and go very far to find the exit wall of parallel drive to reach it costs more. Again we return to the side wall to remove it from parallel backhand shot and define a parallel, thus reaction and definition work.
After 12 balls is changed player.

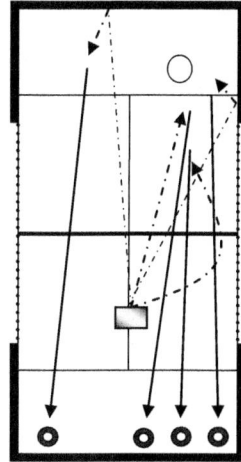

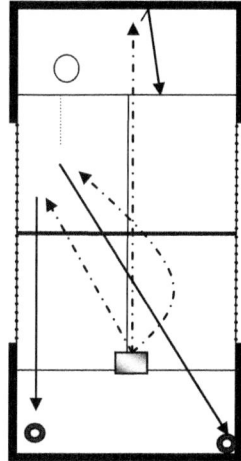

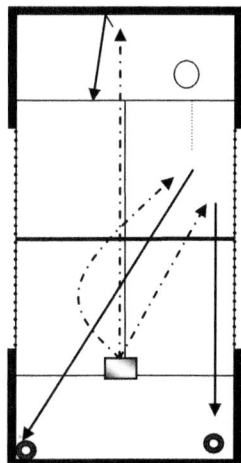

Exercise 0710   Hits: CP – V – Rm

Target: Reaction to a situation
Striking sequence: VD// - CPD – RmX

Description:
Set the player at the bottom of the court, up to the net to parallel forehand volley, back to the bottom to make a forehand against wall in and goes up to the net to finish with a power crossed over shot, with the target the marks on the back of the court.
After 12 balls is changed player.

Exercise 0711   Hits: CP – V – Rm

Target: Reaction to a situation
Striking sequence: VR// - CPR – RmX

Description:
Set the player at the bottom of the court, up to the net to parallel backhand volley, back to the bottom to make a backhand against wall in and goes up to the net to finish with a power crossed over shot, with the target the marks on the back of the court.
After 12 balls is changed player.

EXERCISES COMBINATION: WALL, VOLLEY, VOLLEY

Exercise 0712   Hits: SF – V – Bd

Target: Combination of hits
Striking sequence: BdX – VDX - SFRX

Description:
Located player near the net, hold a crossed over volley tray, rise to the net and make a crossed over forehand volley, and lower your wall to make a crossed over bottom outlet, with the target of the marks on the background court.
After 12 balls is changed player.

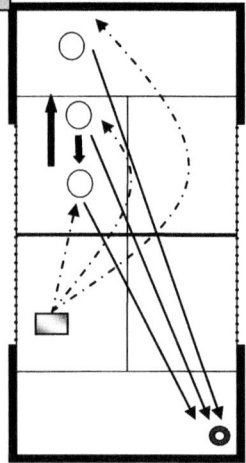

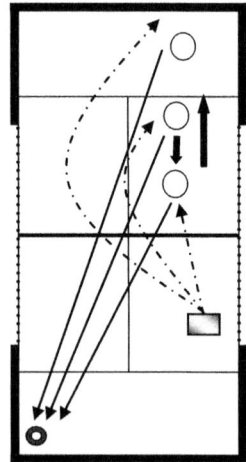

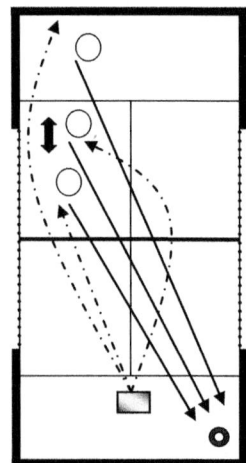

Exercise 0713   Hits: SF – V – Bd

Target: Combination of hits
Striking sequence: BdX – VRX - SFDX

Description:
Located player near the net, hold a crossed over volley tray, rise to the net and make a crossed over backhand volley, and lower your wall to make a crossed over bottom outlet, with the target of the marks on the background court.
After 12 balls is changed player.

Exercise 0714   Hits: SF – V – Bd

Target: Combination of hits to keep the net
Striking sequence: BdX – VDX – SFDX

Description:
Located player in half court will hold a crossed over volley tray, rise to the net to make a crossed over forehand volley and slow enough to make a crossed over forehand bottom outlet, with the target of the marks at the bottom of the court.
After 12 balls is changed player.

Exercise 0715   Hits: SF – V – Bd

Target: Combination of hits to keep the net
Striking sequence: BdX – VRX – SFRX

Description:
Located player in half court will hold a crossed over volley tray, rise to the net to make a crossed over backhand volley and slow enough to make a crossed over backhand bottom outlet, with the target of the marks at the bottom of the court.
After 12 balls is changed player.

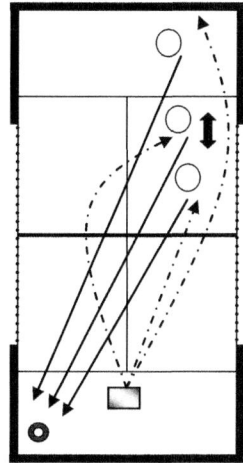

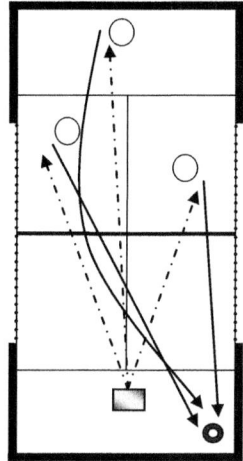

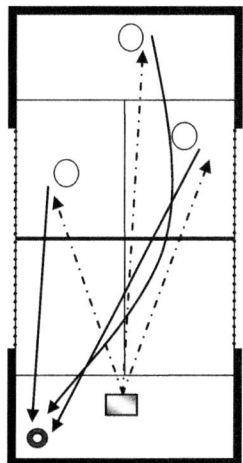

Exercise 0716   Hits: SF – V – Bd

Target: Combination of hits
Striking sequence: BdX – VR// - SFGDX

Description:
Taking 3 players in court, we worked in 3 different positions simultaneously. In the first we do a crossed over volley tray, in another parallel backhand volley and the other crossed over forehand bottom outlet lob, with the target of the mark on the back of the court.
After 12 balls is changed player.

Exercise 0717   Hits: SF – V – Bd

Target: Combination of hits
Striking sequence: BdX – VD// - SFGRX

Description:
Taking 3 players in court, we worked in 3 different positions simultaneously. In the first we do a crossed over volley tray, in another parallel forehand volley and the other crossed over backhand bottom outlet lob, with the target of the mark on the back of the court.
After 12 balls is changed player.

Exercise 0718   Hits: SF – V – Bd

Target: Combination of hits
Striking sequence: VDX – VR// – BdX – VR// - VDX - SFRX

Description:
Set the player near the net, hold a crossed over forehand volley and a parallel backhand volley, it will be delayed to make a crossed over volley tray and retrieve the net closing the middle with a parallel backhand volley and a crossed over forehand volley. Then run in the background to take a crossed over backhand bottom outlet, with the target of the mark on the back of the court.
After 12 balls is changed player.

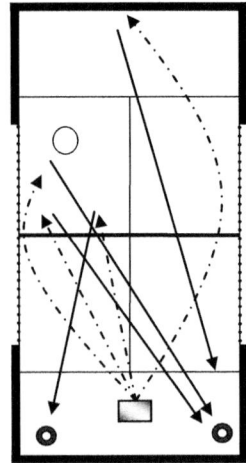

Exercise 0719   Hits: SF – V – Bd

Target: Combination of hits
Striking sequence: VRX – VD// - BdX – VD// – VRX - SFDX

Description:
Set the player near the net, hold a crossed over backhand volley and a parallel forehand volley, it will be delayed to make a crossed over volley tray and retrieve the net closing the middle with a parallel forehand volley and a crossed over backhand volley. Then run in the background to take a crossed over forehand bottom outlet, with the target of the mark on the back of the court.
After 12 balls is changed player.

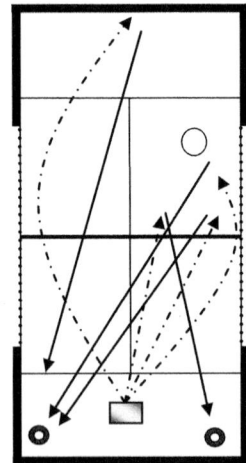

Exercise 0720   Hits: SF – V – Bd

Target: Keep net with relay
Striking sequence: VD// – Bd// – VD – VD – SFG

Description:
Cooperative exercise in which we intend to keep the net. The player drive performs a parallel forehand volley and a parallel volley tray. Then the player backhand closes the middle with a forehand volley. The player of drive you throw a ball close to the grid and return with a forehand volley, but make it a lob and running mate to make a bottom outlet with lob and recover the position.
After 10 balls is changed player.

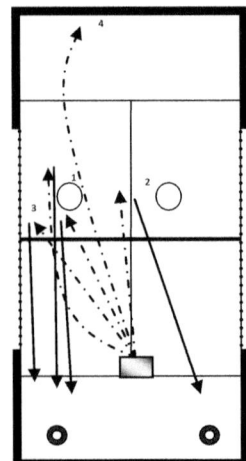

Exercise 0721   Hits: SF – V – Bd

Target: Keep net with relay
Striking sequence: VR// – Bd// – VR – VR – SFG

Description:
Cooperative exercise in which we intend to keep the net. The player drive performs a parallel backhand volley and a parallel volley tray. Then the player forehand closes the middle with a backhand volley. The player of drive you throw a ball close to the grid and return with a backhand volley, but make it a lob and running mate to make a bottom outlet with lob and recover the position.
After 10 balls is changed player.

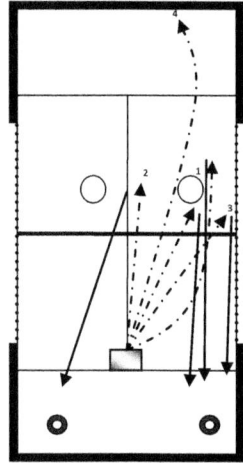

Exercise 0722   Hits: CP – V – Bd

Target: Combination of hits
Striking sequence: CPR – VR middle –BdX

Description:
Set the player at the bottom of the court, retrieves a ball with a backhand against wall, perform up to the middle backhand volley and a crossed over volley tray, with the target of the marks on the back of the court.
After 12 balls is changed player.

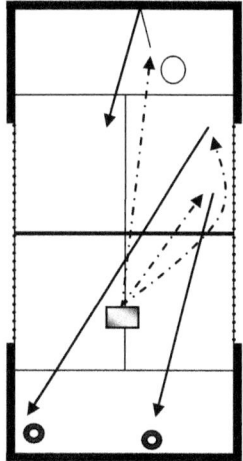

Exercise 0723   Hits: V – Bd – SF – Rm

Target: Combination of hits
Striking sequence: VDX – BdX – VRX – SFR// - Rm//

Description:
Set the player near the net, perform a crossed over forehand volley, a crossed over volley tray (Bd), closed with a crossed over backhand volley, recede to output parallel bottom with which rise backhand to finish with a parallel shot.
Then you can do on the other side with the sequence VRX - BDX - VDX - SFDX - Rm //

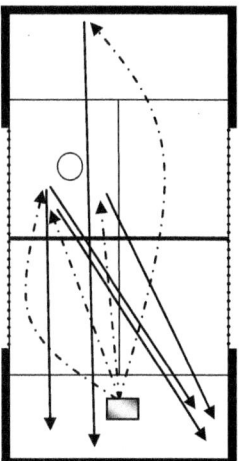

EXERCISES COMBINATION: VOLLEY, SHOT

Exercise 0724   Hits: V – Rm

Target: Play on the net, volley and shot.
Striking sequence: VD middle – RmX

Description:
Set the player at the bottom of the court, will go running to the net and perform a forehand volley from the middle and shot the peak, with the target of the marks on the back of the court.
After the exercise will again row.

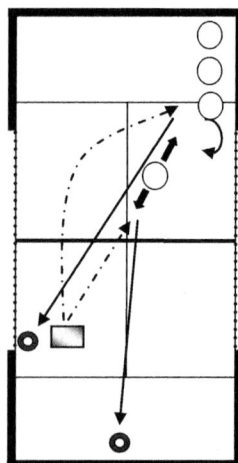

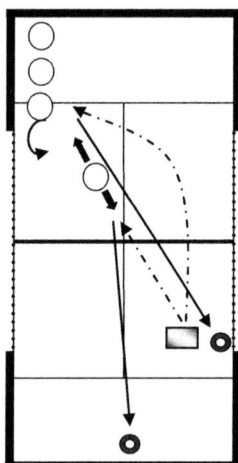

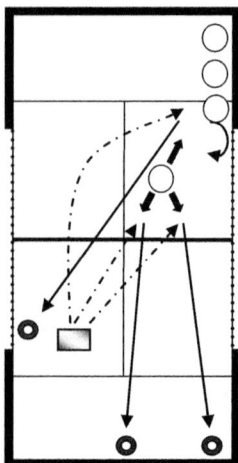

Exercise 0725   Hits: V – Rm

Target: Play on the net, volley and shot.
Striking sequence: VR middle – RmX

Description:
Set the player at the bottom of the court, will go running to the net and perform a backhand volley from the middle and shot the peak, with the target of the marks on the back of the court.
After the exercise will again row.

Exercise 0726   Hits: V – Rm

Target: Play on the net, volley and shot.
Striking sequence: VR// - VD middle – RmX

Description:
Set the player at the bottom of the court, will go running to the net and perform a parallel backhand volley and a forehand volley from the middle and shot the peak, with the target of the marks on the court.
After the exercise will again row.

Exercise 0727   Hits: V – Rm

Target: Play on the net, volley and shot.
Striking sequence: VD// - VR middle – RmX

Description:
Set the player at the bottom of the court, will go running to the net and perform a parallel forehand volley and a backhand volley at the middle and shot the peak, with the target of the marks on the court.
After the exercise will again row.

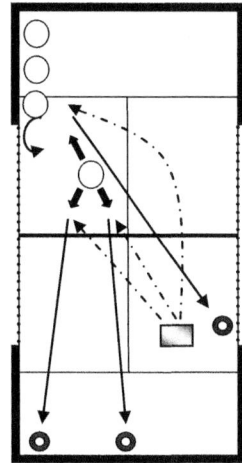

Exercise 0728   Hits: V – Rm

Target: Play on the net, volley and shot.
Striking sequence: VDX - VR middle – RmX

Description:
Set the player at the bottom of the court will go running to the net and perform a crossed over forehand volley, a backhand volley to middle and a shot to the peak, with the target of the marks on the court.
After the exercise will return to the line.

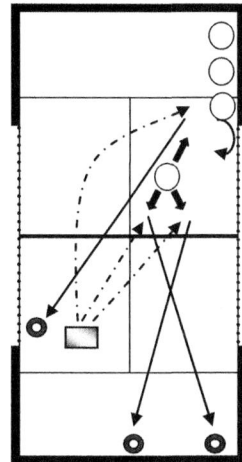

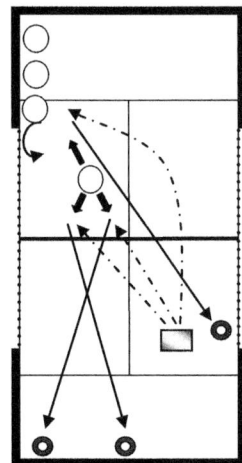

Exercise 0729   Hits: V – Rm

Target: Play on the net, volley and shot.
Striking sequence: VRX - VD middle – RmX

Description:
Set the player at the bottom of the court will go running to the net and perform a crossed over backhand volley, a forehand volley to middle and a shot to the peak, with the target of the marks on the court.
After the exercise will return to the line.

Exercise 0730   Hits: V – Rm

Target: Play on the net, volley and shot.
Striking sequence: VD// - VRX – Rm// - RmX

Description:
Located player near the net, perform a parallel forehand volley, a crossed over backhand volley, a parallel shot and a crossed over shot, with the target of the marks on the back of the court.
After the exercise will return to the line.

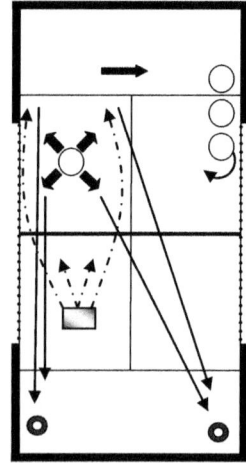

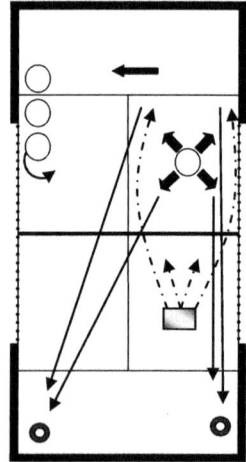

Exercise 0731   Hits: V – Rm

Target: Play on the net, volley and shot.
Striking sequence: VR// - VDX – Rm// - RmX

Description:
Located player near the net, perform a parallel backhand volley, a crossed over forehand volley, a parallel shot and a crossed over shot, with the target of the marks on the back of the court.
After the exercise will return to the line.

Exercise 0732   Hits: V – Rm

Target: Play on the net, volley and shot.
Striking sequence: VD// - Rm// - VR// - Rm //

Description:
Set the player near the net, perform a parallel forehand volley, a parallel shot, a parallel backhand volley and parallel shot, with the target of the mark on the back of the court.
After the exercise will again row.

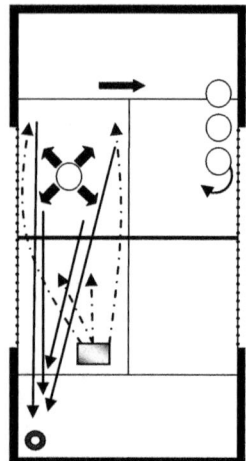

Exercise 0733   Hits: V – Rm

Target: Play on the net, volley and shot.
Striking sequence: VR// - Rm// - VD// - Rm//

Description:
Set the player near the net, perform a parallel backhand volley, a parallel shot, a parallel forehand volley and parallel shot, with the target of the mark on the back of the court.
After the exercise will again row.

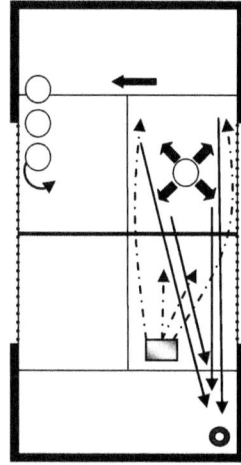

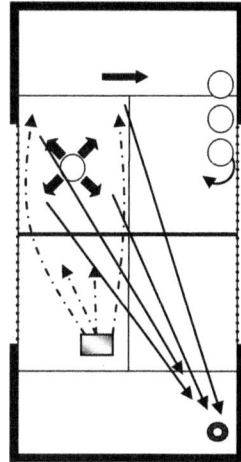

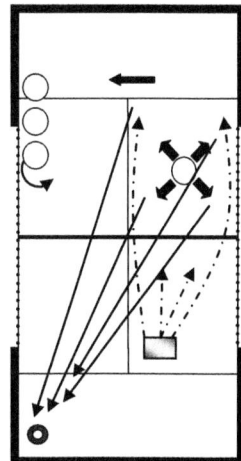

Exercise 0734   Hits: V – Rm

Target: Play on the net, volley and shot.
Striking sequence: VDX - RmX - VRX - RmX

Description:
Located player near the net, hold a crossed over forehand volley, a crossed over shot, a crossed over backhand volley and a crossed over shot, with the target of the marks on the back of the court.
After the exercise will again row.

Exercise 0735   Hits: V – Rm

Target: Play on the net, volley and shot.
Striking sequence: VRX - RmX - VDX - RmX

Description:
Located player near the net, hold a crossed over backhand volley, a crossed over shot, a crossed over forehand volley and a crossed over shot, with the target of the marks on the back of the court.
After the exercise will again row.

Exercise 0736   Hits: V – Rm

Target: Play on the net, volley and shot.
Striking sequence: VR al middle - RmX

Description:
Set the player near the net, perform a backhand volley and a crossed over shot to the middle, with the target of the marks on the back of the court.
After 10 balls is changed player.

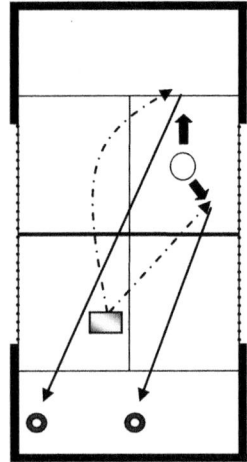

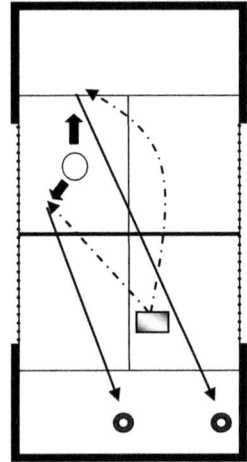

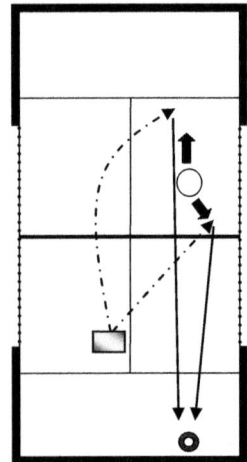

Exercise 0737   Hits: V – Rm

Target: Play on the net, volley and shot.
Striking sequence: VD al middle - RmX

Description:
Set the player near the net, perform a forehand volley and a crossed over shot to the middle, with the target of the marks on the back of the court.
After 10 balls is changed player.

Exercise 0738   Hits: V – Rm

Target: Play on the net, volley and shot.
Striking sequence: VR// - Rm//

Description:
Set the player near the net, perform a parallel backhand volley and a parallel shot, with the target of the mark on the back of the court.
After 10 balls is changed player.

Exercise 0739   Hits: V – Rm

Target: Play on the net, volley and shot.
Striking sequence: VD// - Rm//

Description:
Set the player near the net, perform a parallel forehand volley and a parallel shot, with the target of the mark on the back of the court.
After 10 balls is changed player.

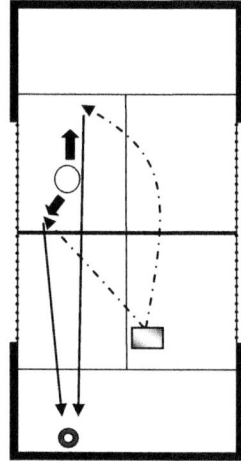

Exercise 0740   Hits: V – Rm

Target: Play on the net, volley and shot.
Striking sequence: VD// - VR// - Rm//

Description:
Set the player near the net, perform a parallel forehand volley and a parallel backhand volley and a parallel shot, with the target of the mark on the back of the court.
After 12 balls is changed player.

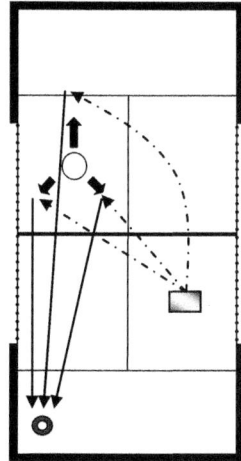

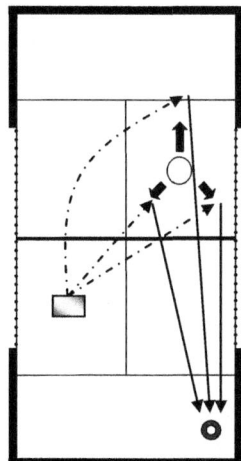

Exercise 0741   Hits: V – Rm

Target: Play on the net, volley and shot.
Striking sequence: VR// - VD// - Rm//

Description:
Set the player near the net, perform a parallel backhand volley and a parallel forehand volley and a parallel shot, with the target of the mark on the back of the court.
After 12 balls is changed player.

Exercise 0742   Hits: V – Rm

Target: Play on the net, volley and shot.
Striking sequence: VR al middle – RmX – VD//

Description:
Located player near the net, perform a backhand volley at the middle, a crossed over shot and a parallel forehand volley, with the target of the marks on the back of the court.
After 12 balls is changed player.

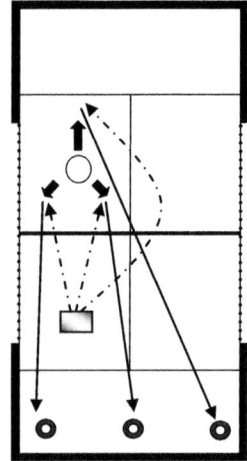

Exercise 0743   Hits: V – Rm

Target: Play on the net, volley and shot.
Striking sequence: VD al middle – RmX – VR//

Description:
Located player near the net, perform a forehand volley at the middle, a crossed over shot and a parallel backhand volley, with the target of the marks on the back of the court.
After 12 balls is changed player.

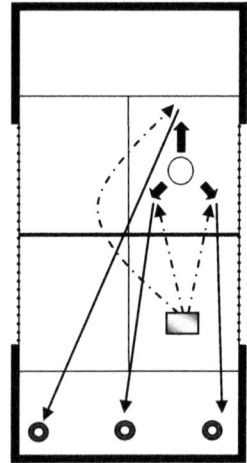

Exercise 0744   Hits: V – Rm

Target: Play on the net, volley and shot.
Striking sequence: VR al middle – RmX – VD// strong

Description:
Located player near the net, perform a backhand volley at the middle, a crossed over shot and a strong parallel forehand volley, with the target of the marks on the back of the court.
After 12 balls is changed player.

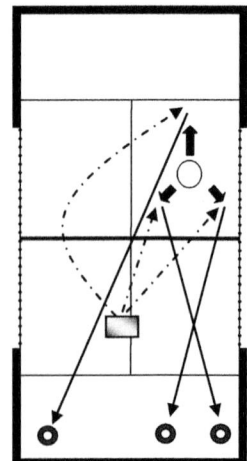

Exercise 0745   Hits: V – Rm

Target: Play on the net, volley and shot.
Striking sequence: VD al middle – RmX – VR// strong

Description:
Located player near the net, perform a forehand volley at the middle, a crossed over shot and a strong parallel backhand volley, with the target of the marks on the back of the court.
After 12 balls is changed player.

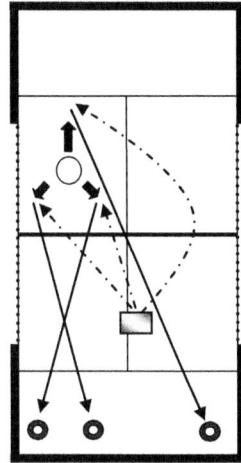

Exercise 0746   Hits: V – Rm

Target: Combination of hits with movement
Striking sequence: VD// o VR// – Rm//

Description:
Located players close to the net, perform a parallel forehand volley or a parallel backhand volley, as the area where they are, and then a parallel shot, with the target of the marks on the back of the court.
After 10 balls position players alternates.

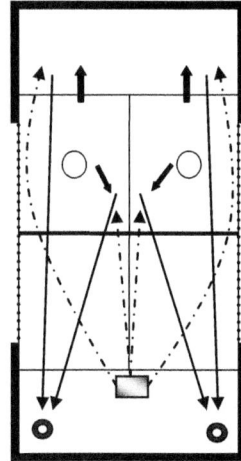

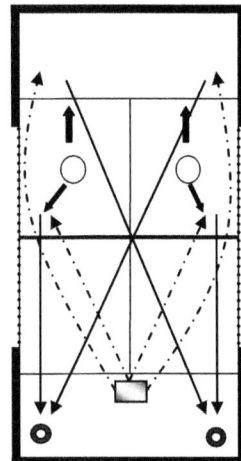

Exercise 0747   Hits: V – Rm

Target: Combination of hits with movement
Striking sequence: VD// o VR// – RmX

Description:
Located players close to the net, perform a parallel forehand volley or a parallel backhand volley, as the area where they are, and then a crossed over shot, with the target of the marks on the back of the court.
After 10 balls position players alternates.

Exercise 0748   Hits: V – Rm

Target: Combination of hits with movement
Striking sequence: VR middle – RmX

Description:
Set the player near the net, perform a backhand volley to the middle and a crossed over shot, with the target of the marks on the back of the court.
After the exercise will again row.

Exercise 0749   Hits: V – Rm

Target: Combination of hits with movement
Striking sequence: VD middle – RmX

Description:
Set the player near the net, perform a forehand volley to the middle and a crossed over shot, with the target of the marks on the back of the court.
After the exercise will again row.

Exercise 0750   Hits: V – Rm

Target: Combination of hits with movement
Striking sequence: VDX – RmX

Description:
Located player near the net, perform a crossed over forehand volley and delayed enough for a crossed over shot to the peak, with the target of the marks on the back of the court.
After the exercise will again row.

Exercise 0751   Hits: V – Rm

Target: Combination of hits with movement
Striking sequence: VRX – RmX

Description:
Located player near the net, perform a crossed over backhand volley and delayed enough for a crossed over shot to the peak, with the target of the marks on the back of the court.
After the exercise will again row.

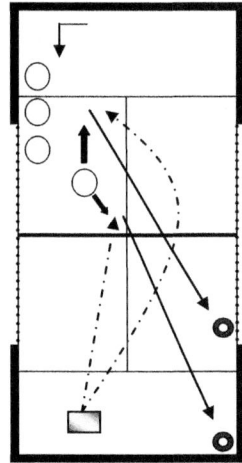

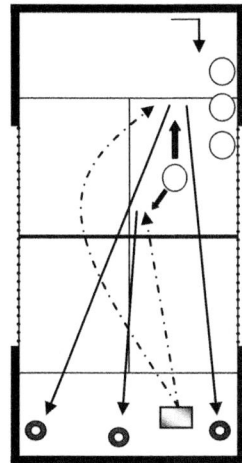

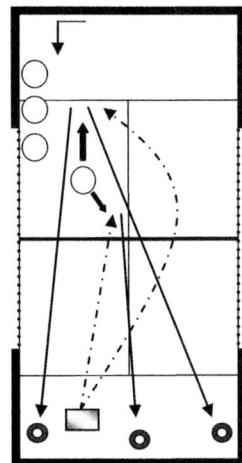

Exercise 0752   Hits: V – Rm

Target: Combination of hits with movement
Striking sequence: RmX – VD middle – Rm//

Description:
Set the player near the net, perform a crossed over shot, will rise to the net for a forehand volley at the middle and slow enough for a parallel shot, with the target of the marks on the back of the court .
After the exercise will again row.

Exercise 0753   Hits: V – Rm

Target: Combination of hits with movement
Striking sequence: RmX – VR middle – Rm//

Description:
Set the player near the net, perform a crossed over shot, will rise to the net for a backhand volley at the middle and slow enough for a parallel shot, with the target of the marks on the back of the court .
After the exercise will again row.

Exercise 0754   Hits: V – Rm

Target: Combination of hits with effort
Striking sequence: RmX – VR middle – VD//

Description:
Located player on the line of serve, hits a crossed over shot to the peak and rise to the net to make a backhand volley at the middle and a parallel forehand volley into the corner, with the target of the marks at the bottom of the court.
After 12 balls is changed player.

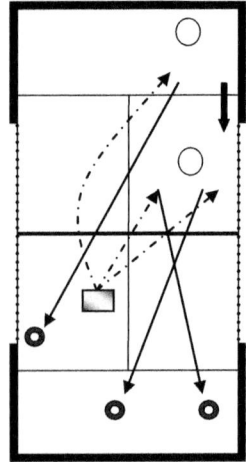

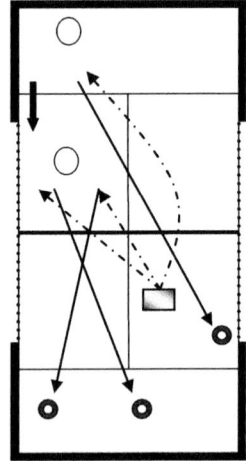

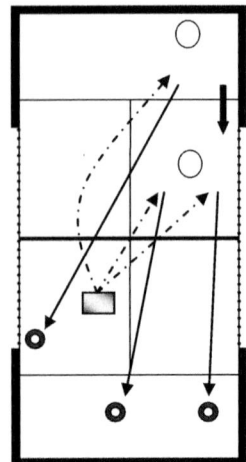

Exercise 0755   Hits: V – Rm

Target: Combination of hits with effort
Striking sequence: RmX – VD middle – VR//

Description:
Located player on the line of serve, hits a crossed over shot to the peak and rise to the net to make a forehand volley at the middle and a parallel backhand volley into the corner, with the target of the marks at the bottom of the court.
After 12 balls is changed player.

Exercise 0756   Hits: V – Rm

Target: Combination of hits with effort
Striking sequence: RmX – VR// – VD middle

Description:
Located player on the line of serve, hits a crossed over shot to the peak and rise to the net to make a parallel backhand volley to the corner and a strong forehand volley to the middle, with the target of the marks at the bottom of the court.
After 12 balls is changed player.

Exercise 0757   Hits: V – Rm

Target: Combination of hits with effort
Striking sequence: RmX – VD// – VR middle

Description:
Located player on the line of serve, hits a crossed over shot to the peak and rise to the net to make a parallel forehand volley to the corner and a strong backhand volley to the middle, with the target of the marks at the bottom of the court.
After 12 balls is changed player.

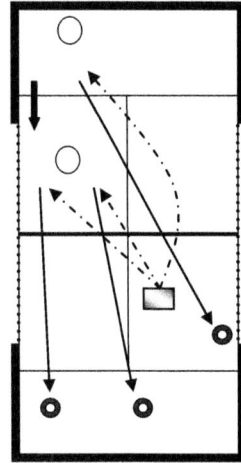

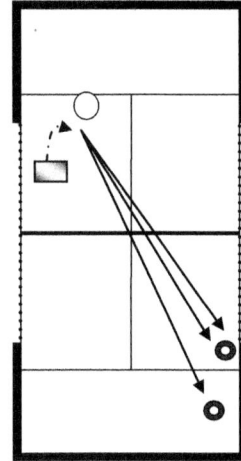

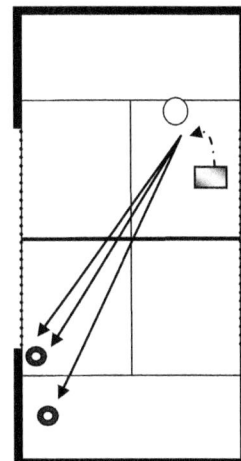

Exercise 0758   Hits: V – Rm

Target: Volley and shot
Striking sequence: VDX – VDX – RmX

Description:
Located players next to the monitor in half court, they throw balls to carry out two forehand volleys to the grid and a crossed over shot, with the target of the marks on the court.
After 12 balls is changed player.

Exercise 0759   Hits: V – Rm

Target: Volley and shot
Striking sequence: VRX – VRX – RmX

Description:
Located players next to the monitor in half court, they throw balls to carry out two backhand volleys to the grid and a crossed over shot, with the target of the marks on the court.
After 12 balls is changed player.

Exercise 0760   Hits: V – Rm

Target: Volley and shot
Striking sequence: VDX – VDX – Rm//

Description:
Located next to the monitor in half court players, they throw balls to carry out two forehand volleys to the grid and a parallel shot, with the target of the marks on the court.
After 12 balls is changed player.

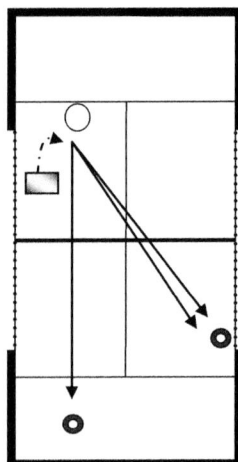

Exercise 0761   Hits: V – Rm

Target: Volley and shot
Striking sequence: VRX – VRX – Rm//

Description:
Located next to the monitor in half court players, they throw balls to carry out two backhand volleys to the grid and a parallel shot, with the target of the marks on the court.
After 12 balls is changed player.

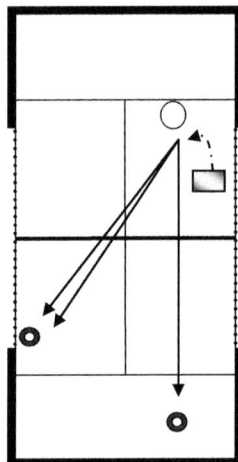

Exercise 0762   Hits: V – Rm

Target: Volley and shot
Striking sequence: VDX – VDX – Rm//

Description:
Set the player at the bottom of the court and the monitor in half court, will throw balls to make two forehand volleys to the grid and a parallel shot, after each stroke will go to the bottom and touch the cone, so all hits he will be thrown forward with race, with the target of the marks on the court.
After 12 balls is changed player.

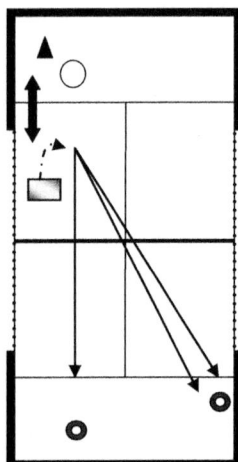

Exercise 0763   Hits: V – Rm

Target: Volley and shot
Striking sequence: VRX – VRX – Rm//

Description:
Set the player at the bottom of the court and the monitor in half court, will throw balls to make two backhand volleys to the grid and a parallel shot, after each stroke will go to the bottom and touch the cone, so all hits he will be thrown forward with race, with the target of the marks on the court.
After 12 balls is changed player.

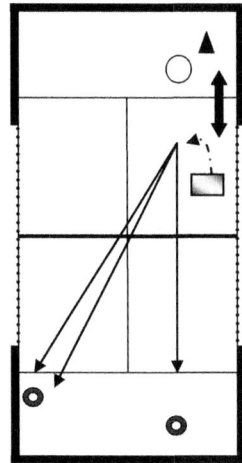

Exercise 0764   Hits: V – Rm

Target: Shot plane
Striking sequence: Rm// - VR//

Description:
Set the player near the net, made shot parallel using flat shoulders with low speed to start to do it and a parallel backhand volley with the target of the mark on the back of the court.
After 10 balls is changed player.

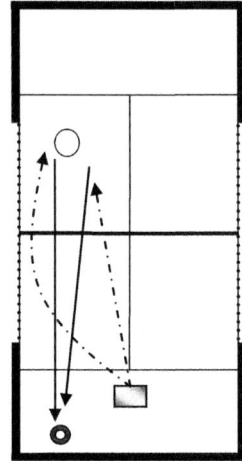

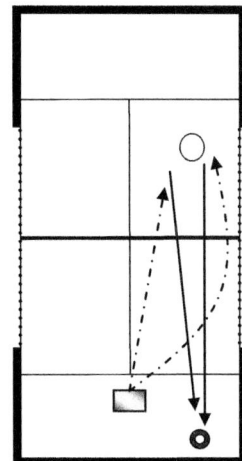

Exercise 0765   Hits: V – Rm

Target: Shot plane
Striking sequence: Rm// - VD//

Description:
Set the player near the net, made shot parallel using flat shoulders with low speed to start to do it and a parallel forehand volley with the target of the mark on the back of the court.
After 10 balls is changed player.

Exercise 0766   Hits: V – Rm

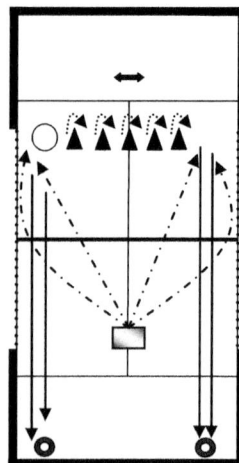

Target: Lateral displacement
Striking sequence: VD// - Rm// - VR// - Rm//

Description:
Located player in the back of the court at the height of the peak will hold a parallel forehand volley and a parallel shot, and moves laterally without touching the cones and always with the opposite leg to the movement ahead (with this movement we simulate the position of the volley), and upon arrival we will make a parallel backhand volley and a parallel shot.
After 8-ball player is changed.

Exercise 0767   Hits: V – Rm

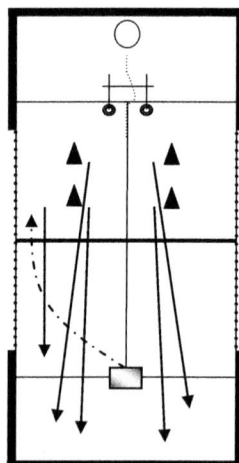

Target: Volley displacement
Striking sequence: Jump–VD//– VR// – VD// –VR//-Rm//

Description:
Located player in the back of the court at the height of the T will make a jump over the bar and a parallel forehand volley and a parallel backhand volley with lateral displacement upward, finishing with a parallel shot.

Exercise 0768   Hits: V – Rm

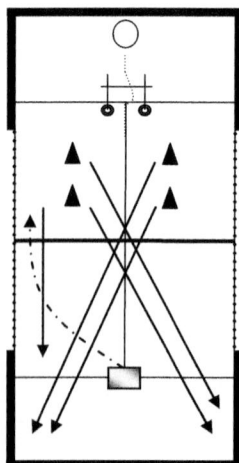

Target: Volley displacement
Striking sequence: Jump–VDX – VRX – VDX – VRX-Rm//

Description:
Located player in the back of the court at the height of the T will make a jump over the bar and a crossed over forehand volley and a crossed over backhand volley with lateral displacement upward, finishing with a parallel shot.

Exercise 0769   Hits: V – Rm

Target: Combination of hits
Striking sequence: VD middle – VR// – VD middle – Rm//

Description:
Set the player at the bottom of the court, perform an approach forehand volley to the middle and go up to the net to make a parallel backhand volley. You return to the starting position for another approach forehand volley to the middle and ends with a power parallel shot, with the target of the marks on the back of the court.
After 12 balls is changed player.

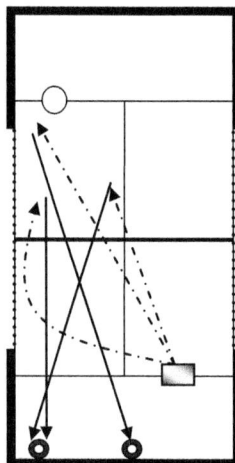

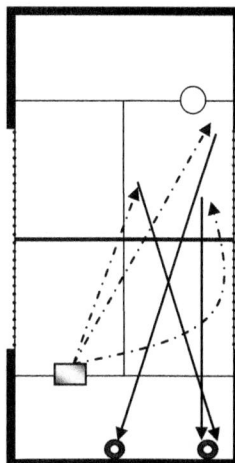

Exercise 0770   Hits: V – Rm

Target: Combination of hits
Striking sequence: VR middle – VD// – VR middle – Rm//

Description:
Set the player at the bottom of the court, perform an approach backhand volley to the middle and go up to the net to make a parallel forehand volley. You return to the starting position for another approach backhand volley to the middle and ends with a power parallel shot, with the target of the marks on the back of the court.
After 12 balls is changed player.

Exercise 0771   Hits: V – Rm

Target: Combination of hits
Striking sequence: RmX – VRX

Description:
Set the player near the net, hits a crossed over shot and rise to the net for a crossed over backhand volley to the grid, with the target of the marks on the court.
After 10 balls is changed player.

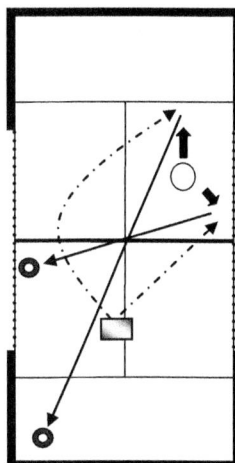

Exercise 0772   Hits: V – Rm

Target: Combination of hits
Striking sequence: RmX – VDX

Description:
Set the player near the net, hits a crossed over shot and rise to the net for a crossed over forehand volley to the grid, with the target of the marks on the court.
After 10 balls is changed player.

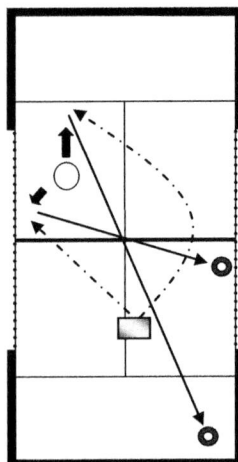

EXERCISES COMBINATION: VOLLEY, VOLLEY TRAY

Exercise 0773   Hits: V – Bd

Target: Combination of strokes moving
Striking sequence: VDX – VRX – BdX

Description:
A player works with the monitor to finish the ball trolley. Located near the net, perform a crossed over forehand volley, a crossed over backhand volley and a crossed over volley tray, returning back to the starting position. The target will be the mark on the corner of the court. The other two players perform control ball, one from the bottom and the other on the volley.
After completing the ball trolley position players alternates.

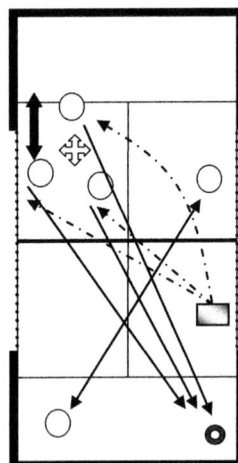

Exercise 0774   Hits: V – Bd

Target: Alternate hits moving
Striking sequence: VRX – VDX – BdX

Description:
A player works with the monitor to finish the ball trolley. Located near the net, perform a crossed over backhand volley, a crossed over forehand volley and a crossed over volley tray, returning back to the starting position. The target will be the mark on the corner of the court. The other two players perform control ball, one from the bottom and the other on the volley.
After completing the ball trolley position players alternates.

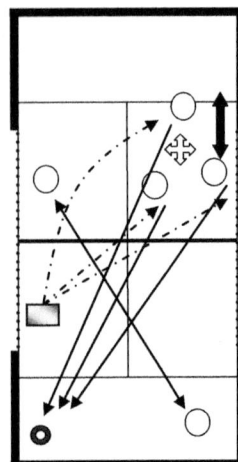

Exercise 0775   Hits: V – Bd

Target: Keep net with volley and volley tray (Bd)
Striking sequence: VD// - Bd// - VD// - Bd//

Description:
Set the player near the net, alternate parallel forehand volleys and parallel volley trays (Bd) to the target in the background court line.
After 12 balls is changed player.

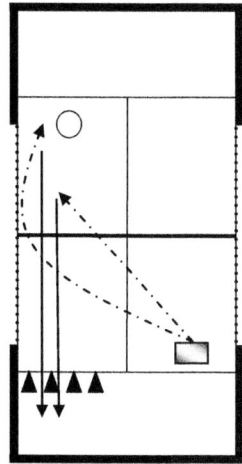

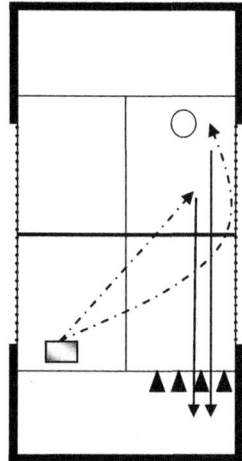

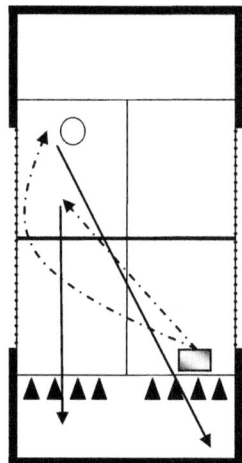

Exercise 0776   Hits: V – Bd

Target: Keep net with volley and Volley Tray (Bd)
Striking sequence: VR// - Bd// - VR// - Bd//

Description:
Set the player near the net, alternate parallel backhand volleys and parallel volley trays (Bd) to the target in the background court line.
After 12 balls is changed player.

Exercise 0777   Hits: V – Bd

Target: Keep net with volley and Volley Tray (Bd)
Striking sequence: VD// - BdX - VD// - BdX

Description:
Set the player near the net, alternate parallel forehand volleys and crossed over volley trays (Bd) to the target in the background court line.
After 12 balls is changed player.

Exercise 0778   Hits: V – Bd

Target: Keep net with volley and Volley Tray (Bd)
Striking sequence: VR// - BdX - VR// - BdX

Description:
Set the player near the net, alternate parallel backhand volleys and crossed over volley trays (Bd) to the target in the background court line.
After 12 balls is changed player.

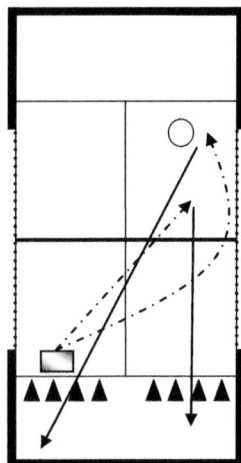

Exercise 0779   Hits: V – Bd

Target: Keep net with volley and Volley Tray (Bd)
Striking sequence: VDX - BdX - VDX - BdX

Description:
Set the player near the net, alternate crossed over forehand volleys and crossed over volley trays (Bd) to the target in the background court line.
After 12 balls is changed player.

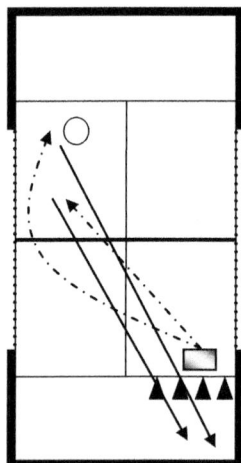

Exercise 0780   Hits: V – Bd

Target: Coordination of movements in volley and Volley Tray (Bd)
Striking sequence: VDX - BdX

Description:
Located the player near cones located in the middle of the court, will make a jump over them to attack with a crossed over forehand volley. Then perform a lateral displacement to exceed the other cone and perform a lateral displacement to stand back and make a crossed over volley tray (Bd). Important lateral displacements and placement prior to volley tray (Bd).
Then it is done on the other side with a crossed over backhand volley and a crossed over volley tray.

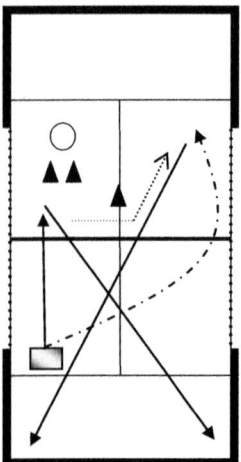

Exercise 0781   Hits: V – Bd

Target: Combination of volley and Volley Tray (Bd)s
Striking sequence: BdX–VRX–BdX–VRX–BdX-VRX

Description:
Located player near the net, alternate to height of each black cone a crossed over volley tray and to height of each white cone a crossed over backhand volley, with the target of the mark on the corner of the court. The volley trays will be progressively longer.
After finishing the series, the player returns to the line.

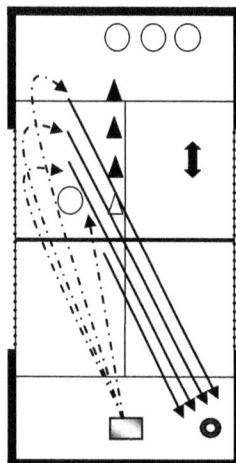

Exercise 0782   Hits: V – Bd

Target: Combination of volley and Volley Tray (Bd)s
Striking sequence: BdX–VDX–BdX–VDX–BdX-VDX

Description:
Located player near the net, alternate to height of each black cone a crossed over volley tray and to height of each white cone a crossed over forehand volley, with the target of the mark on the corner of the court. The volley trays will be progressively longer.
After finishing the series, the player returns to the line.

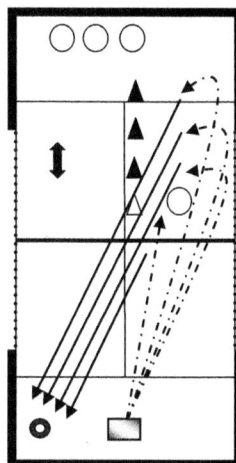

Exercise 0783   Hits: V – Bd

Target: Combination of volley and Volley Tray (Bd)s
Striking sequence: BdX–VD//–BdX–VD//–BdX-VD//

Description:
Located player near the net, alternate to height of each black cone a crossed over volley tray and to height of each white cone a parallel backhand volley, with the target of the mark on the corner of the court. The volley trays will be progressively longer.
After finishing the series, the player returns to the line.

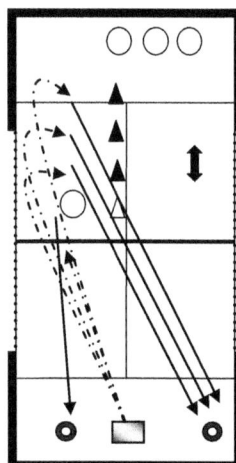

Exercise 0784   Hits: V – Bd

Target: Combination of volley and Volley Tray (Bd)s
Striking sequence: BdX–VR//–BdX–VR//–BdX-VR//

Description:
Located player near the net, alternate to height of each black cone a crossed over volley tray and to height of each black cone a parallel forehand volley, with the target of the mark on the corner of the court. The volley trays will be progressively longer.
After finishing the series, the player returns to the line.

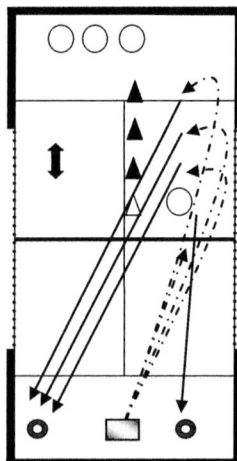

Exercise 0785   Hits: CP – V – Bd

Target: Combination of hits with movement
Striking sequence: CP – VD// - BdX

Description:
Set the player at the bottom of the court, retrieves a ball against wall, up to the net for a parallel forehand volley and a crossed over volley tray, with the target of marks the bottom of the court.
After 12 balls is changed player.

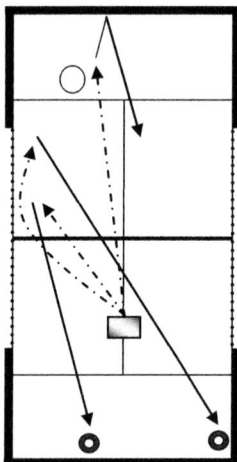

Exercise 0786   Hits: CP – V – Bd

Target: Combination of hits with movement
Striking sequence: CP – VR// - BdX

Description:
Set the player at the bottom of the court, retrieves a ball against wall, up to the net for a parallel backhand volley and a crossed over volley tray, with the target of marks the bottom of the court.
After 12 balls is changed player.

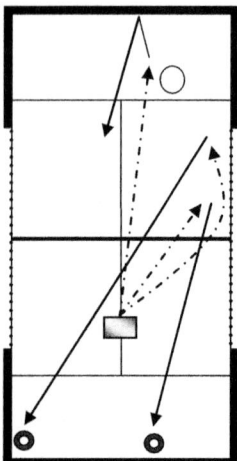

Exercise 0787   Hits: V – Bd

Target: Combination of hits
Striking sequence: VDX – VR// - BdX

Description:
Located player near the net, hold a crossed over forehand volley and a parallel backhand volley, and backward enough to make a crossed over volley tray (Bd), with the target of the marks on the back of the court.
After 12 balls is changed player.

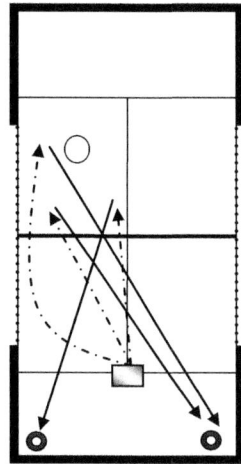

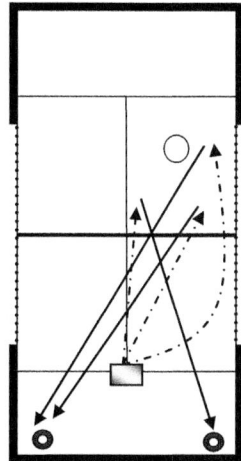

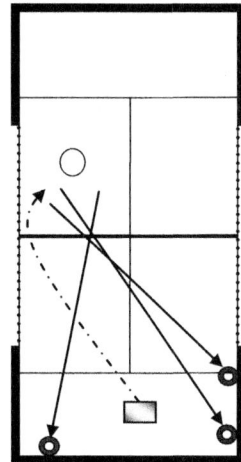

Exercise 0788   Hits: V – Bd

Target: Combination of hits
Striking sequence: VRX – VD// - BdX

Description:
Located player near the net, hold a crossed over backhand volley and a parallel forehand volley, and backward enough to make a crossed over volley tray (Bd), with the target of the marks on the back of the court.
After 12 balls is changed player.

Exercise 0789   Hits: V – Bd

Target: Combination of volley and volley tray (Bd)
Striking sequence: BdX - VR// - BdX - VDX

Description:
Set the player near the net, hold a crossed over volley tray to recover the net and make a parallel backhand volley. It will be delayed again to make a crossed over volley tray and make a crossed over forehand volley, the entire target marks on the back of the court.
After 12 balls is changed player.

Exercise 0790   Hits: V – Bd

Target: Combination of volley and volley tray (Bd)
Striking sequence: BdX - VD// - BdX - VRX

Description:
Set the player near the net, hold a crossed over volley tray to recover the net and make a parallel forehand volley. It will be delayed again to make a crossed over volley tray and make a crossed over backhand volley, the entire target marks on the back of the court.
After 12 balls is changed player.

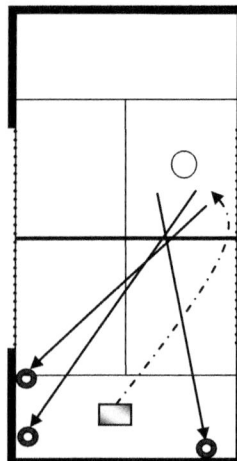

Exercise 0791   Hits: V – Bd

Target: Combination of volley and Volley Tray (Bd)s
Striking sequence: VD// - Bd// - VRX - BdX

Description:
Set the player near the net, perform a parallel forehand volley, it will be delayed for a parallel volley tray and close the middle with a crossed over backhand volley and again delayed to make a crossed over volley tray, all with the target of brands located on the back of the court.
After 12 balls is changed player.

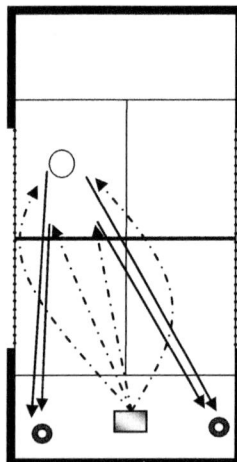

Exercise 0792   Hits: V – Bd

Target: Combination of volley and Volley Tray (Bd)s
Striking sequence: VR// - Bd// - VDX - BdX

Description:
Set the player near the net, perform a parallel backhand volley, it will be delayed for a parallel volley tray and close the middle with a crossed over forehand volley and again delayed to make a crossed over volley tray, all with the target of brands located on the back of the court.
After 12 balls is changed player.

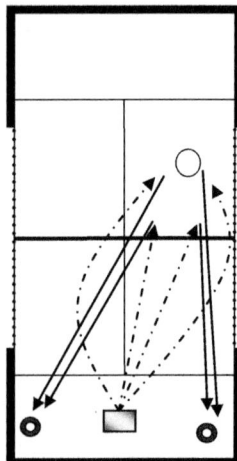

Exercise 0793   Hits: V – Bd

Target: Combination of volley and Volley Tray (Bd)s
Striking sequence: VD// –Bd// – VD// - Bd//

Description:
The monitor throws balls by hand to return the pupil to monitor the following balls: white low ball of forehand, volley tray (Bd) on the bottom line, white low ball of forehand, volley tray (Bd) on line and repeat the exercise.
All soft balls are returned to the monitor.
After 12 balls is changed player.

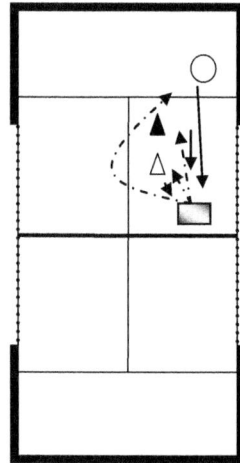

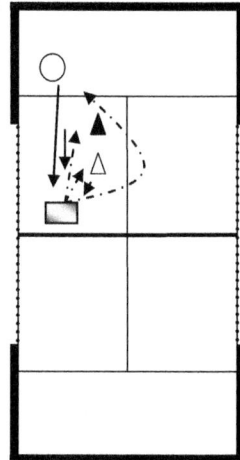

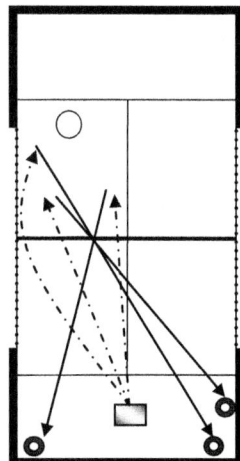

Exercise 0794   Hits: V – Bd

Target: Combination of volley and Volley Tray (Bd)s
Striking sequence: VR// –Bd// – VR// - Bd//

Description:
The monitor throws balls by hand to return the pupil to monitor the following balls: white low ball of backhand, volley tray (Bd) on the bottom line, white low ball of backhand, volley tray (Bd) on line and repeat the exercise.
All soft balls are returned to the monitor.
After 12 balls is changed player.

Exercise 0795   Hits: V – Bd

Target: Keep net
Striking sequence: VR// - BdX - VDX

Description:
Set the player near the net, trying to keep the net with a parallel backhand volley, a crossed over volley tray and a crossed over forehand volley tray, with the target of the marks on the back of the court.
After each volley tray (Bd), we close the middle, as it is possible for a ball instead.
After 12 balls is changed player.

Exercise 0796   Hits: V – Bd

Target: Keep net
Striking sequence: VRX - BdX – VD//

Description:
Set the player near the net, trying to keep the net with a crossed over backhand volley, a crossed over volley tray and a parallel forehand volley tray, with the target of the marks on the back of the court.
After each volley tray (Bd), we close the middle, as it is possible for a ball instead.
After 12 balls is changed player.

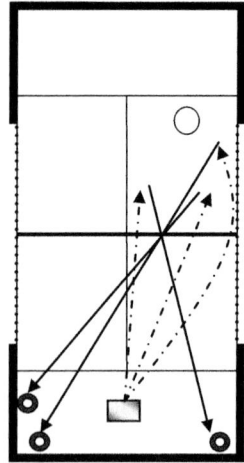

Exercise 0797   Hits: V – Bd

Target: Close the middle after viper (víbora)
Striking sequence: BdX – VR//

Description:
Set the player near the net, we try to keep it and close the middle with a parallel backhand volley after each power crossed over volley tray (Viper), with the target of the marks on the back of the court.
After 10 balls is changed player.

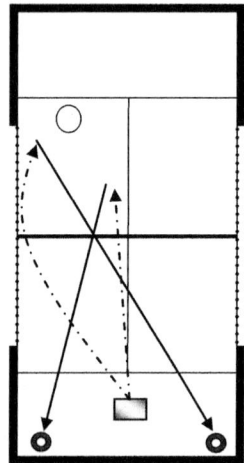

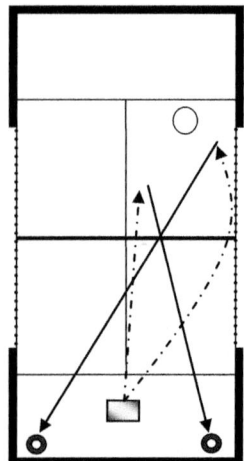

Exercise 0798   Hits: V – Bd

Target: Close the middle after viper (víbora)
Striking sequence: BdX – VD//

Description:
Set the player near the net, we try to keep it and close the middle with a parallel forehand volley after each power crossed over volley tray (Viper), with the target of the marks on the back of the court.
After 10 balls is changed player.

Exercise 0799   Hits: SF – V – Bd

Target: Attack crossed over
Striking sequence: VRX – BdX – VD x3 – CPD

Description:
Set the player near the net, hold a crossed over backhand volley and a crossed over volley tray to keep the net, then hit three power crossed over forehand volleys, with the target of the marks on the back of the court, and end running in crossed over to a ball against wall of forehand, with the target of the mark on the corner of the court.
After 12 balls is changed player.

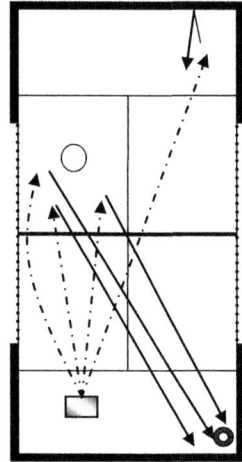

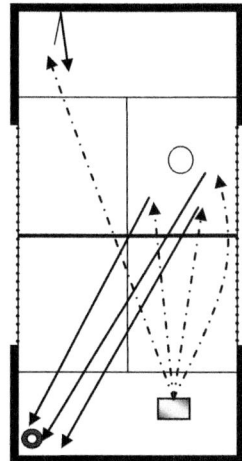

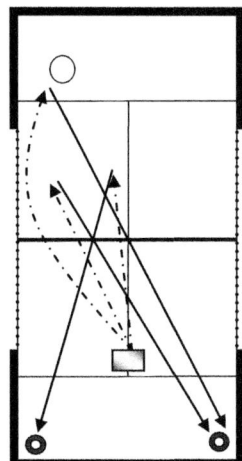

Exercise 0800   Hits: SF – V – Bd

Target: Attack crossed over
Striking sequence: VDX – BdX – VR x3 – CPR

Description:
Set the player near the net, hold a crossed over forehand volley and a crossed over volley tray to keep the net, then hit three power crossed over backhand volleys, with the target of the marks on the back of the court, and end running in crossed over to a ball against wall of forehand, with the target of the mark on the corner of the court.
After 12 balls is changed player.

Exercise 0801   Hits: V – Bd

Target: Combination of hits
Striking sequence: BdX – VR// - VDX

Description:
Set the player on the bottom line, hold a crossed over volley tray (Bd) that will rise to the net closing the middle to make a parallel backhand volley and a crossed over forehand volley, with the target of the marks at the bottom of the court.
After 12 balls is changed player.

Exercise 0802   Hits: V – Bd

Target: Combination of hits
Striking sequence: BdX – VD// - VRX

Description:
Set the player on the bottom line, hold a crossed over volley tray (Bd) that will rise to the net closing the middle to make a parallel forehand volley and a crossed over backhand volley, with the target of the marks at the bottom of the court.
After 12 balls is changed player.

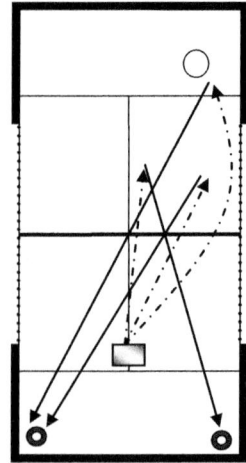

Exercise 0803   Hits: V – Bd

Target: Relay on the net
Striking sequence: VD// – VD// – BdX – VR// – VRX

Description:
Exercise relay between partners. The player of the drive performs two parallel forehand volleys to progress to the net, you do a lob and the partner of the left covers her back and makes a crossed over volley tray). There is an exchange of positions. The drive is now closed the backhand and makes a parallel backhand volley and backhand player who is now in the drive closes the center with crossed over backhand volley.

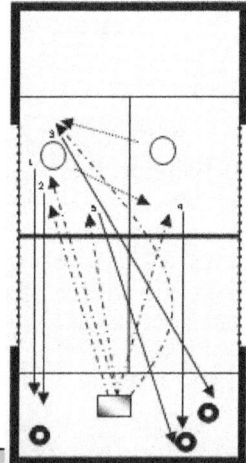

EXERCISES COMBINATION: VOLLEY TRAY (BD), SHOT

Exercise 0804   Hits: Bd – Rm

Target: Volley tray (Bd) and shot
Striking sequence: BdX – BdX – RmX

Description:
Located monitor at the back of the court with the player, will throw balls to make two volley trays to the grid and a crossed over shot, with the target of the marks on the court.
After 12 balls is changed player.

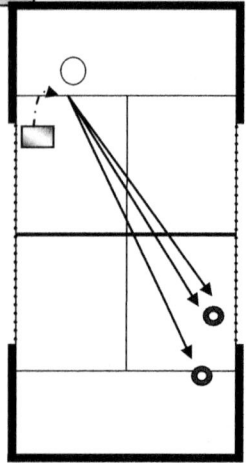

Exercise 0805   Hits: Bd – Rm

Target: Volley tray (Bd) and shot
Striking sequence: BdX – BdX – RmX

Description:
Located monitor at the back of the court with the player, will throw balls to make two volley trays to the grid and a crossed over shot, with the target of the marks on the court.
After 12 balls is changed player.

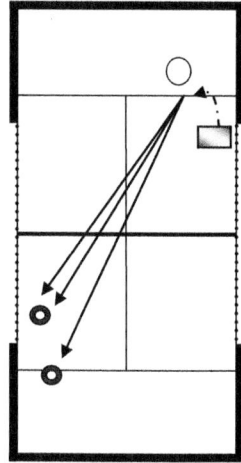

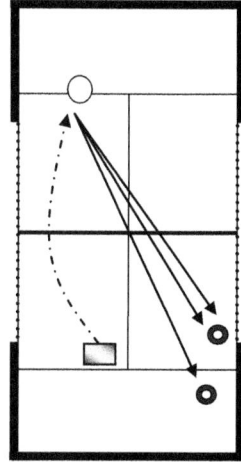

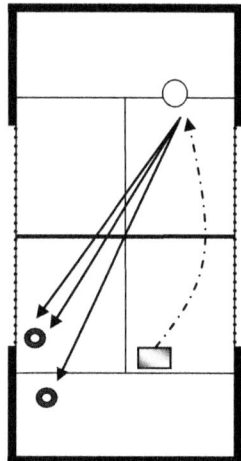

Exercise 0806   Hits: Bd – Rm

Target: Volley tray (Bd) and shot
Striking sequence: BdX – BdX – RmX

Description:
Located monitor at the back of the court with the player, will throw balls to make two volley trays to the peak and a crossed over shot, with the target of the marks on the court.
After 12 balls is changed player.

Exercise 0807   Hits: Bd – Rm

Target: Volley tray (Bd) and shot
Striking sequence: BdX – BdX – RmX

Description:
Located monitor at the back of the court with the player, will throw balls to make two volley trays to the peak and a crossed over shot, with the target of the marks on the court.
After 12 balls is changed player.

Exercise 0808   Hits: Bd – Rm

Target: Volley tray (Bd) and shot
Striking sequence: BdX – BdX – Rm//

Description:
Set the monitor in half court with the player, will throw balls to make two crossed over volley trays and a parallel shot, with the target of the marks on the court.
After 12 balls is changed player.

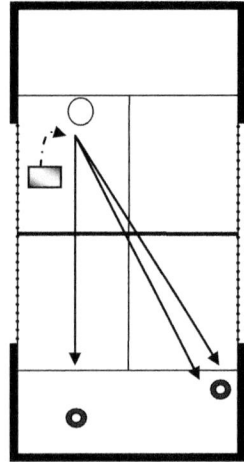

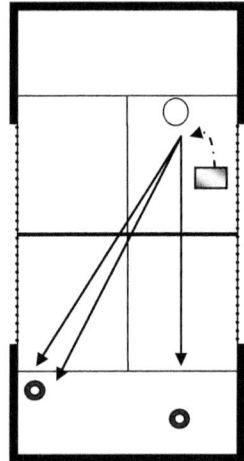

Exercise 0809   Hits: Bd – Rm

Target: Volley tray (Bd) and shot
Striking sequence: BdX – BdX – Rm//

Description:
Set the monitor in half court with the player, will throw balls to make two crossed over volley trays and a parallel shot, with the target of the marks on the court.
After 12 balls is changed player.

Exercise 0810   Hits: Bd – Rm

Target: Volley tray (Bd) and shot
Striking sequence: BdX – Bd// – RmX

Description:
Located monitor in half court with the player will throw balls to perform a crossed over volley tray, a parallel volley tray and a crossed over shot, with the target of the marks on the court and after every shot will go to the bottom and touch cone, so all hits will be thrown forward with race.
After 12 balls is changed player.

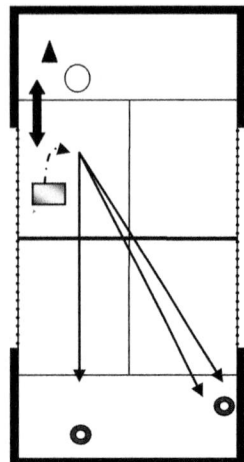

Exercise 0811   Hits: Bd – Rm

Target: Volley tray (Bd) and shot
Striking sequence: BdX – Bd// – RmX

Description:
Located monitor in half court with the player will throw balls to perform a crossed over volley tray, a parallel volley tray and a crossed over shot, with the target of the marks on the court and after every shot will go to the bottom and touch cone, so all hits will be thrown forward with race.
After 12 balls is changed player.

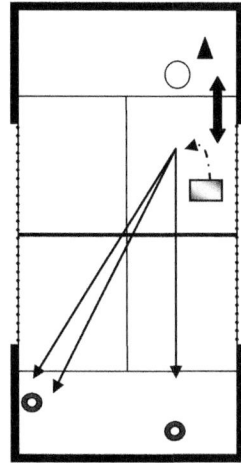

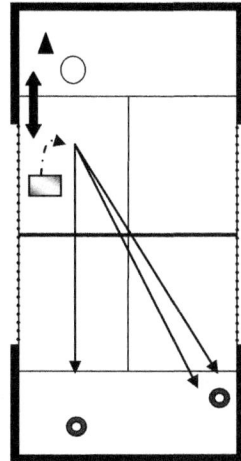

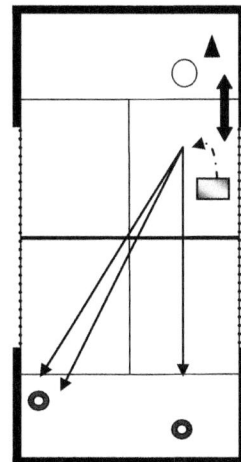

Exercise 0812   Hits: Bd – Rm

Target: Volley tray (Bd) and shot
Striking sequence: BdX – BdX – Rm//

Description:
Located monitor in half court with the player will throw balls to perform two crossed over volley tray and a parallel shot, with the target of the marks on the court and after every shot will go to the bottom and touch cone, so all hits will be thrown forward with race.
After 12 balls is changed player.

Exercise 0813   Hits: Bd – Rm

Target: Volley tray (Bd) and shot
Striking sequence: BdX – BdX – Rm//

Description:
Located monitor in half court with the player will throw balls to perform two crossed over volley tray and a parallel shot, with the target of the marks on the court and after every shot will go to the bottom and touch cone, so all hits will be thrown forward with race.
After 12 balls is changed player.

Exercise 0814   Hits: V – Bd – Rm

Target: Combination of hits
Striking sequence: VDX – BdX - RmX

Description:
Located player near the net performs a crossed over forehand volley, a crossed over volley tray and a crossed over shot, with the target of the mark on the back of the court.
After 12 balls is changed player.

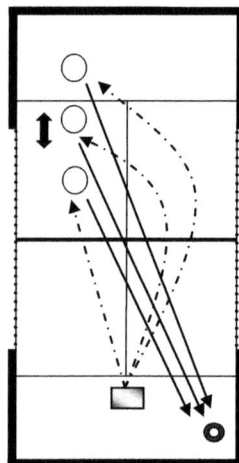

Exercise 0815   Hits: V – Bd – Rm

Target: Combination of hits
Striking sequence: VRX – BdX - RmX

Description:
Located player near the net performs a crossed over backhand volley, a crossed over volley tray and a crossed over shot, with the target of the mark on the back of the court.
After 12 balls is changed player.

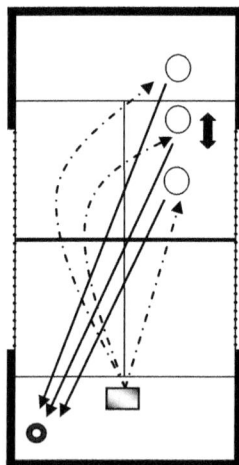

Exercise 0816   Hits: V – Bd – Rm

Target: Combination of hits
Striking sequence: VDX – BdX – Rm//

Description:
Located player near the net performs a crossed over forehand volley, a crossed over volley tray and a parallel shot, with the target of the mark on the back of the court.
After 12 balls is changed player.

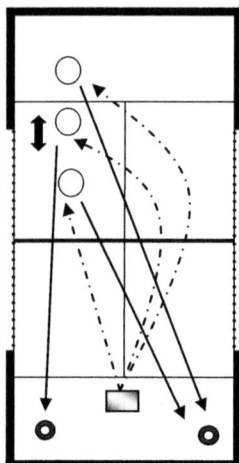

Exercise 0817   Hits: V – Bd – Rm

Target: Combination of hits
Striking sequence: VRX – BdX – Rm//

Description:
Located player near the net performs a crossed over backhand volley, a crossed over volley tray and a parallel shot, with the target of the mark on the back of the court.
After 12 balls is changed player.

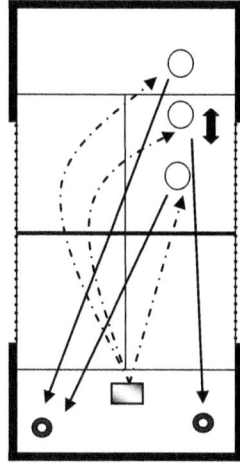

Exercise 0818   Hits: V – Bd – Rm

Target: Combination of hits in attack
Striking sequence: Bd// - VD// - Let D – VR// - Rm//

Description:
Set the player near the net performs all the hits in parallel with the following sequence: parallel volley tray (Bd), parallel forehand volley, let forehand, attack with a power parallel backhand volley and ends with a parallel shot with the target of the marks on the back of the court.
After 12 balls is changed player.

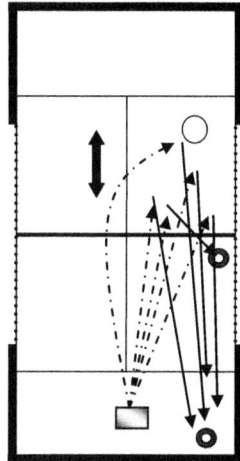

Exercise 0819   Hits: V – Bd – Rm

Target: Combination of hits in attack
Striking sequence: Bd// - VR// - Let R – VD// - Rm//

Description:
Set the player near the net performs all the hits in parallel with the following sequence: parallel volley tray (Bd), parallel forehand volley, let forehand, attack with a power parallel backhand volley and ends with a parallel shot with the target of the marks on the back of the court.
After 12 balls is changed player.

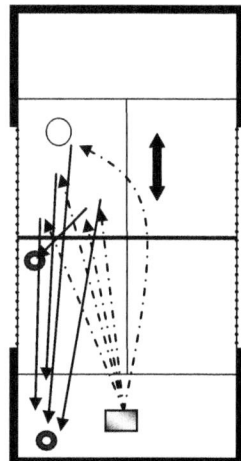

Exercise 0820   Hits: V – Bd – Rm

Target: Combination of hits
Striking sequence: VRX – Let D – BdX – RmX

Description:
Set the player near the net combines the following hits: crossed over backhand volley, let to the grid of forehand, crossed over volley tray and a crossed over shot, with the target of the marks on the court.
After 12 balls is changed player.

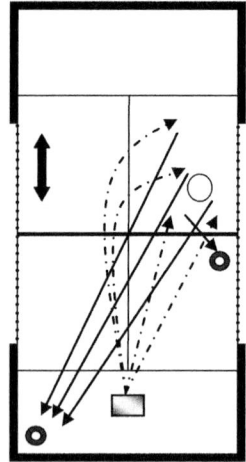

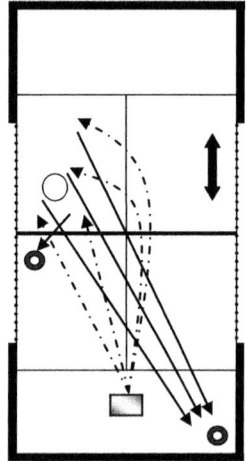

Exercise 0821   Hits: V – Bd – Rm

Target: Combination of hits
Striking sequence: VDX – Let R – BdX – RmX

Description:
Set the player near the net combines the following hits: crossed over forehand volley, let to the grid of forehand, crossed over volley tray and a crossed over shot, with the target of the marks on the court.
After 12 balls is changed player.

Exercise 0822   Hits: V – Bd – Rm

Target: Combination of hits
Striking sequence: VDX – VR// - BdX – VDX – VR// - RmX

Description:
Located player near the net will hold a crossed over forehand volley and a parallel backhand volley, be delayed to make a crossed over volley tray to recover the net and follow with a crossed over forehand volley and a parallel backhand volley. It will end with a power crossed over shot. All hits to the target of the marks on the court.
After 10 balls is changed player.

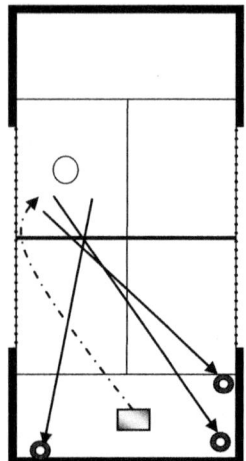

Exercise 0823   Hits: V – Bd – Rm

Target: Combination of hits
Striking sequence: VRX – VD// - BdX – VRX – VD// - RmX

Description:
Located player near the net will hold a crossed over backhand volley and a parallel forehand volley, be delayed to make a crossed over volley tray to recover the net and follow with a crossed over backhand volley and a parallel forehand volley. It will end with a power crossed over shot. All hits to the target of the marks on the court. After 10 balls is changed player.

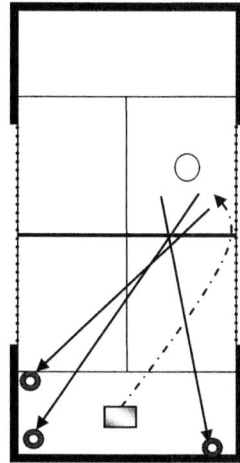

Exercise 0824   Hits: V – Bd – Rm

Target: Combination of hits
Striking sequence: VDX x3– VR// x3 - BdX – Rm//

Description:
Located player near the net, he makes six volleys alternating crossed over forehand and crossed over backhand, it will be delayed to make a crossed over volley tray and ends with a power parallel shot, with the target of the marks on the back of the court.

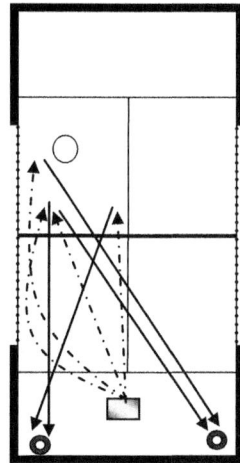

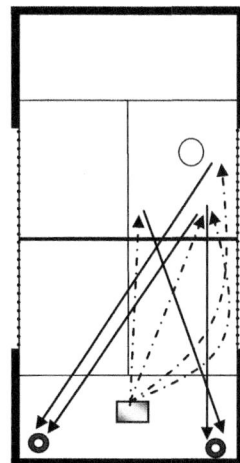

Exercise 0825   Hits: V – Bd – Rm

Target: Combination of hits
Striking sequence: VD// x3 – VRX x3 - BdX – Rm//

Description:
Located player near the net, he makes six volleys alternating crossed over forehand and crossed over backhand, it will be delayed to make a crossed over volley tray and ends with a power parallel shot, with the target of the marks on the back of the court.

Exercise 0826   Hits: V – Bd – Rm

Target: Combination of hits
Striking sequence: BdX – VDX – RmX

Description:
Located player on the line of serve, hold a crossed over volley tray with which he will go to the net to make a short crossed over forehand volley and back down to make a crossed over shot, with the target of the marks on the court.
After 12 balls is changed player.

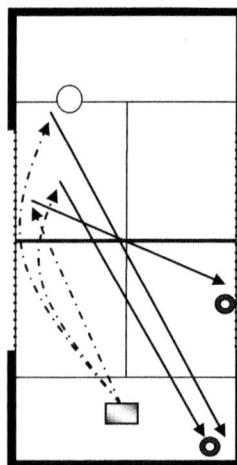

Exercise 0827   Hits: V – Bd – Rm

Target: Combination of hits
Striking sequence: BdX – VRX – RmX

Description:
Located player on the line of serve, hold a crossed over volley tray with which he will go to the net to make a short crossed over backhand volley and back down to make a crossed over shot, with the target of the marks on the court.
After 12 balls is changed player.

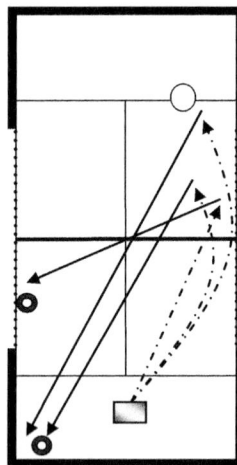

Exercise 0828   Hits: V – Bd – Rm

Target: Combination of hits
Striking sequence: Bd// – VD// - Rm//

Description:
Located player on the line of serve, perform a parallel volley tray which will rise to the net to make a parallel forehand volley and back down to make a parallel shot with the target of the bottom of the court.
After 12 balls is changed player.

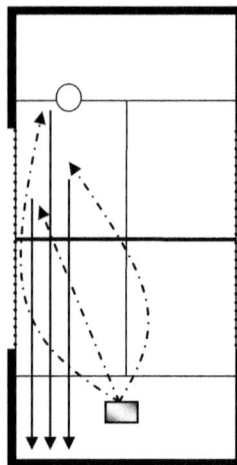

Exercise 0829   Hits: V – Bd – Rm

Target: Combination of hits
Striking sequence: Bd// – VR// - Rm//

Description:
Located player on the line of serve, perform a parallel volley tray which will rise to the net to make a parallel backhand volley and back down to make a parallel shot with the target of the bottom of the court.
After 12 balls is changed player.

EXERCISES COMBINATION: FOREHAND, BACKHAND, WALL, VOLLEY, SHOT

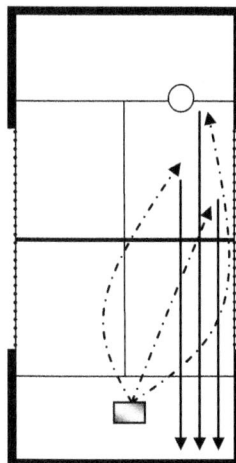

Exercise 0830   Hits: D – R – SF – SL – V – Rm

Target: Combination of hits
Striking sequence: R – SLD – SFR – Grid D – VR - Rm

Description:
Located player in the back of the court and upward movement, perform the following combination of hits; backhand, side exit forehand, exit background backhand, forehand to the grid, volley backhand and shot, all hits crossed over to the target of the marked area in the corner of the court.

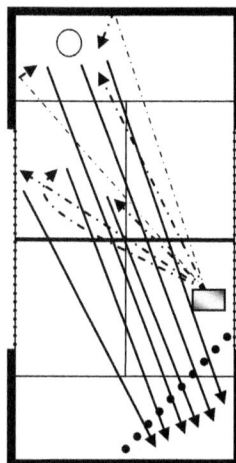

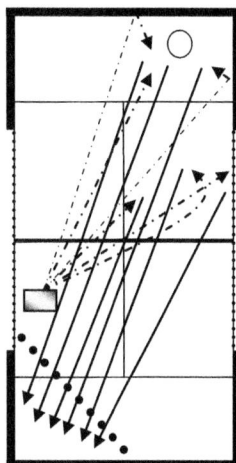

Exercise 0831   Hits: D – R – SF – SL – V – Rm

Target: Combination of hits
Striking sequence: D – SLR – SFD – Grid R – VD - Rm

Description:
Located player in the back of the court and upward movement, perform the following combination of hits; forehand, side exit backhand, exit background forehand, backhand to the grid, volley forehand and shot, all hits crossed over to the target of the marked area in the corner of the court.

Exercise 0832   Hits: D – R – SF – SL – V – Rm

Target: Combination of hits
Striking sequence: R – SLD – SFR – Grid D – VR - Rm

Description:
Located player in the back of the court and upward movement, perform the following combination of hits; backhand, side exit forehand, exit background backhand, forehand to the grid, volley backhand and shot, all hits crossed over to the target of the marked area in the corner of the court.

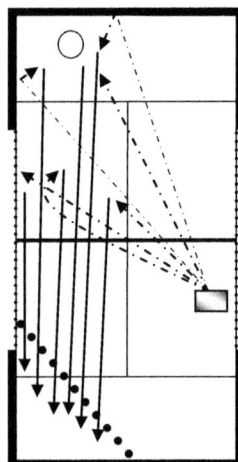

Exercise 0833   Hits: D – R – SF – SL – V – Rm

Target: Combination of hits
Striking sequence: D – SLR – SFD – Grid R – VD - Rm

Description:
Located player in the back of the court and upward movement, perform the following combination of hits; backhand, side exit forehand, exit background backhand, forehand to the grid, volley backhand and shot, all hits crossed over to the target of the marked area in the corner of the court.

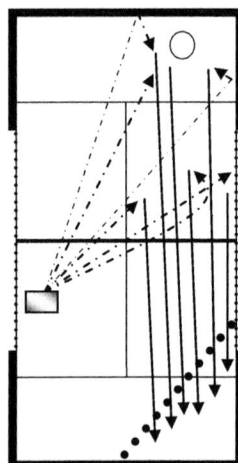

EXERCISES COMBINATION: SERVE, VOLLEY

Exercise 0834   Hits: Sq – V

Target: Win the net after the serve
Striking sequence: Serve – V middle

Description:
A player makes an open server and go up to the net to perform a volley to the center, with the target of the mark on the back of the court, the rest or return the other player has made the center.
After 20 balls position players alternates.

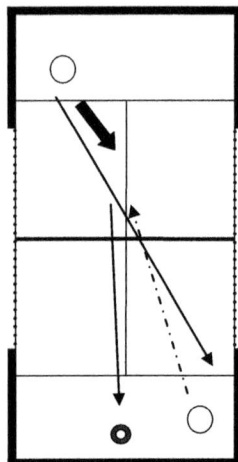

Exercise 0835   Hits: Sq – V

Target: Win the net after the serve
Striking sequence: Serve – V middle

Description:
A player makes an open server and go up to the net to perform a volley to the center, with the target of the mark on the back of the court, the rest or return the other player has made the center.
After 20 balls position players alternates.

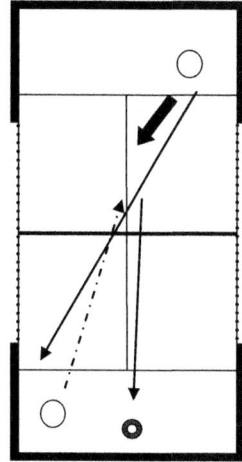

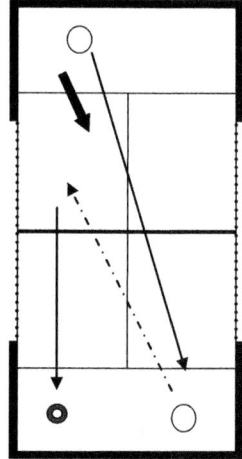

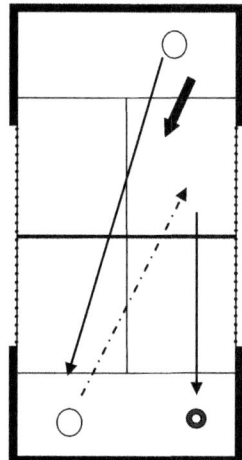

Exercise 0836   Hits: Sq – V

Target: Win the net after the serve
Striking sequence: Serve – VD//

Description:
A player takes a server to the middle and go up to the net for hits a parallel forehand volley, with the target of the mark on the back of the court, the rest or return the other player has made open.
After 20 balls position players alternates.

Exercise 0837   Hits: Sq – V

Target: Win the net after the serve
Striking sequence: Serve – VR//

Description:
A player takes a server to the middle and go up to the net for hits a parallel backhand volley, with the target of the mark on the back of the court, the rest or return the other player has made open.
After 20 balls position players alternates.

Exercise 0838   Hits: Sq – V

Target: Win the net after the serve
Striking sequence: Serve – VDX

Description:
A player takes a server to the middle and go up to the net for hit a crossed over forehand volley, with the target of the mark on the back of the court, the rest or return the other player has made open.
After 20 balls position players alternates.

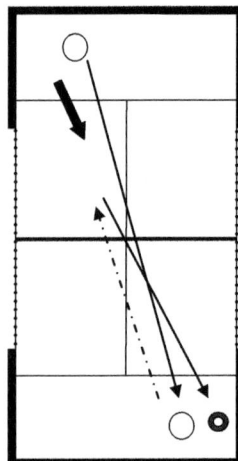

Exercise 0839   Hits: Sq – V

Target: Win the net after the serve
Striking sequence: Serve – VRX

Description:
A player takes a server to the middle and go up to the net for hit a crossed over backhand volley, with the target of the mark on the back of the court, the rest or return the other player has made open.
After 20 balls position players alternates.

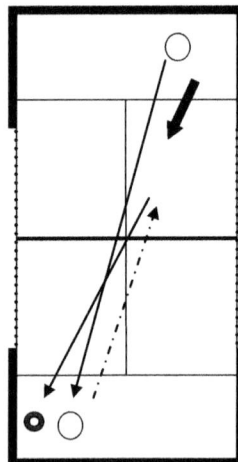

Exercise 0840   Hits: Sq – Rm

Target: Win the net after the serve
Striking sequence: Serve – RmX

Description:
Players take a server and uploaded to the net where the monitor throws them a ball to you for a crossed over shot, with the target of the mark on the corner of the court. After the shot, the monitor will throw a ball to the opposite corner to get back when you touch.

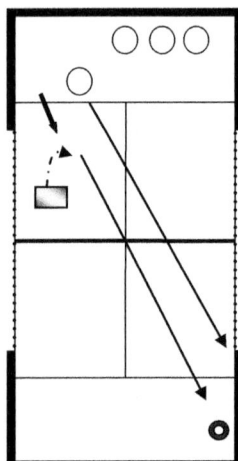

Exercise 0841   Hits: Sq – Rm

Target: Win the net and shot
Striking sequence: Serve – RmX

Description:
Players take a server and uploaded to the net where the monitor throws them a ball to you for a crossed over shot, with the target of the mark on the corner of the court. After the shot, the monitor will throw a ball to the opposite corner to get back when you touch.

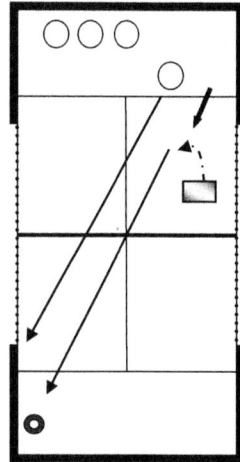

Exercise 0842   Hits: G – V

Target: Combination of hits with effort
Striking sequence: GR// - VR// – VR middle – VRX

Description:
Set the player at the bottom of the court, hits a parallel backhand lob, rise to the net and make a backhand volley to each of the brands in the bottom of the court. After 12 balls is changed player.

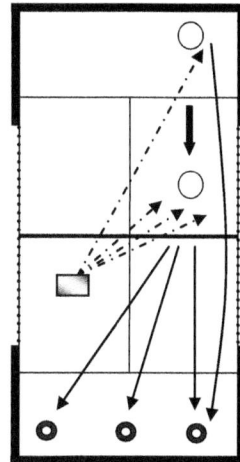

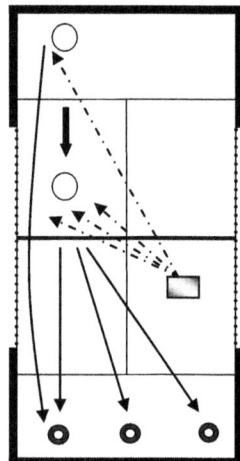

Exercise 0843   Hits: Gb – V

Target: Combination of hits with effort
Striking sequence: GD// - VD// – VD middle – VDX

Description:
Set the player at the bottom of the court, hits a parallel forehand lob, rise to the net and make a forehand volley to each of the brands in the bottom of the court. After 12 balls is changed player.

Exercise 0844   Hits: G – V

Target: Combination of strokes moving
Striking sequence: GDX – GRX – VDX – VRX

Description:
Set the player at the bottom of the court, hits a crossed over forehand lob and a crossed over backhand lob, go up to the net and perform a crossed over forehand volley and a crossed over backhand volley, returning back to the starting position. The target will be the square marked in the corner.
After 12 balls is changed player.

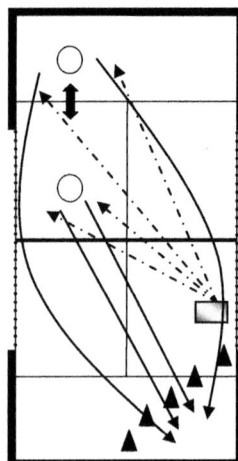

Exercise 0845   Hits: G – V

Target: Combination of strokes moving
Striking sequence: GDX – GRX – VDX – VRX

Description:
Set the player at the bottom of the court, hits a crossed over forehand lob and a crossed over backhand lob, go up to the net and perform a crossed over forehand volley and a crossed over backhand volley, returning back to the starting position. The target will be the square marked in the corner.
After 12 balls is changed player.

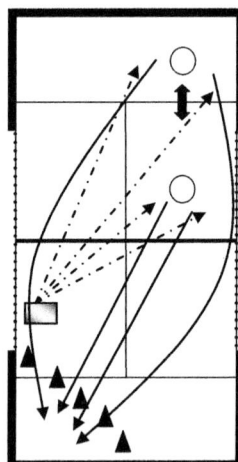

Exercise 0846   Hits: G – V

Target: Combination of strokes moving
Striking sequence: GDX – GRX – VDX – VRX

Description:
A player works with the monitor to finish the ball trolley. Located player in the back of the court, perform a crossed over lob from forehand side and a crossed over backhand lob, go up to the net and perform a crossed over forehand volley and a crossed over backhand volley, returning back to the starting position. The target area will be marked in the corner of the court. The other two players will perform control ball, one from the bottom and the other on the net.
Upon completion of the ball trolley, the position of the players alternate.

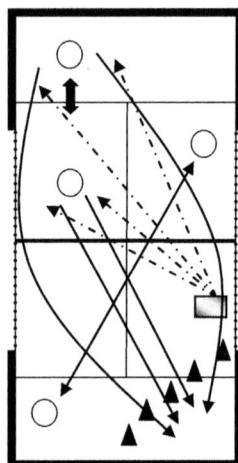

Exercise 0847   Hits: G – V

Target: Alternate hits moving
Striking sequence: GDX – GRX – VDX – VRX

Description:

A player works with the monitor to finish the ball trolley. Located player in the back of the court, perform a crossed over forehand lob from forehand side and a crossed over backhand lob, go up to the net and perform a crossed over forehand volley and a crossed over backhand volley, returning back to the starting position. The target area will be marked in the corner of the court. The other two players will perform control ball, one from the bottom and the other on the net.

Upon completion of the ball trolley, the position of the players alternate.

EXERCISES COMBINATION: SERVE, VOLLEY, SHOT

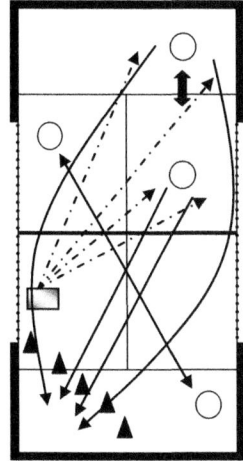

Exercise 0848   Hits: Sq – V – Rm

Target: Win the net after the serve
Striking sequence: Serve – VD// - Rm//

Description:

Set the player at the bottom of the court, hits a serve and go up to the net for a parallel forehand volley and a parallel shot, with the target of the mark on the back of the court. After the shot, it will go to the opposite side and catch a ball launch monitor him to do the exercise.

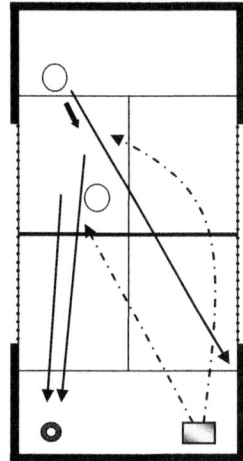

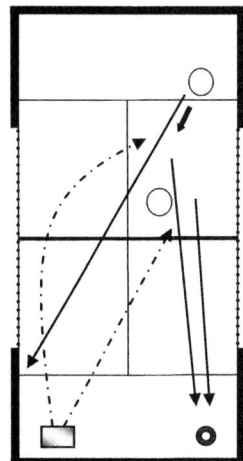

Exercise 0849   Hits: Sq – V – Rm

Target: Win the net after the serve
Striking sequence: Serve – VR// - Rm//

Description:

Set the player at the bottom of the court, hits a serve and go up to the net for a parallel backhand volley and a parallel shot, with the target of the mark on the back of the court. After the shot, it will go to the opposite side and catch a ball launch monitor him to do the exercise.

Exercise 0850   Hits: Sq – V – Rm

Target: Win the net after the serve
Striking sequence: Serve – VD// - RmX

Description:
Set the player at the bottom of the court, hits a serve and go up to the net for a parallel forehand volley and a crossed over shot, with the target of the mark on the back of the court. After the shot, it will go to the opposite side and catch a ball launch monitor him to do the exercise.

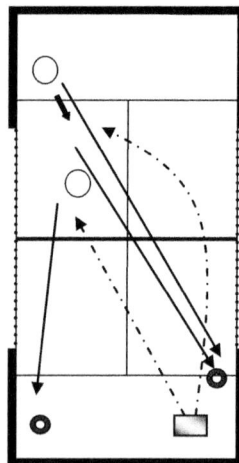

Exercise 0851   Hits: Sq – V – Rm

Target: Win the net after the serve
Striking sequence: Serve – VR// - RmX

Description:
Set the player at the bottom of the court, hits a serve and go up to the net for a parallel backhand volley and a crossed over shot, with the target of the mark on the back of the court. After the shot, it will go to the opposite side and catch a ball launch monitor him to do the exercise.

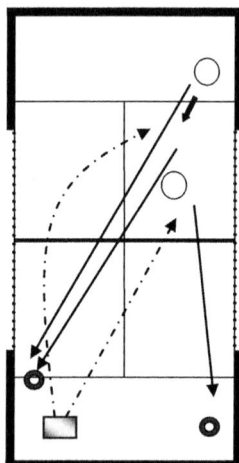

Exercise 0852   Hits: Sq – V – Rm

Target: Win the net after the serve
Striking sequence: Serve – VDX – RmX

Description:
Set the player at the bottom of the court, hits a serve and go up to the net for a crossed over forehand volley and a crossed over shot, with the target of the mark on the back of the court. After the shot, it will go to the opposite side and catch a ball launch monitor him to do the exercise.

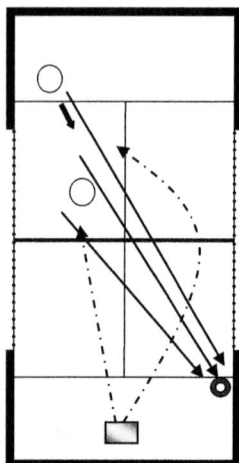

Exercise 0853   Hits: Sq – V – Rm

Target: Win the net after the serve

Striking sequence: Serve – VRX – RmX

Description:
Set the player at the bottom of the court, hits a serve and go up to the net for a crossed over backhand volley and a crossed over shot, with the target of the mark on the back of the court. After the shot, it will go to the opposite side and catch a ball launch monitor him to do the exercise.

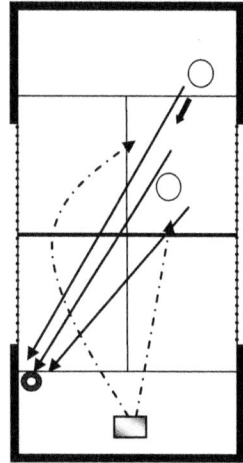

EXERCISES COMB.: SERVE, VOLLEY, VOLLEY TRAY (BD),

Exercise 0854   Hits: Sq – V – Bd – Rm

Target: Combination of hits after Australian serve

Striking sequence: Serve – VD// - VR// - Bd// - VD// - VR// - Rm//

Description:
Set the player at the bottom of the court, hits a serve and go up to their side of the net where will hit the next combination of hits; parallel forehand volley, parallel backhand volley, parallel volley tray (Bd), parallel forehand volley, parallel backhand volley and parallel shot, with the target of the mark on the back of the court.
After the last blow, the monitor will throw a ball to serve again when you touch.

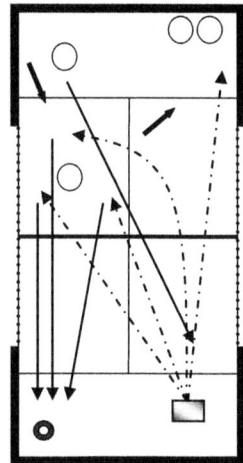

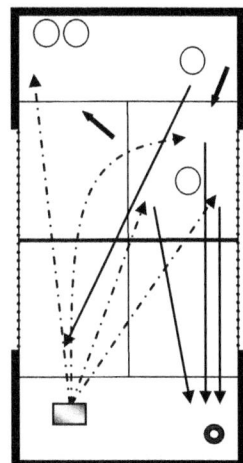

Exercise 0855   Hits: Sq – V – Bd – Rm

Target: Combination of hits after Australian serve

Striking sequence: Serve – VD// - VR// - Bd// - VD// - VR// - Rm//

Description:
Set the player at the bottom of the court, hits a serve and go up to their side of the net where will hit the next combination of hits; parallel forehand volley, parallel backhand volley, parallel volley tray (Bd), parallel forehand volley, parallel backhand volley and parallel shot, with the target of the mark on the back of the court.
After the last blow, the monitor will throw a ball to serve again when you touch.

Exercise 0856   Hits: Sq – V – Bd – Rm

Target: Combination of hits after Australian serve

Striking sequence: Serve – VD middle – VR middle – Bd middle – VD middle – VR middle – Rm middle

Description:
Set the player at the bottom of the court, hits a serve and go up to their side of the net where will hit the next combination of hits; the middle forehand volley, backhand volley to the middle, volley tray to the middle, forehand volley to the middle, backhand volley to the middle and a shot to the middle, with the target of the mark on the back of the court.
After the last blow, the monitor will throw a ball to serve again when you touch.

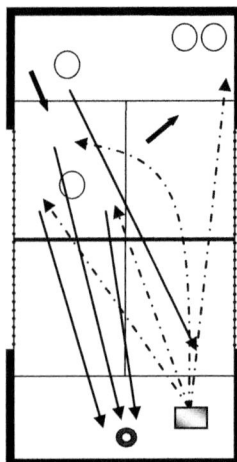

Exercise 0857   Hits: Sq – V – Bd – Rm

Target: Combination of hits after serve

Striking sequence: Serve – VD middle – VR middle – Bd middle – VD middle – VR middle – Rm middle

Description:
Set the player at the bottom of the court, hits a serve and go up to their side of the net where will hit the next combination of hits; the middle forehand volley, backhand volley to the middle, volley tray to the middle, forehand volley to the middle, backhand volley to the middle and a shot to the middle, with the target of the mark on the back of the court.
After the last blow, the monitor will throw a ball to serve again when you touch.

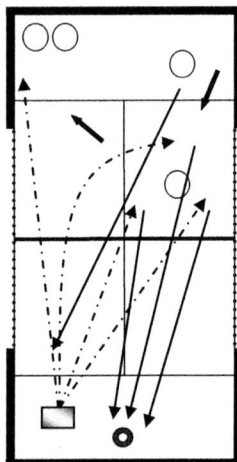

Exercise 0858   Hits: Sq – V – Rm

Target: Combination of hits after serve
Striking sequence: Serve – VD// – VR// – Rm//

Description:
Set the player at the bottom of the court, hits a serve and go up to the net where perform a parallel forehand volley, a parallel backhand volley and a parallel shot, with the target of the marks on the court, after which will go to the opposite side where the monitor will throw another ball to repeat the exercise.

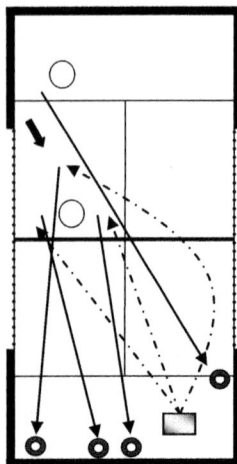

Exercise 0859   Hits: Sq – V – Rm

Target: Combination of hits after serve
Striking sequence: Serve – VD// – VR// – Rm//

Description:
Set the player at the bottom of the court, hits a serve and go up to the net where perform a parallel forehand volley, a parallel backhand volley and a parallel shot, with the target of the marks on the court, after which will go to the opposite side where the monitor will throw another ball to repeat the exercise.

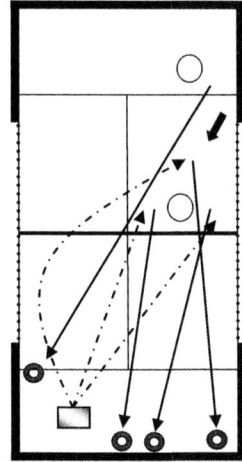

Exercise 0860   Hits: Sq – V – Rm

Target: Combination of hits after serve
Striking sequence: Serve – D middle – VDX – VR// - RmX

Description:
Set the player at the bottom of the court, hits a serve and go up to the net with a short forehand ball to the middle. And located on the net, will hold a crossed over forehand volley to the middle and a parallel backhand volley, finishing with a crossed over power shot.
Once the exercise is completed, the player will go to the other side and the monitor will throw a ball to repeat the exercise when you touch.

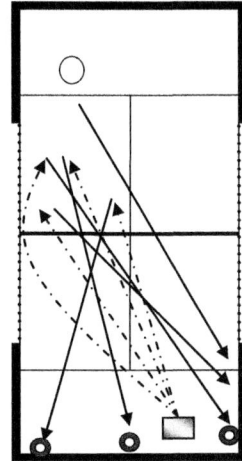

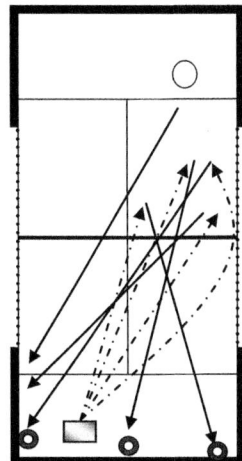

Exercise 0861   Hits: Sq – V – Rm

Target: Combination of hits after serve
Striking sequence: Serve – R middle – VRX – VD// - RmX

Description:
Set the player at the bottom of the court, hits a serve and go up to the net with a short forehand ball to the middle. And located on the net, will hold a crossed over forehand volley to the middle and a parallel backhand volley, finishing with a crossed over power shot.
Once the exercise is completed, the player will go to the other side and the monitor will throw a ball to repeat the exercise when you touch.

Exercise 0862   Hits: Sq – V – Rm

Target: Combination of hits after serve
Striking sequence: Serve – VR// – RmX

Description:
Set the player at the bottom of the court, hits a serve and go up to the net to make a parallel backhand volley and a crossed over shot, to the target of the marks on the court.
Once the exercise is completed, the player will go to the other side and the monitor will throw a ball to repeat the exercise when you touch.

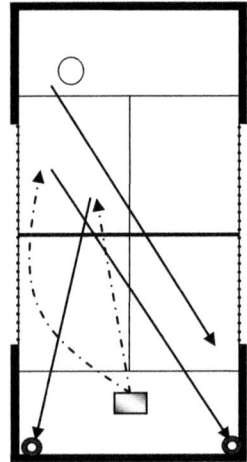

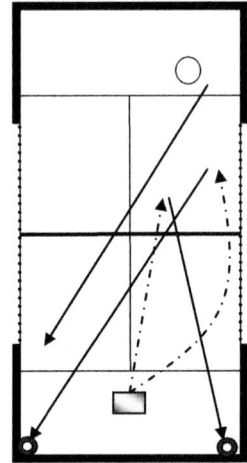

Exercise 0863   Hits: Sq – V – Rm

Target: Combination of hits after serve
Striking sequence: Serve – VD// – RmX

Description:
Set the player at the bottom of the court, hits a serve and go up to the net to make a parallel forehand volley and a crossed over shot, to the target of the marks on the court.
Once the exercise is completed, the player will go to the other side and the monitor will throw a ball to repeat the exercise when you touch.

Exercise 0864   Hits: Sq – V – Bd – Rm

Target: Combination of hits after serve
Striking sequence: Serve – VDX - VRX - BdX - VDX - VRX - RmX

Description:
Set the player at the bottom of the court, hits a serve and go up to their side of the net where will hit the combination of following hits: crossed over forehand volley, crossed over backhand volley, crossed over volley tray, crossed over forehand volley, crossed over backhand and crossed over shot, with the target of the marks on the court.
After the last blow, the monitor will throw them a ball to serve again when you touch.

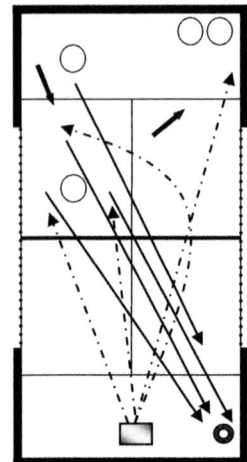

Exercise 0865   Hits: Sq – V – Bd – Rm

Target: Combination of hits after serve

Striking sequence: Serve – VDX - VRX - BdX - VDX - VRX - RmX

Description:
Set the player at the bottom of the court, hits a serve and go up to their side of the net where will hit the combination of following hits: crossed over forehand volley, crossed over backhand volley, crossed over volley tray, crossed over forehand volley, crossed over backhand and crossed over shot, with the target of the marks on the court.
After the last blow, the monitor will throw them a ball to serve again when you touch.

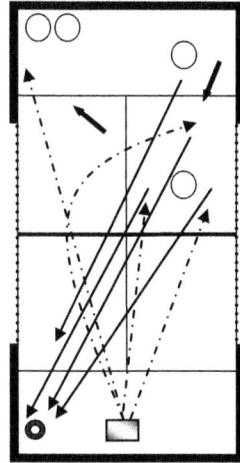

EXERCISES COMBINATION: REST OR RETURN VOLLEY,

Exercise 0866   Hits: Rest or return – V – Bd

Target: Rest or return and win the net

Striking sequence: Rest or return – VD// – BdX

Description:
Set the player at the bottom of the court, takes a rest or return to serve of the monitor will go up to the net for a parallel forehand volley and a crossed over volley tray, with the target of the marks on the back of the court.

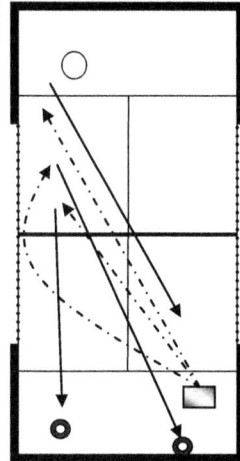

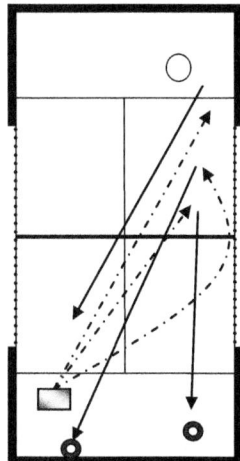

Exercise 0867   Hits: Rest or return – V – Bd

Target: Rest or return and win the net

Striking sequence: Rest or return – VR// – BdX

Description:
Set the player at the bottom of the court, takes a rest or return to serve of the monitor will go up to the net for a parallel backhand volley and a crossed over volley tray, with the target of the marks on the back of the court

Exercise 0868   Hits: Rest or return – V

Target: Rest or return y volley
Striking sequence: Rest or return – V

Description:
With two players on court, a player will be crossed over below the monitor to serve his teammate strong volley and try to win the point. The game continues crossed over until the end point.
After 10 balls position players alternates.

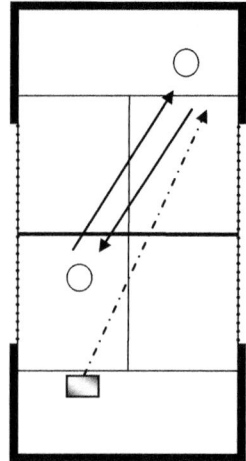

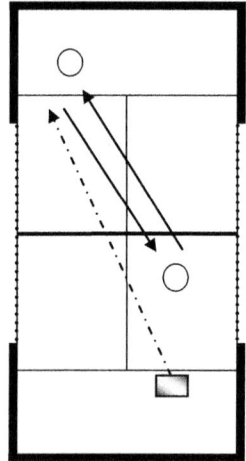

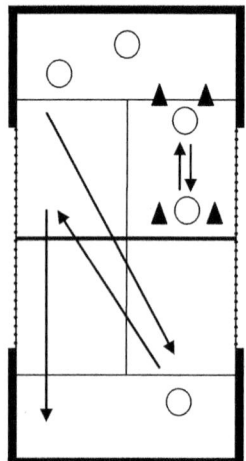

Exercise 0869   Hits: Rest or return – V

Target: Rest or return y volley
Striking sequence: Rest or return – V

Description:
With two players on court, a player will be crossed over below the monitor to serve his teammate strong volley and try to win the point. The game continues crossed over until the end point.
After 10 balls position players alternates

Exercise 0870

Target: Working with 5 pupils

Description:
A pupil near the ball trolley Ball, held serve and go up to the net to a parallel volley.
Another pupil subtract only crossed overlooking the volley of his partner.
2 pupils will control volley between cones.
One pupil will perform proprioceptive exercises (squats, rubber arms,) as shown in the monitor.
After 1' position players alternates.

Exercise 0871   Hits: Stairs – Bd – V

Target: Coordination of movements
Striking sequence: Stairs – BdX – VDX short

Description:
Located next to the stairs of coordinating, made the movements on it and at the end of her run in crossed over to the other court to make a crossed over volley and a short crossed over forehand volley to the grid.

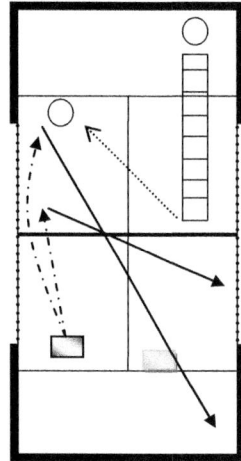

Exercise 0872   Hits: SF – SDP – V – Bd

Target: Gesture of the hits- Warm-up
Striking sequence: SF – SDP – V – Bd

Description:
Four pupils work simultaneously in different positions:
1. Forehand background out, Backhand output background
2. Output double wall with turn on both sides
3. Forehand volley and Backhand volley displacement
4. Volley Tray (Bd) and turn the net
First we will do this without a ball and then the monitor will be done with each in all positions.
After 1' position of the players is alterned.

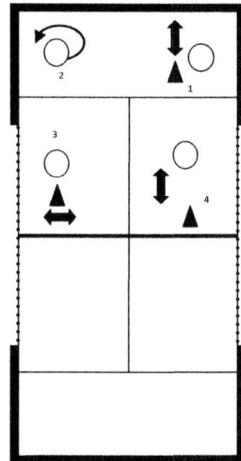

Exercise 0873

Target: Exercise plyometric and fence
Striking sequence: Jump – 2-1-2-1-2-1 and return

Description:
Exercise plyometric with fence. Set the player at the bottom of the court, starting with jump of fence and does jump about two cones, then on 1 with the sequence 2-1 - 2 - 1 - 2 - 1 and return jump with one leg on each cone.
When mastered, it will be held in each volley hitting a jump.

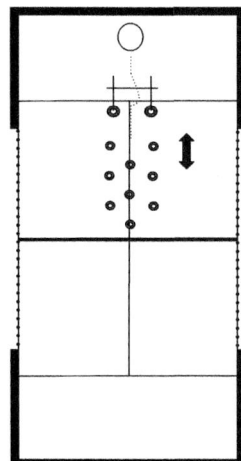

COMPETITION EXERCISES

Exercise 0874   Hits: Sq

Target: Win the net after the serve and continue
Striking sequence: Serve and play

Description:
Faced two players in parallel from the back of the court, a player will make a serve in parallel and continue the point with the player is left. Players are limited to half court and then 10 points on serve is changed.
The first to reach 20 points win.
We will do the same on the opposite side.

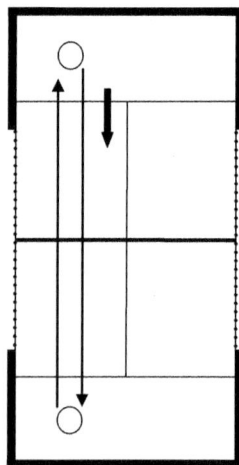

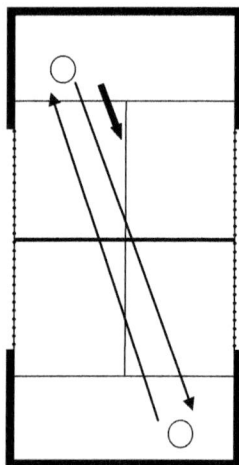

Exercise 0875   Hits: Sq

Target: Win the net after the serve and continue
Striking sequence: Serve and play

Description:
Faced two players in crossed over from the back of the court, a player will make a serve in crossed over and continue the point with the player is left. Players are limited to half court and then 10 points on serve is changed.
The first to reach 20 points win.
We will do the same on the opposite side.

Exercise 0876   Hits: R – Bd

Target: Reaction to a situation
Striking sequence: R – Bd

Description:
With two players on court, a player hits a ball to the middle and then tries to return the volley tray on the grid of his teammate. The game continues crossed over until the point end.
The first to reach 10 win and position switches.
The exercise will be repeated on the opposite side.

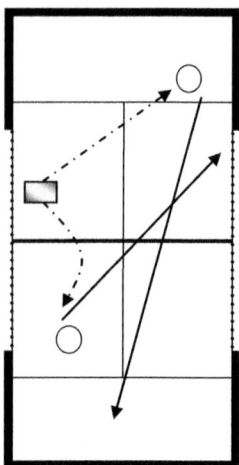

Exercise 0877   Hits: Sq

Target: Win the net after the serve and continue

Striking sequence: Serve – Rest or return with lob and play

Description:
Faced two players in crossed over from the back of the court, a player will make a serve in crossed over, the player remains will continue the point with a lob. Players are limited to crossed over half court and then 10 points on serve is changed.
The first to reach 20 points win.

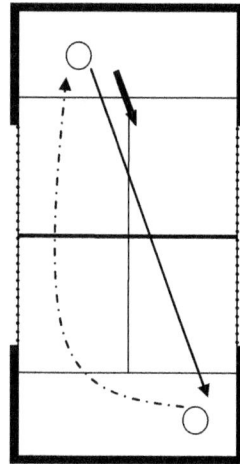

Exercise 0878   Hits: V

Target: Coordination gesture - ocular

Striking sequence: Cadet, double cadet, cadet below ...

Description:
Two opposing players hit the ball after boat, carrying only cadet, double cadet, cadet or below.
When it is mastered by both players, they can perform battle in which they implement the hits and contrast the need to repeat.

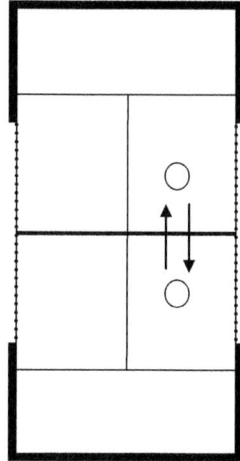

Exercise 0879   Hits: Sq – Rest or return – V

Target: Win the next after the serve and continue

Striking sequence: Serve – Rest or return – Volley and play

Description:
The top player takes a server in crossed over and rises to perform a parallel volley the rest or return and will continue the point. Players are limited to the average player taking the court.
After 10 balls position players alternates.
Then you can do the opposite.

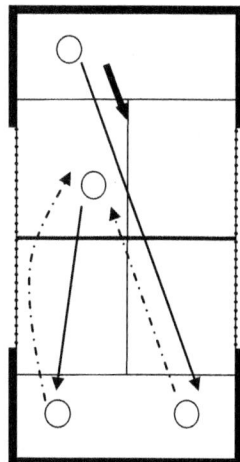

Exercise 0880   Hits: D

Target: Keep the ball in play
Striking sequence: D

Description:
Match to 11 points from four players who hit freely from the back of the court. The target is that players hit to 10 forehands and then they can win the point. No matter that become backhand hits, but not counted. It is a cooperative exercise.
After reaching 11 points rotate their position players left. Then it becomes just backhand.

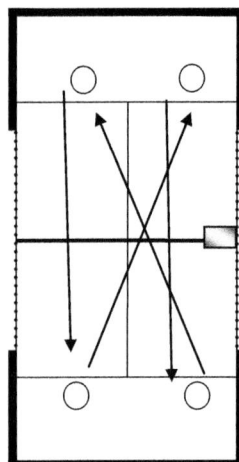

Exercise 0881   Hits: Sq – Rest or return – G

Target: Win the net after the serve and continue
Striking sequence: Serve – Rest or return - Lob and play

Description:
The top player hits a server in crossed over and rise to the net to hit the rest or return parallel to lob the player below and continue the point. Players are limited to the average player taking the court.
After 10 balls position players alternates.

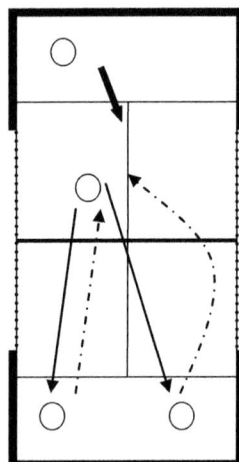

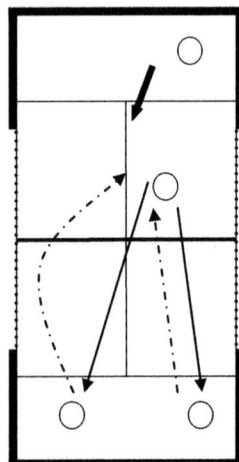

Exercise 0882   Hits: Sq – Rest or return – G

Target: Win the net after the serve and continue
Striking sequence: Serve – Rest or return - Lob and play

Description:
The top player hits a server in crossed over and rise to the net to hit the rest or return parallel to lob the player below and continue the point. Players are limited to the average player taking the court.
After 10 balls position players alternates.

Exercise 0883   Hits: Sq - V

Target: Win the net after the Australian serve
Striking sequence: Serve – volley and play

Description:
The player takes an Australian server up to the side wall and go up to the net to hit the middle the rest of the Player and will continue to the point. Players are limited to the average player taking the court.
After 10 balls position players alternates.

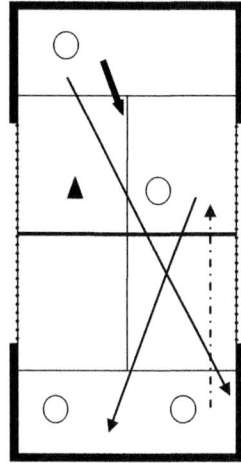

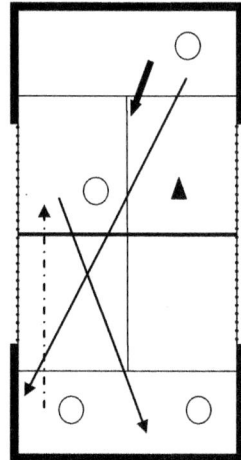

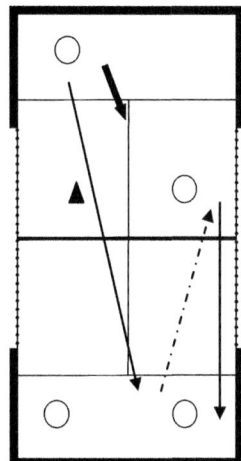

Exercise 0884   Hits: Sq – V

Target: Win the net after the Australian serve
Striking sequence: Serve – volley and play

Description:
The player takes an Australian server up to the side wall and go up to the net to hit the middle the rest of the Player and will continue to the point. Players are limited to the average player taking the court.
After 10 balls position players alternates.

Exercise 0885   Hits: Sq – V

Target: Win the net after the Australian serve
Striking sequence: Serve – volley and play

Description:
The top player hits an Australian server to the middle and go up to the net to hit parallel or parallel return of the player who remains and will continue to the point. Players are limited to the average player taking the court.
After 10 balls position players alternates.

Exercise 0886   Hits: Sq – V

Target: Win the net after the Australian serve
Striking sequence: Serve – volley and play

Description:
The top player hits an Australian server to the middle and go up to the net to hit parallel or parallel return of the player who remains and will continue to the point. Players are limited to the average player taking the court. After 10 balls position players alternates.

Exercise 0887   Hits: Sq – Rest or return

Target: Serve Australian
Striking sequence: Serve and play

Description:
The top player takes an Australian server up and rises to the net to cover your area and continue the point with his partner. The receiver will do to the area you want and continue to point the two players against the net. Players are limited to the average remaining court player.
After 10 balls position players alternates. Then you can do the opposite.

Exercise 0888   Hits: Free

Target: Keep the ball in play
Striking sequence: Free

Description:
Match to 11 points from four players who hit freely from the back of the court. The target is to pass the ball 20 times without failure by the net and then you can win the point. It is a cooperative exercise.
After reaching 11 points rotate their position players left.

Exercise 0889   Hits: SF

Target: Down wall
Striking sequence: Down wall and play

Description:
Located two players near the net, the monitor will launch a lob to execute a drop wall against the player is alone in the net. Return after this set will continue respecting the middle of the court of the player is alone.
After 10 balls position players alternates.
Then it is made from the other side.

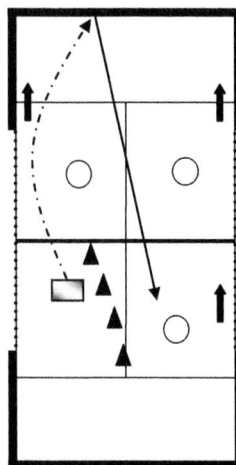

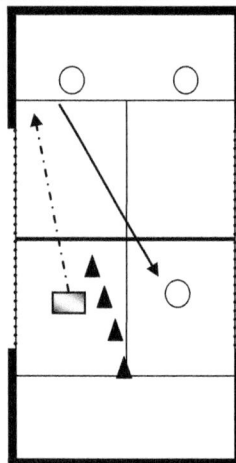

Exercise 0890   Hits: Rm / Bd

Target: Shot / Volley tray (Bd)s without seeing the origin
Striking sequence: Shot or Volley Tray (Bd)

Description:
Located two players on the net and two at the bottom, throw balls from the monitor outside the court for the players to make a volley tray or a shot, and continue to finish the point.
After 10 points the position of the players alternate.

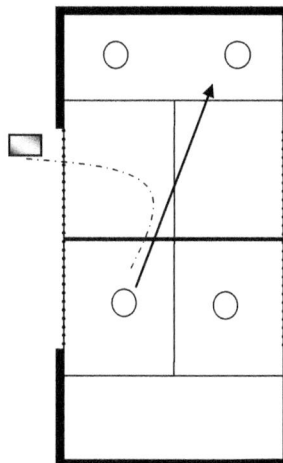

Exercise 0891   Hits: SF

Target: Advance shot , Wall background
Striking sequence: Down Wall and play

Description:
Located two players at the bottom of the court and another near the net, the monitor will execute a shot against the background wall to make a return against the player is alone in the net. He returns after this respect will continue playing half the court the player is alone.
After 10 balls position players alternates. Then it is made from the other side.

Exercise 0892   Hits: SF

Target: Wall output without seeing the origin
Striking sequence: SF

Description:
Faced four players at the bottom of the court, carried wall outlets to the balls thrown by the monitor from outside the court, and will continue to finish the point.
After 10 points the position of the players alternate.

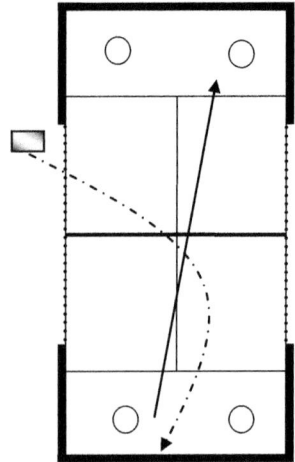

Exercise 0893   Hits: SF

Target: Advance to a shot in lateral wall and background wall
Striking sequence: Down wall and play

Description:
Located two players at the bottom of the court and another near the net, the monitor will execute a rebound shot looking at the side and bottom wall to make a return against the player who is on the net alone. Return after this set will continue respecting the middle of the court of the player is alone.
After 10 balls position players alternates.
Then it is made from the other side.

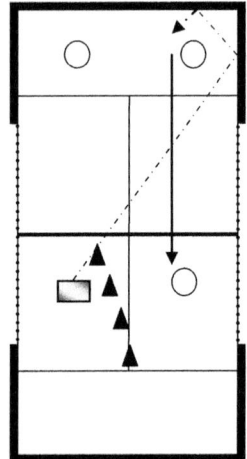

Exercise 0894   Hits: Bd o Rm

Target: Bd o Rm to balls that are thrown at players
Striking sequence: Bd o Rm

Description:
Faced four players at the bottom of the court, players who are next to monitor will be thrown to the ground a ball to have a high bounce and hold a crossed over volley tray or a crossed over shot and continue the game.
After 10 points the position of the players alternate.

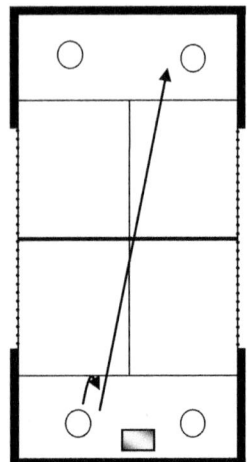

Exercise 0895   Hits: Rm

Target: Advance a shot high rebound
Striking sequence: Down wall and play

Description:
Located two players at the bottom of the court and another near the net, the monitor will execute a shot with high rebound in the background wall to make a return against the player who was in the net and lowered to the bottom of the court to try to return. Return after this set will continue respecting the middle of the court of the player is alone.
After 10 balls position players alternates.

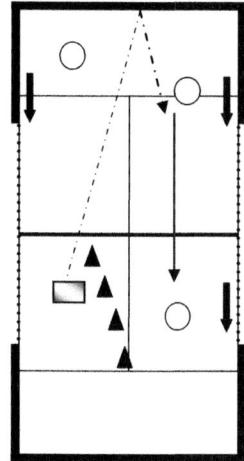

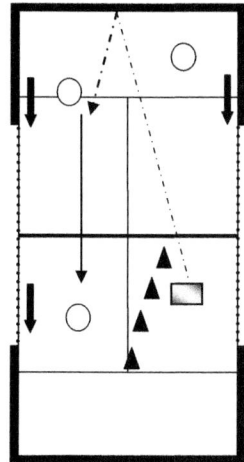

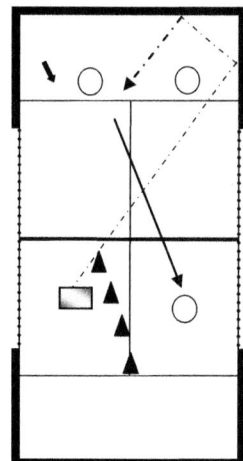

Exercise 0896   Hits: Rm

Target: Advance a shot high rebound
Striking sequence: Down Wall and play

Description:
Located two players at the bottom of the court and another near the net, the monitor will execute a shot with high rebound in the background wall to make a return against the player who was in the net and lowered to the bottom of the court to try to return. Return after this set will continue respecting the middle of the court of the player is alone.
After 10 balls position players alternates.

Exercise 0897   Hits: Rm

Target: Help a shot of side and bottom
Striking sequence: Down Wall and play

Description:
Located two players at the bottom of the court and another near the net, the monitor will execute a long shot looking rebound in the side and bottom wall to support team mate returned against the player that is in the takes place net. Return after this set will continue respecting the middle of the court of the player is alone.
After 10 balls position players alternates.

Exercise 0898   Hits: Rm

Target: Help a shot of side and bottom
Striking sequence: Down Wall and play

Description:
Located two players at the bottom of the court and another near the net, the monitor will execute a long shot looking rebound in the side and bottom wall to support team mate returned against the player that is in the takes place net. Return after this set will continue respecting the middle of the court of the player is alone.
After 10 balls position players alternates.

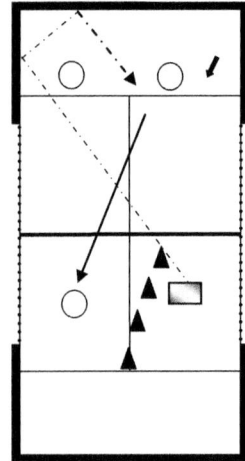

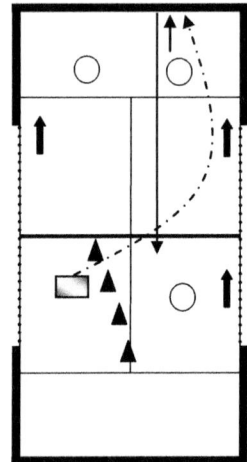

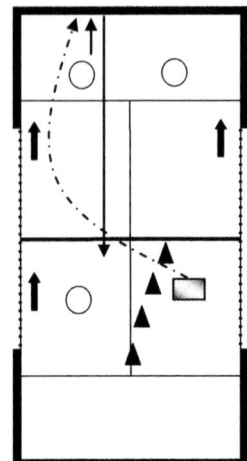

Exercise 0899   Hits: CP

Target: Parallel against wall
Striking sequence: Against wall and play

Description:
Located two players at the bottom of the court and another near the net, the monitor runs a blow for the player is required to make a parallel against wall that return parallel Against the player is in the net. After this return will continue respecting the half court of the player is alone.
After 10 balls position players alternates.

Exercise 0900   Hits: CP

Target: Parallel against wall
Striking sequence: Against Wall and play

Description:
Located two players at the bottom of the court and another near the net, the monitor runs a blow for the player is required to make a parallel against wall that return parallel Against the player is in the net. After this return will continue respecting the half court of the player is alone.
After 10 balls position players alternates.

Exercise 0901   Hits: CP

Target: Crossed over against wall
Striking sequence: Against wall and play

Description:
Located two players at the bottom of the court and another near the net, the monitor runs a blow for the player is required to make a return crossed over against wall against the player is in the net. After this return will continue respecting the half court of the player is alone. After 10 balls position players alternates.

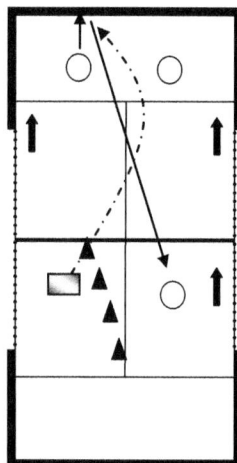

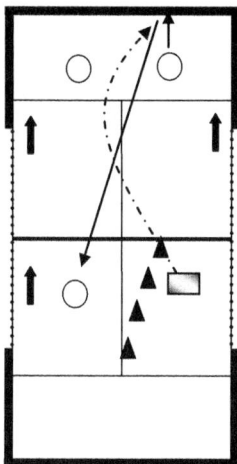

Exercise 0902   Hits: CP

Target: Crossed over against wall
Striking sequence: Against wall and play

Description:
Located two players at the bottom of the court and another near the net, the monitor runs a blow for the player is required to make a return crossed over against wall against the player is in the net. After this return will continue respecting the half court of the player is alone. After 10 balls position players alternates.

Exercise 0903   Hits: All

Target: Singles matches on average parallel court
Striking sequence: Serve and striking free

Description:
Having 6 players on court, the separated into two teams to play singles matches in parallel at half court. By having 6 players, who lose out singles match and one player enters the net.
After 2' position players alternates.

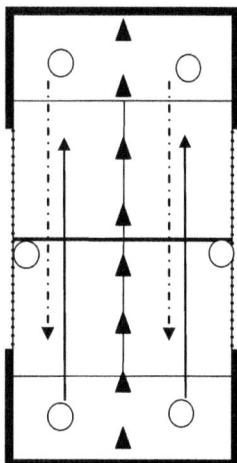

Exercise 0904   Hits: All

Target: Singles matches on average parallel court
Striking sequence: King of the court

Description:
Singles matches in parallel in half court. The attacking players must make two points with any player defending and cannot play twice in a row with the same opponent. The serve will have to enter into the square serve.

Exercise 0905   Hits: All

Target: Singles matches on average crossed over court
Striking sequence: King of the court

Description:
Singles matches in crossed over half court. The attacking players must make two points with any player defending and cannot play twice in a row with the same opponent. The serve will have to enter into the square serve.

Exercise 0906   Hits: CP

Target: Singles matches on average parallel court
Striking sequence: King of the court without bounce

Description:
Singles matches in crossed over half court. The attacking players must make two points with any player defending and cannot play twice in a row with the same opponent. The serve will have to enter into the square serve. The attacking player cannot help but throw the ball, so he made only volleys and volley trays.

Exercise 0907   Hits: All

Target: Singles matches on average parallel court
Striking sequence: King of the court parallel without bounce

Description:
Singles matches in parallel in half court. The attacking players must make two points with any player defending and cannot play twice in a row with the same opponent. The serve will have to enter into the square serve. The attacking player cannot help but throw the ball, so he made only volleys and volley trays.

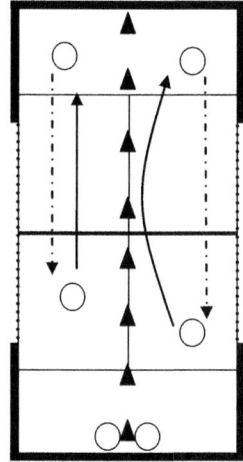

Exercise 0908   Hits: All

Target: Win the net
Striking sequence: Free

Description:
Singles matches in crossed over half court. The attacking players must make defending and never win the net. Whoever wins the net or point wins. The attacking players must make two points with any player defending and cannot play twice in a row with the same opponent.

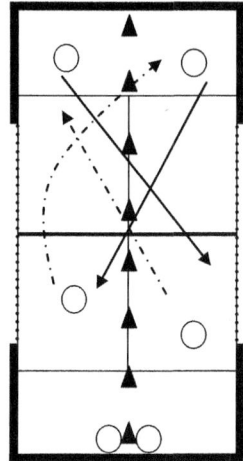

Exercise 0909   Hits: All

Target: Singles matches on average crossed over court
Striking sequence: Free

Description:
Singles matches in crossed over half court. Players who earn the point, taken out and placed in the court above. The serve will have to enter into the square serve.

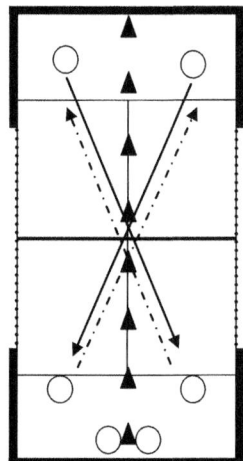

Exercise 0910   Hits: Free

Target: Defense and attack
Striking sequence: Free

Description:
Having at least 6 players on court, the players separated pairs. The couple who wins two points or makes a "winner" defends on the back of the court and court changes.

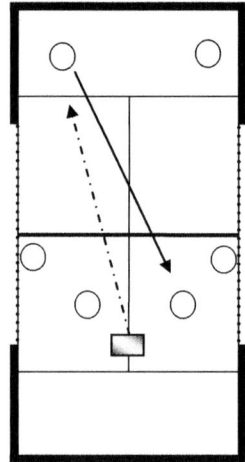

Exercise 0911   Hits: All

Target: Singles matches on average crossed over court
Striking sequence: King of the court crossed over counting

Description:
Singles matches in crossed over half court. Players count the hits to perform. If the attacking player wins, he added, and the first to reach 100 with either player wins the court.

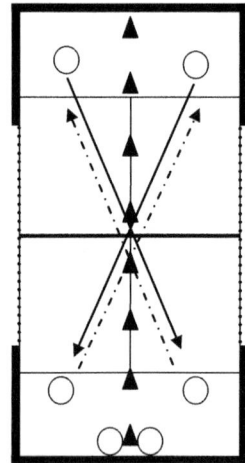

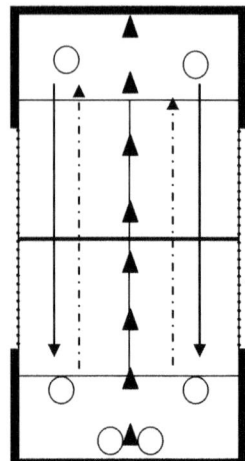

Exercise 0912   Hits: All

Target: Singles matches on average parallel court
Striking sequence: King of the court parallel counting

Description:
Singles matches in parallel in half court. Players count the hits to perform. If the attacking player wins, he added, and the first to reach 100 with either player wins the court.

Exercise 0913   Hits: All

Target: Win the net after the serve and continue
Striking sequence: Serve and play

Description:
With the ball trolley beside players, they perform a serve and continue to monitor the point crossed over to finish. They may only play half court marked.

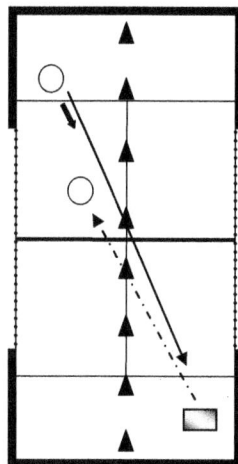

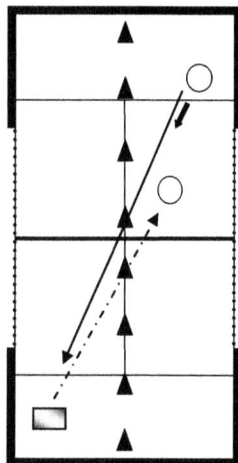

Exercise 0914   Hits: All

Target: Win the net after the serve and continue
Striking sequence: Serve and play

Description:
With the ball trolley beside players, they perform a serve and continue to monitor the point crossed over to finish. They may only play half court marked.

Exercise 0915   Hits: D – R – SF – SL – SDP

Target: Defending the bottom of the court
Striking sequence: Free

Description:
They placed two players in the back of the court, they will defend the balls thrown by the monitor directing his balls to the area marked on the court.
After 10 balls position players alternates.

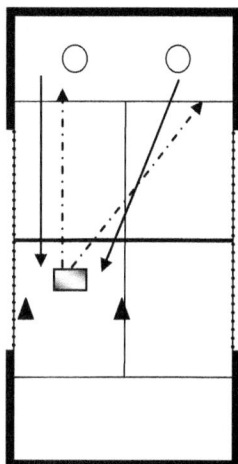

Exercise 0916   Hits: All

Target: Winning the point from an initial position
Striking sequence: DX - Free

Description:
Mini game to 11 points, which begins with a crossed over forehand. Defending players can win the point, but never doing lobs.
Once you reach 11, players will rotate to the left.

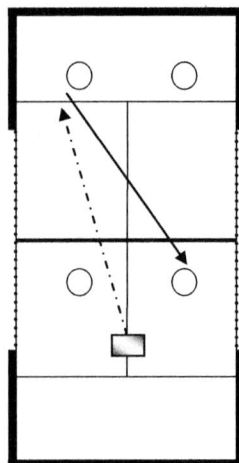

Exercise 0917   Hits: All

Target: Winning the point from an initial position
Striking sequence: RX - Free

Description:
Mini game to 11 points, which begins with a Backhand blow crossed over. Defending players can win the point, but never doing lobs.
Once you reach 11, players will rotate to the left.

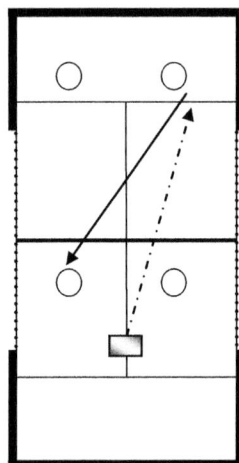

Exercise 0918   Hits: All

Target: Winning the point from an initial position
Striking sequence: DX - Free

Description:
Mini match best of 5 points, which begins with a crossed over forehand. Defending players can win the point, but never doing lobs.
If the player who plays with the monitor loses, he gets out and enters the fellow who is out. If on the contrary, the player's forehand goes outside, the left holds the forehand position and entering, it is in left.

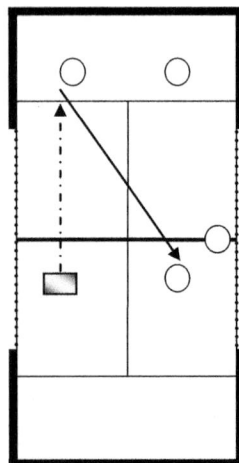

Exercise 0919   Hits: All

Target: Winning the point from an initial position
Striking sequence: RX - Free

Description:
Mini match best of 5 points, which begins with a crossed over backhand. Defending players can win the point, but never doing lobs.
If the player who plays with the monitor loses, he gets out and enters the fellow who is out. If on the contrary, the player's forehand goes outside, the left holds the forehand position and entering, it is in left.

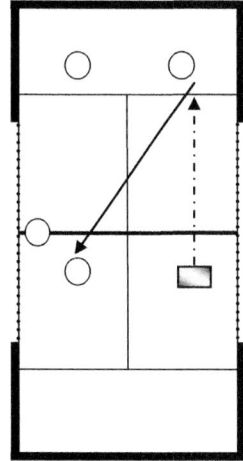

Exercise 0920   Hits: All

Target: Winning the point from an initial position
Striking sequence: SLDX - Free

Description:
Mini game to 11 points, which begins with a crossed over forehand output side. Defending players can win the point, but never doing lobs.
Once you reach 11, players will rotate to the left.

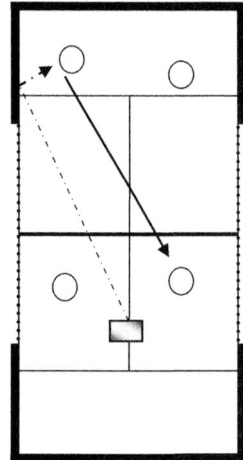

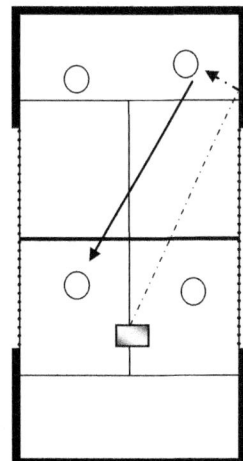

Exercise 0921   Hits: All

Target: Winning the point from an initial position
Striking sequence: SLRX - Free

Description:
Mini game to 11 points, which begins with a crossed over backhand output side. Defending players can win the point, but never doing lobs.
Once you reach 11, players will rotate to the left.

Exercise 0922   Hits: All

Target: Winning the point from an initial position
Striking sequence: SLDX - Free

Description:
Mini match best of 5 points, which begins with a crossed over forehand output side. Defending players can win the point, but never doing lobs.
If the player who plays with the monitor loses, he gets out and enters the fellow who is out. If on the contrary, the player's forehand goes outside, the left holds the forehand position and entering, it is in left.

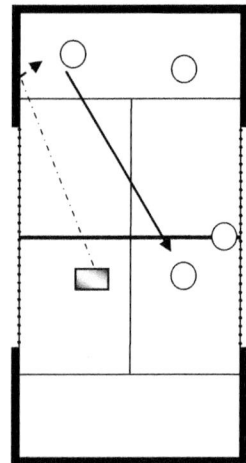

Exercise 0923   Hits: All

Target: Winning the point from an initial position
Striking sequence: SLRX - Free

Description:
Mini match best of 5 points, which begins with a crossed over backhand output side. Defending players can win the point, but never doing lobs.
If the player who plays with the monitor loses, he gets out and enters the fellow who is out. If contrary, the player on the left comes out, that of forehand in the left position and entering, it is in the right.

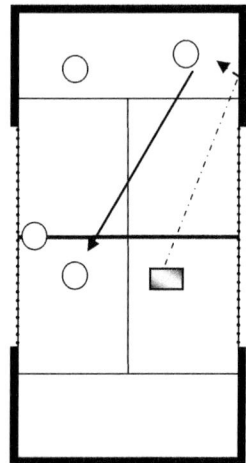

Exercise 0924   Hits: All

Target: Winning the point from an initial position
Striking sequence: SFRX - Free

Description:
Mini game to 11 points, which is started by a crossed over backhand bottom outlet. Defending players can win the point, but never doing lobs.
Once you reach 11, players will rotate to the left.

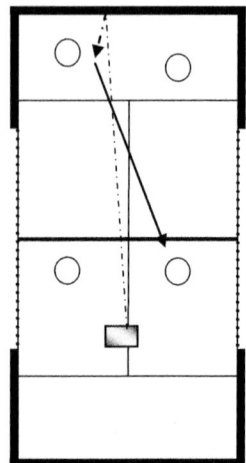

Exercise 0925   Hits: All

Target: Winning the point from an initial position
Striking sequence: SFDX - Free

Description:
Mini game to 11 points, which is started by a crossed over forehand bottom outlet. Defending players can win the point, but never doing lobs.
Once you reach 11, players will rotate to the left.

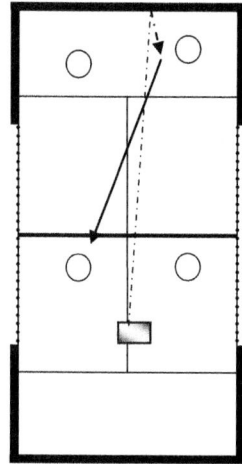

Exercise 0926   Hits: All

Target: Winning the point from an initial position
Striking sequence: SFRX - Free

Description:
Mini match best of 5 points, which is started by a crossed over backhand bottom outlet. Defending players can win the point, but never doing lobs.
If the player who plays with the monitor loses, he gets out and enters the fellow who is out. If on the contrary, the player's Forehand goes outside, the left holds the Forehand position and entering, it is in left.

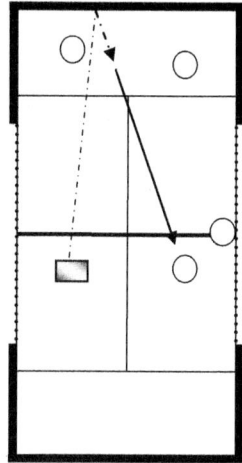

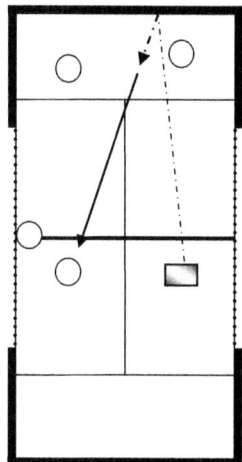

Exercise 0927   Hits: All

Target: Winning the point from an initial position
Striking sequence: SFDX - Free

Description:
Mini match best of 5 points, which is started by a crossed over forehand bottom outlet. Defending players can win the point, but never doing lobs.
If the player who plays with the monitor loses, he gets out and enters the fellow who is out. If on the contrary, the player's Forehand goes outside, the left holds the Forehand position and entering, it is in left.

Exercise 0928   Hits: All

Target: Winning the point from an initial position
Striking sequence: VDX - Free

Description:
Mini game to 11 points, which begins with a crossed over forehand volley. Defending players can win the point, even making lobs.
Once you reach 11, players will rotate to the left.

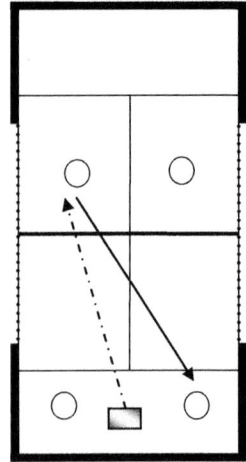

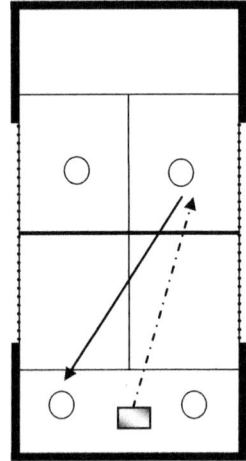

Exercise 0929   Hits: All

Target: Winning the point from an initial position
Striking sequence: VRX - Free

Description:
Mini game to 11 points, which begins with a crossed over backhand volley. Defending players can win the point, even making lobs.
Once you reach 11, players will rotate to the left.

Exercise 0930   Hits: All

Target: Winning the point from an initial position
Striking sequence: VDX - Free

Description:
Mini match best of 5 points, which begins with a crossed over forehand volley. Defending players can win the point, even making lobs.
If the player who plays with the monitor loses, he gets out and enters the fellow who is out. If on the contrary, the player's forehand goes outside, the left holds the forehand position and entering, it is in left.

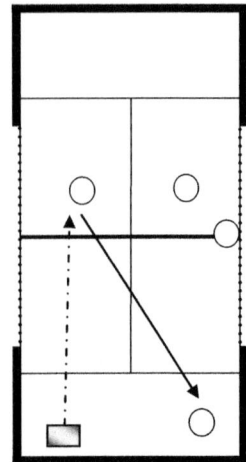

Exercise 0931   Hits: All

Target: Winning the point from an initial position
Striking sequence: VRX - Free

Description:
Mini match best of 5 points, which begins with a crossed over backhand volley. Defending players can win the point, even making lobs.
If the player who plays with the monitor loses, he gets out and enters the fellow who is out. If on the contrary, the player's forehand goes outside, the left holds the forehand position and entering, it is in left.

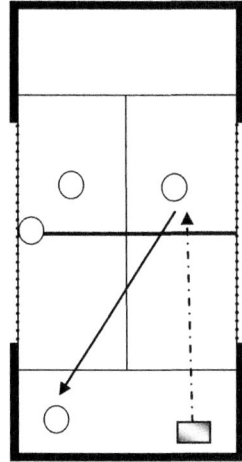

Exercise 0932   Hits: All

Target: Winning the point from an initial position
Striking sequence: RmX - Free

Description:
Mini game to 11 points, which begins with a crossed over shot. Defending players can win the point, even making lobs.
Once you reach 11, players will rotate to the left.

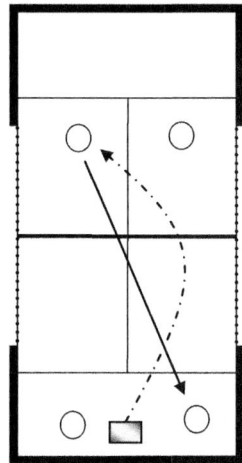

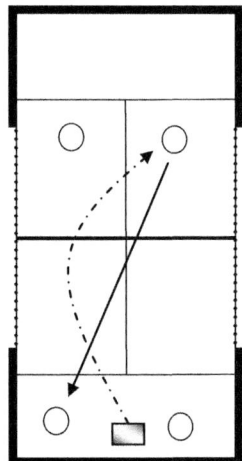

Exercise 0933   Hits: All

Target: Winning the point from an initial position
Striking sequence: RmX - Free

Description:
Mini game to 11 points, which begins with a crossed over shot. Defending players can win the point, even making lobs.
Once you reach 11, players will rotate to the left.

Exercise 0934   Hits: All

Target: Winning the point from an initial position
Striking sequence: RmX - Free

Description:
Mini match best of 5 points, which begins with a crossed over shot. Defending players can win the point, even making lobs.
If the player who plays with the monitor loses, he gets out and enters the fellow who is out. If on the contrary, the player's forehand goes outside, the left holds the forehand position and entering, it is in left.

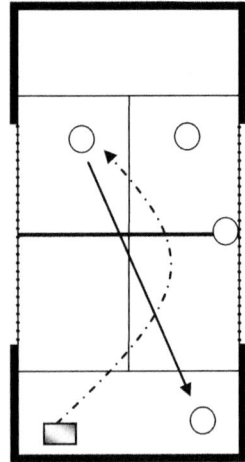

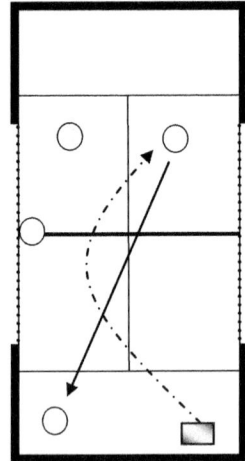

Exercise 0935   Hits: All

Target: Winning the point from an initial position
Striking sequence: RmX - Free

Description:
Mini match best of 5 points, which begins with a crossed over shot. Defending players can win the point, even making lobs.
If the player who plays with the monitor loses, he gets out and enters the fellow who is out. If on the contrary, the player's forehand goes outside, the left holds the forehand position and entering, it is in left.

Exercise 0936   Hits: All

Target: Winning the point from an initial position
Striking sequence: BdX - Free

Description:
Mini game to 11 points, which begins with a crossed over volley tray. Defending players can win the point, even making lobs.
Once you reach 11, players will rotate to the left.

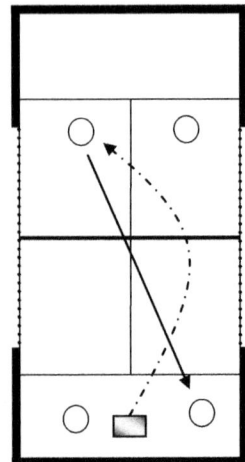

Exercise 0937   Hits: All

Target: Winning the point from an initial position
Striking sequence: BdX - Free

Description:
Mini game to 11 points, which begins with a crossed over volley tray. Defending players can win the point, even making lobs.
Once you reach 11, players will rotate to the left.

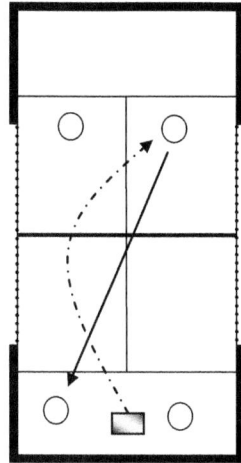

Exercise 0938   Hits: All

Target: Winning the point from an initial position
Striking sequence: BdX - Free

Description:
Mini match best of 5 points, which begins with a crossed over volley tray. Defending players can win the point, even making lobs.
If the player who plays with the monitor loses, he gets out and enters the fellow who is out. If on the contrary, the player's forehand goes outside, the left holds the forehand position and entering, it is in left.

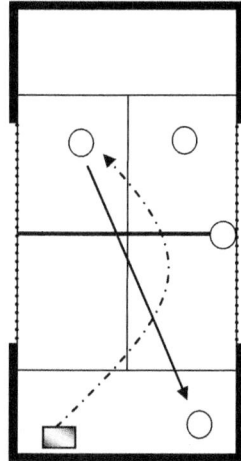

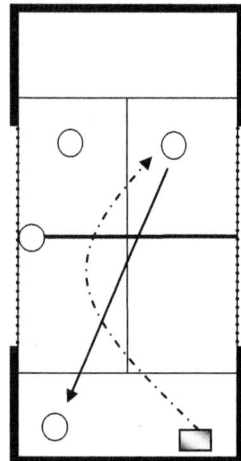

Exercise 0939   Hits: All

Target: Winning the point from an initial position
Striking sequence: BdX - Free

Description:
Mini match best of 5 points, which begins with a crossed over volley tray. Defending players can win the point, even making lobs.
If the player who plays with the monitor loses, he gets out and enters the fellow who is out. If on the contrary, the player's forehand goes outside, the left holds the forehand position and entering, it is in left.

Exercise 0940　Hits: All

Target: Winning the point from an initial position
Striking sequence: High ball X - Free

Description:
Mini game to 11 points, which begins with a lob monitor and answered with a crossed over. Defending players can win the point, even making lobs.
Once you reach 11, players will rotate to the left.

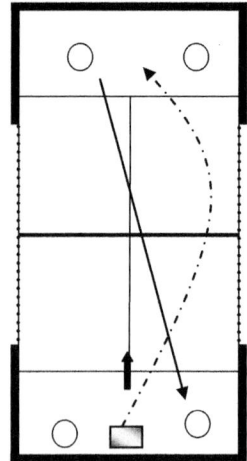

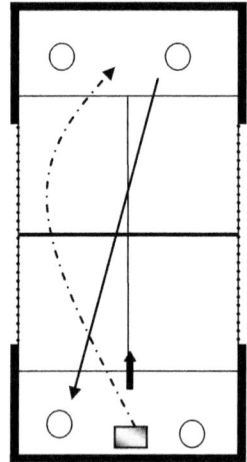

Exercise 0941　Hits: All

Target: Winning the point from an initial position
Striking sequence: High ball X - Free

Description:
Mini game to 11 points, which begins with a lob monitor and answered with a crossed over. Defending players can win the point, even making lobs.
Once you reach 11, players will rotate to the left.

Exercise 0942　Hits: All

Target: Winning the point from an initial position
Striking sequence: SFR// - Free

Description:
Mini game to 11 points, which begins with a parallel backhand background below. Defending players can win the point, even making lobs. They can even play against the monitor.
After reaching 11 points, players rotate the position.

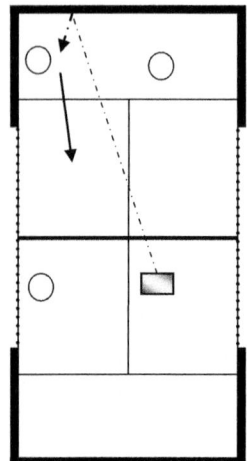

Exercise 0943   Hits: All

Target: Winning the point from an initial position
Striking sequence: SFD// - Free

Description:
Mini game to 11 points, which begins with a parallel forehand background below. Defending players can win the point, even making lobs. They can even play against the monitor.
After reaching 11 points, players rotate the position.

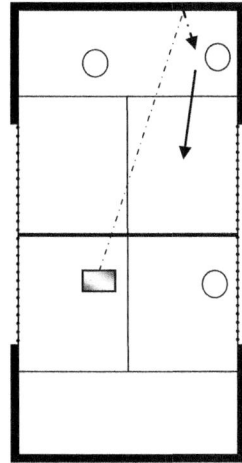

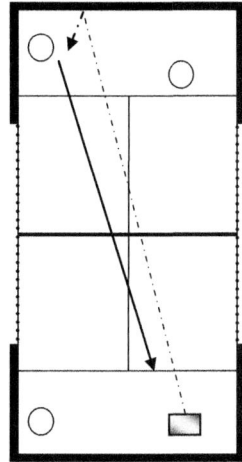

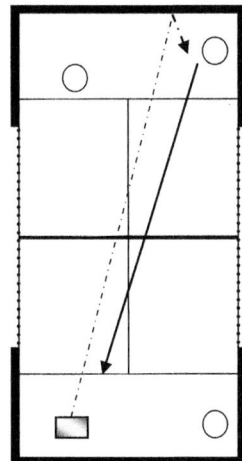

Exercise 0944   Hits: All

Target: Winning the point from an initial position
Striking sequence: SFRX - Free

Description:
Located players and the monitor on the back of the court, we'll play mini games to 11 points, in which they start with a crossed over backhand background out against the monitor. Defending players can win the point, even making lobs, but not on the first ball.
After reaching 11 points, players rotate the position.

Exercise 0945   Hits: All

Target: Winning the point from an initial position
Striking sequence: SFDX - Free

Description:
Located players and the monitor on the back of the court, we'll play mini games to 11 points, in which they start with a crossed over forehand background out against the monitor. Defending players can win the point, even making lobs, but not on the first ball.
After reaching 11 points, players rotate the position.

Exercise 0946 Hits: All

Target: Winning the point from an initial position
Striking sequence: Low ball DX - Free

Description:
Located players and the monitor near the net, we'll play mini games to 11 points, in which you start with a low crossed over forehand. Defending players can win the point, even making lobs, but not on the first ball.
After reaching 11 points, players rotate the position.

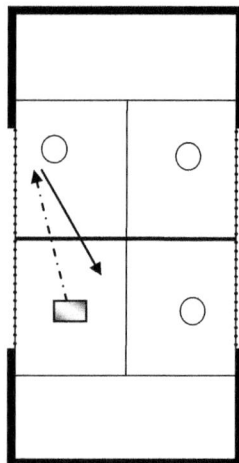

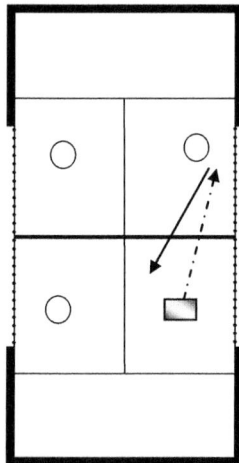

Exercise 0947 Hits: All

Target: Winning the point from an initial position
Striking sequence: Low ball RX - Free

Description:
Located players and the monitor near the net, we'll play mini games to 11 points, in which you start with a low crossed over backhand. Defending players can win the point, even making lobs, but not on the first ball.
After reaching 11 points, players rotate the position.

Exercise 0948 Hits: All

Target: Winning the point from an initial position
Striking sequence: RmX - Free

Description:
Two players placed close to the net and monitor and another player in the back of the court, play mini games to 11 points, which begins with a crossed over. Defending players can win the point, even making lobs.
Once you reach 11, players will rotate to the left.

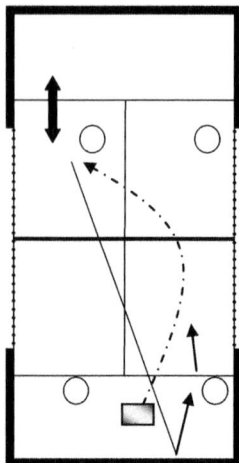

Exercise 0949   Hits: All

Target: Winning the point from an initial position
Striking sequence: RmX - Free

Description:
Two players placed close to the net and monitor and another player in the back of the court, play mini games to 11 points, which begins with a crossed over. Defending players can win the point, even making lobs. Once you reach 11, players will rotate to the left.

Exercise 0950   Hits: All

Target: Winning the point from an initial position
Striking sequence: Rm// - Free

Description:
Two players placed close to the net and monitor and another player in the back of the court, play mini games to 11 points, which begins with a parallel shot. Defending players can win the point, even making lobs.
Once you reach 11, players will rotate to the left.

Exercise 0951   Hits: All

Target: Winning the point from an initial position
Striking sequence: Rm// - Free

Description:
Two players placed close to the net and monitor and another player in the back of the court, play mini games to 11 points, which begins with a parallel shot. Defending players can win the point, even making lobs.
Once you reach 11, players will rotate to the left.

333

Exercise 0952   Hits: All

Target: Winning the point from an initial position
Striking sequence: BdX - Free

Description:
Two players placed close to the net and another players in the back of the court, play mini games to 11 points, in which one player start with a crossed over volley tray against to volley. Defending players can win the point, even making lobs.
Once you reach 11, players will rotate to the left.
Then you can make pulling the tray to the player backhand volley.

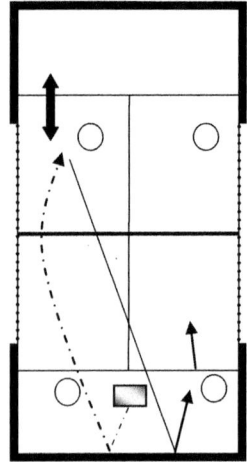

Exercise 0953   Hits: All

Target: Match volleys
Striking sequence: Serve and play

Description:
Located two players on each side of the court, which is bounded by lines serve, they will play a game with the rules of volleyball, passing the ball above the string located above the net. When passing the net, the ball may be hit a maximum of 3 times between partners before being returned to the opposite field.
Whoever wins the point makes a serve.
Once you reach 11 points are changed partners.

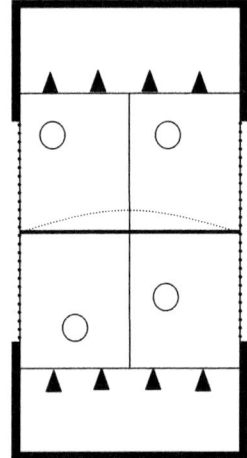

Exercise 0954   Hits: All

Target: Winning the point from an initial position
Striking sequence: Bd// - Free

Description:
They placed two players close to the net and monitor and another player in the back of the court, play mini games to 11 points, in which you start with a parallel volley tray to the parallel against wall parallel making monitor. Defending players can win the point, even making lobs.
Once you reach 11, players will rotate to the left.

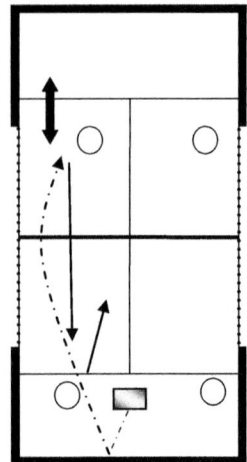

Exercise 0955   Hits: All

Target: Speed after striking
Striking sequence: Serve and play

Description:
Two players placed on each side of the court, played a game in which the pulling wall must touch the net before the ball back to them. If they touch the ball before touching the net, they cannot win the point. Once touched the net, they can win.
At 11 points, the position of the players alternate
Then it is done with the returners, they cannot win the point until the two players touch the net.

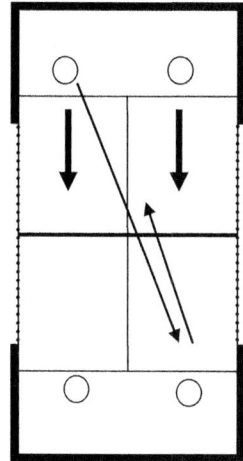

Exercise 0956   Hits: All

Target: Striking and movement
Striking sequence: Serve – Free

Description:
Matches 3 to 3 in which a player cannot repeat striking, therefore, hit and move to one of his team mates cover your area. It is a cooperative work.

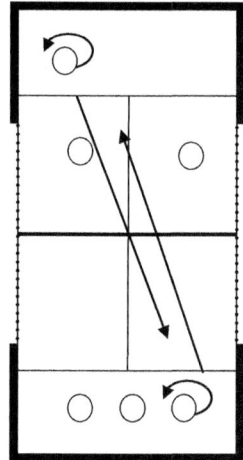

Exercise 0957   Hits: All

Target: Striking and movement
Striking sequence: Serve – Free

Description:
Matches 2 to 2 in a half court in parallel in which a player cannot repeat striking, therefore, it will strike and move to his partner cover your area. It is a cooperative work.

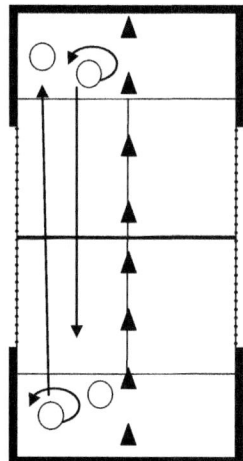

Exercise 0958   Hits: All

Target: Striking and movement
Striking sequence: Serve – Free

Description:
Matches 2 to 2 crossed over in court in which a player cannot repeat striking, therefore, will strike and move to his partner cover your area. It is a cooperative work.

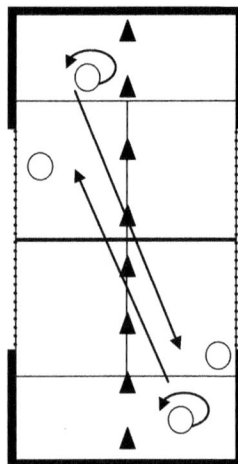

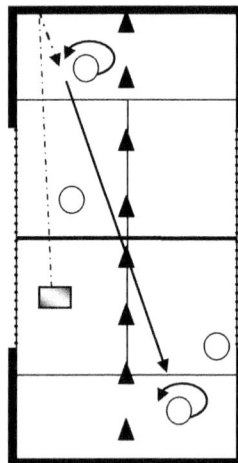

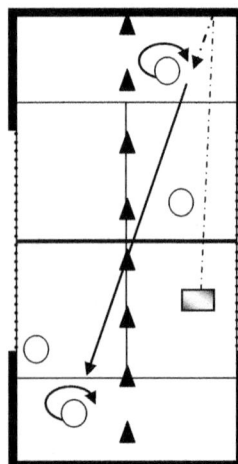

Exercise 0959   Hits: All

Target: Striking and movement
Striking sequence: SFDX – Free

Description:
Matches 2 to 2 crossed over half court in which output begins with crossed over forehand background out, in which a player cannot repeat striking, therefore, it will strike and move to his partner cover your area. It is a cooperative work.

Exercise 0960   Hits: All

Target: Striking and movement
Striking sequence: SFRX – Free

Description:
Matches 2 to 2 crossed over half court in which output begins with crossed over backhand background out, in which a player cannot repeat striking, therefore, it will strike and move to his partner cover your area. It is a cooperative work.

Exercise 0961   Hits: All

Target: Approach the game
Striking sequence: D - free

Description:
Matches 2 to 1 to any court, where the first ball is played against the players on defense and must go against volley player who stands alone. From that ball, you can play anywhere on the field. Whoever loses the position. If he wins he is alone, he goes to the bottom with the other player.
Then you can do in the other zone volley.

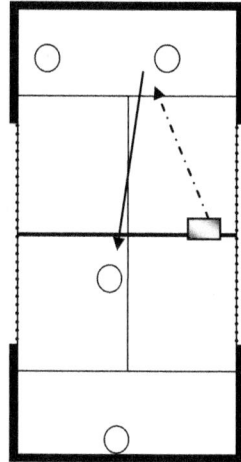

Exercise 0962   Hits: All

Target: Approach the game
Striking sequence: SFRX - free

Description:
Individual game against crossed over backhand background output after hit of the monitor. The first ball should go down from the return can be made even lobs. The player, who manages to make 3 points before, will occupy the position of the monitor.

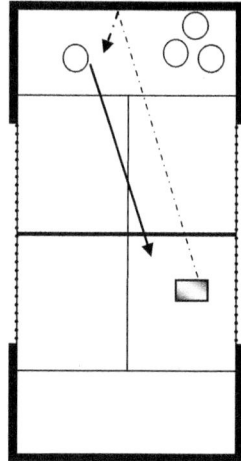

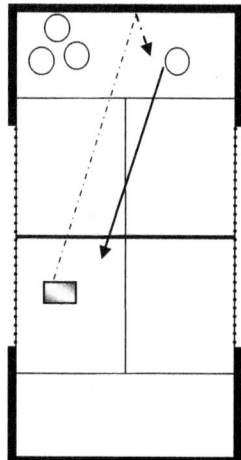

Exercise 0963   Hits: All

Target: Approach the game
Striking sequence: SFDX - free

Description:
Individual game against crossed over forehand background output after hit of the monitor. The first ball should go down from the return can be made even lobs. The player, who manages to make 3 points before, will occupy the position of the monitor.

Exercise 0964   Hits: All

Target: Approach the game
Striking sequence: SLDX - free

Description:
Individual game crossed over against the monitor after crossed over forehand output side. The first ball should go down from the return can be made even lobs.
The player, who manages to make 3 points before, will occupy the position of the monitor.

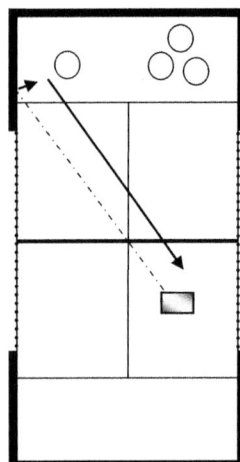

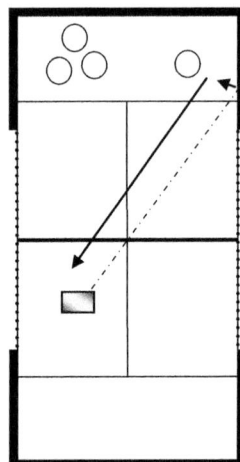

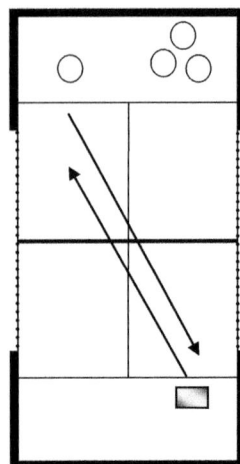

Exercise 0965   Hits: All

Target: Approach the game
Striking sequence: SFRX - free

Description:
Individual game crossed over against the monitor after crossed over backhand output side. The first ball should go down from the return can be made even lobs.
The player, who manages to make 3 points before, will occupy the position of the monitor.

Exercise 0966   Hits: All

Target: Approach the game
Striking sequence: Serve - free

Description:
Individual game crossed over against the monitor after serve.
The player, who manages to make 3 points before, will occupy the position of the monitor.

Exercise 0967   Hits: All

Target: Approach the game
Striking sequence: Serve - free

Description:
Individual game crossed over against the monitor after serve.
The player, who manages to make 3 points before, will occupy the position of the monitor.

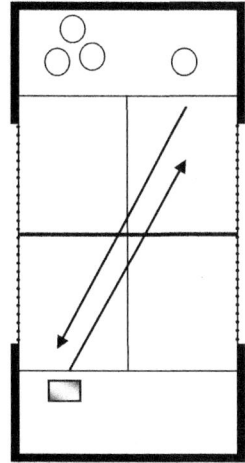

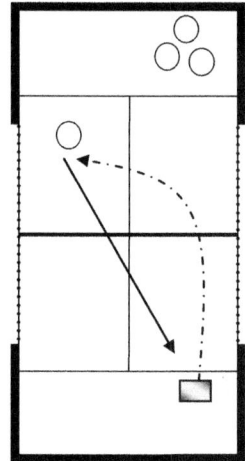

Exercise 0968   Hits: All

Target: Approach the game
Striking sequence: BdX - free

Description:
Individual game crossed over against the monitor after crossed over volley tray.
The player, who manages to make 3 points before, will occupy the position of the monitor.

Exercise 0969   Hits: All

Target: Match with area reduction
Striking sequence: Serve and play

Description:
Games 1 against 1 to 2 against 2 in the areas bounded by cones. They can hit before launching. The serve is made behind the line of serve.

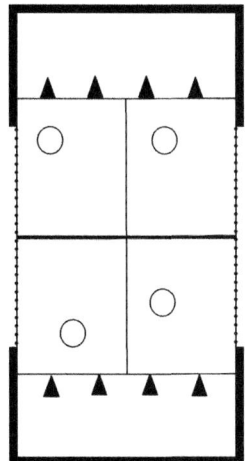

Exercise 0970   Hits: All

Target: Approach the game
Striking sequence: RmX - free

Description:
Individual game crossed over against the monitor after crossed over shot.
The player, who manages to make 3 points before, will occupy the position of the monitor.

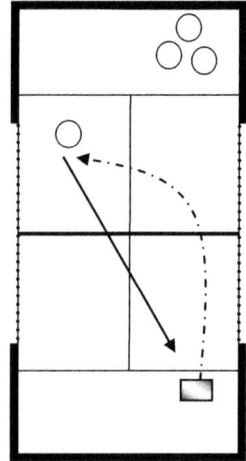

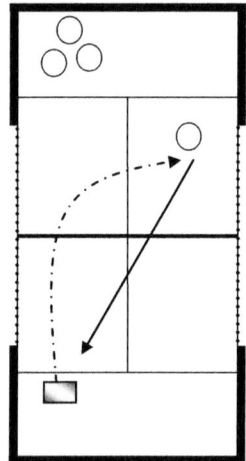

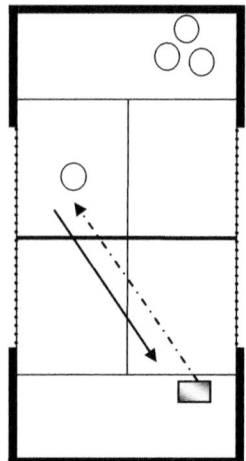

Exercise 0971   Hits: All

Target: Approach the game
Striking sequence: RmX - free

Description:
Individual game crossed over against the monitor after crossed over shot.
The player, who manages to make 3 points before, will occupy the position of the monitor.

Exercise 0972   Hits: All

Target: Approach the game
Striking sequence: VDX - free

Description:
Individual game crossed over against the monitor after crossed over forehand volley.
The player, who manages to make 3 points before, will occupy the position of the monitor.

Exercise 0973   Hits: All

Target: Approach the game
Striking sequence: VRX - free

Description:
Individual game crossed over against the monitor after crossed over backhand volley.
The player, who manages to make 3 points before, will occupy the position of the monitor.

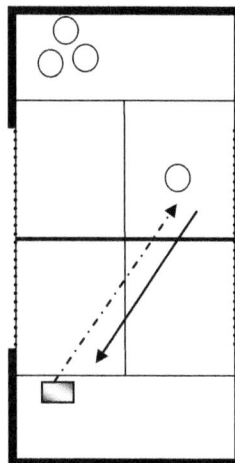

Exercise 0974   Hits: All

Target: Approach the game
Striking sequence: Sq – V and play

Description:
With two players on court, a player will be crossed over below the monitor to serve his teammate makes a strong volley and try to win the point. The game continues crossed over until the end point.
After 10 balls position players alternates.
It can be done on the other side.

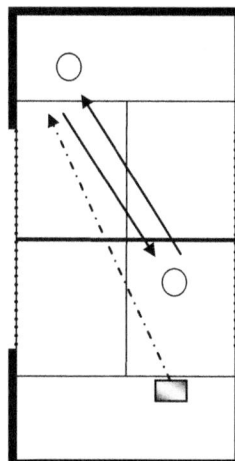

PEQUE-PÁDEL: CHILDREN EXERCISES

Exercise 0975   Peque-Pádel

Target: Hits moving
Exercise name: Baseball

Description:
2 teams. A team bats the ball and throwing the monitor has to run the bases. The other team has to catch the ball to try to eliminate the other team. Not worth the ball to the grid, Wall or net. To remove the air must take it or put it in the trolley Ball bearings before the players take the base.

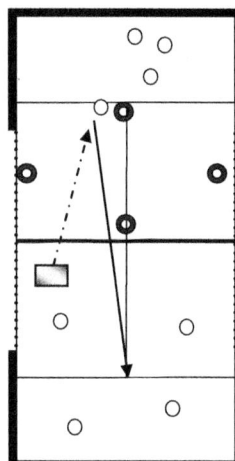

Exercise 0976   Peque-Pádel

Target: Coordination hits
Exercise name: The river

Description:
Important game for learning hits forehand and backhand. A pupil placed over another, with 3 cones between them with the following progression:
1. Both pupils without paddle, making boat in front of them.
2. One with paddle and the other without. Concept of hitting the side waist position.
3. Both pupils with paddle ball bouncing in the marked area.
4. Both pupils paddle but by middle of the net.

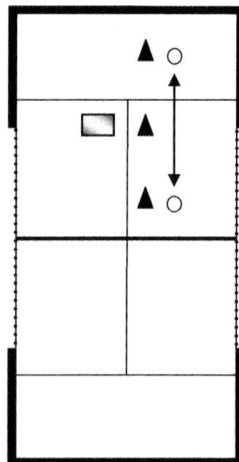

Exercise 0977   Peque-Pádel

Target: Coordination of movements
Exercise name: The sandwich

Description:
We put the kids in pairs and press a ball between two paddles with moving in different directions. If they drop the ball again begin.
After 1' changes pairs among all children.

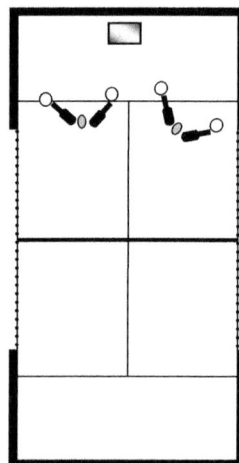

Exercise 0978   Peque-Pádel

Target: Psychomotor
Exercise name: The volcano

Description:
We place the ball trolley in the center of a circle that will have previously marked with cones, and learners outside. From there without entering it they should try to make paddles pulling balls fall to the ground against them. Win pupil achieve his paddle remains the last in the ball trolley.

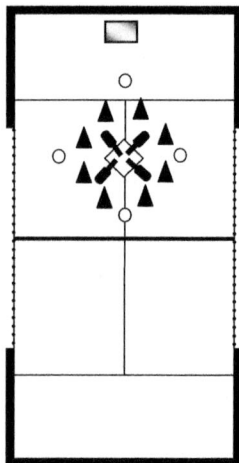

Exercise 0979   Peque-Pádel

Target: Psychomotor
Exercise name: Race balls

Description:
Pupils stood behind the service line and the monitor signal will cast his ball to roll on the floor and try to get to the net as soon as possible by pushing the paddle.
After taking the paddle is done with the left hand.

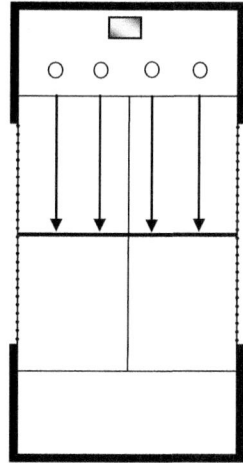

Exercise 0980   Peque-Pádel

Target: Psychomotor
Exercise name: The pan

Description:
Pupils stood behind the service line and the monitor just across the net, with his paddle as many balls as number of pupils but one has. He launched the ball towards the pupils and they must take each into a ball, a pupil who is left without a fault point's ball well up to 5 faults that will be eliminated and a ball to keep playing and have a winner will be removed.

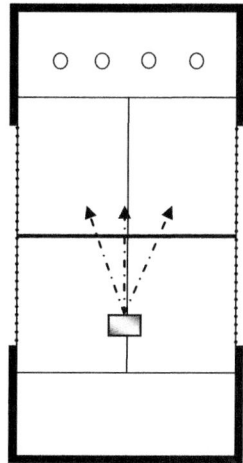

Exercise 0981   Peque-Pádel

Target: Psychomotor
Exercise name: Mom Chicken

Description:
Pupils placed in the midline in single row, must prevent the ball touch the pupil who is first in line but backs, which is moved by his team mate. To do this, grabbing her by the waist, they must travel through space. Win pupil who have a less number of failures.

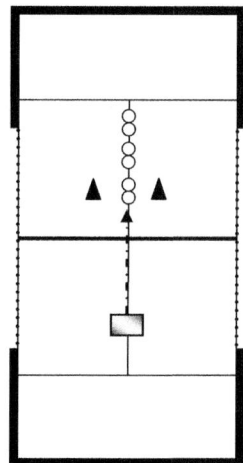

Exercise 0982   Peque-Pádel

Target: Psychomotor
Exercise name: The Marcianitos

Description:
The monitor is placed behind the net and pupils on the other side, on the midline of the field (in a line), and between two cones. They should avoid being touched with the ball thrown by the monitor and if they are made must run to the bottom wall and placed last in the row. Pupil who will win when there are no balls in the ball trolley is the first in line.

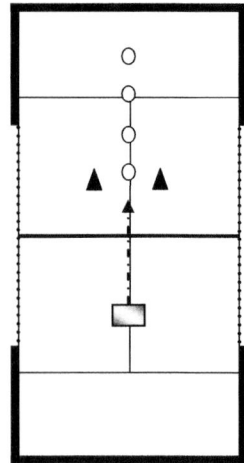

Exercise 0983   Peque-Pádel

Target: Targeting and coordination
Exercise name: The Target

Description:
All children placed his paddle on the grid and from the line of cones as target will throw paddles with ball. They may not approach or throw a ball over. Win owner of the paddle remaining in the grid.

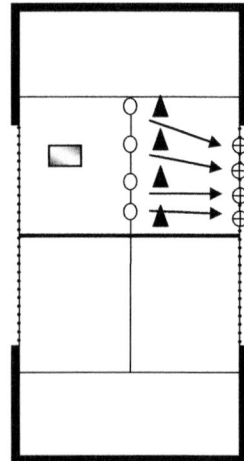

Exercise 0984   Peque-Pádel

Target: Avoid the balls and read the rebounds
Exercise name: Kill Chickens

Description:
Traditional Mata Pollos in the area where children should avoid the balls thrown by the monitor, who will launch directly or bouncing on the walls to become familiar with the rebounds. The child 'gives him the ball, will be eliminated.

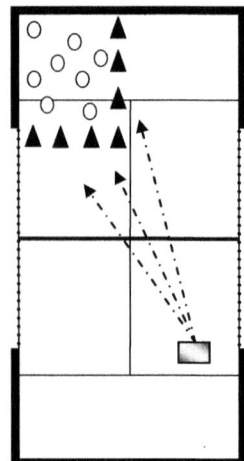

Exercise 0985   Peque-Pádel

Target: Coordination hits
Exercise name: The Yo-Yo

Description:
With an elastic ball and support to pupils to practice the striking of forehand or backhand, to see which pupil achieves a higher number of hits with a maximum of one boat.

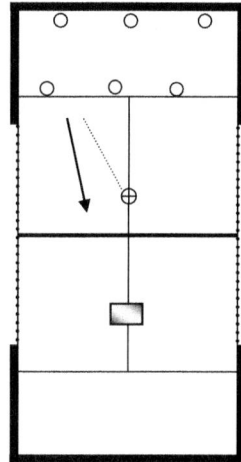

Exercise 0986   Peque-Pádel

Target: Introduction to the games
Exercise name: Padel Mini Match

Description:
Using a mini net padel or string, we divide half court at the halfway line and play games in pairs.
After 2' alternating the position of the players.

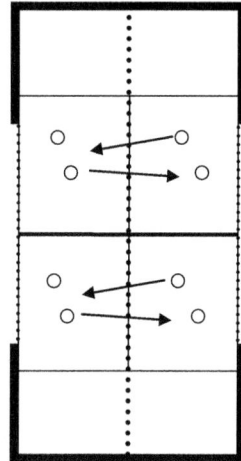

Exercise 0987   Peque-Pádel

Target: Coordination of movements

Striking sequence: The cat and mouse

Description:
With more than padel ball, we place two pupils on both sides of the middle line and the rest of pupils on it. They should spend trying to ball center colleagues not intercept the pass. You are binding let the ball bounce once overshoot the line formed by peers. If someone intercepts the pass is changed automatically for which failed.

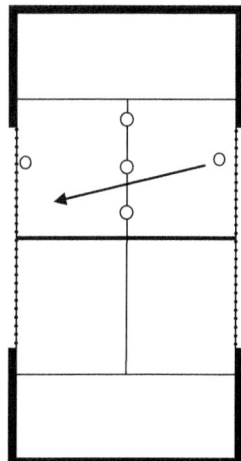

Exercise 0988   Peque-Pádel

Target: Learning Forehand
Striking sequence: D

Description:
All players are at least 2 side of the court and hit a forehand from the back of the court trying the ball bounce on the other side of the court. If they do not succeed or fail, they pass to the other side. If they are getting get hit the ball before it touches the ground, exchange position.

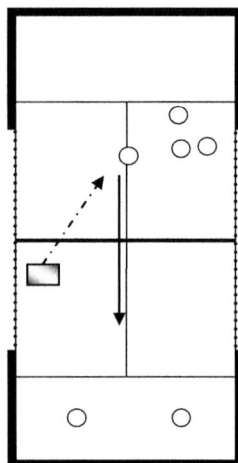

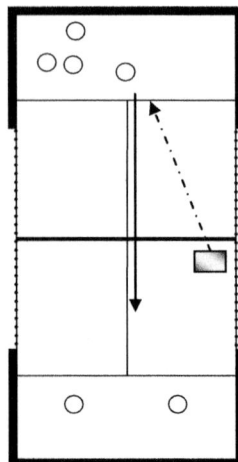

Exercise 0989   Peque-Pádel

Target: Psychomotor
Exercise name: Rain of stars

Description:
Each pupil gets a cone (which used as a basket) to catch the balls that the monitor has launched high. They can catch any ball whenever they are bouncing. Every time you manage to catch a ball, they take with his paddle that has left over the service line. The pupil will gain at the end of the trolley ball has more balls in his possession.

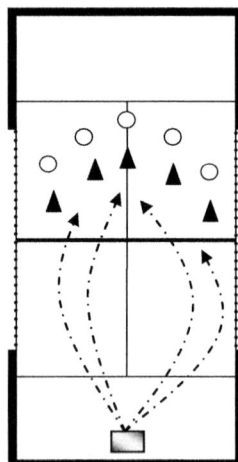

Exercise 0990   Peque-Pádel

Target: Learning backhand
Striking sequence: R

Description:
All players are at least 2 side of the court and hit a backhand from the back of the court trying the ball bounce on the other side of the court. If they do not succeed or fail, they pass to the other side. If they are getting get hit the ball before it touches the ground, exchange position

Exercise 0991   Peque-Pádel

Target: Launch control in hand
Exercise name: The Frontón

Description:
Mark an area in the background wall and a line of cones at half court. Pupils from this line of cones, launched balls against the wall to serve as a background for this area. The player, who achieves more hits, wins the game.

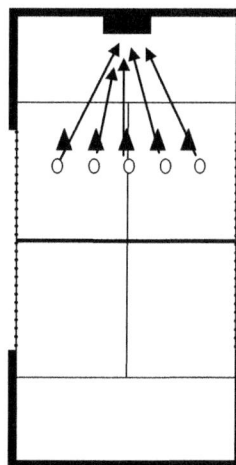

Exercise 0992   Peque-Pádel

Target: Learning hit forehand volley
Striking sequence: VD

Description:
All players are at least 2 side of the court and hit a forehand volley from the middle of the court trying the ball bounce on the other side of the court. If they do not succeed or fail, they pass to the other side. If they are getting get hit the ball before it touches the ground, exchange position.

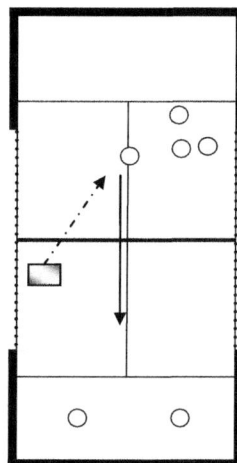

Exercise 0993   Peque-Pádel

Target: Coordination of movements
Exercise name: Relay race

Description:
It is a team relay race, where pupils will have the area marked with cones relay keeping the ball on the paddle. One pupil drop will begin its journey from the beginning. The change is also made ball without the ball lands and avoiding touching it with his hand.

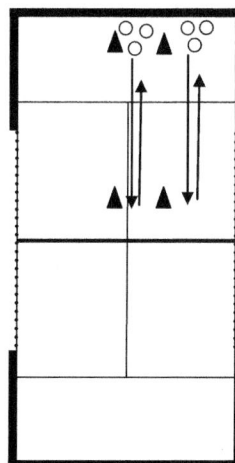

Exercise 0994 Peque-Pádel

Target: Learning backhand volley
Striking sequence: VR

Description:
All players are at least 2 side of the court and hit a backhand volley from the middle of the court trying the ball bounce on the other side of the court. If they do not succeed or fail, they pass to the other side. If they are getting get hit the ball before it touches the ground, exchange position.

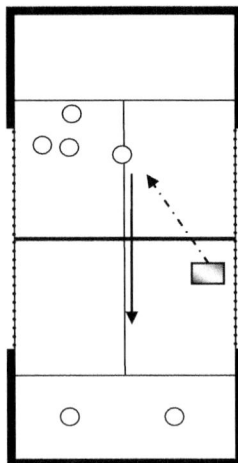

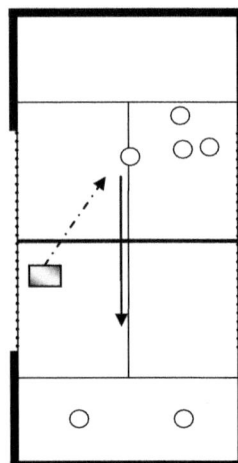

Exercise 0995 Peque-Pádel

Target: Displacements
Exercise name: Pacman

Description:
It is used as the only way around the court lines without departing from them. Each pupil will take a ball on the paddle and must keep it there without crashing to the ground, and if it becomes the Pacman and have to chase.

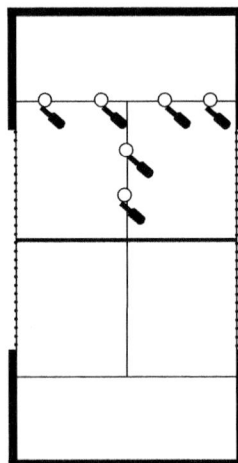

Exercise 0996 Peque-Pádel

Target: Learning volley tray (Bd) stroke
Striking sequence: Bd

Description:
All players are at least 2 side of the court and hit a volley tray from the middle of the court trying the ball bounce on the other side of the court. If they do not succeed or fail, they pass to the other side. If they are getting get hit the ball before it touches the ground, exchange position.

Exercise 0997   Peque-Pádel

Target: Psychomotor
Exercise name: Paddle passes

Description:
We are partners and gripped by hand, give one to each pair. The monitor will launch to the couples and depending on the side where the ball goes, the couple will pass the paddle to hit the ball.

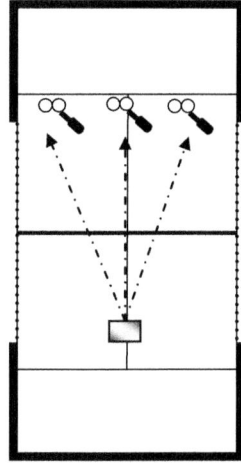

Exercise 0998   Peque-Pádel

Target: Learning shot hit
Striking sequence: Rm

Description:
All players are at least 2 side of the court and hit a shot from the middle of the court trying the ball bounce on the other side of the court. If they do not succeed or fail, they pass to the other side. If they are getting get hit the ball before it touches the ground, exchange position.

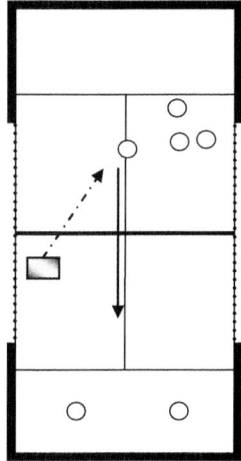

Exercise 0999   Peque-Pádel

Target: Psychomotor
Exercise name: The goalkeeper

Description:
We put a goal on the bottom line, to where they should go with it, forehand or backhand pupil. These launch the ball into the goal and try to score a goal. The goalkeeper may take his paddle and keep her goal, but if not avoided, will leave the target and leave the place to the player that has marked the pupil.

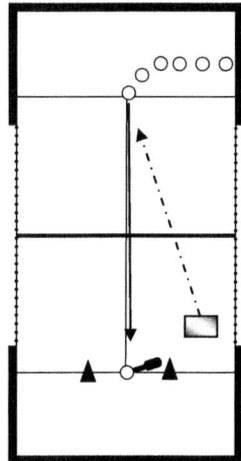

Exercise 1000   Peque-Pádel

Target: Learning serve
Exercise name: The Target

Description:
We mark various objects with cones in the serve area and pupils will perform serves about them. Win pupil who get a larger number of successes by making your serve touch any of the cones with or without bounce.
Then you can do from the other side.

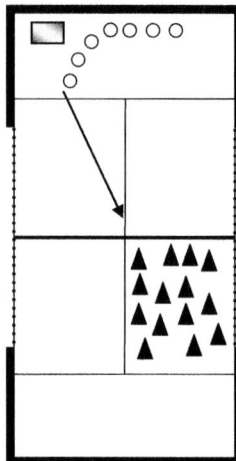

Exercise 1001   Peque-Pádel

Target: Psychomotor
Exercise name: Top the ball does not fall

Description:
The monitor throws balls up in the form of meteorites and pupils should beat them up before they stop bouncing in order to keep as many balls in the air.

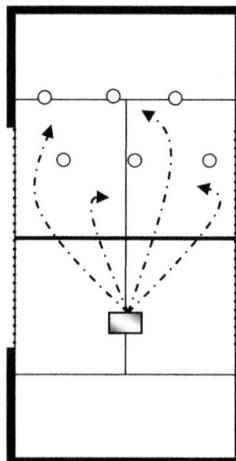

CLASS SCHEDULE SHEET

CLUB PÁDEL TORREJÓN

Nº DE ALUMNOS

OBJETIVO DE LA SESIÓN   DERECHA

TEMPORADA: 2010 - 2011

PRIMER TRIMESTRE

NIVEL   INICIACIÓN / MEDIO

MONITOR   JUAN JOSÉ MOYANO VÁZQUEZ

SESIÓN

EN PISTA: CONTROL DEL GOLPE DE DERECHA A DISTINTAS DIRECCIONES Y PROFUNDIDADES, ALTERNANDO EL GOLPEO PLANO, LIFTADO Y CORTADO.

.- EMPUÑADURA
.- CONTROL DE FUERZA
.- MIRAR LA BOLA
.- POSICIÓN DEL CUERPO CON RESPECTO A LA POSICIÓN DE LA BOLA

	CONOS
4	CONOS
1	CADENA

351

PADEL REVIEWS

Iciar Montes, 2010 World Champion and Player # 3 of the PPT: "From the outside, this sport is very misleading, difficult to assess the true level of the players. What you see are the bright hits, plasticity execution or "winners" isolated. But to know how he plays really have to get inside, feeling the difficulty of his hits, if they come adjusted Wall, give little rebound, what kind of effect and variety used, how come their lobs and which zone the strip, how to defend and he puts the ball in areas....; all that, from the outside is so difficult to see, is what gives you the true level courts player. "

Patty Llaguno, 2010 World Champion and Player # 3 of the PPT: "For me the padel is a sport where I face situations arising from my life while doing what I love. Therefore, every game is a situation and every day I learn something new. "

Valeria Pavon Player No. 5 PPT: "Who is afraid of losing, is already defeated. If you run what you are asked, you will be good. If you run twice, you will be better. "

Alejandra Salazar, Player # 5 of PPT: "If you do not dream, you never find what is beyond your dreams."

Vanessa Martinez Zamora, Player No. 16 PPT: "Not everything is cooked inside the court. Watch games, players analyze and make your strategies. The padel is not only good to give the beanbag. "

Miguel Lamperti, PPT Player No. 5 "always train as if it were the first day, and after they have won or lost the last game, every time you go to court, full Push yourself to be the best."

Gaston Malacalza Player # 23 of PPT: "The Padel is a sport, a job, a hobby, fun and in my case, my life .... Training is everything, is the basis for a good race. "

Pitu Losada, Champion of Spain 2010 and No. 25 of the PPT Player: "The Padel is a team sport which must be taught and understand it well."

Rodrigo Ovide, Coach Padel: "Smart is not the one who knows everything but one who knows how to use what little he knows.

The Padel is a mental sport where besides playing padel.

Basic tips:

1. Have fun, whether playing or teaching.

2. Search challenges to keep you motivated.

3. Win the last point of the match. "

Roby Pampin, Coach Padel (Argentina): "When you start in this sport you never learn though you find enough, you learn just when you think you get stuck, it means I start to grow as a player."

Beatriz Arranz: "The Padel is a sport that captivates the very beginning, but if you keep working and it will be like your love ... .. not only captivate you but will thrill and you can not live without him."

Joao, Portuguese Padel Federation: "We are always eager to play and play at the highest points in all to try to win the game but without forgetting that the most important and the best way to get there is when we had fun and we took advantage our passion for this sport to play our best padel."

Alvaro ABL Sport: "From your reaction speed depends anticipate the trajectory of your execution speed effectiveness of technical gestures, speed resistance levels optimal competitiveness to win the game."

David Cuesta Alonso: "The Padel, like chess, is a mental game, not just physical, requires tranquility and knows how to play as required every play."

Bjorn Borg, Swedish tennis player ". My problems go away when the ball has passed the net" "Winning or losing a game depends on the desire you have to play the final goal" "If you are afraid to lose, do not deserve to win... "" you've got to lose to know how to win "

Padel Barranqueras: "It's just Padel ...... but I like it."

Padel Alzira: "Speed, coordination, reflexes, cunning and placement .... More than a sport. "

Juanjo: "It's no problem to fall, we all do, the important thing is to get up, and the sooner the better."

Matias Diaz Sangiorgio, player # 5 of PPT: "Discipline, Patience and Consciousness"

SPECIAL THANKS

A Carolina Navarro, Ceci Reiter and Vanessa Zamora by make
the prologue and contribute their experience in completing the book.

Makin'Events Company, for their unconditional support.

Carolina Navarro Björk:
Current world No. 1
11 times champion of Spain Absolute
couples world champion 2000 and 2006.
World champion selections 1998, 2000 and 2010.
6 years Champion Spain Team:
2007, 2008, 2009, 2010 and 2011.
Bronze medal for sporting merit, awarded by the Royal House
  and collected from King Juan Carlos I
Silver medal at the National Sports Awards (FEP)
MASTER champion PPT 2007, 2008 and
2009.www.carolinanavarro.com

Cecilia Reiter:
Current world No. 1
World champion in 2004 and 2006 with Argentina
www.cecireiter.com

Vanessa Martínez Zamora:
2010:
Ranking couple 5 Padel Pro Tour
Champion Spain Team 1st Cat. With Higueron
Selected to represent Spain to Cancun 2010 World
Championship.
www.vanessazamora.com

THANKS

To Iciar Montes, Patty Llaguno, Valeria Pavón, Alejandra Salazar, Vanessa Martínez Zamora, Miguel Lamperti, Gastón Malacalza, Pitu Losada, Rodrigo Ovide, Beatriz Arranz, Joao, Álvaro, David Cuesta, Matías Díaz.

To my colleagues who directly or indirectly contributed to enriching this work.

All students who passed through my courts, with which I could implement each and every one of my exercises and games.

All monitors, players and teachers (Andrés, Chema, Ángel, Chemi, Maxi, Cato,...), who taught me the way to progress and improve.

To Adidas Padel "All for Padel" for its sports support and cooperation in this and future projects in common.

To Club Pádel Torrejón, in which the last 8 years I have been able to implement my classes.

To Club de Pádel Soto Torrejón, for the transfer of photos from your Club.

To the photographer José David Sacristán, author of the cover photo.

REFERENCES

.- Manuales de apoyo del Curso de Monitor de Pádel por la Federación de Pádel de Madrid.

.- Libro Curso de Monitor de Pádel Adaptado, impartido por Kiki de la Rocha, Presidenta de la Asociación de Pádel Adaptado.

.- 400 Juegos y Ejercicios con conos, de José María Cañizares Márquez. Editorial Wanceulen.

.- www.sportfactor.es Red social de deportes

.- www.esferapadel.com La web del Pádel

.- Juanjo Moyano: juanjo.moyano@gmail.com

PHOTOGRAPH

.- José David Sacristán – www.josedavidsacristan.es / info@josedavidsacristan.es

Printed in Great Britain
by Amazon

19105763R10208